TELEPEN

60 0056334 2

DATE DUE FOR RETURN

24. JUN 07

KU-545-199

COMPETITION POLICY IN THE
EUROPEAN COMMUNITY

The Royal Institute of International Affairs is an unofficial body which promotes the scientific study of international questions and does not express opinions of its own. The opinions expressed in this publication are the responsibility of the authors.

The Institute gratefully acknowledges the comments and suggestions of the following who read the manuscript on behalf of the Research Committee: Miriam Camps, Professor Otto Kahn-Freund, and John Pinder.

COMPETITION POLICY IN THE EUROPEAN COMMUNITY

THE RULES IN THEORY AND PRACTICE

D. L. McLachlan
Economic Affairs Officer in the Shipping Division of the United Nations Conference on Trade and Development

and

D. Swann
Reader in Economics, The Queen's University of Belfast

Issued under the auspices of the
Royal Institute of International Affairs

OXFORD UNIVERSITY PRESS
LONDON   NEW YORK   TORONTO
1967

*Oxford University Press, Ely House, London W.*1

GLASGOW NEW YORK TORONTO MELBOURNE WELLINGTON
CAPE TOWN SALISBURY IBADAN NAIROBI LUSAKA ADDIS ABABA
BOMBAY CALCUTTA MADRAS KARACHI LAHORE DACCA
KUALA LUMPUR HONG KONG TOKYO

© Royal Institute of International Affairs, 1967

C C

PRINTED IN GREAT BRITAIN
BY EBENEZER BAYLIS AND SON, LTD
THE TRINITY PRESS, WORCESTER, AND LONDON

To Frances and Beryl

CONTENTS

PART III

MANAGING THE COMPETITIVE ECONOMY

PART IV
CONCLUSION

ABBREVIATIONS

ATIC:	Association Technique de l'Importation Char-bonnière
BKA:	Bundeskartellamt
BLEU:	Belgium-Luxembourg Economic Union
Bull. ECSC:	*Bulletin of the European Coal and Steel Com-munity*
Bull. EEC:	*Bulletin of the European Economic Community*
COBECHAR:	Comptoir Belge des Charbons
DKV:	Deutscher Kohlen-Verkauf
ECE:	(United Nations) Economic Commission for Europe
ECSC:	European Coal and Steel Community
EEC:	European Economic Community
EFTA:	European Free Trade Association
FAO:	Food and Agriculture Organization
GATT:	General Agreement on Tariffs and Trade
GEORG:	Gemeinschaftsorganisation Ruhrkohle GmbH
ICLQ:	*International and Comparative Law Quarterly*
IMF:	International Monetary Fund
JO:	*Journal Officiel*
JPE:	*Journal of Political Economy*
NIESR:	National Institute of Economic and Social Research
OECD:	Organization for Economic Co-operation and Development
OEEC:	Organization for European Economic Co-opera-tion
OKU:	Oberrheinische Kohlenunion
QJ Econ.:	*Quarterly Journal of Economics*
PEP:	Political and Economic Planning
R & D:	Research and Development
SCPA:	Société Commerciale des Potasses d'Alsace
UNICE:	Union des Industries de la Communauté Euro-péenne
WuW:	*Wirtschaft und Wettbewerb*

Preface

THE main theme of this book is, at least conceptually, a relatively simple one. It is an assessment of the roles on the one hand of market forces and competition, and on the other of various forms of intervention by Community and national authorities, in some of the spheres of economic and social activity which fall within the purview of the Paris and Rome Treaties.[1] Having said this it is necessary to add a number of qualifications. Firstly, although we confine ourselves to a discussion of policy in the European Coal and Steel Community and the European Economic Community, Euratom enters into our discussion, if only marginally, in connexion with energy policy. Secondly, in dealing with the economic policy which falls within the ambit of the two treaties, it is not our intention to discuss in turn every field of economic policy. Our plan is more selective than that. The fundamental problems of economic life are ultimately threefold—what goods are to be produced and in what quantity, how are they to be produced, and for whom are they to be produced. This statement of the problems which face all economies, however organized, is one which can be found in the most elementary texts on Economics—it is none the less useful for that. Clearly such problems can be solved by a *laissez-faire* policy which leaves the course of economic events to be determined by the play of market forces and competition. On the other hand it is possible to solve them by a central control over the deployment of factors of production, allocation of investment funds, and the pricing and distribution of final output. Alternatively it is possible to have some admixture of the two approaches. What we are aiming to do in this book is to analyse the way in which these questions are answered within the context of Community policy. For example, it is without doubt true that the creation of greater competition through the removal of trade barriers, the suppression of cartels, and so forth is a prime aim of policy in both the ECSC and EEC. It would, however, be a great mistake

[1] Throughout this book the Rome Treaty refers to that treaty which created the European Economic Community.

xi

to assume that this is the end of the matter and that *laissez-faire* is therefore the rule. There are important sectors of the Community economy in which the forces of the market will not be free but will instead be managed—this is pre-eminently true in the case of agriculture. Then again in the Coal and Steel Community, although competition and free market forces have a role to play, the actual process of price competition is governed by rules laid down in the Paris Treaty. In addition over a long period the High Authority has used its various powers to guide investment in the light of forecasts of future demand. Then again a balanced view of the two Communities must take into account not just the policies designed to unleash the force of competition but also those social and regional policies designed to cope with its consequences. This then is our main theme. It is also our intention to try to show how policies in various spheres fit together to form a coherent whole.

We intend to look critically at the goals set by the treaties and we shall also ask whether the policies pursued are in fact well adapted to secure their achievement. We are also aware that the Paris and Rome Treaties are products of the early and mid 1950s. Since then the European Community has changed, but so has the outside world and the relationship between the two. It is therefore necessary to ask whether the passage of time calls for new emphases in policy and new powers to be conferred upon the Community authorities.

In order not to prolong the book unduly we have had to concentrate our attention upon certain areas of policy. As an example of this selectivity, we have tended to concentrate most of our attention upon the market for final goods and services. We recognize that factor mobility as between states is important if competition is to achieve its ends, but we have tended to take it for granted and have thus avoided any lengthy discussion of it. Again in discussing planning, our main interest is in that aspect which relates to the securing of balanced growth as between industries and enterprises, rather than the coordination of macro-economic policies. It has not been our intention to provide a general guide to the whole of Community economic and social policy, even though there is a high degree of interdependence between all the various fields of Community policy and as a result it is difficult to draw a line.

Throughout we have run the discussion of ECSC and EEC policy in harness. This has two main benefits in that it provides an excellent opportunity for making comparisons and for the drawing of lessons from the earlier experiment.

Parts I and II of the book are devoted to elaborating the policies followed in both the ECSC and EEC for increasing the competition between enterprises in the various member states. In Part I the emphasis is upon policies for sweeping away those obstacles to competition which arise from the activities of member state governments. In Chapter I, after a brief discussion of the theory behind the establishment of free movement of goods, we discuss the actual process of pulling down tariff and quota barriers. Fiscal factors can also distort the free flow of goods and factors of production, and policies to deal with such problems are discussed in Chapter 2. In Chapter 3 we discuss the policy for dealing with state aids or subsidies and Chapter 4 is concerned with the other major obstacles to trade which are governmental in origin. In Part II it is recognized that the beneficial effects of the pulling down of state barriers could be undone if, as fast as these barriers fell, private—or for that matter state—enterprises erected others in their place. For example the Community market could be divided up by price or quota agreements which could restrict competition when enterprises in one member state exported to another member.

A Community anti-trust policy is therefore necessary. In Chapter 5 we discuss the philosophy which lies behind it. In Chapter 6 we provide instances of the types of cartel which could prevent the goal of greater competition from being achieved. Chapter 7 contains an account of the rules of cartel policy in the two Communities together with an account and appraisal of actual Decisions and Judgments to date. It is more or less universal practice to divide discussions of anti-trust policy into two parts—agreements between otherwise independent enterprises (cartels) and the problems of size. In the Communities the latter part resolves itself into the twin problems of mergers and market domination. Again firms which merge or acquire a dominant position could hold back the interpenetration of markets. The subject of concentration policy is dealt with in Chapter 8, which is also a convenient point to discuss the problem of size of enterprise in Europe and the United States and the allied subject of research and development. The special pricing régime for steel provides the basis of the first part of Chapter 9 and this is followed by a discussion of ECSC transport policy which is intimately connected with steel pricing.

Having discussed how greater competition is to be created and maintained and the play of market forces is to be facilitated, in Part III we try to show how erroneous it would be to see the two treaties purely in the light of the content of Parts I and II. Chapter 10 is devoted to a discussion of the managed markets of transport, agriculture, and energy. Here, with differing emphases, some guidance over the course of economic events is to be exercised by Community and national authorities. Then in Chapter 11 we give further evidence of the fact that the two treaties are not concerned solely with the creation of more competition. Not only is provision made for retraining and resettlement of workers displaced both by the new competition and by subsequent changes in the fortunes of individual industries, but there is in the Six an active regional policy which both the High Authority and the EEC Commission have done much to encourage and coordinate. In the Note to Chapter 11 we discuss the form of industrial planning that has been actively pursued by the ECSC for many years. In our Part Four, 'A Concluding Assessment', we attempt to show what effect the pulling down of trade barriers and suppressing of restrictive practices has had on the flow of intra-Community trade. In the ECSC steel market, unlike that of the UK, competition has been a reality since the early 1950s and this provides an excellent opportunity to measure the effects of competition. The Concluding Assessment also provides an opportunity for us to take an overall view of competition policy in the two Communities and to suggest possible lines of development for the future.

Acknowledgements

WHEN the research upon which this book is based first began, the UK was negotiating terms for entry into the Common Market. In retrospect those seem to have been the halcyon days of the European Community. In Brussels there seemed every prospect that the 'ever closer union' to which the preamble of the Rome Treaty refers was within the grasp of the Six. For the UK there was a fair prospect that membership would be secured. The rude awakening to which the UK was subjected needs no elaboration here. Not only that, but subsequently on more than one occasion the very existence of the Community itself seemed in doubt. But as this book goes to press the prospect before the Community now seems much brighter than in the dark days that followed the crises on agricultural policy. With the solid achievement of agreements on agriculture, the customs union, and the negotiating mandate for the Kennedy Round behind it, the Community seems to have passed the point of no return, at least on the economic plane. Equally encouraging to the authors is the fact that the UK has decided to make a second attempt to join the Community—although as we write the outcome is surrounded with uncertainty. The most that can be said is that all the major parties, with varying degrees of enthusiasm, are in favour of membership and that in the country at large a growing body of responsible opinion sees the future of the UK increasingly in a European context. If we do join, it is our hope that this book will throw some light on a vital area of policy which will be of intimate concern to us as members. Even if we do not join, the policy which the Community pursues in the field of competition policy is of considerable intellectual interest. Moreover, since our trade is increasingly orientated towards Europe, and since many of the problems of the Six are also our problems, for example, the question of competition with US giant enterprises, Community policy is of practical importance and interest for the UK.

If the political uncertainties surrounding the Common Market have not conspired to assist us in our research, we must set against this the help and encouragement we have received from many quarters. We would like to thank the Royal Institute of International Affairs which has sponsored this study. We are particularly indebted to Andrew Shonfield, the Director of Studies, who first encouraged us to write this book and whose observations and criticisms have been of great value to us. We also owe a great debt to the Information Service of the European Communities. The members of that Service have not only constantly supplied us with information, but have been unfailingly helpful in arranging visits to Brussels and Luxembourg. We would particularly like to thank Roy Pryce, Russell Lewis, and Derek Prag in the UK, Diarmid McLaughlin in Luxembourg, and Jean Moreau in Brussels.

We have derived much benefit from discussions with Community officials in Brussels and Luxembourg. They have been most generous in giving up time not only to talk to us but also to read and comment upon most of the chapters in this book. At the EEC Commission our thanks are due to Professor L. Duquesne de la Vinelle, Dr F. Froschmaier, R. Giry, J. Hasse, G. Heerkens, R. Jaume, Dr N. Koch, Dr H. B. Krohn, H. Lavenir, J. van Lierde, A. Prate, A. Reinarz, P. Romus, Dr W. Schlieder, Dr M-D Hesse, H. Schumacher, Dr I. Schwartz, Dr W. Stabenow, Dr H-R Watermann and Dr H. Zünkler. At Luxembourg we especially appreciated the opportunity to talk to P. Olivier Lapie, a Member of the High Authority. We are also grateful to the following members of the staff of the High Authority: J. Abraham, C. Goudima, Dr H. Kutscher, P. Maillet, J. Petrick, D. Rabe, and Dr W. Renner. The Statistical Office of the European Communities has supplied us with data and for this we would like to thank Professor R. Wagenführ and Dr F. Grotius.

We also gained considerable insight into the problems of Community policy by looking at it from the point of view of those engaged in British industry. For this we are indebted to P. Evans and W. L. Richardson at the British Iron and Steel Board, J. Driscoll and his staff at the British Iron and Steel Federation and E. F. Schumacher at the National Coal Board.

Our thanks are also due to Miriam Camps, Professor Otto Kahn-Freund, and John Pinder whose comments on and criticisms of the final draft not only helped to remove errors and obscurities in the argument but also led to a most useful alteration

in the plan of the book. For much painstaking typing our thanks
are due to Miss Audrey Allen, Miss Grace Jamison, Miss
Margaret Norman, and Mrs Betty Sullivan. We are also indebted
to the editors of *The Economic Journal* and the *Scottish Journal
of Political Economy* and the Directors of the Royal Institute of
International Affairs and Political and Economic Planning for
permission to draw upon some of our works which they have
published.

We gratefully acknowledge financial assistance from several
institutions: the Royal Institute of International Affairs, the
Carnegie Trust for the Universities of Scotland, the Clement-
Wilson Trust, and the Research Funds of Queen's University,
Belfast and the University of St. Andrews.

In thanking all who have assisted us in our task, we must add
that any errors that have found their way into the text are
entirely our responsibility. Similarly no other individuals or
organizations should necessarily be associated with any views
we have expressed.

Finally we owe a very special debt to our wives and families
who have without complaint borne with our absences and with
the constant mental involvement which writing this book has
entailed.

D. L. McL.
D. S.

May 1967

PART I

The Promotion of Competition— Its Impact upon State Policy

I

Steps Towards a Customs Union

THE subject-matter of this book is economic integration: this can of course take many forms. At one end of the spectrum we have the free trade area, in which tariffs and quotas in respect of the trade flowing between the member states are removed but each country retains its own tariff and quota protection with respect to trade with third countries. The European Free Trade Association is a typical example of this, although agriculture has largely but not totally been excluded from the free trade arrangements. Next comes the customs union, which, besides suppressing barriers to the free movement of goods and services between members, requires the equalization of tariffs *vis-à-vis* imports from third countries. Next we have the concept of the common market, which in addition to fulfilling the conditions required by a customs union, also provides for the free movement of factors of production. Then there is the economic union, which goes beyond a common market by requiring some harmonization of national economic policies. Finally, at the end of the spectrum comes total economic integration, which pushes economic union to the point of more or less total unification of national policies, presumably under a supranational political authority.[1]

Where does the EEC stand in this spectrum? First, we should note that although discussions of the EEC often centre upon its customs union aspect, it is in fact more than that since it involves free movement of factors. Then again the phrase 'The Common Market' is often used to describe the EEC (and indeed the ECSC) but clearly the existence of common policies in agriculture and transport and harmonization in fiscal and other fields pushes the EEC beyond the level of a common market to that of an economic union, and indeed this seems to be the best description of it. It

[1] We base our distinctions on those in B. Balassa, *The Theory of Economic Integration* (1962), p.2.

should perhaps be mentioned that the EEC Commission in discussing the implementation of the Rome Treaty (particularly in respect of harmonizing national policies) often refers to the goal of creating within the EEC conditions resembling those of a single internal market in respect of price determination and of the free movement of commodities and factors. This suggests a high degree of economic unification.

The ECSC is a more difficult creature to pin down. It has features more akin to a free trade area than a customs union, in that under the Paris Treaty tariffs *vis-à-vis* third countries were not required to be, and indeed are not, set at a common level. On the other hand the Paris Treaty goes beyond the customs union stage to that of a common market by providing for the free movement of labour—and yet there is no provision in that treaty for free movement of the other factors. There are, however, elements of an economic union in the ECSC in that common rules exist in respect of pricing. It should be added that such common rules apply to the activities of enterprises rather than to state policy, although there are substantial state interests in the Community coal and steel industries. It is clear that the ECSC is a hybrid creation which defies being placed clearly and unambiguously in any one of the categories discussed above. Those who dislike this ambiguity may take comfort in the possibility that the fusion of the treaties, following the fusion of the ECSC and EEC executives, may well lead to a harmonization of ECSC policy with that of the EEC—rather than the other way round. We could then regard the ECSC as no longer being a separate entity but as a more or less integral part of an economic union with possibly a common external tariff for coal and steel products.

I. THE BASIC THEORY OF CUSTOMS UNIONS

Theoretical discussions of customs unions tend to assume that the only obstacles to trade are tariffs. In practice, however, many other obstacles exist which, if not dealt with, would impede the workings of a customs union and jeopardize any advantageous effects which it might otherwise have. Although it is analytically convenient to begin a study of economic integration with tariff questions, realism requires that this should be complemented by a discussion of non-tariff barriers. We examine the latter in subsequent chapters.

Present understanding of the theoretical implications of customs unions is based upon the pioneer study of this subject by Professor Jacob Viner.[2] The theoretical issues were subsequently developed by Professor James Meade[3] and others.[4]

(a) The Static Analysis

It is not difficult to recognize that, from the point of view of resource allocation, the world-wide abolition of tariffs would have positive advantages. The nature of the advantages can be recognized by considering the disadvantageous effects which the existence of tariffs has from the angles of production and consumption. First, the tariff gives rise to a shift in production from lower-cost foreign producers to higher-cost domestic sources of supply of particular commodities. Secondly, it alters the relative prices of foreign and home-produced goods causing consumers to shift from higher valued foreign goods to lower valued domestically produced goods.

(i) *Production Effects of a Customs Union.* Although a customs union clearly represents a free trade arrangement between a group of countries, it would be a mistake to assume that because universal free trade implies a definite improvement on the production side, a customs union must inevitably have the same implications. The problem as Viner saw it was that, on the one hand the establishment of a customs union could, for example, lead to production being shifted from a higher-cost member of the union to a lower-cost member, on the other hand it could lead to a shift from a lower-cost outside supplier to a higher-cost member. Whether a customs union represented an improvement or a deterioration in the production side depended on the balance of such effects.

A numerical example is supplied in Table 1 (p. 7) to illustrate this point. We assume (1) that the world consists of two countries I and II, who wish to form a customs union, and a third outside country which we term III; (2) that only three commodities are

[2] *The Customs Union Issue* (1950).

[3] *The Theory of Customs Unions* (1955).

[4] For a review of these developments see the survey article by R. G. Lipsey, who has himself made a substantial contribution in this field, 'The Theory of Customs Unions: A General Survey', *Econ. J.*, lxx/279 (Sept. 1960), pp. 496–513.

produced: A, B, and C; (3) that prior to the customs union country I applied a 50 per cent *ad valorem* tariff to all imports but after the formation of the union the tariff only applies to imports from country III.

In the case of Good A, the lowest-cost producer is country III which is outside the proposed union. Prior to the union Good A produced by country III (with duty applied) undersells A produced by country I, or A produced by country II (with duty applied). But after the union, A produced in II ceases to have duty applied and undersells A produced in III (bearing duty) and A produced in I. This is trade diversion. In the case of Good B the lowest-cost producer is country II. But even prior to the union B produced in II does not enter I, because the customs duty renders B produced in II uncompetitive with B produced in I. But after the union B produced in II ceases to have duty applied and enters I and undersells B produced in I— here we have trade creation. In the case of Good C, the lowest-cost producer is I, which produces the good before and after the union—as a result neither trade diversion nor trade creation occurs.

Therefore in judging a customs union we have to take into account the fact that it can, for example, shift production away from the lowest-cost producer to a higher-cost member of the union, and that this trade diversion is a departure from a previously more rational pattern of resource allocation. On the other hand the union can shift production away from a less efficient to a more efficient member of the union and such trade creation represents a shift to a more economic pattern of resource allocation. Viner therefore concluded that whether or not a customs union was beneficial depended on the balance of these two effects.

How can this balancing be carried out? Viner gave no precise answer. Meade, however, indicates that the answer will be as follows. In the case of Good A in Table 1, suppose that country I imports 1 million units first from III and then from II; the original cost was £12 million but is now £14 million. The cost of trade diversion—the extra cost incurred by virtue of obtaining supplies from the higher-cost source—is therefore £2 million. In the case of Good B, suppose country I consumes half a million units; then the saving of trade creation is £2·5 million,

TABLE I

Trade Creation and Trade Diversion in a Customs Union

(£)

Good	Cost or cost plus duty per unit	Country III exporting to country I	Flow of trade	Goods produced by country I	Flow of trade	Country II exporting to country I	Results
Good A	Cost	12		20		14	Trade diversion
	Cost plus duty prior to customs union	18	→	20	No trade	21	
	Cost plus duty after customs union	18	No trade	20	↓	14	
Good B	Cost	14		17		12	Trade creation
	Cost plus duty prior to customs union	21	No trade Country I produces B	17	No trade Country I produces B	18	
	Cost plus duty after customs union	21	No trade	17	→	12	
Good C	Cost	16		10		12	Neither trade creation nor trade diversion. Country I is the lowest cost producer and provides C before and after the union.
	Cost plus duty prior to customs union	24	No trade	10	No trade	18	
	Cost plus duty after customs union	24	No trade	10	No trade	12	

so that on balance in this particular hypothetical case, from the production side, the customs union is beneficial.

The above analysis is, however, based upon Viner's simplifying assumptions. The first is that the elasticity of demand for the goods in question is zero, that is to say demand is totally inelastic. This simplifies matters considerably, since in calculating the gains and losses we can assume that any change in the price of A or B[5] resulting from the formation of the union will not cause the quantities consumed in I, pre- and post-union, to differ. The second simplifying assumption is that supply curves are infinitely elastic—clearly the absence of such an assumption would complicate the calculation of gains and losses since costs will change with movements along supply curves.

Suppose that these assumptions are relaxed, what difficulties arise and what solutions can be found? We will deal mainly with the problem arising on the demand side. Assume that demand is not totally inelastic but, as is usually the case, the quantity bought responds to price changes, the relationship being the usual negative one. Let us take the case of Good A in the above example. We shall assume that originally, at a price of £18 per unit, country I consumed 1 million units of A produced in country III, but that, after the union, Good A becomes available to consumers in I at a price of £14 per unit. Suppose that demand is highly elastic and the quantity bought at £14 is 3 million tons. The problem is how shall we treat the extra 2 million tons which is being traded to country I now but was not so before? Here we have to bring into consideration the value to the consumers of this extra trade. Consumers pay £18 for the first million tons and £14 for the last, or third, million tons and, if we take these prices to measure the satisfaction derived, we may, following Meade, split the difference and say that each extra million tons is worth £16 per ton to consumers. The cost of producing those extra units is assumed to be constant at £14 per unit. Meade would argue that on the extra 2 million tons traded there is a £2 per ton excess of consumers' value over producers' cost. Thus there is an extra gain of £4 million, which can be set against the loss from trade diversion. This is something which Viner did not allow for and which is favourable to the case for a customs union. This gain from trade also applies

[5] We can ignore C since there was no change pre- and post-union.

in the case of Good B, where trade creation in any case exists. It should perhaps be observed that when Meade speaks of the excess of consumer value over producer cost he is assuming that the price of each ton of A in country II is equal to the cost of producing that ton, that is, £14. Consumers in II therefore derive £14 worth of satisfaction from a ton of Good A consumed but, on average, extra tons of A in country I are worth £16 to consumers—hence the gain from trade.

(ii) *Consumption Effects of a Customs Union.* In discussing the consumption effects of a customs union we will follow the Meade approach and assume that each of the countries can produce only one product and that there is full employment—in other words the elasticity of supply is zero. Under these circumstances there can be no production effects—that is to say the production of a good cannot shift from a high-cost to a low-cost producer or vice-versa. However, we can consider whether the creation of a customs union will have favourable or unfavourable consumption effects. We once more adopt a three-country model, but this time country I produces only Good A, country II only Good B, and country III only Good C. Also, a unit of each costs £100 to produce. Initially country I imposes an *ad valorem* import duty of 20 per cent, country II a duty of 50 per cent, and country III a duty of 100 per cent. Suppose that subsequently countries I and II form a customs union. What are the consumption effects?

In country I imported B now falls in price because of the abolition of import duty. If we assume that price provides a measure of marginal utility, the consumer in A will derive £120 of utility from a unit of B priced at £100 as opposed to £100 of utility from a unit of domestically produced A priced at £100. The consumer in I will buy more B and less A. The reverse occurs in country II. If we consider this in isolation, then the expansion of trade between country I and II will lead to positive consumption gains.

If this were the end of the matter, we could conclude that on the consumption side the customs union was unambiguously beneficial. However, against this trade expansion between country I and country II we must set the possibility of a trade contraction between country I and country III, and country II and country III. When, for example, the price of imported B falls in country I, consumers will shift not only from A to B but also from C (imported from country III), which has not fallen in price, to B. (In country II consumers will shift not only from B to A but also from C to A.) Two effects are now manifest. Both country I and country II buy less from country III. Also because of the expanded sales of A and B, taking countries I and II together, there will be less A and B to sell to country III. Trade in both directions between country I and country III and country II and country III will contract and here there will be a loss. For example, country I would prefer more C and less A, country III would prefer more A and less C.

This leads us to the conclusion that, as on the production side, so on the consumption side the union can have both advantageous and disadvantageous effects. Whether it is beneficial or not depends on the balance of the effects of trade expansion and contraction. Briefly we can say that where the balance will lie will depend upon two factors. In the first place it will depend upon the structure of tariffs from which the union starts, since this will give rise to different price ratios in each country. The latter measure the gains and losses which can be obtained from expanding or contracting trade. It should be noted that the *initial* ratio of prices only measures the gain or loss on the *first* unit of trade expansion or contraction. The second factor will be the structure of demand in the countries concerned. Thus, as Meade observes, if A and B are good substitutes for each other, but C is a poor substitute for both, the formation of a union will lead to much trade expansion and little trade contraction.

(iii) *Assessing the Probable Effects of Customs Unions.* The static analysis of customs unions does not of itself provide a basis for categorically commending or rejecting them. Whether they are good or bad depends upon the particular circumstances. The theory does, however, suggest certain generalizations which can be applied in judgment, although it must be admitted that there is no substitute for measurement in deciding the actual results of a union. These are some of the more important. (1) A customs union is more likely to lead to a net increase in economic welfare if the economies of the partners are actually very competitive but are potentially complementary. If they produce similar products but efficiencies differ, they will each contract their relatively inefficient industries and expand their efficient ones, and there will be a beneficial increase in mutual trade without much diversion of imports or exports from other markets. If, on the other hand, their economies were complementary, for example one concentrating mainly on producing raw materials, the other on manufactured goods, the prospects of gains on the production side would be correspondingly small. (2) A customs union is more likely to increase economic welfare the higher the initial duties on imports from partners. The higher the duties, the higher the inefficiencies which are being protected and the greater the gains from trade after such protection is removed. (3) The production effects of a customs union will be the more advantageous the lower its tariff against the outside world.[6] (4) A union is more likely to raise welfare the greater the proportion of world production, consumption, and trade covered by it. For example, the larger the union becomes the greater the probability that trade creation will outweigh trade diversion, until, in the case of a union embracing the world, trade diversion would cease to exist.

(b) The Dynamic Analysis

So far the argument has been almost totally static. On the production side the union causes a shift of production leading to once-for-all gains or losses associated with trade diversion and trade creation. But we also need to consider two dynamic aspects of a customs union. One relates to the economies of scale, the other to increased competitive pressure. Indeed, it seems to us that concentration upon the above static analysis fails to take into account what might well be the most important feature of a customs union, which is that its beneficial effects are likely to spring not so much from the reallocation of production with given techniques and facilities as from the development of entirely new methods of production.

(i) *Economies of Scale.* There may be substantial unexploited internal[7] economies of scale caused perhaps by the limited size of national markets.[8] Suppose the creation of a customs union

---

[6] Professor Meade also adds: the lower the tariff level in export markets outside the union.

[7] There may of course be external economies to be derived from the process of forming a customs union.

[8] Scitovsky however is of the view that although the size of national markets may inhibit the full exploitation of scale economies, this latter result arises in the

leads to a diversion of trade from a more efficient outside supplier to a less efficient member country. This would normally be counted as a disadvantage. But if, because of the increased market now available to the member country, it undertakes additional investment, enabling it to take advantage of the economies of scale, then the cost of supplies coming from the member country may fall below that of diverted supplies, thus wiping away the loss due to trade diversion. Gains from economies of scale could of course also arise in the case of trade creation. However, some economists, of whom Professor H. G. Johnson is one, have doubted the existence of any significant benefits in this sphere.[9] Taking as his example the United Kingdom, Johnson doubts whether there are significant unexploited economies of scale in an economy of this size (particularly when account is taken of the fact that the world market has been open to UK products). In our opinion the matter is not quite so straightforward. In the first place, it may be that the UK economy is big enough to accommodate a firm of optimum size. But where, for example, only one firm can be accommodated, the problem of monopoly arises, particularly if tariff or other protection exists. In this case the advantage of economic integration is that optimum size and competition between optimum units can co-exist.

Then again the argument that national markets can accommodate optimal firms does not really meet the EEC size problem at all. The problem in the EEC, as we have indicated, has been in the past one of too many sub-optimal firms, caused by a combination of factors such as market imperfections, a preference for high-margin low-volume strategy, and a correlated preference for an easy life rather than one which involves making incursions into competitors' territory. The increased impersonal competition in an integrated market could push the inefficient firms out and allow the rest to grow to a more efficient size. Informed opinion in the EEC would probably generally agree that there are substantial economies of scale yet to be exploited. Secondly, although international trade provides a means of increasing

main from too many firms, each producing too many models, types, and varieties of product—see T. Scitovsky, *Economic Theory and Western European Integration* (1958), pp. 24–32.

[9] H. G. Johnson, 'The Criteria of Economic Advantages', *Bull. Oxford Univ. Inst. Statist.*, xix (Feb. 1957), p. 35.

sales and output and reaping scale economies, the existence of different national official standards, and so forth, may well set limits to the economies to be derived from export sales. Firms may boost output by exports but these may consist of limited outputs of various models, each designed for a particular market. It is at this point that the policy of harmonization of standards within the EEC becomes particularly important, as this will enable economies of long runs to be secured. Thirdly, discussions about the pros and cons of customs unions tend to consider the advantages of greater firm size almost entirely under the heading of conventional economies of scale, stressing particularly the technical economies related to plant size. But if Community firms grow in size because of the extra demand arising from trade diversion, or if some firms grow at the expense of others as a result of trade creation, this may have real dynamic advantages in that there is a tendency for the amount spent on research and development, as a ratio to employment or output, to increase up to a point with size. This is discussed at greater length in Chapter 8.

(ii) *Increased Competition.* There are some reasons for believing that the degree of competition may increase as a result of the formation of a union. In the first place, industrial structures undergo a change. National monopolies become community oligopolies, the situation in established oligopolies becomes more fluid, with a reduction of oligopolistic collusion and mutual awareness. Secondly, there is the possibility of a psychological change. Scitovsky, writing in 1958, observed that in Western Europe, where national markets were relatively small, relations between competitors were friendly and personal.[10] Competition expresses itself in terms of a willingness of competitors to expand at each other's expense. He argues that this was not likely to occur in the accommodating atmosphere which then characterized the national industries in the Six. He illustrates the problem with a numerical example which assumes that economies of scale exist. Suppose that in one state, prior to the union, industry consists of five firms of approximately equal size. Suppose also that the industry's demand increases by 100,000 per annum and that this is the optimum capacity of a plant using the best techniques known, although existing sub-optimal plants have an

10 Scitovsky, pp. 123–6.

annual capacity of 20,000 per annum. The industry can deal with the growth of demand either by each firm providing one extra sub-optimal plant per annum or by one firm building an optimal plant. But if the latter occurs market shares will be disturbed temporarily (but not permanently if each firm in turn was responsible for such annual expansions). Scitovsky argues that in an oligopolistic situation, in which the price structure allows adequate profits even with sub-optimal plant, disturbances of market shares will probably not occur.

Under circumstances such as these one of the benefits of economic integration is that the opening up of other national markets may induce some firms—which might not be willing to precipitate a change in relative shares in their own national markets—to attempt to make incursions into other national markets where the personal relationship does not exist.[11] Correspondingly, each firm must now be aware that its own national market share can now no longer be regarded as secure and it might be encouraged because of this to look less favourably on the preservation of its less efficient compatriots. Of course this growth of more aggressive business conduct is all the more likely to occur if there are important differences in the business strategies and attitudes as between the different national industries. C. D. Edwards has drawn attention to this factor. He points out that

Countries with a homogeneous culture probably tend to be less competitive than countries that are culturally more diversified; collusion and monopoly flourish best in coherent groups. Group solidarity promotes collusion. Similarity among members of the group limits the variety of competitive ventures that must be suppressed. But when the customary modes of thought and loyalties of differing segments of the business community are diverse, agreement among these segments is likely to be difficult and the members of each segment are likely to offer a different kind of competitive threat to the rest.[12]

[11] Ibid. p. 133.
[12] C. D. Edwards, 'Size of Markets, Scale of Firms, and the Character of Competition' in E. A. G. Robinson, ed., *Economic Consequences of the Size of Nations* (1960), p. 127. We drew attention to this fact in trying to explain the more competitive nature of the ECSC steel market as compared with that existing in the UK (see D. Swann and D. L. McLachlan, 'Steel Pricing in a Recession: an Analysis of United Kingdom and ECSC Experience', *Scottish JPE*, xxii/4 (1965), p. 92).

An intensification of the degree of competition could indeed be a permanent force serving to accelerate technical progress and the rate of economic growth. It may well be that the main benefits from a customs union lie not so much in the static but quantifiable aspects discussed under the heading of trade creation and diversion, as in those dynamic but unquantifiable factors which give rise to greater competition. Economists, as Streeten has observed,[13] tend to focus their attention when assessing the gains of integration upon the quantifiable aspects, neglecting or dismissing the less quantifiable.

2. TARIFFS AND QUOTAS IN THE EEC AND ECSC

(a) EEC

The most substantial barrier to the free movement of goods between states must be ascribed to the existence of import duties and quotas. How substantial were these barriers at the time of the signing of the Rome Treaty? Data are available showing the average tariff level of each of the Six in 1955—this average refers to the tariff level on each member state's imports as a whole and not that on imports from the other five only. The problem which arises here is how to measure the effective height of a tariff, an exercise which led Viner to comment that 'there is no way in which the "height" of a tariff as an index of its restrictive effect can be even approximately measured, or, for that matter, even defined with any degree of significant precision.'[14] Nevertheless at least some rough indication of the relative heights of the tariffs of the member states can be given. One method is to calculate an unweighted average of each national tariff—a procedure which requires that tariff classifications are comparable. Such an unweighted average is a better indicator of the effectiveness of a tariff than an average weighted by value of imports, the reason being that in applying the latter a deceptively low average figure is obtained. This arises from the fact that a relatively high tariff effectively restricts imports, so reducing the weighting factor in the averaging process. Balassa has illustrated this point by drawing on two continental studies

---

[13] P. Streeten, *Economic Integration; Aspects and Problems*, (1961), p. 37.
[14] Viner, *Customs Union Issue*, pp. 66–67.

of tariff levels in the Six, one weighted, the other unweighted.[15] The results are shown in Table 2, where on a weighted basis

TABLE 2

Weighted and Unweighted Average Tariff Levels of the Six in 1955

	Unweighted Average	Weighted Average
Belgium–Luxembourg	9·5	4·3
Netherlands	9·5	5·5
Western Germany	15·5	5·6
Italy	17·3	7·1
France	18·1	5·1

Source: Unweighted data: R. Bertrand, 'Comparaison du niveau des tarifs douaniers des pays du marché commun', *Cahiers de l'Inst. de Science Économique Appliquée*, Serie R, No. 2, Feb. 1958, p. 7. Weighted data: H. C. Binswanger, 'Der Zollschutz in den Ländern der europäischen Wirtschaftsgemeinschaft und in der Schweiz', *Aussenwirtschaft*, Mar.–June 1959, p. 131 (cited by Balassa, p. 46).

protectionist France appears as a low-tariff country whereas in part it is low imports caused by relatively high tariffs which has caused this result. The unweighted data indicate that the members of Benelux were relatively low-tariff countries, Western Germany lay in between, with France and Italy the most heavily protected. These relative positions are confirmed by an investigation (relating however to 1952) by J. Black,[16] in which he determined for each of sixteen tariff headings the percentage of the heading (not trade) with a duty of 11 per cent or over and averaged these percentages on an unweighted basis. The percentages resulting for Italy, France, Western Germany, and Benelux were 87, 82, 65, and 43 per cent respectively.

Article 9 of the Rome Treaty begins by saying 'The Community shall be based upon a customs union.' This has two main implications. First, tariffs on trade flowing between the member states have to be eliminated, and, secondly, tariffs in respect of

---

[15] Balassa, table 1, p. 46.
[16] J. Black, 'The Implications of the Proposed European Free Trade Area', in G. D. N. Worswick, ed., *The Free Trade Proposals* (1960), table xvi, p. 20.

trade with third countries have to be equalized in order to form a common customs tariff—often referred to as the common external tariff.

(i) *The Elimination of Internal Tariffs.* Article 12 introduces a 'standstill' requirement by binding member states not to introduce new customs duties on imports (or exports) within the Community or to increase those duties already in existence. Article 13 requires the duties existing on 1 January 1957 to be eliminated not later than by the end of the transition period, that is by the end of 1969.[17] Article 14 prescribes a time table for this process of dismantling tariff protection, and in Table 3 (p. 18) we show the progress so far achieved in the industrial and agricultural sectors. It will be noted that in 1961 and 1962 there were accelerated cuts putting the Community ahead of schedule. If present plans are fulfilled, intra-Community customs duties will have been eliminated by 1 July 1968.

Two other points are worthy of notice. One is that Articles 12 and 13 between them require that in respect of charges having effects which are equivalent to import duties, existing ones should not be increased nor should new ones be imposed, and that they should be eliminated within the transition period. These charges refer to such things as taxes, which cannot be described as import duties but nevertheless have the same effect in that they apply to imports only. Such taxes would not include charges, levied on imports, equivalent in amount to taxes—as for example turnover taxes—levied on the same good produced domestically.[18] The second point is that Article 16 requires the abolition during the transition period of customs duties on exports or charges having an equivalent effect.

(ii) *Safeguards.* It is worth noting that, under Article 226 of the Rome Treaty, if during the transition period there are serious difficulties in a sector and these persist, or if there are difficulties which might result in a region suffering grave hardship, a member state can seek the approval of the Commission to take protective measures. This has a direct relevance to the process of dismantling tariffs (and quotas). In practice the number of

---

[17] Customs duties of a fiscal character also have to be reduced along with the general reduction in customs duties proper.

[18] The imported good would of course have had turnover tax remitted upon export.

TABLE 3

Reductions of Internal Customs Duties in the EEC

(per cent)

	1.1.59	1.7.60	Acceleration of 1.1.61	1.1.62	Acceleration of 1.7.62	1.7.63	1.1.65	1.1.66
Industrial products:								
1. Individual reductions made in 1 Jan. 1957 level	10	10	10	10	10	10	10	10
2. Cumulative reduction	10	20	30	40	50	60	70	80
Agricultural products (Annexe II of Treaty)								
1. Individual reductions made in 1 Jan. 1957 level	10	10	5*	10	5†	10	10	5 / 10
2. Cumulative reduction at 1.1.66	10	20	25* / 20	35* / 30	35 / 30†	45 / 40†	55 / 50†	65 / 60

* Reduction for non-liberalized agricultural products only.
† Reduction for liberalized agricultural products only.
‡ Reduction for certain liberalized agricultural products only.

Source: EEC, *9th Gen. Rep.* (1966), p. 44.

instances where exceptions have been made are few. The process of dismantling protective barriers has been achieved with relatively little fuss.

Most of the special measures have been for the benefit of Italy. For example, in 1962 the first accelerated tariff reduction was waived in respect of imports of lead-covered cable into Italy.[19] The most interesting example of special action under Article 226 concerns imports of Italian refrigerators into France. In 1963, because of the disturbance caused by Italian competition, the Commission permitted the levying of a tax on Italian refrigerators entering the French market. The tax (in addition to the 7·5 per cent import duty) was only temporary, being 12 per cent from 17 January 1963 to 30 April, then 9 per cent from 1 May to 30 June, and 6 per cent from 1 to 31 July—thereafter it was abolished. The upsurge of Italian refrigerator exports to France followed the abolition of quotas and cuts in the import duties in 1962—it will be remembered that in 1962 there were two tariff cuts, one of 10 and one of 5 per cent. The French industry appears to have been particularly vulnerable, since imports from Italy increased sixfold between 1961 and 1962—and imports from other Community countries also increased three-fold. Employment in the French industry decreased by about one-third over this period, five out of fifteen producers ceased producing refrigerators and stocks rose to about 190,000 units at the end of 1962, equivalent to about 20 per cent of annual French consumption. The Italian government strenuously resisted the idea that the upsurge of exports to France was due to dumping and the Commission did not take that view either. The Italian industry was indeed highly competitive, and as a result was able to offer better profit margins to French dealers as an inducement to hold stocks and push sales of Italian models, and as a means of enabling dealers to offer tempting discounts below oatalogue prices, which were incidentally similar to those of comparable French models. The Italian government objected to the Commission's decision in favour of temporary protection and contested the matter in the European Court of Justice. The argument turned upon such matters as whether or not the French refrigerator industry constituted a 'sector of the economy'

---

[19] A list of some of the earlier decisions is to be found in EEC, *6th Gen. Rep.* (1963) pp. 45–47. Subsequent measures also appear in later *General Reports*.

within the meaning of Article 226. The upshot of this case was that the Court upheld the Commission's decision.[20]

It is convenient while discussing the subject of dismantling tariffs to say a few words about quotas. Articles 31 and 32 contain the main provisions in this field, since they introduce a standstill requirement and call for the abolition of quotas by the end of the transition period.[21] At the time of the signing of the Rome Treaty quotas were, however, no longer the major hindrances to trade which they had been in the period immediately following the last war—a fact which is to be ascribed to the measures of liberalization evolved within the framework of the IMF, the GATT, and, above all, the OEEC. By 1957 the percentage of imports from all other members of the Community not yet liberalized was for West Germany 16, Benelux 3, Italy 3, and France 25 per cent.[22]

(iii) *Establishing the Common External Tariff.* Basically the principle for establishing the common external tariff is laid down in Article 19, which declares that the duty to be applied by all member states in respect of imports from third countries will be the (unweighted) arithmetical average of the import duties of the four customs territories of the Community on 1 January 1957.[23] There are, however, a number of exceptions to this rule. For products on List A of the treaty the duties in the list were to be substituted for duties calculated by arithmetical average. For products in Lists B, C, D, and E the tariff levels derived by averaging could not exceed 3, 10, 15, and 25 per cent respectively.[24] For goods on List F duties were laid down in the list; and duties for goods in List G were to be determined by negotiation between the member states. The actual establishment of the external tariff was to be brought about gradually. Article 23 required tariffs, which on 1 January 1957 were less than 15 per cent above or below the final common level, to be brought

[20] See 'Re Electric Refrigerators: The Italian Government v. EEC Commission (Case 13/63)', *Common Market Law Reports*, ii, pt. 8, 1963, pp. 289–314.
[21] The actual procedure for abolishing quotas, which began with the globalization of bilateral quotas, is dealt with in Article 33.
[22] F. Ortoli, 'The Customs Union' in H. K. Junckerstorff, ed., *International Manual on the European Economic Community* (1963), p. 105.
[23] But in the case of Italy the relevant duties were those operating prior to the temporary 10 per cent reduction in force on 1 Jan. 1957.
[24] In respect of List E goods, where a Benelux duty was 3 per cent or less, that duty was to be raised to 12 per cent for averaging purposes.

to the common level on 1 January 1962. In all other cases there was to be, on 1 January 1962, a 30 per cent reduction of the difference between the 1957 and the final external tariff level. Another 30 per cent adjustment was to be made on 1 January 1966 and the common external tariff was to be fully established by the end of the transition period at the latest. In practice it has been agreed that the completing adjustment will be made on 1 July 1968. It will be seen from Table 4 that, in respect of industrial goods, accelerated adjustments have been made.

TABLE 4

The Establishment of the Common External Tariff of the EEC

(*per cent*)

	Acceleration 1.1.61	1.1.62	Acceleration 1.7.63	1.1.66	Proposed adjustment 1.7.68
Industrial products					
Adjustments made	30		30		40
Cumulative adjustment	30		60		100
Agricultural products					
Adjustments made		30		30	40
Cumulative adjustment		30		60	100

Source: EEC, *8th Gen. Rep.* (1965), p.33.

Finally, we make a few brief comments upon the height of the common external tariff. It has been contended that the effect of using the unweighted rather than the weighted average has been to push the tariff up. The point of this charge is that an unweighted average gives the same weight to the higher Italian and French tariffs as it does to the lower German and Benelux tariffs although the volume of trade in the latter was greater than in the former. There does not, however, appear to be any substance in this claim. Thus, taking the structure of imports into the Community in 1958 and applying an unweighted tariff gives an average percentage incidence of 7·6 per cent while the weighted average gives a figure of 9·1 per cent. (Taking the import data for 1958 the average incidence of the original common external tariff by products would be for food 15·1 per cent, for raw materials 0.1 per cent, for processed goods 7 per cent, for capital goods 12½ per cent, and for industrial products 17.3 per cent.)[25] Community officials maintain that the external tariff is moderate, although it must be observed that it would have been lower if the temporary Italian cut of 10 per cent in force on 1 January 1957 and the German cut of 25 per cent introduced later in 1957 had been incorporated. We should also mention that cuts in the common external tariff were negotiated in the 'Dillon Round' concluded in 1962,[26] and at the time of writing final offers are being prepared for the 'Kennedy Round'.

(b) ECSC

Article 4 of the Paris Treaty declares that all import and export duties and quantitative restrictions on the movement of coal and steel within the Community are prohibited. The treaty entered into force on 25 July 1952, and after a six-month preparatory period, the common market for coal, iron ore, and scrap came into existence—that is on 10 February 1953. The problem of abolishing import duties hardly arose, since, with one exception, there were no such duties on these products. The exception was Italy, which imposed a 15 per cent duty on coke imports, and this was allowed to continue on a degressive basis, being finally eliminated at the expiration of the five-year transition period.[27] Imports of these products were also generally free from quantitative restriction. In the case of iron and steel products, the common market for which was established on the 1 May 1953, the situation was different. All the Community countries had duties on iron and steel imports, the levels being shown in Table 5.

In practice the French and German duties were in suspension and the Italian rates continued to be applied during the transition period,[28] so that only the Benelux rates were actually removed in

[25] Data on incidence from Ortoli, in Junckerstorff, p. 103.

[26] The Community was prepared to make an across-the-board cut of 20 per cent but this was not taken up, and in the end the cuts negotiated represented less than half this offer.

[27] This ended on 10 Feb. 1958, five years after the establishment of the common market for coal.

[28] The Italian rates were progressively reduced and finally abolished at the end of the transition period. In the case of pig-iron final abolition took place in 1955.

TABLE 5

Iron and Steel Import Duties of the Six in 1952

(per cent)

	Pig-iron	Crude & semi-finished steel	Hot-finished steel products	Finished steel products
Benelux	0–1	1–2	1–6	6–8
France	5	7–10	10–18	10–22
West Germany	12	15–18	15–25	15–28
Italy	11–20	11–15	15–20	15–23

Source: H. Mendershausen, 'First Tests of the Schuman Plan', *R. Econ. & Statist.*, xxxv/4 (Nov. 1953), table 2, p. 277.

1953. However, the effect of the treaty was to prevent the French and German rates ever being applied to intra-Community trade at a later date. Quantitative restrictions were also removed from steel exports within the Community and quantitative import restrictions, which were important in the case of France, were also abolished. A separate régime existed for special steels. These were not integrated into the common market until 1 August 1954, and in the case of Italy a progressive reduction of duties over the transition period was allowed.

It should also be mentioned that the High Authority had to deal with miscellaneous protective devices. For example, the Italian government charged an 'administrative duty' of ½ per cent on imports of ECSC treaty products and the Belgian government made the issue of licences for the import of coal from the Ruhr subject to certain transport regulations.[29] These and other obstacles were removed as a result of efforts by the High Authority and the latter also strove successfully to reduce the burden of formalities and administrative procedures imposed upon goods passing over national frontiers. The EEC Commission is also aware of the latter problem.

On the external side the Paris Treaty does not call for a common external tariff, and an equalization of import duties has

[29] W. Diebold, *The Schuman Plan* (1959), pp. 151–2.

2*

not in fact been achieved. As we have seen, duties were not levied on imports of coal,[30] iron ore, and scrap from third countries, but duties on imports of iron and steel from third countries did exist, and when the common market for steel was opened the French and West Germans reimposed their suspended import duties. Since 1952 there has been a considerable reduction in iron and steel duties.[31] For example, at the outset of the common market in steel some German rates were lowered to the French level. Then again in 1956 German rates were reduced unilaterally to combat inflation and in the same year ECSC protection was reduced in GATT negotiations. The main negotiations were with the US and Austria, although concessions were extended to other GATT members. In 1957 an agreement was concluded between the Community and the UK in which the latter reduced its import duties, in exchange for which the Six agreed to apply a new 'harmonized' set of duties. (The latter did not of course involve equalization of national rates. The Benelux tariff was in fact moved upwards but on balance a substantial reduction in Community protection was brought about.) Further reductions also occurred in the Dillon Round. By 1963 Community protection was well below the 1952 level. Tariff rates for semi-finished and finished steel products in 1963 lay between 4 and 10 per cent[32] whereas, as we can see from Table 5, the 1952 level lay for the most part in the 6–28 per cent range. However, in January 1964 the High Authority recommended the raising of import duties on iron and steel products to the minimum Italian level, which averaged 9 per cent, and this was acted upon, although only on a temporary basis.[33] This action was taken as a defence, during the steel recession which began in 1961, against low-price steel imports coming, in some cases, from countries enjoying higher domestic protection than the ECSC. Nevertheless the Community level of protection still remains well below the 1952 level and indeed well below some of its major competitors.

[30] The exception was, of course, Italian coke duties.
[31] For an interesting discussion of the reductions up to 1958 see Diebold, ch. 17.
[32] ECSC High Authority Doc., No. 6943/63f, (1963), table 8.
[33] A specific duty of $7 per metric ton was also imposed on pig-iron imports— see ECSC, *12th Gen. Rep.* (1964), pp. 46–48. For the background to these decisions see ch. 9, below.

It is also worth noting that in the case of coal, as a result of the deteriorating position of Community coal—a subject which we deal with later in Chapter 3 and also in Chapter 10 on managed markets—in 1959 the German government imposed an import duty of 20 DM per metric ton (equal to 36 per cent of the 1959 import price)[34] on all coal entering Germany from outside the Community over and above a duty-free quota.[35]

[34] J. E. Meade, H. H. Liesner, and S. J. Wells, *Case Studies in European Economic Union* (1962), p. 250.
[35] ECSC, *12th Gen. Rep.* (1964), p. 134.

2

Fiscal Factors in an Economic Union

I. INDIRECT TAXES

ALTHOUGH customs duties and quotas may initially constitute the biggest obstacle to the free movement of goods, once they have been removed or substantially reduced the problems posed by indirect taxes begin to obtrude.

(a) Turnover Taxes

This form of tax was one which posed considerable problems during the early years of the Schuman Plan. Indeed, understanding of this subject was greatly increased as a result of the Tinbergen Report[1] which the High Authority called for in order to reach a settlement on the Franco-German turnover-tax dispute in 1952.[2] The following discussion is limited to the more recent aspects of the problem as they have appeared in the EEC.

A turnover tax is a general tax upon production. As far as the Community is concerned, it is possible to distinguish two forms of this tax.

(i) *Added Value Taxes.* The first is the added value tax—*la taxe sur valeur ajoutée*. Basically the principle of this type is that the tax is paid at each stage in the productive process upon the value added at each stage. The final price of a product (in the absence of turnover tax) is equal to the sum of the values added at each stage in the productive process. Because of this it makes no difference whether the tax is collected at several stages or as a single payment on the final product. The tax collected will be the same in either case—the tax is therefore neutral as between production which is carried out in a vertically integrated

---

[1] *Rapport sur les problèmes posés par les taxes sur le chiffre d'affaires dans le marché commun* (1953).

[2] We do not propose to discuss this topic—rather the reader who wishes to follow it up is recommended to read the discussion by Liesner in Meade, Liesner, & Wells, pp. 310–36. This is in our opinion the best treatment of the subject and we have derived much benefit from Liesner's work in this field.

firm and production carried out by several separate firms with tax levied at the intermediate stages.

The value added tax is applied in France—the actual rate being applied to the *tax-inclusive* value added.[3] The tax is applied, in general, up to the wholesale stage of distribution and applies to a very wide range of goods including the supply of coal, electricity, and gas, and the construction of buildings.[4] The general rate is 20 per cent of tax-inclusive values but certain classes of goods are taxed at different rates—as little as 6 per cent or as much as 25 per cent.

(ii) *Cascade Taxes*. The second type of turnover tax is the cascade or cumulative version. With variations, this is applied in all the other five member states, although Western Germany is proposing to shift over to the French approach. The West German cascade system covers a wide range of goods and services including investment goods and building construction. It consists of a standard levy of 4 per cent of the tax-inclusive selling price and applies to all stages of production and distribution, including the retail stage, though with exceptions. There are some reduced rates and exemptions. The important point to note is the cumulative nature of the tax. Tax is applied at each stage upon the whole selling value including tax. If the product is used in further production the selling price of the resulting product upon which tax is charged will be inflated by tax paid at the previous stage. Unlike the added value tax, under the cascade system the cost of producing a given product excluding tax (that is the value added) may be the same whether produced by a vertically integrated firm or by a vertical series of independent enterprises, but the tax paid on the product of the latter will be greater than that levied on the former.

(iii) *Systems of Application*. Next, it is important to distinguish two systems which can be employed in applying turnover taxes— these are the origin and destination principles. Under the origin principle the tax is levied in the country of origin, that

---

[3] The tax is actually levied on gross output and an allowance is made for tax paid at previous stages.

[4] The main exceptions are unprocessed farm and fishery products and some lightly processed foodstuffs. A separate services tax—*la taxe sur la prestation de service*—is applied in a wide range of consumer and business services. A useful discussion of the French indirect tax system can be found in *Report of the Committee on Turnover Taxation* (Richardson Committee), Cmnd. 2300, 1964.

is, the country in which the good is produced and irrespective of the country in which it is consumed. Under the destination principle the tax is levied in the country in which the good is consumed irrespective of where it was produced. This latter system involves the application of export rebates and counter-vailing import duties. Two examples will illustrate the principle. Suppose there are two countries A and B producing Good X. Suppose the cost of production is the same in each, that is £100, but that A applies an added value tax of 10 per cent and B of 20 per cent. According to the origin principle, when A produces a unit of X it levies a tax of £10, and if it is exported it enters B's market at a price of £110. Likewise B levies a tax of £20 on each unit of X produced and any of its X exported enters A's market at £120. According to the destination principle, in its ideal form, when good X is exported to B an export rebate of £10 (equal to the added value tax levied) is granted while on entry into B a compensating import duty of £20 would be levied.

We shall see later that it appears possible that within the EEC there will be a change over in the present system from the destination to the origin principle. What are the implications of such a shift if national rates differ? The first relates to the allocation of resources, the second to the external balance.

(iv) *Effects on Resource Allocation.* We can follow the effects on resource allocation by means of a simple comparative cost analysis using a two-country, two-commodity model in which each country employs an added value tax but A applies a 50 per cent rate and B a 100 per cent rate. The conclusion of the Tinbergen Report was that the allocation of resources would not be affected by a shift from one system to another. The reason for this was that, in the case of country A, on the basis of the destination principle both products would be exempt from the 50 per cent tax, and, therefore, the relative costs of producing the two products for export would not be affected. Under the origin principle both goods bear a tax of 50 per cent and again relative costs would be unchanged. The same considerations apply in the case of country B. The shift from one system to another would not, of itself, affect the distribution of resources in the trade between the two countries, since with given demand conditions, this depends on comparative cost conditions.

(v) *Effects on the External Balance.* When, however, we come to consider the question of external balance, we observe a difference. A shift from the destination to the origin principle would have an effect on the external balance. Let us assume that trade between the two countries was in balance prior to the change over and that exchange rates were temporarily fixed. When the change to the origin principle occurs the country which levies the higher rate of turnover tax, country B in our example, would find that, even though its industries might be as efficient as those in A, it would not be able to sell its products in competition with those of A, since its export price level would rise above the price level of its rival A by virtue of having its higher domestic rate of tax applied to its exports rather than the lower domestic rate of its rival. A balance-of-trade deficit will, therefore, arise. The country (A) with the lower rate of tax would find its export price level had fallen relatively to the price level of its rival (B). The situation could, however, be corrected by B devaluing or deflating. In our example, equilibrium of the balance of trade could be re-established by a devaluation by B of 25 per cent. (It should, of course, be emphasized that the situation in the EEC is much more complicated than this model. Tax systems differ, general rates differ, and different goods are accorded reduced rates or exemptions.)

(vi) *The Problem in the EEC.* We are now in a position to consider the problem of turnover taxes as it actually affects the EEC. But before doing so we must briefly note what the Rome Treaty provisions are in this matter. These are found in Articles 95 to 99. Articles 95 and 96 relate to discrimination in respect of internal charges—a member state must not apply to products of other member states charges in excess of those applied directly or indirectly to similar products of its own, and in respect of exports a member state shall not accord drawbacks in excess of internal charges imposed directly or indirectly. These two points relate to the question of export drawbacks and countervailing import duties discussed earlier in connexion with turnover taxes. (They are in a sense interim provisions since, as we shall see, it is envisaged that a common turnover tax system with equal national rates will be adopted such that export rebates and countervailing import charges would cease to be a problem. In the case of excise duties the possibility of retaining the destination principle could, however, mean that Articles 95 and 96 could continue to be applied in practice.)

Article 97 declares that in respect of the cumulative multi-stage turnover tax (that is, the type which is, for example, applied in Western Germany) the export drawbacks and counter-vailing import charges can be based upon average rates. (This again will probably prove to be only an interim provision in practice since the West German system, which gives rise to this provision, will not be adopted generally if the Commission has its way.)

Article 98 states that in respect of charges other than turnover taxes, excise duties, and other forms of indirect tax, export drawbacks and compensating import duties are not allowed except in special circumstances. Article 99 requires the Commission to consider how the further integration of the Common Market can be achieved by harmonization of national legislation in respect of turnover taxes, excise duties, and other forms of indirect tax.

With the latter requirement in mind, the Commission quite early on in the development of the Common Market turned its attention to the question of harmonization of turnover taxes. In 1959 a group of governmental experts on fiscal questions concluded that the diversity of turnover tax systems in the Common Market was prejudicial to its development and that harmonization was desirable. As a result three working groups were set up, consisting of experts representing the member states and the Commission, to consider aspects of the turnover tax question. The Fiscal and Financial Committee, chaired by Professor Fritz Neumark, composed of university professors (including Professor Carl Shoup) and attended by members of the staff of the EEC Commission, has also considered the problem at length.[5] This committee was set up by a decision of the EEC Commission of 5 April 1960. Its task was to study how differences in member-state public finance hindered the establishment of a common market and how such differences could be eliminated.

The two major problems which have faced the Commission and its advisers have been, first, whether the origin or destination

---

[5] Translations of both the reports of the working groups and the Neumark Committee can be found in International Bureau of Fiscal Documentation, *The EEC Reports on Tax Harmonization* (1963).

principle should be adopted and, secondly, what type of turnover tax should be the basis of the Community system.

(vii) *Choice of System for the EEC.* There are two major drawbacks to the destination principle. The first is that it inevitably requires export drawbacks and countervailing import charges. These are difficult to calculate, especially in the case of a cascade tax. As Shoup observes:

it may be extremely difficult to estimate closely how much of a general sales tax is embodied, so to speak, in any particular item of export, so complicated are the processes of manufacture and the channels of commerce. Indeed, absolute precision would require taking into account sales-tax collections going far back; exported textiles have been produced on taxed steel that was itself produced by taxed machinery, and so on.[6]

Because of such practical difficulties, the West German authorities have, as permitted by the treaty, calculated broad average rates of rebate. But unintended distortions can occur. Also, difficulties of accurate calculation can cloak deliberate discrimination in the form of excessive export drawbacks and import charges. The second major disadvantage is a psycho-political one. Thus while tariff frontiers will be removed, machinery will have to be maintained to calculate export drawbacks and to apply import charges—this means that fiscal frontiers would still exist.

For reasons of this kind it has been suggested that the origin principle should be adopted. It would, however, appear that if this were done but different national rates were applied, then, if exchange rates remained unchanged, the lower-rate countries would undersell the higher-rate countries and this could give rise to substantial economic difficulties. The Neumark Committee, however, suggested a common rate in all countries, which would appear to dispose of this problem.

In Table 1 we show the percentage of total tax revenue raised by turnover taxation: it is clear that this forms an important proportion of total tax revenues. It is to be expected that harmonization would lead to significant changes in revenue. For example, in France and Belgium reductions would be likely to

[6] C. S. Shoup, 'Taxation Aspects of International Economic Integration', in *Aspects financiers et fiscaux de l'intégration économique internationale* (1954), p. 94.

TABLE I

Percentage of Total Tax Revenue Raised by Turnover Taxes in 1959

Western Germany	25·3
France	34·7
Belgium	29·1
Netherlands	19·0
Italy	20·4
Luxembourg	16·2

Source: Report of the [Neumark] Fiscal and Financial Committee (1963), p. 114.

occur while in the Netherlands the opposite effect would be likely. The question arises, how can tax revenue be maintained in countries like France and Belgium, other things being equal? One suggestion was that the common turnover tax be supplemented by a tax at the retail stage which could be varied according to national necessity and thus compensate for changes in turnover tax revenue caused by harmonization. The Neumark Committee suggested that goods at the retail stage do not normally enter into international trade, so no notable disturbance of such trade would arise if differences existed in the national retail sales tax rates.

(viii) *Choice of Type of Tax.* The second major problem concerns the type of turnover tax to be adopted. The Commission's advisers favoured the French-type added value tax and this point has now been generally accepted by the member state governments. The basic reason for selecting the added value tax is that it is 'neutral' while the cascade system is not.[7] Thus, under the

[7] The cascade system has never been regarded as a potential model for common usage. At one stage the idea of a production tax levied at a single stage, the last in the production process, was considered. It was, however, pointed out that this tax would present a financing problem for the final producer, who would have to pay the tax to the revenue authorities but credit terms to purchasers might prevent him recovering it quickly. The alternative was considered that the tax be levied at several stages in the production process; but the possibility that such a tax would not be neutral, as between enterprises which were vertically integrated and those that were not, led to the favouring of the added value form of turnover tax. We should point out that a shift to a single-stage tax would have involved a radical change in tax policy, and this appears to have been considered too much of an upheaval although it would reduce the number of collection points.

cascade system, the amount of tax paid depends, other things being equal, upon the number of separate stages in the productive process at which raw materials and semi-finished products are sold by one enterprise to another. This provides a powerful incentive to vertical integration, while by contrast the added value system neither encourages nor discourages it.

Two possible consequences arise out of the cascade system's bias to vertical integration. The first is that, although in fact it may be more efficient to specialize in one stage of the productive process, the tax system may discourage this. It may, of course, be the case that on balance there is no advantage in specializing and that the integrated and non-integrated enterprises are equally efficient. But even then the integrated concern enjoys an artificial advantage. The second is connected with market power. Commentators generally content themselves with alluding to the stimulus to concentration. It should, however, be noted that, normally, economists would be more alarmed by the prospect of greater *horizontal* concentration, that is, where the number of sellers of a particular product is reduced (or where a greater proportion of total sales is in the hands of a given number of firms). Are there, from the point of view of competition, any reasons for fearing *vertical* concentration? On the face of it the answer is yes—it could enable certain firms to suppress competition. A firm which integrated backwards could control supplies of raw materials, semi-finished products, and so forth and therefore could force competitors either out of business or to conform. Of course what we are really saying here is that this problem only arises if there is *horizontal* concentration at an earlier stage of production, and it is not immediately clear that this is any more likely to occur when vertical integration exists than in its absence. It could of course be argued that by vertically taking over other enterprises, a firm could accumulate financial resources which would put it in a better position to integrate horizontally and endure price-wars.[8]

[8] A point which is generally overlooked is that the 'amount' of competitive activity in a totally vertically-integrated industry would appear to be less than that in one in which vertical integration is less or non-existent. For example, if it is non-existent, then at each stage in the productive process competitive sales exist. In a totally vertically-integrated industry competition only occurs when selling to the final consumer. If there are no economies to be derived from vertical integration, then there is a loss of competition with no compensating gain in productive efficiency.

The other aspect of neutrality relates to productive techniques. The Richardson Committee, for example, indicates that while the value-added system is neutral as between capital- and labour-intensive methods of production, the cascade system penalizes investment, because a firm which purchases equipment from outside will have to bear the tax in the cost of its purchases.[9]

(ix) *Progress up to February 1967*. In February 1967, after a long delay, the Council of Ministers agreed to the adoption of a common turnover tax of the value-added type. Two directives were adopted. The first[10] requires the common value-added tax to come into force on 1 January 1970 at the latest and national laws must be promulgated early enough for this date-line to be complied with.

The second directive[11] concerns the methods of application of the common turnover tax which each state must incorporate in its tax law. The common tax is to be a general tax, levied, in principle, at each stage of the economic process in such a way that it falls on the value added at each point. In principle the tax will be charged on the deliveries of all goods up to and including the retail stage. As we have seen, the Neumark Committee suggested the possibility that the tax should only extend to the wholesale stage, and that a separate sales tax be levied at the retail stage. The level of the latter would be determined by the impact of turnover tax rate harmonization on national tax revenue. This idea has not been adopted. However, until such time as fiscal frontiers are finally abolished, member states will be free to limit the field of application of the tax up to and including the wholesale stage. In one of its draft directives the Commission was of the opinion that services 'of only local significance' could be excluded, since fiscal disparities in this field are not apt to cause disturbances in the conditions of competition between member states. On the other hand, many services do enter into the cost of producing goods, and they should be covered by the tax. This line of thinking has been embodied in the present directive. Services will only be taxed if they have a marked direct or indirect effect on the price of goods. A list of such services has been specified, and it includes the assignment of patents and trade

[9] Cmnd. 2300, pp. 13 & 15.
[10] *JO*, 14 Apr. 1967.
[11] Ibid.

marks, freight transport and warehousing, but not banking services. It is up to member states to decide whether they will tax services lying outside the list, and, if so, at what rate. The latter will include services rendered by doctors, hairdressers, and others who usually supply their services only to private individuals.

How turnover tax policy will evolve in the future must be a matter of speculation. It is, however, clear that following the introduction of a common system of value-added tax, the intention is that the next stage should consist of harmonization of value-added tax rates. In addition it would also appear from statements made at the time of the adoption of the two above directives that the origin system will be adopted. This is not absolutely certain but the reference to the abolition of compensatory import taxes and export drawbacks seems to point in this direction.

(x) *Fiscal Violations of the Treaty.* The Commission has had to deal with cases of violations of the treaty in the field of indirect taxes which have come to its notice. There are several of these and we shall only cite a few instances. In 1963, for example, Italy was induced to abolish a rate differential in the single-stage turnover tax as between domestic and imported products.[12] Belgium was also influenced to do away with turnover tax discrimination in respect of imported spirits, pigs for slaughter, and pigmeat.[13] Subsequently the Belgian government put an end to discrimination in this field in respect of certain types of slaughter cattle and meat.[14] The Belgian government also submitted a bill to Parliament to abolish the exemption from turnover tax which Belgian government departments enjoyed when purchasing Belgian, as opposed to imported, goods.[15] Agreement to these changes has not always been easily obtained. Thus, in its 1963 *General Report*, the Commission indicated that it had to compel by a Decision the West German government to end its practice of applying a higher turnover tax on imported worsted yarns than on the German product.[16]

Perhaps the most interesting case in this field concerns the export drawback which the Italian government allowed on a very

---

[12] EEC, *6th Gen. Rep.* (1963), p. 79.
[14] EEC, *7th Gen. Rep.* (1964), p. 85.
[16] EEC, *6th Gen. Rep.* (1963), p. 90.

[13] Ibid.
[15] Ibid.

large range of engineering products. The drawback of taxes on production was computed at a flat rate per kilogramme of the products or classes of products concerned. The Commission attacked the practice on the ground that it was a violation of Article 96, since the Italian system treated as eligible for drawback certain charges which could not be said to be of the type allowed by that article. The matter was taken to the Court of Justice, which ruled against the Italian government, indicating that company-registration charges, stamp duty, mortgage charges, charges on government concessions, and taxes on motor vehicles and advertising did not constitute the direct or indirect charges which could be allowed in drawbacks. As for the other taxes of the kind which could be allowed, the Commission had objected to the flat-rate basis of their calculation, on the ground that they were equivalent to average rates rather than actual. The Court required the Italian government to establish that the drawback did not exceed the amount of tax borne in each case.[17]

(b) Excise Duties

These too pose a problem for the EEC, because certain products are taxed in some member states but not in others and because in the case of those which are taxed in all or some states, the rates tend to vary. The fact that this situation would interfere with the proper working of competition can be easily seen. Suppose we assume two countries, both of whom produce only tobacco and wine. As a result of tariffs they have not hitherto traded with each other but now they form a customs union. Should they adopt the origin or destination principle if distortions are to be avoided? Suppose that X applies a (high) excise duty solely on tobacco and Y does likewise with wine. Under the origin principle producers of tobacco in X will (*ceteris paribus*), because of the tax burden which they alone bear, find their sales falling off in X and Y. Similar reasoning would lead us to expect producers of wine in Y to find sales falling off in Y and X. Production of tobacco in Y and of wine in X would both expand. Such results would not, however, necessarily be the reflection of differing factor endowments but of differences in tax rates on particular products. The application of the destination principle

[17] European Communities' Court of Justice, *Recueil de la Jurisprudence de la Cour*, 1966, xi/10, pp. 1057–80.

would eliminate this problem, but then we would have a fiscal frontier. The Neumark Committee was aware of this and considered the possibility of adopting the origin principle together with an equalization of excise duty rates in all states. However, the Committee recognized that equalization in this field would severely disturb the raising of revenue. As a result it concluded that rates would have to differ and the destination principle, with its attendant fiscal frontiers, would have to be accepted. There are grounds for thinking that the Commission does not agree with this as a solution. At the moment the problem is being studied.

The destination principle does not, however, remove all forms of distortion.[18] We have so far been considering the optimization of production, and the destination principle fulfils this condition. But we should also consider the optimization of trade. If we were to do so we would conclude in our example above that the destination principle does not optimize trade. This is because the imposition of taxes and their consequent effects on the relative prices of tobacco and wine in X and Y would cause consumers in X to buy more wine and less tobacco than they would otherwise do. On the other hand consumers in Y would buy more tobacco and less wine than they would otherwise do. There would be a gain from a shift of wine from X to Y and tobacco from Y to X.

Clearly where excise rates differ from product to product, as in our example, neither the origin nor the destination principle would lead to a full optimum. In principle the real solution is to adopt the origin principle and apply in all states an equal rate on all goods subject to excise taxes. Fiscal frontiers would also then disappear.

2. DIRECT TAXES

(a) Disparities in the EEC

The free movement of factors of production provided for by the Rome Treaty is part of a policy for achieving a better allocation of resources. It is clear that direct taxes can impede this process. Although the treaty makes no explicit reference to the question of harmonizing direct taxation, Articles 100 to 102,

---

[18] Not all writers take cognizance of this point—see for example R. Sannwald and J. Stohler, *Economic Integration* (1959), pp. 211–12.

dealing with approximation of laws, provide for the possibility
of harmonization where discrepancies in legislation between
states interfere with competition and produce distortions.
Clearly the harmonization of direct taxes could be brought
within the terms of these articles, and possible policy in this
field has already been subjected to study, for example by the
Neumark Committee.

In the ECSC the only taxes explicitly dealt with are those
equivalent in effect to import or export duties. These are
recognized by Article 4 of the Paris Treaty to be incompatible
with the treaty and therefore prohibited. Fiscal policy is virtually
left entirely in the hands of the member-state governments. In
this sense the Rome Treaty is the more supranational of the
two. Quite early on, the High Authority considered the question
of the tax burden on the coal and steel industries but reached
the conclusion that national differences did not lead to serious
distortions. The turnover tax dispute which broke out a little
later caused the subject of taxation to be reconsidered at length.
Direct taxation was not dealt with in any detail—the Tinbergen
Committee touched upon it only in passing, although this is
not surprising in view of the fact that the mandate of the
Committee concerned indirect taxes. Of course the fact that the
Paris Treaty does not provide for free movement of capital
means that the elimination of differences in direct taxes on investment income in order to bring about a better distribution of
resources is not really a relevant problem. However, the problem,
at least conceptually, does arise in the case of differences in
taxes on income from employment[19] since there is free movement of labour in the ECSC.

Within the EEC the existence of differences in taxes on income
from investment does clearly raise a problem. Suppose in a
two-country customs union model that the tax on income from
investment is 50 per cent in A and only 25 per cent in B, then
capital will tend to flow from A to B. It will continue to flow to
B until the accumulation of capital in B leads to a situation in
which the returns net of tax in A and B are equal. But in such a
situation the return before tax will be much higher in A than in B,
and this implies that the distribution of the factor of production

[19] See, however, the discussion of this problem as it affects the EEC, pp.
40–41.

capital is distorted—an international excess burden arises. We are of course assuming that businessmen do in fact seek to maximize returns net of tax. In so far as this is so, the need for harmonization of taxes on investment income is therefore clear.

Do disparities of a significant kind exist? The answer appears to be in the affirmative. Peggy B. Musgrave, in a valuable empirical investigation into the taxation of investment income in the EEC,[20] has compared the domestic tax rate on investment income in each member state with the rate if the investment were made in each of the other five member states. The data are shown in Table 2 below. They indicate, for instance, that in the case of a West German corporation investing in a corporation in other member states, the tax rate would be between 27 and 7 per cent lower than it would be if the investment were in West Germany. This example relates to an investment made in a

TABLE 2

Percentage Tax Differentials on Income from Investment as between Domestic and Foreign Investment

	Direct investment (substantial interest)		Portfolio investment (minor interest)	
	Earnings fully retained	Earnings fully distributed	Earnings fully retained	Earnings fully distributed
Belgium	+8 to +27	+14 to +19	+8 to +27	+14 to +19
France	−20 to +7	−19 to −5	−20 to +7	−17 to −10
W. Germany	−27 to −7	−6 to +13	−27 to −7	−1 to +7
Italy	−8 to +19	+5 to +19	−8 to +19	+5 to +19
Luxembourg	−15 to +12	+5 to +30	−15 to +12	−4 to +5
Belgium	−15 to +12	−7 to +8	−15 to +12	−2 to +6

Notes: + indicates tax rate on foreign investment is higher; − indicates tax rate on foreign investment is lower. Investments in this table are assumed to be made by one corporation in another.

Source: Musgrave, *Public Finance*, xx/3-4 (1965), p. 289, table 2.

[20] 'An Evaluation of Investment Income Taxation within the European Common Market', *Public Finance*, xx/3-4 (1965), pp. 248-95.

subsidiary (substantial interest)—earnings being fully retained. The table suggests the existence of a significant international excess burden.

What are the solutions to the problem? The most obvious one,[21] and it has been suggested by the Neumark Committee, is that member states should equalize their profits taxes. The Committee proposes a rate of 50 per cent on ploughed back profits and one of 25 per cent (but not less than 15 per cent) on profits distributed.[22]

(b) Shifting the Tax Burden

Before leaving the subject of direct taxes on investment income, some reference should be made to the possibility of shifting, that is to say the passing on of the tax to the consumer in the form of higher prices. Under conditions of international perfect competition taxes cannot be shifted and equalization of tax rates, *ceteris paribus*, would equalize burdens on investment income and thus prevent any distortion from arising. If shifting is possible, it gives rise to no problem, provided the shifting is the same in all states, but, if this is not so, tax burdens differ and distortions arise. It is probably worth noting that the removal of trade barriers and the anti-trust policy are intended to increase competition, and therefore shifting may become more difficult. However, if the degree of competition is not equal as between states or indeed as between industries then distortions can arise.[23]

(c) Income from Employment

The Neumark Committee did not think that harmonization of income taxes to any considerable degree would be politically feasible or economically necessary for the proper working of the Common Market. The Committee felt that differences in rates, for example, would not lead to the distorting effects evident in the

---

[21] For other solutions see Musgrave, *Public Finance*, xx/3–4 (1965), pp. 291–3.

[22] This is in marked contrast to the British system, which tends to discriminate against distributed profits. The Community system must be regarded as an important contribution towards a more rational allocation of capital between alternative industrial uses.

[23] In connexion with the free movement of capital it should be noted that in order to remove distortions arising from discriminatory rates and double taxation in respect of stamp duties and capital duties, the EEC Commission proposes the abolition of the former and the harmonization of the latter.

case of capital because the latter is highly mobile while labour is less so. This seems to be accepted by the EEC Commission. In border areas and more generally in respect of professional classes this may be less true and in the long run greater political unification and better transport facilities may also render it less true. But then if there is greater political unification the major obstacle to harmonization of rates and so forth will decline. The Neumark Committee did, however, think that some harmonization of the type of income tax and the methods of taxable-income computation was needed.

3. FISCAL HARMONIZATION

The Rome Treaty provides specifically only for the harmoniza tion of indirect taxation. In the case of direct taxes harmonization may, therefore, appear to be more difficult to achieve. But it is worth noting that the sheer existence of a Common Market is tending to bring about a greater degree of harmony between national tax systems. Pressures are bound to develop whereby those who are at a disadvantage by virtue of their national tax system as compared with that in other states will press for their system to be brought into line. Also, as tax systems are revised, there is a tendency to imitate the best systems in other member states—this is clearly so in the case of the German decision independently to adopt the French added value turnover-tax system.

It would also appear that there is a need to bring the tax system in the ECSC into line with that of the EEC—a process which would be facilitated by the merger of the three Communities.

3

The Problem of State Aids

I. THE ECSC RULES AND POLICY

THE possibility that state aids or subsidies can distort the conditions of competition and give rise to a misallocation of resources is not difficult to recognize. Because of this both the Paris and Rome Treaties make specific provisions for dealing with them. Article 4 of the Paris Treaty flatly forbids subsidies. The rules for the transitional phase[1] granted special powers to the High Authority to cope with the problem of adaptation to the process of opening up national markets and if necessary subsidies could be authorized. The transitional rules also required member governments to notify subsidies to the High Authority for scrutiny.

Although the Paris Treaty takes an uncompromising stand on subsidies, the experience of the ECSC has been mixed. In the early years the High Authority was able to get rid of some subsidies, but in the case of the Belgian coal industry, and the French nationalized Charbonnages de France (whose losses have been covered by the French government), subsidization continued and the High Authority has now been forced to accept subsidies to coal producers as an integral part of its common energy policy. It must be added that to a large degree the fact that coal subsidies have not been abolished must be ascribed to an unfortunate turn of events in the market for coal.

(a) Subsidies in the French Coal Industry

The High Authority achieved a number of early successes in dealing with the French coal industry. In one of the early cases the High Authority had to deal with the problem of subsidies paid to briquetting plants on the Atlantic coast. The reason for the payment of these subsidies was that the plants could no

---

[1] Section 13 of the Convention containing the Transitional Provisions.

longer obtain supplies of British coal and had to rely on French supplies. As a result they were at a competitive disadvantage compared with briquetting plants close to the domestic coalfields. The High Authority required these subsidies to be phased out and this was eventually accomplished, although in so far as the briquetting plants depended on third-country supplies, they received the subsidy generally available to reduce the price of imported supplies (mainly US coal) down to the French level. The French government also subsidized imports of coking coal and coke, most of which was German in origin, destined mainly for Lorraine. The reason for the subsidies lay in the fact that Lorraine coal is not well adapted to the process of cokeification unless mixed with Ruhr coal. In order to stimulate the use of Lorraine coal for coking (it was part of French policy to reduce dependence on imports of coke) a subsidy was granted on imports of Ruhr coal, since in the absence of such a subsidy the price of Lorraine-produced coke would have been so high that the French steel industry would have turned to other sources of supply.

The High Authority ultimately required the subsidy to be wound up and it was in fact terminated in 1957. However, despite the stimulus of this subsidy, the Lorraine output of coke was inadequate to meet local needs, and since supplies from the Nord/Pas-de-Calais field were not available in sufficient quantity, coke had to be imported from Germany. But as the Nord price was below the German price,[2] a subsidy was paid on coke imports to bring their price down to the French level. This subsidy was, however, largely removed by the end of the transition period (1958) because the development of the common market and the elimination of differential pricing and transport discrimination cheapened supplies of Ruhr coke and rendered subsidies unnecessary. Finally, the subsidy on French coal exports from Lorraine and the Saar to South Germany, necessitated by the lower price of German coal, was eliminated completely. The elimination was assisted by the relatively faster rise of German coal prices, reforms in transport which enabled

---

[2] It should be remembered that these cases occurred at a time when price controls still existed. These had originally been applied by governments but were taken over and operated by the High Authority. National price ceilings were not necessarily uniform.

Saar and Lorraine producers to take advantage of their geographical position, and the fact that the High Authority's
zonal price arrangements allowed the French producers to
absorb freight on deliveries to South Germany.[3]

(*b*) *Subsidies in the Belgian Coal Industry*

The Belgian coal industry provided an altogether tougher
problem. It was realized at the time of the signing of the Paris
Treaty that special arrangements would have to be made to
accommodate it. The Belgian industry is divided into two zones,
the Campine Basin in the north and the Southern Basin—the
latter being an extension of the French Nord/Pas-de-Calais

TABLE I

*Output per Man-Shift and Total Output of the Main ECSC
Coal-producing Regions in 1953*

	Southern Basin	Campine Basin	Ruhr	Nord/ Pas-de-Calais	Saar	Lorraine	Dut Limb
OPMS (kg.)	1,075*	1,428*	1,486	1,277	1,676	2,088	1,5
Total output ('000 metric tons)	20,577	9,483	115,551	27,554	16,418	12,001	12,2

* Estimates.

Source: ECSC, *12th Gen. Rep.* (1964), statist. annex, tables 2 & 3.

field. The Southern Basin was particularly inefficient owing to a
combination of poor geological conditions, old equipment, and
small pits—the pits of the Borinage being the most inefficient
of all. Table 1 indicates the output per man-shift in the main
coal-producing regions of the ECSC in 1953. The figures show
that both Belgian coal basins were among the lowest in terms of
output per man-shift, and that two-thirds of Belgian output was
concentrated in the South where the output per man-shift was
the lowest of any major field. Since 10 per cent of the industrial

[3] Diebold, p. 199.

labour force in Belgium worked in the coal industry, the combined inefficiency of the Belgian industry and the reliance placed upon it as a source of income and employment meant that the opening up of national markets might prove disastrous for Belgium if there were no adequate transitional safeguards. Whether such difficulties would actually arise was of course dependent upon the general supply and demand conditions for coal (in fact energy as a whole) within the Community. As it transpired there was for a number of years a general shortage, punctuated, however, by a recession in 1953/4. Nevertheless, once the situation of 'coal at any cost' has passed, the logic of a common market suggested that if any branch of the Community industry had to contract, the Belgian one looked like heading the list—unless some remarkable upsurge of efficiency were to occur.

In the light of the vulnerability of the Belgian coal industry the treaty laid down special transitional provisions for its benefit. Unless Community production was falling, Belgian coal output was not to fall at more than 3 per cent per annum. A levy was to be placed upon producers whose average costs were below the weighted mean of the Community as a whole, the proceeds of which were to be allocated to the Belgian (and Italian)[4] colliery companies—aid so granted by the High Authority had to be matched by equivalent aid from the respective national governments.

The Belgian industry received three forms of subsidy. One consisted of a deficiency-payments system to enable Belgian coal to be sold at a price similar to that paid elsewhere in the Community. The finance allocated to the colliery companies by the High Authority for this purpose was exactly matched in amount by the Belgian government. Secondly, in times of slack demand, for example 1953/4, the Belgian industry experienced difficulties in exporting, and so export subsidies were granted, when needed, by the High Authority and Belgian government in equal amounts. Thirdly, prior to the entry into force of the treaty, colliery companies, mainly in the Borinage, had received special 'contractual subsidies' and it was decided that these could continue. The amounts paid by the Belgian government under this third heading were not necessarily matched by the

[4] In the interests of brevity we have chosen to concentrate on the Belgian case as this was quantitatively far more important than the Italian one.

High Authority—the latter's contribution tending to fall over time.

The original scheme for assisting the Belgian industry was due to end in February 1958, that is to say at the end of the five-year transitional period. (It should be noted that the levy on the efficient producers was degressive and funds ran out by 1958.) During that period the Belgian industry received £45 million[5] by way of subsidies from the High Authority and the Belgian government. There were two other features of the transitional scheme which were to be important in the light of future developments. One was that the Belgian government was allowed to introduce trade barriers, with respect to coal, between Belgium and the rest of the Community for four years after the end of the transitional phase. Also the Belgian government could, with High Authority approval, continue to grant subsidies.

The general emphasis in this period was upon keeping the Belgian industry profitable. It involved the assumption that, as a result, the industry would be able to find funds to modernize. In this way it would increase efficiency and eventually be able to compete on equal terms with the mines in the rest of the Community.[6] At this time there was, as we indicated earlier, a scarcity of coal and the emphasis was therefore upon increasing the average efficiency of existing producers rather than upon closing down inefficient branches of the Community industry. The original arrangement was not, however, free from criticism. It was a general scheme and it came to be recognized that the system should be made more selective. In 1955 the High Authority therefore decided that collieries whose coals could be sold in the common market without assistance should be removed from the scheme. Other enterprises in the Campine had their assistance reduced. Assistance was, however, increased to the main Borinage companies for modernization on the understanding that nine pits which were beyond redemption should be closed. In 1957 further selectivity was introduced. Twenty-one mining companies were considered capable of paying their way without further assistance. Four Borinage collieries were judged incapable of adapting themselves to competitive conditions and their subsidies were terminated. The Belgian government continued

---

[5] ECSC, *7th Gen. Rep.* (1959), statist. annexe, table 16.
[6] There is reason to doubt whether this was ever a feasible proposition.

to cover their losses and the High Authority undertook to assist discharged workers with its readaptation funds. (We shall discuss the work of the High Authority in the South—particularly the Borinage—in respect of redundancy and the introduction of new sources of employment in Chapter 11 on Social and Regional Policy.) Subsidies were to continue in respect of all the remaining colliery companies until the end of the transition period, after which the High Authority would cease to assist, although the Belgian government could continue its subsidies for two more years.

The question which arises is this. Did the distribution of £45 million really achieve the objective of adapting the Belgian coal industry to competitive conditions? The answer would appear to be in the negative. Belgian prices continued to be well out of line with Ruhr prices although some narrowing of the gap had been achieved. In 1953 the ratios of Belgian to Ruhr prices for low-volatile, semi-bituminous, bituminous, and high-volatile bituminous coal were 142, 120, 112, and 129. By 1957 the ratios were 162, 127, 128, and 131 respectively.[7] We may also ask what precisely had been the impact of subsidization and the threat of having eventually to stand on its own feet, and whether these had provided the means and stimulus to invest at a rapid rate. There is clear evidence of a distinct impact on investment. Between 1954 and 1957 both the Campine and the South had invested at a significantly faster rate than the rest of the Community—the rate of investment being measured in Belgian francs per ton of coal produced. By 1957 the level of investment in the Campine and South was 38 per cent and 32 per cent greater than that in the rest of the Community.[8] But the productivity increase between 1953 and 1957 was 4 per cent in the South, 10 per cent in the Campine and 10 per cent in the Community as a whole.[9] The performance in the South was particularly bad, but even taking the Belgian coal industry as a whole it must be concluded that what was in effect subsidized investment had not been particularly efficacious. It is true that,

---

[7] Source of data as in table 2, p. 50.
[8] See data by Liesner in Meade, Liesner, & Wells, table 5, p. 301.
[9] Calculated from ECSC, *12th Gen. Rep.* (1964), statist. annexe, table 3. These figures do not tally with those quoted by Diebold (p. 211) and Liesner (p. 301) since the data used by them have now been revised.

3

given the need to produce as much coal as possible, the subsidization of investment did at least help to keep down the price of marginal supplies of Belgian coal. This helped to keep down the Community coal-price level, a fact which commended itself to the governments of the Six, who were anxious to avoid inflation. On the other hand it seems probable that, as far as increasing productivity was concerned, the £45 million could have been better spent in other coalfields. This too could have been anti-inflationary, and to an even greater degree. But had the subsidies not been made available to the Belgian industry (and if also the more efficient producers had, by virtue of not paying the levy, invested at a faster rate) then as soon as the first recession had come along or the coal shortage had eased, the impact of unemployment in Belgium would have been all that much more severe.[10]

After 1957 the energy situation began to change. In 1958 substantial excess supplies of coal emerged on the Community market and this change was not a temporary phenomenon but was a reflection of a fundamental shift in the energy market caused by increasing competition from oil (and US coal). We shall not pursue this matter here as it is analysed in detail in Chapter 10. It was inevitable that the Belgian coal industry would feel the impact particularly severely, all the more so as High Authority subsidies had ceased at the beginning of 1958.[11] In 1959 the Belgian government had to assist the industry generally with subsidies to cover losses, and in the same year the High Authority agreed to limits being placed upon the coal trade between Belgium and the rest of the Community. Imports into Belgium in 1960 were to be only 86 per cent of the 1959 level, while exports from Belgium to the rest of the Community were to be left virtually at that level. No time limit was placed upon this partial sealing off. From 1958 onwards pit closures began to take place at an altogether more rapid pace than in the transition phase and the renewed deficiency payments scheme of 1959 was authorized on the understanding that a programme

[10] The immediate impact of not subsidizing the Belgian industry (temporary recessions apart) would not necessarily have been severe. Given the shortage of coal, Community prices would have risen to cover the costs of the Belgian supplies. Since the price of US coal was at this period well above the Belgian level, the Community would probably still have preferred Belgian supplies.

[11] 'Contractual subsidies' to mining companies in the South had continued.

of closures would be implemented. Subsequently the High Authority required that the Belgian government subsidy scheme begun in 1959 should be eliminated by 1963. Also, from the beginning of 1963, the Belgian market was reopened.

It might therefore appear that the ending of subsidies was in sight, but this was not to be. In 1962 the Belgian industry conceded a wage claim and in 1963 the Belgian government applied to the High Authority for permission to grant a BF255–million subsidy to offset the extra wage costs. The High Authority agreed. It could hardly do otherwise for the plain fact was that as a result of the changed energy situation one member state after another was introducing special measures to assist its coal industry.[12] These took several forms—relief from part of colliery company social security contributions, subsidies to nationalized collieries, assistance with rationalization schemes. The High Authority viewed these disparate forms of assistance with alarm and decided to exert its authority by calling for harmonization within the framework of a common energy policy—we discuss this at greater length in Chapter 10.

Before leaving this subject it should be noted that a considerable contraction of output had been achieved in the Belgian coal industry. Thus although between 1953 and 1957 Belgian coal production remained more or less static, between 1957 and 1964 it fell by 27 per cent (a decline at about three times the Community rate)—and virtually all the decline occurred in the relatively inefficient Southern Basin. Whereas there had been 120 pits in operation in Belgium in 1957, the number had been reduced to 58 by the end of 1964.[13] By 1964 output per man-shift, as compared with 1953, had increased by 38 per cent in the Campine, 49 per cent in the South, and 65 per cent in the Community as a whole.[14] There was little sign of the Belgian industry catching up. The Campine had kept pace with the Community between 1953 and 1957 but over the longer period had fallen behind. The South, however, was closer to the Community over the longer period but was still well behind. As far as prices are concerned, we have already shown that

---

[12] It should be remembered that the French government had been offsetting the losses of Charbonnages de France even in the years of coal scarcity.
[13] ECSC, *13th Gen. Rep.* (1965, German), table 21, p. 133.
[14] Ibid. statist. annexe, table 3. (The 1964 figures are estimates.)

between 1953 and 1957 Belgian prices increased faster than Ruhr prices. But between 1957 and 1964 the tendency was reversed. This is shown in Table 2, in which we show that in the case of bituminous coal the Belgian industry was underquoting the Ruhr in 1964. In the other three products, however, the Belgian industry was still uncompetitive with the Ruhr.

TABLE 2

The Ratio of Belgian to Ruhr Coal Prices* 1953, 1957, and 1964

	Low-volatile†	Semi-bituminous‡	Bituminous§	High-volatile bituminous ‖
1953	142	120	112	129
1957	162	127	128	131
1964	135	120	90	110

* Published price lists (Apr. 1953, Apr. 1957, Jan. 1964).
† Low-volatile small nuts.   ‡ Semi-bituminous singles.
§ Bituminous washed duff or coking fines.
‖ High-volatile No. 2 nuts doubles.

Source: ECSC, *12th Gen. Rep.* 1964, statist. annexe, table 13, and *11th Gen. Rep.* 1963, statist. annexe, table 13–14.

2. THE EEC RULES AND POLICY

In the case of the Rome Treaty, Articles 92 to 94 deal with state aids. Article 92 declares that generally state aids which distort or threaten to distort competition, by favouring certain enterprises or the production of certain goods, and which affect inter-state trade adversely are incompatible with the treaty. However, some aids are compatible with the treaty. These are, first, aids of a social character granted to individuals (such as free school milk), secondly, aid to make good damage caused by natural disaster (for example, the Fréjus disaster), thirdly, aids to regions of the German Federal Republic affected by the division of Germany. Also other forms of aid may be deemed compatible with the treaty. These include, first, aids to promote the development of backward regions, secondly, aids to promote an important project of common European interest or remedy a serious disturbance in an economy of a member state, thirdly, aids to facilitate the development of certain activities (for example the film industry)[15] or certain economic regions, provided the aid does not adversely affect trading conditions to such an extent as would be contrary to the common interest, fourthly, other aids specified by the Council by qualified majority vote on a proposal of the Commission. The distinction between regional aid under the first and third categories is somewhat obscure, but it seems likely that the first refers to aids to really chronically backward areas while the third presumably refers to regions with problems of a less intractable kind which can, after limited assistance, achieve some kind of 'take-off'. We shall not discuss regional state aids here since they will be considered in Chapter 11. Aids in the field of transport and agriculture will be discussed in the chapter dealing with these industries. We shall concentrate in this chapter on aids to specific industries and general export aids.

Where aids are to be approved the EEC Commission requires that two main criteria be satisfied. First, an aid must never be admitted if it creates a competitive advantage. In other words aids are merely permitted to offset disadvantages. Secondly, it is desirable that aids be selective, that is they are granted to those who really need them rather than in a blanket fashion (a lesson learnt by the High Authority), and that they should be temporary, decreasing in amount over time so as to compel the recipient to make increasing attempts to become self-sufficient.

(a) Some Decisions by the Commission

The Commission has already dealt with a number of aids and we shall discuss some of these cases. As an example, in the field of fiscal policy, the Commission succeeded in 1959 in persuading the French government to modify a provision whereby French producers purchasing French equipment were granted more rapid depreciation in connexion with tax assessment. In 1960 the Commission obtained the agreement of the French government to the abolition of aids to staple-fibre production, silk spinning, and *haute couture*—these were abolished as from the beginning of 1961.[16] In 1960 the West German

---

[15] Aids granted to the shipbuilding industry existing on 1 Jan. 1957, in so far as they were necessary only to offset the absence of customs protection, were required to be scaled down in line with the abolition of customs duties.

[16] EEC, *4th Gen. Rep.* (1961), p. 72.

government agreed to put an end to the price equalization fund designed to encourage synthetic rubber production at the expense of natural rubber.[17] In the same year the Commission obtained the approval of the Italian government to the cancellation of tax reliefs in connexion with the purchase of motor cars of Italian manufacture.[18] Later the Italian government also removed discriminatory features in connexion with loans for the purchase of agricultural machinery.[19] More recently the Commission has called upon member-state governments to adjust the aids granted to their industries processing farm products so that comparable conditions apply whether the supplies come from ordinary domestic producers, nationalized sources, or other member states.[20]

Aids have been approved in a number of cases. In the case of the French paper-pulp producers state aids have been approved, the legality of such aid being the compensation for the French agreement to the external tariff level on this product (List G).[21] The Commission approved state aid to compensate German lead and zinc mines. This was to compensate for losses in 1963 caused by distortions on the world market. As world prices subsequently began to rise the Commission stated that the compensation could not be renewed.[22] In 1963 it also approved state subsidies to keep down the interest on loans for technical development in civil aircraft construction, the reason for this concession being the difficult conditions the industry was experiencing at the time.[23]

(b) Export Aids

In drawing up its inventory of aids, which was completed in 1964, the Commission has become aware of aids made available to exporters. In 1964, it made a proposal[24] about the steps which should be taken to deal with the problem. We shall not list these exhaustively but indicate some of the more important instances together with the Commission's proposal. Thus in France a *carte d'exportateur* is issued to firms which export

---

[17] Ibid.   [18] EEC, *4th Gen. Rep.* (1961), p. 72.
[19] Ibid. *5th Gen. Rep.* (1962), p. 83.
[20] Ibid. *7th Gen. Rep.* (1964), pp. 76–77.
[21] Ibid. *4th Gen. Rep.* (1961), pp. 76–77.
[22] Ibid. *7th Gen. Rep.* (1964), p. 75.
[23] Ibid.   [24] Ibid. pp. 73–74.

more than a certain percentage of their turnover (there is also an absolute minimum). The *carte d'exportateur* entitled the firm to tax benefits. The Commission proposes that this aid be abolished. In both Belgium and France the rediscount rate for export credits is ½ per cent below the standard rate. This can hardly be regarded as a crucial matter but the Commission recommends that the practice be abolished. State guaranteed financing arrangements (medium- and long-term credit) are available in all member states and this suggests that distortions are not likely to occur. However, the Commission suggests that it be kept informed about the number and size of consignments covered by these arrangements in each state—presumably it would like to eliminate any significant differences in the coverage of such schemes which might emerge. As a final example of export aid we quote the system in Italy and France whereby capital-goods producers who enter into fixed-price contracts can obtain state-guaranteed insurance against increases in costs. The Commission appears to take the view that such risks cannot really be insured against and therefore to imply that the state is bearing some of the risk. It therefore considers that this form of insurance be abolished.

(c) Aids to the Shipbuilding Industry

One of the most prominent examples of state aids in the Communities is the shipbuilding industry. This is particularly the case in France and Italy. In both countries direct subsidies have been given to enable the industry both to sell below its own costs of production and to convert to alternative lines of production. In France the subsidy system was introduced by the Law of 24 May 1951, and in Italy by Law no. 522 of 1954, the Tambroni Law.[25]

In the case of France these subsidies have been used since 1960 to bring about a concentration of production by reducing the number of yards. Aids have also been available to bring about a conversion to other forms of employment, this being particularly important as alternative occupations in the coastal

---

[25] OECD, *The Situation in the Shipbuilding Industry* (1965), pp. 40–41 & 62–63. The failure of the OECD to bring about fairer conditions of competition as between the leading countries producing ships has led the Commission to propose methods of giving the Community special treatment—see p. 55 below.

areas concerned were not available. The aid there included, among other things, an investment premium granted to established shipbuilding firms for projects designed to create employment outside shipbuilding itself. As far as aids for actual shipbuilding are concerned, the Commission has negotiated with the French government step-by-step reductions in the building subsidies. By 1963 it reported that aid had been reduced since the entry into force of the treaty by 45 per cent.[26] As far as reconversion aid is concerned, the Commission has allowed this to continue. For example, in 1965 the Commission authorized for one year the reconversion programme, which at that stage was reported as being 80 per cent complete.

As far as the Italian shipbuilding subsidies are concerned, it was assumed that the subsidies begun in 1954 would be reduced by 10 per cent annually so as to be eliminated by 1964. However, a deterioration in the Italian industry's position since 1957 led the Italian government in 1961 to re-establish aid at the level achieved in 1957—which was about 75 per cent of the 1954 level.[27] The return to the higher scale of subsidies in 1961 was submitted to the Commission for approval and was accepted by the latter provided it brought about intensive efforts to improve the industry's competitive position.[28] It was also assumed that this aid would be abolished by the end of 1964 and some reductions in it were in fact achieved.

However, although it was originally expected that the Italian subsidies would end in 1964, and that the French subsidies would be progressively phased out, this does not appear to have happened. In the first place there is no reference in the later reports of the Commission to pressing the French reductions beyond the 45 per cent level already achieved. As far as the Italian government is concerned, it has proposed the continuation of the subsidies for a number of years and has been unwilling to commit itself to the rate at which they should be tapered.

The resistance which appears to have been encountered from France and Italy to the abolition of aids appears to have stemmed from the deterioration in the international competitive position of the Community shipbuilding industry as illustrated by the fact

[26] EEC, *6th Gen. Rep.* (1963), p. 69.
[27] OECD, *Shipbuilding Industry*, p. 41.
[28] EEC, *4th Gen. Rep.* (1961), p. 72.

that the share of the six Community countries in total world tonnage launched fell from about 40 per cent in 1954 to 33 per cent in 1956–60 and 28 per cent in 1962–3.[29]

The Commission now appears to have accepted that a continuation of subsidies is necessary. Its concern is now to harmonize them throughout the Community. It has therefore suggested that a common rate of subsidy of 10 per cent of the contract price of a ship should be adopted by all the member states for a trial period from 1967 to 1969, although it could be renewed subsequently.[30] This 10 per cent is based upon the Commission's estimate that support measures in Japan in respect of shipbuilding-plate price concessions and long-term agreed facilities for ship exports amount to 10 per cent of the prices of Japanese ship exports. It should be noted that in following this policy the Community is not attempting to bridge the gap between its own level of costs and those in, for example, Japan. It is merely placing its own shipyards on what it regards as an equal competitive footing with Japan in respect of aid granted. The Commission recognizes that the only way to bridge the competitive gap fully will be by a modernization and rationalization programme. Also, it proposes that the aid granted should be brought into the open and supervised by the Community so as to guarantee equal treatment to all Community yards.

[29] EEC, *L'industrie de la construction navale dans les pays de la CÉE, Études Série Industrie*, no. 4, 1964, p. 5.

[30] Agence Europe, *Europe Documents*, no. 317, 26 Apr. 1964. The aid would be applicable to ships destined for Community owners as well as those destined for non-Community owners. If aid was available solely for the export of ships Community owners would tend to place orders in third countries to avoid being placed at a competitive disadvantage.

4

Adjusting Other State Activities

I. STATE TRADING MONOPOLIES

ONE form of state activity that could impede the integration process is the kind of intervention which takes the form of endowing a particular organization with the exclusive right to import a particular commodity into the national territory. If the privileged organization limits its imports, then established domestic suppliers are protected and producers in other member states find that the national market remains closed to them even when tariffs and quotas have been dismantled.

A problem of this kind had proved a cause of considerable dispute within the ECSC in its early years. In addition to nationalizing coal production in the Charbonnages de France in 1946, the French government had also granted the exclusive right to import coal to the Association Technique de l'Importation Charbonnière (ATIC). Even the largest buyers of imported coal, such as the French steel firms, could not conclude contracts independently with, say, their Ruhr suppliers, but had to do so via ATIC. The High Authority took the view that this kind of limitation on the buyer's freedom was incompatible with the Paris Treaty and, after protracted litigation, was able to secure the French government's agreement to a reduction in the role of ATIC as a result of which it lost its power to veto contracts in respect of coal imports from other Community countries.[1]

The basic ingredients of the ATIC situation were also present in respect of other products in France, Germany, and Italy when the Rome Treaty was being negotiated and, perhaps learning from difficulties thrown up by the ATIC case, Article 37 of the Rome Treaty was designed specifically to ensure the adjustment of

---

[1] An important reason for French obstinacy in this case was the perfectly understandable one that as long as Ruhr coal sales remained in the hands of a powerful private cartel (GEORG), then centralization of buying power was a necessary kind of insurance against exploitation.

state trading monopolies to the needs of integration. It provides that the member states will adjust state trading monopolies in such a way that, by the end of the transitional period, all discriminations between nationals of member states in conditions of supply or marketing of goods will be eliminated. By the same token, the member states are also bound by a standstill agreement not to introduce any new measures that conflict with these principles.

It may be mentioned here parenthetically that state trading monopolies are conceptually quite different from nationalized industries, and that the specific attack upon the former in Article 37 should not be construed as an attack upon nationalization. To put it at its simplest, state trading monopolies have been given their privileges with the purpose of supporting some 'higher' functions of the state. In practice this usually means that the monopoly earnings of the sales organizations accrue to the state as part of its fiscal revenues. Nationalized industries, on the other hand, are in principle simply examples of public rather than private ownership of industrial capital, and their organization and policies are in the first instance largely the result of their specific industrial postures rather than any extra-industrial aims that are required of them by the state. However, it is clear that in practice the nationalization of an industry makes it easier for the government to use the industry concerned in pursuit of general policy objectives, such as price stability and regional employment policy, and that it is, therefore, to some extent misleading to regard nationalized industries as involving nothing more than the substitution of public for private ownership of capital. Be that as it may, however, the treaties make no distinction between public and private ownership, and a state's right to nationalize or denationalize an industry is not affected by its adherence to the treaties, although abuse of economic power by nationalized enterprises is subject to the same checks as abuse by private ones. It should be clearly understood, therefore, that it is not the ordinary run of nationalized industry whose adjustment is called for in Article 37 of the Rome Treaty. Thus the activities of the Deutsche Bundesbahn, ENI, and Renault, for example, are not affected by this set of requirements.

The industries that enjoy privileges as state trading monopolies are listed on p. 58 in Table 1, which also indicates briefly the reason for their privileged position.

TABLE I

State Trading Monopolies in the EEC

State	Products	Type of monopoly
Germany	Matches	Fiscal
	Alcohol	Fiscal
France	Raw & manufactured tobacco	Fiscal
	Matches	Fiscal
	Gunpowder	Fiscal; public security & national defence
	Alcohol	Fiscal
	Potash	Common selling organization of purely commercial character
	Newsprint	Purchasing group of purely commercial character
	Petroleum	Complex system of import licences favouring franc-zone crude and state-owned Union Générale des Pétroles
Italy	Raw & manufactured tobacco	Fiscal
	Cigarette paper	Fiscal
	Matches, phosphorus, lighters, flints	Fiscal
	Salt	Fiscal
	Sulphur	Economic and social support for Sicily
	Quinine	Health policy
	Sweetening agents	Health policy
	Bananas	Relations with Somalia

Source: Information supplied by EEC Commission.

As might be expected in dealing with long-established positions of national privilege, the Commission has had to proceed cautiously. One result of this is that discussion of these monopolies in the Commission's *General Reports* is very sketchy and not all the suggestions and comments that the Commission has put before the relevant governments have been made public. The brief remarks that follow should, therefore, be regarded as only a very limited introduction to this range of problems.

The general lines of the Commission's approach are exemplified in the way it has tried to deal with the state trading monopoly for potash in France. Although steps had been taken to create freer trading conditions for these products in 1959 and 1960 it was observed that the Société Commerciale des Potasses d'Alsace (which enjoyed the exclusive rights to import) did not in fact increase its imports in line with the new possibilities. The Commission therefore issued a Recommendation outlining how non-discriminatory trading conditions could be brought about by the SCPA.[2] It considered that branded fertilizers from the other member states should be sold through the sales organization of the SCPA in such a way that the same margin would be applied to such imported goods as to the equivalent domestic products. In the case of crude potash and other basic materials necessarily sold at uniform prices, the principle of non-discrimination between the nationals of the member states should take the form of giving preference to the cheaper supplies. In the case of several sources of supply being equally favourable, then orders should be allocated among them in a reasonable way. Import possibilities along these lines were to be provided in 1962 to an amount equivalent to 5 per cent of national production in 1960 and this amount should thereafter be increased by 15 per cent annually. The implementation of these proposals would, therefore, gradually place suppliers in the other member states in a position of equality with the Mines Domaniales des Potasses d'Alsace by the end of the transitional period.

These policies recommended in respect of the French potash monopoly are typical of the general principles followed by the Commission in this field. The general nature of the adjustments required of state trading monopolies in fact amount to liberalization under three main headings:

1. to increase imports gradually up to a level determined only by available outlets on the home markets;
2. to eliminate gradually the disparity of margins between the

[2] Text of Recommendation in *WuW*, Jan. 1963, p. 48.

delivery price and the sale price applied to national products on the one hand and to imported products on the other, and to fix the delivery price of the products of the monopolies at a normal level compared with their average cost price;

3. gradually to adjust the marketing conditions of domestic and imported products, particularly in the supply of retailers, market prospecting and advertising.[3]

Unfortunately sufficient information is not available to permit us to show how rapidly imports of the relevant products have grown for states in which these monopoly conditions prevail in certain fields. Imports of tobacco products from other member states have certainly increased into France and Italy, in both of which state trading monopolies exist for these products. This is shown in Table 2.

TABLE 2

Imports of Tobacco Products from Other Member States
(Millions of units of national currency)

State	1959	1960	1961	1962	1963	1964*
France	2	3·4	5·4	10·95	14·46	14·23
Italy	320	1,160	1,850	3,769	4,604	5,764

* Based on figures for first six months.
Source: EEC, *6th Gen. Rep.* (1963), p. 24; *8th Gen. Rep.* (1965), p. 46.

However, in the cases of the French monopolies for matches and alcohol and the Italian match monopoly the governments appear to have greeted the Commission's Recommendations with something less than enthusiasm and the Commission has not ruled out the possibility of having to take further action should the need arise. In the important case of the French petroleum monopoly the Commission has also had to consider whether the French Decrees of 1963 that provide for the control of the market well beyond 1970 have created a new discriminatory system that breaks the standstill agreement of Article 37.

[3] EEC, *5th Gen. Rep.* (1962), p. 30.

2. TECHNICAL AND ADMINISTRATIVE
OBSTACLES TO TRADE

In each of the member states, rules are often laid down regarding the standards and qualities of goods sold in national markets. These rules often differ considerably and the disparities encourage the separation of markets and limit the free movement of goods. This problem occurs in connexion with a wide variety of products. For example there are differing national technical standards in the case of motor vehicles. These relate to such things as traffic indicators and braking and lighting systems. Judging from the work of the Commission similar problems arise in connexion with measuring instruments, paints and lacquers, fertilizers, and household electrical appliances. In the field of food legislation national standards relating to colouring and preserving agents, and so forth differ widely. Pharmaceutical products also pose problems. Differences in health requirements in respect of animal products will also have to be ironed out if really free movement of goods is to be established in the agricultural sector.

There are two problems here. In the case of proprietary medicines, for example, generally a product cannot be introduced on to a national market without obtaining the approval of the relevant governmental body. The existence of such national administrative controls gives rise to the possibility that foreign medical products could be deliberately kept off the national market. If the rules upon which decisions were based were imprecise or not made public, then it would be difficult to object to an adverse decision. Discrimination of this kind may not be a major problem but the difference between national standards clearly is. The existence of such differences means that a producer who wishes to sell throughout the Community has to vary his product to satisfy each national standard.[4]

Clearly if the Community wishes to facilitate competition

---

[4] Despite a steady increase in the consumption of proprietary medicines the Commission has observed that inter-state trade has remained at a low level. It ascribes this to the inhibiting influence of administrative controls and differing standards. It is, however, worth observing that this is a field in which the consumer finds it difficult to make objective choices, and where he may therefore prefer to consume those products which have been nationally advertised over a long period.

between the enterprises in each state and if it wishes to obtain the economies of long runs, then a harmonization of standards is essential.[5] That such harmonization is provided for in the Rome Treaty has already been pointed out in the discussion on taxation. Not only would such harmonization and the subsequent increase in efficiency directly benefit the Community but it is directly relevant to the problems of producing on a scale comparable to that of US enterprises—an issue which is a major preoccupation within the Community at the present time. It seems to us that the possibility of harmonizing standards is one which could pay some of the greatest dividends to member states and needs to be pressed ahead as rapidly as possible.

We shall not go into great detail about the work which is taking place in this field. Suffice it to say that several Regulations have been issued and a considerable number have been drafted or are in the process of being prepared.[6] It is however doubtful whether the harmonization procedure under Article 100 is really well adapted to the problem. For example, in 1965 the Council adopted a Regulation on the application of legal and administrative provisions relating to proprietary medicines.[7] This took two years to negotiate. It was originally discussed by a working party of national experts and went the rounds of the European Parliament and the Economic and Social Committee before being thrashed out in Council. This is a long-winded procedure, and the Commission is aware of its weaknesses[8] and has suggested, in the context of technical obstacles to trade, that the Council should transfer the process of elaborating common technical standards to the Commission under special Council directives.

[5] Other advantages may accrue. The regulation on harmonization of administrative provisions relating to proprietary medicines, which we discuss below, lays down that a medicine cannot be introduced on to the market if there is no therapeutic effect or if insufficient proof is provided. The German technical experts refused to accept this condition and no progress could be made by the working party on this subject. The Council of Ministers, however, disposed of the problem without much difficulty and accepted the therapeutic test. It seems possible that improved national standards may arise from these technical and administrative confrontations.

[6] A list of Regulations issued and drafted as at June 1965 can be found in EEC, *8th Gen. Rep.* (1965), pp. 86–101. It is also worth noting that harmonization of such things as sanitary regulations in respect of meat and live animals is also necessary before the common agricultural policy can operate properly.

[7] *JO*, 9 Feb. 1965.

[8] EEC, *7th Gen. Rep.* (1964), p. 80.

Flexible machinery is needed, since, as the Commission observes, the rapidity of scientific change poses the problem as to whether the standards that have been established by Community machinery can be changed quickly enough to keep pace. One case which is worth discussing in detail is that of proprietary medicines. The first Regulation in this field deals with unifying procedures in connexion with requests to authorize the introduction of such products on the market and grants or refusals of such requests. It should be noted that the existing first Regulation only unified national procedures. An authorization under a national procedure only remains valid for that state. The ultimate aim is that an authorization granted in one state will be automatically valid in all; and it is expected that regulations will in due course bring this about. But it should be noted that even the first regulation does improve the position of a manufacturer in one state trying to obtain an authorization in another, since the conditions under which an authorization can be refused have been closely defined. This will reduce the possibility of an outside manufacturer being kept out for bogus reasons.[9]

3. FREEDOM TO SUPPLY SERVICES AND THE RIGHT OF ESTABLISHMENT

So far our emphasis has been upon what the Rome Treaty calls the free movement of goods. This is a situation in which goods produced by an enterprise established in one member state can without hindrance be supplied to consumers in another. But it is also equally important that the same kind of freedom should exist in respect of services. The situation envisaged here is that a national (this term includes enterprises) who is established in one member state renders services to a national in another. The problem is that this may require the national rendering the service to travel to another state and render it there.[10] It is clear that a number of problems arise here. For example there must be freedom for foreigners to come and go, freedom to receive

[9] Problems of the kind mentioned in this section have not been of any great relevance in the ECSC.

[10] It is of course possible that the receiver of the services may travel to the country of the national rendering the services, or that only the service across the frontier (for example a chemical analysis)—the persons remaining in their respective domiciles.

payment and transfer it to the home country, and there is the problem of recognizing the technical or other qualifications of the person rendering the services. Articles 59 and 66 of the Rome Treaty provide for the freedom to supply services.[11] The word services does not include labour, the latter being dealt with under the article relating to the free movement of labour. (The latter is dealt with in Chapter 11.)

It is of course possible that a national established in one state, wishing to compete with a national established in another, may need to establish himself in the latter. This would apply equally to the rendering of services and the production of goods. This Right of Establishment is provided for by Articles 52 and 58 of the Rome Treaty.[12] It should be noted that the Right of Establishment applies to those engaged in non-wage-earning activities.

There would be little point in a tedious discussion of the numerous Regulations and Recommendations already in force or drafted. Substantial progress has been made in this field and we can confine our discussion to an outline of the main measures already implemented and to mentioning some of the special problems involved in this field.

In 1963 a Regulation was adopted removing all prohibitions of, or obstacles to, the payment for services where the payment restriction was the only limiting factor on their supply.[13] In 1964 a Regulation was approved by Council removing restrictions relating to travel and residence as they affect the freedom to supply services and of establishment.[14] In the same year Regulations were issued relating to the freedom to supply services and establishment in non-wage-earning activities in the wholesale trade (internal, export, import, and transit trade),[15] and to activities serving trade and industry (representatives, travellers, brokers, &c.).[16] These were followed later in 1964 by Regulations for freedom of establishment and supply of services

[11] There is no parallel to these provisions in the Paris Treaty. It should also be noted that freedom of movement of services in respect of transport is governed by the transport title of the Rome Treaty. The liberalization of services in banking and insurance is to be effected in line with the liberalization of the movement of capital.

[12] The Right of Establishment in respect of factor of production enterprise is paralleled in the Rome Treaty by the freedom of movement of labour (Arts. 48–51) and capital (Arts. 67–73). The Paris Treaty limits itself to providing for the free movement of labour—Art. 69.

[13] *JO*, 10 June 1963.   [14] Ibid. 4 Apr. 1964.   [15] Ibid.   [16] Ibid.

in connexion with processing industries (textiles, chemicals, metallurgy, electrical, automobile, &c, together with direct selling whether wholesale or retail),[17] and mining and quarrying (special arrangements apply in the oil and natural gas sector).[18] In the same year a Regulation was adopted establishing freedom to supply services in agriculture and horticulture.[19] In addition transitional measures were embodied in a directive relating to the co-ordination and recognition of diplomas.[20]

There are three problems in this sphere which deserve special attention. One is the problem of qualifications. Clearly the right to establish or supply services is of little relevance in itself if, for example, the qualification obtained by a national in one state is not acceptable when he wishes to render a service in another. There is, therefore, a need for a national recognition of diplomas and a co-ordination of conditions for admission to and practice in the liberal professions.[21] The Commission has found this task impossible to complete within the short space of time allocated in 1961 in the General Programmes for bringing about freedom to establish and supply services. As a result interim measures have been adopted pending final solutions.

The second major problem concerns the abolition of laws, regulations, and administrative practices whereby firms in other member states are wholly or partly excluded from tendering for work for central and local authorities or other bodies which conclude contracts under public law. The Commission submitted a draft Regulation to the Council in March 1964 dealing with this problem,[22] but at the time of writing it has not yet been adopted. The Commission has proposed freedom of establishment and to supply services in the field of public-works contracting. It has also proposed the adoption of common rules relating to the

---

[17] *JO*, 23 July 1964.

[18] Ibid. For oil and natural gas see EEC, *8th Gen. Rep.* (1965), pp. 51 & 169–70.

[19] *JO*, 8 Jan. 1965.   [20] Ibid. 23 July 1964.

[21] Art. 57 of the Rome Treaty provides for this. The Paris Treaty (Art. 69) binds member states to renounce restrictions, based on nationality, on the employment of *workers* in the coal and steel industries. Member states were required to work out a common definition of skilled jobs and conditions of qualification. This article would only parallel the Rome Treaty articles relating to services if the word 'workers' used above related to the type of activities defined in the Rome Treaty articles as services.

[22] EEC, *7th Gen. Rep.* (1964), pp. 57–58.

suspension, during the transitional period, of the award of public contracts to non-nationals. Liberalization should also be extended to public-works concessions and to work contracts awarded by national railway boards. In July 1964 the Commission also submitted to the Council a draft Regulation providing for the co-ordination of national procedures for the award of such contracts. According to the instructions of the Council of Ministers in Annex II of the General Programme on freedom of establishment and freedom to supply services, the Regulation was required to provide for general notification of contracts, common criteria on qualifications and adjudication, and strict rules on technical specifications in contracts. A body to settle disputes would also be provided.[23]

The third problem relates to company law.[24] Under Article 58 of the Rome Treaty, companies and firms formed according to the law of a member state and having their registered office, central administration, or principal place of business in the Community shall, from the point of view of the right of establishment, be treated in the state in which they are established in the same way as nationals of that state. Article 220 of the treaty calls for the member states to enter into negotiations with a view to ensuring the mutual recognition of companies and firms, as defined in Article 58, and a draft convention to this effect has been drawn up.[25] The treaty recognizes that problems could arise if companies established themselves in other member states. For example, differences in the national laws relating to the protection of shareholders against companies, or creditors against companies, differ from state to state. The directors of a company established in member state B might consider, on the basis of the law in home country A, that certain practices in relation to shareholders were permissible, whilst the shareholders in country B might have a different view of their rights on the basis of the law of country B. Because of this, Article 54 (3,g) of the Rome Treaty requires co-ordination of national company law to the extent that is necessary to render equally the guarantees demanded from companies for the protection of shareholders and creditors. In 1964 the Commission submitted a

[23] EEC, *7th Gen. Rep.* (1964), p. 79.
[24] The legal background to this problem is dealt with by W. Scholz and others, 'The Right of Establishment in the EEC', in Junckerstorff, pp. 233—66.
[25] EEC, *8th Gen. Rep.* (1965, English, mimeo.), pp. 105–6.

Directive to the Council to implement Article 54 (3,g).[26] This Directive, which still awaits Council approval, deals only with the protection of creditors and only with joint-stock companies and limited partnerships. The basic aim of the Directive is to guarantee some minimum standard of protection for creditors by requiring, firstly, the publication of company articles, statutes, and financial statements, secondly, that a third party must be in a position to verify that a person acting in the name of a company is in fact empowered to represent it, and, thirdly, that third parties should be able to ascertain easily whether or not the company is validly organized.

[26] Draft directives have been drawn up for other types of enterprise.

PART II

The Promotion of Competition—
Its Impact upon Enterprises

5

Anti-Trust and Integration

1. CARTELS, CONCENTRATION, AND INTEGRATION

'IT is . . . no exaggeration to state that economically, the Rome
Treaty is basically a Treaty for more competition . . . [competi-
tion] has been considered as one of the principal pillars on which
our building rests.'[1] This statement, made by a senior member
of the staff of the EEC Commission, highlights the important
role which anti-trust policy is expected to play in the creation of
the EEC. There can be no doubt that, as Monnet described it,
'Europe's first anti-trust law' was also expected to play an important if not quite such a crucial role in the creation of the Coal
and Steel Community.

Why was anti-trust policy expected to play such an integral
part in the creation of these two Communities?

One of the most obvious aims of both treaties is the removal of
trade barriers such as customs duties, quotas, and so on, between
member states so as to establish free trade. 'The European
Economic Community takes the classical aim of free trade and
seeks to fulfil it as completely as possible.'[2] Such a statement
could equally well be applied to the Coal and Steel Community.
It was anticipated in both cases that variations in efficiency
existed as between enterprises, or indeed whole industries, in the
different member states and that tariff and other barriers to intra-
community trade allowed the inefficient enterprises or industries
to persist. If, however, these barriers were removed, the inefficient would be faced with competition from more efficient
outsiders.[3] In either event the general level of productive

---

[1] R. Mussard, 'The Regulation of Restrictive Business Practices under the
Common Market Treaty', *ICLQ*, Suppl. Publ. no. 4 (1962), p. 17.

[2] P. Verloren van Themaat, 'Rules of Competition and Restrictive Trade
Practices', *ICLQ* Suppl. Publ. no. 1 (1961), p. 76. The idea of creating a
single market was of course also very much inspired by the political desire to
create something analogous to a single state.

[3] The need for such a stimulus was recognized by the more perceptive

efficiency would rise, either because the less efficient would be forced to reorganize and re-equip or because they would be supplanted by the more efficient.[4] It is of course possible that, rather than close down entirely, firms would narrow their range of products, weeding out the ones which they produced relatively inefficiently. In other words, there would be greater specialization with all its attendant advantages.

Productive efficiency would also rise if member-state markets were too small to reap all the economies of large-scale production. The removal of barriers would in such cases have a twofold advantage, in that the more efficient would be able to supplant the less efficient but would also, in expanding themselves grow more efficient still.[5]

The above arguments are essentially, in the way in which they have been presented, of a static, once-for-all kind. Thus, prior to the removal of trade barriers, variations in productive efficiency exist as between states and there are unexploited economies of scale. After the barriers have been dismantled these disparities in productive efficiency tend to disappear and economies of scale are more fully if not totally exploited. However, there are what may be termed dynamic benefits from the

---

politicians before the Schuman Plan was proposed. According to Reynaud, 'We need German competition in order to rouse French enterprise from its slumbers' (quoted in Diebold, p. 92).

[4] Too much should probably not be made of the idea that because of difference in efficiency between states the competitive process will lead to the absolute contraction or closing down of some enterprises. During a period of rapid expansion such as has been experienced by the Six since the signing of the Paris Treaty it is more likely that competition in such circumstances will result in a smaller share in the overall development going to the less efficient and a larger share to the more efficient. Such a view would appear to be held by the High Authority of the ECSC—see *5th Gen. Rep.* (1957), p. 17. A recognition of this point is important since it is possible to believe mistakenly that, because bankruptcies and closures have been few, the freeing of trade cannot have had the anticipated effects upon efficiency.

[5] It is perhaps worth noting that where there are no great differences in efficiency between firms over the whole range of their production, competition would not necessarily bring about this growth in the scale of output even though there were unexploited economies of large-scale production. In this case only mergers or specialization agreements would accomplish this end. For this reason the EEC Commission favours the removal of legal and psychological barriers to mergers across frontiers (subject to the requirements of Art. 86) and the conclusion of specialization, rationalization, joint purchasing, and joint research agreements—see speech by H. von der Groeben, *European Parliamentary Debates*, 16 June 1965.

removal of trade barriers. These relate to the increased competition which can arise and which can, over time, stimulate a faster rate of innovation. Competition within an integrated economic system is likely to be greater than it is in a purely national framework for a number of reasons. In the first place, integration gives rise to a potentially more competitive market structure. As we indicated earlier, national monopolies become Community oligopolies—the situation in established oligopolies is likely to become comparatively fluid with a lessening of oligopolistic collusion and coordination. Secondly, an integrated multi-national market is likely to embrace a more heterogeneous attitude towards business strategy than would a national market.

It is perhaps interesting to note, in connexion with the above discussion about market structures and economies of scale, that those who were involved in drawing up the *actes préparatoires* of the Rome Treaty were aware that in some industries economies of scale were such as to be only compatible with a monopoly at the national level. The attraction of the integration process was that consumers could continue to enjoy the benefits of large-scale production but also have the added benefit of competition between erstwhile monopolies.[6] Thus the Spaak Report points out that:

This fusion of markets will open up vast outlets for the employment of the most modern techniques. There are some types of production calling for such huge resources or for machinery with such a large output that they are no longer within the capability of a single market. But above all, in many branches of industry, the national markets offer the chance of attaining optimum dimensions only to enterprises having a de facto monopoly. The strength of a vast market lies in the fact that it reconciles mass production with the absence of monopoly.[7]

If these are the benefits which the freeing of trade could bring,

[6] National unitary monopolies may not have been a major problem on the eve of the European Economic Community, but if we also take into account enterprises which had a dominant position in the national market, then the problem was probably real enough. For example, in the synthetic-fibre industry, where the economies of scale are very considerable, the French production of polymide 66 (nylon) was monopolized by Rhodiaceta-Rhone-Poulenc whilst in Italy Snia Viscosa was the predominant producer of polyamide 6. For more on this subject see D. P. O'Brien, 'Patent Protection and Competition in Polyamide and Polyester Fibre Manufacture', *J. Industrial Econ.*, xii/3 (1964).

[7] Comité Intergouvernemental créé par la Conférence de Messine, *Rapport des chefs de délégation aux Ministres des Affaires Étrangères* (1956), pp. 13–14.

then it is equally clear that these ends could be frustrated if the reduction of state-created tariff and quota barriers were accompanied by the erection of private barriers to trade. Such barriers might take many forms. For example, enterprises in the various member states might enter into formal agreements to fix a common price or to allocate markets geographically or otherwise. Alternatively, a dominant enterprise in one state might use its influence over distributors to establish exclusive dealing arrangements thus barring the way to the foreign competitor. Then again in oligopolistic markets enterprises might refrain from making incursions into each other's traditional territory. Whatever the techniques adopted the problem is plain enough. Hans von der Groeben, member of the EEC Commission and Head of the Directorate General for Competition put the matter to the European Parliamentary Assembly as follows:

It is . . . beyond dispute—and the authors of the Treaty were fully aware of this—that it would be useless to bring down trade barriers between Member States if the Governments or private industry were to remain free through economic and fiscal legislation, through subsidies or cartel-like restrictions on competition, virtually to undo the opening of the markets and to prevent, or at least unduly to delay the action needed to adapt them to the Common Market.[8]

2. THE PHILOSOPHY OF COMPETITION IN THE COMMUNITIES

So much for the relationship between anti-trust and trade liberalization. We can now proceed to consider in detail the philosophy which lies behind the reliance upon competition.

Both treaties seek to bring about a competitive order because it is held that competition will guarantee something approaching the optimum allocation of resources. This seems to be what the Paris Treaty is striving to say when Article 2 speaks of the need for the Community to establish conditions which of themselves will assure 'The most rational distribution of production at the highest possible level of productivity.' The Rome Treaty does not explicitly lay down any such requirement although this might be inferred from Article 3, which calls for the establish-

[8] *European Parliamentary Assembly Debates*, 19 Oct. 1961 (official trans.).

ment of a system ensuring that competition will not be distorted.[9] Von der Groeben has, however, put the matter more explicitly by saying that competition must be protected

because in the Common Market competition has an important part to play in giving guidance to producers, and because any distortion of competition is a threat to the best supply of goods in the Community. In all our six national economies the day to day coordination of individual economic plans and measures depends on the functioning of the market; the supplies the consumers wish to have and those the producers are able to provide are so attuned to one another by the play of prices that the maximum of satisfaction results.[10]

The idea that the Common Market can lead to an optimum allocation of resources must however be treated with some caution. As has been observed by Liesner in his study of the Coal and Steel Community,[11] theoretical models aimed at demonstrating the advantageous effect of free trade on resource allocation usually assume the existence of perfect markets. In practice perfect competition can rarely if ever be said to exist. In the case of the steel industry, for example, perfect competition is simply inconceivable. Although individual steel products may be reasonably homogeneous, the number of enterprises is characteristic of oligopoly rather than polypoly. In the case of Rome Treaty products such as, for example, artificial fibres and automobiles the industrial structures, as again dictated by technical considerations, are oligopolistic. That perfect competition is in fact largely unattainable in practice is of course recognized. As von der Groeben points out:

[9] The words 'distorted' and 'restricted' are sometimes used by European commentators as if they were interchangeable. Much confusion can be avoided by realizing that this is only partially the case. 'Distortion' as used in Art. 3 of the Rome Treaty is a generic term that covers any interference with the natural forces of free competition. For example, a distortion of competition would occur when enterprises in a particular industry in one member state received a subsidy that was not granted to enterprises in the same industry in another member state. The less efficient may survive at the expense of the more efficient. But a distortion of competition can equally be caused in the private sector itself as a result of cartels or monopolies. It is this latter kind of distortion, consisting of such things as collective agreement of prices, allocation of markets, control of production, &c. that are known as restrictions.

[10] *European Parliamentary Assembly Debates*, 19 Oct. 1961. This is perhaps an excessively optimistic view of the capabilities of the market mechanism.

[11] Meade, Liesner, & Wells, p. 200.

Our view of the advantages of competition in the Common Market does certainly not mean—and here I should like to forestall a further possible misunderstanding—that we start from the ideal of perfect competition, or that we believe this could be put into general practice.[12]

However, it is generally recognized that if the optimum as defined by assuming perfect competition is unattainable, the optimal ends of free trade are more nearly approached the more that collusion and monopolistic restraints are swept away, and it is in this light that the anti-trust rules of the treaties should be viewed. This would seem to be the line of argument which von der Groeben is following when he says of EEC anti-trust policy that: 'We are on the contrary convinced that competition can fulfil most of its functions even in an imperfect market. . . . We must therefore endeavour to put into practice that degree of competition which is feasible under the conditions of the market concerned.'[13]

On the subject of the relationship between competition, monopoly, and technical progress the attitude of von der Groeben is that there is no proof of a conflict between competition and innovation. According to him, competition forces businessmen continuously to seek more efficient techniques. It is true that a monopolist may be in a position to spend considerable amounts on technical research but the compulsion to do so may be lacking. Instead, he may prefer to continue using old and fully amortized plants rather than to undertake costly new investment. It is indeed oligopolies which are the standard-bearers of technical progress because they are locked in a tough, competitive struggle for performance and quality with their rivals.[14]

(a) Differing Emphases in the Treaties

Although it is true from what has gone before that there is a parallel between the ECSC and the EEC in the important role which each assigns to competition, it is important to recognize that there are certain differences between the two treaties largely arising from the comparatively non-specific nature of the Rome Treaty as compared with the more detailed individual provisions of the Paris Treaty. In the case of the EEC the reliance which is,

---

[12] *European Parliamentary Assembly Debates*, 19 Oct. 1961.
[13] Ibid.　　　　[14] Ibid.

in general,[15] now coming to be placed upon competition and free market forces largely arises from the fact that the authors of the Rome Treaty provided for no other form of guidance and control. As von der Groeben observes, there is in the present state of political integration no question of sweeping powers to control prices, production, investment, &c. being conferred upon a central Community authority. An economy based on competition is therefore 'in harmony with the federalist make-up of our Community'.[16] But in the case of the ECSC, while it is true that the mechanisms of competition are elaborated in greater detail than they are in the Rome Treaty, it is equally true that the Paris Treaty contains provisions enabling the High Authority to apply price floors and ceilings, production quotas, and consumption priorities.

However, such *dirigiste* aspects of the treaty attracted considerable opposition, some of it coming from the US, which was an influential occupying power with definite views on this matter, and in order to dispel suspicion at the time of treaty negotiations, Monnet suggested that: 'It would be understood that certain of the powers conferred on the Authority would be of a precautionary character and that the Authority would direct its activities so as to avoid use of these powers save in exceptional circumstances.'[17]

A glance at the treaty suggests that this condition was fulfilled, in that some of these powers require the existence of a manifest crisis before they can be applied; and in any case the High Authority is first required to attempt indirect solutions such as co-operating with governments to boost demand. In practice these powers do not appear to have been invoked, but nevertheless they exist, and to this extent the Paris Treaty, at least in principle, has a somewhat different orientation from that which established the EEC. However, in one important respect, namely programming, the Paris Treaty is clearly more *dirigiste* than the Rome Treaty and in this sphere the High Authority has been quite active. The powers to draw up General Objectives of growth of coal and steel output, to vet investment projects to see

---

[15] We say 'in general' because some sectors, particularly agriculture and transport, are in some degree exceptions to this rule. Indeed the whole of Part III is devoted to elaborating upon the exceptions to the competitive rule.

[16] *European Parliamentary Assembly Debates*, 10 Oct. 1961.

[17] *Summary of the Working Document submitted by the French Experts* quoted in Diebold, p. 65.

whether they conform to the Community's growth or technological requirements, and to give financial assistance to those projects which it favours, constitute an influence over the course of economic events which the EEC Commission does not generally possess.[18]

If we ask why the emphasis of the treaties is different the answer must be somewhat speculative. First, at the time of the ratification of the Paris Treaty there were numerous cases of governmental control over the treaty products. It is not therefore surprising that the signatories, knowing that they were also embarking upon a novel experience in economic integration within a free market context, should require that some controls should be retained in case of serious disequilibria. Secondly, as one might expect, the treaty bears the imprint of some of its leading protagonists. This is particularly the case with respect to the programming provisions of the treaty, which bear the imprint of Jean Monnet, the founder of the French planning system. However, by the time the Rome Treaty was drafted the economic climate had changed considerably. The treaty, coming as it did on the high tide of European recovery, seems to have been conceived in a mood of considerable optimism about the capabilities of a free market system. Also the process of economic integration in coal and steel had proved to be much less disruptive than might have been anticipated, a factor which was itself partly the result of rapid growth. But the emphasis in the Rome Treaty on competition and market forces—and it is most noticeable that those who drafted it and those charged with implementing it have been more forward than their predecessors in extolling its virtues—also appears to be in some degree the reflection of a specifically German influence, namely the neo-liberal school of Freiburg.[19]

(b) *The influence of German Neo-Liberalism*

The principal task of policy according to neo-liberal thinking is the creation of a socio-economic system which consists, first, of a legal framework guaranteeing private property in consumer

---

[18] This subject is dealt with below in greater detail in the 'Note on Investment Planning in the ECSC', pp. 428–39.

[19] For an illuminating account of the thinking of this school see H. Oliver, 'German Neoliberalism,' *QJ Econ.*, lxxiv (1960), pp. 117–49.

and producer goods, freedom of opportunity of labour and enterprise, and freedom of contract; secondly, and of prime importance, a system in which vigorous competition determines prices, outputs, incomes; thirdly, a governmental system in which egalitarian and stabilization policies exist in a form and to an extent which is compatible with the fundamental individualistic order. In principle the latter implies something considerably short of a welfare state. (In practice the distinction is by no means so clear cut.) The advantages of such a policy are in part economic—as for example the optimum allocation of resources referred to above by von der Groeben, whose pronouncements appear to be in some degree inspired by neo-liberal ideas. But in addition there is a political aspect which is well summed up by Hallstein, who points out that: 'Besides the known economic and social advantages, an economic order based on competition has the decisive political advantage that it guarantees personal freedom to an extent not attainable in any other economic order.'[20]

The basic idea here is twofold. First, that greater freedom exists when economic decision-making is decentralized by being left to the play of market forces. The alternative is to vest the making of such decisions in the state, and this involves increasing the power of the state over the individual. Secondly, if the economy is to be market-oriented, it is necessary to have as much competition as possible. This prevents entrepreneurs from building up unchecked positions of power which can be used to exploit consumers or to limit the opportunity of other entrepreneurs to engage in the same line of business. The parallel between this line of thinking and the philosophy which lies behind American anti-trust is quite close.[21]

Indeed the importance of competition goes further than this. If a free-enterprise market economy is the best guarantee of personal freedom, the survival of such a system depends upon a willingness of entrepreneurs to compete. If they are not willing, but prefer instead to form cartels or whatever, they will ultimately come to be regarded as dispensable. Thus Erhard, whose philosophy of the social market economy is to a marked extent based upon neo-liberal ideas, observes:

[20] W. Hallstein, 'Der Weg zur gemeinsamen Politik', *Europäische Gemeinschaft*, Nov. 1962, p. 8.
[21] See A. D. Neale, *The Antitrust Laws of the USA* (1960), p. 422.

4

The businessman can justify his existence only as long as he is prepared to fulfil the function of a free businessman, with all its opportunities but also with all its risks. He remains irreplaceable and untouchable only as long as he is willing to prove himself in free competition in a free market. As soon as the businessman tries to limit the risks by collective agreements, or attempts to remove them entirely—i.e., if he aims at shifting through cartels the individual decision from the level of his own undertaking to the level of branches and associations, then I believe the demands for joint management can no longer be opposed and certainly not with any justification or conviction. By forming cartels the businessman deprives himself of his proper function; eventually he becomes an official and thus is replaceable.[22]

The neo-liberal objection to programming or planning[23] is essentially the same—it edges the entrepreneur from the centre of the stage and encourages the idea that he is not indispensable.

In conclusion it is clear that the view of competition which is generally accepted as the 'Community' view, is in practice very largely a German one, and is particularly strongly held by German members of the EEC Commission. It does not necessarily follow that these ideas would be echoed so enthusiastically by, say, Italian or French economists, government officials, or politicians.

3. CRITIQUES OF COMPETITION

Not all opinion has favoured reliance upon competition as an instrument of economic integration and economic progress. Before, however, proceeding to discuss the views under these two heads it is perhaps necessary to justify separating the appraisal of competition into these two compartments. In a sense economic integration gives rise to economic progress in that it brings in its train all the economic benefits discussed above in connexion with competition and customs unions. It is, however, possible to consider competition, not as the vehicle of economic integration, but as a means of generating more rapid innovative activity. For example, some economists have not considered con-

[22] L. Erhard, *Prosperity through Competition* (1958), p. 134.
[23] We are thinking here of the publication by the Central Authorities of targets which may, at the one extreme, merely be guides to entrepreneurs in their decision-making about output and investment (but which may be made effective by inducements), and at the other extreme may be mandatory.

ventional competitive market structures as being well suited to technical advance and have favoured an element of monopoly. There is of course good reason to consider competition under the heading of technical progress, since Article 2 of the Rome Treaty states that one of the major tasks of the Community is to secure 'a harmonious development of activities, a continuous and balanced expansion . . . an accelerated raising of the standard of living'.

One of the fascinating problems of competition policy in the two Communities is whether the conventional competitive model which is generally regarded as essential to the full realization of the benefits of a customs union (see Liesner's remarks on page 75 above) does not conflict with the requirements of technical progress. It must be remembered that in some degree the benefits of a customs union are of a once-for-all character. That is to say that the union involves a dismantling of barriers and as a result there may be a once-for-all movement to a better allocation of resources—whether this is so depends upon the considerations discussed in our treatment of the theory of customs unions. On the other hand market structures other than the conventional competitive one may generate more rapid technological advance and this is a continuing process over time.

(a) Business Attitudes to Competition

Before we begin to consider what we may term the intellectual reservations about competition, it is necessary to note that competition has been opposed in some industrial circles, albeit largely for reasons of self-interest. There was, for example, strong opposition in certain quarters to the contents of the Paris Treaty. The treaty was regarded as *dirigiste*. The charge of *dirigisme* related not merely to the influence given to the High Authority in the matter of investment but also to the pricing rules and, above all, to the rules relating to cartels and concentrations. A lack of *dirigisme* must not, of course, be equated with the existence of a competitive free market economy. *Dirigisme* in the eyes of these businessmen was a term applied to any interference by officialdom which prevented them from doing what they wanted, including not competing. Thus in Germany, although in general the coal and steel industries were favourable to the idea of economic integration, there was a strong current of feeling that this should be accomplished by means of a treaty stripped of *dirigiste* powers and in which the emphasis would be upon co-operation between the interested industries. The anti-competition view was perhaps best illustrated in Germany by the virtually solid support in the coal and steel industries, not only amongst employers but also amongst trade unions, for the joint non-competitive sales of coal at prices fixed by the Gemeinschaftsorganisation Ruhrkohle (GEORG), the Ruhr coal cartel. These attitudes were summed up in a leading editorial in 1955 which called for a revision of the treaty in respect of the anti-trust rules and added:

Let the members of the High Authority and all those possessed of the theory of free competition who loudly demand that cartel ghosts must be hunted in the coal sector, recognise their mistake in the last hour and be wise enough to draw the consequences from their recognition.[24]

In the French steel industry objections to the anti-trust rules were likewise strong, and opinion was firmly in favour of a cartelization approach to industrial integration.[25]

By contrast the competition rules of the Rome Treaty did not evoke the same kind of opposition from other industrial circles and it is worth while considering why. In some degree the contrast must be ascribed to the fact that coal and steel had a long history of cartelization which had become an accepted way of doing business. The idea of being launched on the high seas of international competition was therefore bound to cause some alarm. The conditions of 1957 were, however, considerably different. The creation of the common market in coal and steel had passed off in a remarkably smooth way. The High Authority's régime had not proved unduly onerous. The European economy was in a phase of rapid expansion and the main problem was one of finding supplies rather than sales. Finally, the proposed anti-trust rules were less *dirigiste*. Pricing was left virtually untouched and it seemed that mergers were to be completely uncontrolled.

(b) *Academic Reservations regarding Competition*

We can now turn to the intellectual critiques of competition,

[24] 'Montan-Union und Gemeinschaftsverkauf', in *Kohlenwirtschaftszeitung.* no. 17, 1955, pp. 4 ff, quoted in E. B. Haas, *The Uniting of Europe* (1958), p. 166,
[25] See particularly J. Ferry and R. Chatel, *L'acier* (1953), pp. 99, 107, & 117.

but in doing so we should note that these critiques have dwelt not so much upon whether competition was an appropriate instrument, as upon the twin problems of what model of competition should be adopted and *to what extent* competition could be relied upon to achieve the desired economic ends. Few critics have recommended a total rejection of competition.

(i) *Competition as a Vehicle of Economic Integration.* Some economists have questioned whether, in principle, competition is always the best instrument for bringing economic integration about. Thus Tinbergen has suggested that

in the field of specialisation and interplant co-operation . . . direct steps seem to promise more than indirect forces of competition might, in the end, perform. In order to obtain the most efficient concentration of production, say of certain spare parts or semi-finished goods, in a few plants, making long production runs possible, deliberate schemes of co-operation and direct conversations probably will be the quickest way.[26]

Byé too, in the context of the proposed Franco-Italian customs union, observed that both partners would have been bound to benefit from: 'The disappearance of certain competitive struggles, from a pooling of market research and advertising and from mutual adaptation of their conditions of production.'[27]

These two views do not, as has been indicated, involve a rejection of competition but a limitation of it. They antedate the Communities, and in some degree it will be shown that the rules of competition of both Communities make some concession to these ideas.

More recently the relationship of integration and competition has been taken up by Louis Phlips.[28] His view is essentially a development of an idea in J. M. Clark's *Studies in the Economics of Overhead Costs.* Phlips does not argue against competition as a means of integration but only about the form. Essentially he believes that imperfections of competition may aid the interpenetration of markets. His attack is directed against the idea,

---

[26] J. Tinbergen, *Selected Papers* (1959), p. 150.

[27] M. Byé, 'Customs Unions and National Interests', *Internat. Econ. Papers,* no. 3, 1953, p. 222.

[28] L. Phlips, 'Common Markets: Towards a Theory of Market Integration', *J. Industrial Econ.,* x (1962), pp. 81–92.

which is widely held in the EEC, that perfect transparency of the market is an essential feature of a common market competition model. He defines a transparent market as one, 'in which sellers have a precise knowledge of the prices, terms of sale and of the qualities of their competitors' products, and in which buyers have a precise knowledge of the prices, terms of sale and of the qualities of all sellers' products', and transparency so defined appears to mean much the same thing as the traditional perfect knowledge of the perfect competition model.

According to Phlips, if producers in one member state are to penetrate into the markets of another, imperfect transparency may aid the process. A foreign producer attacking a new market must expend considerable time and effort in making himself known and attracting custom. He may attempt to build up his sales by offering a low price. If the market were perfectly transparent, customers would rapidly shift their custom to him[29] and this might bring a quick competitive response from domestic producers. This in turn might dislodge the foreign producer before he had had time enough to establish his products with consumers. But if the market is imperfectly transparent it may take time before buyers know that the foreign producer is entering the market, what price he is offering, what the delivery conditions are like, and so forth. Meanwhile domestic producers will continue to enjoy the patronage of their old clientele although some will be attracted away as time elapses. This time-lag caused by imperfect transparency on the demand side gives the foreign producer the breathing-space to establish himself in the market. If there is also a time-lag before domestic producers can obtain the necessary information to mount an effective competitive riposte (imperfect transparency on the supply side), this further assists the foreign producer in building up a strong market position.

(ii) *Competition and Technical Progress.* The most detailed argument on this score has been put forward by Professors Vito, Marchal, Wessels, and Woitrin in a report for a conference on

---

[29] A lower price may not, for all consumers, overcome the effect of product differentiation in holding consumers to the products of any particular domestic producer. Phlips appears to assume that if the foreign producer's price is low enough it will attract a significant number.

Technical Progress in the Common Market in 1960.[30] Their criticism is twofold. First, they reject the conventional competitive model as being the one most conducive to economic progress. Secondly, they suggest alternatives to the conventional competitive mechanism as a means of guaranteeing that the fruits of technical progress are equitably shared out.

The four professors first maintain that those who drafted the Rome Treaty in particular 'were captives of an outdated conception of competition'. They are here referring to the view that the essential feature of a competitive market structure is large numbers. Their argument, however, is that the essence of competition is the willingness and ability to grow at the expense of others. True competition, which they designate as workable competition, involves rivalry in respect of market shares. They instance the example of the numerous family and craftsmen businesses in France which, although they fulfil the requirements of large numbers, instead of having the desire to expand at each other's expense remain 'in an immobile rut'. Not only do these businesses abstain from the necessary innovative activity but their smallness and their attitudes to new methods and outside capital preclude them from doing so. The professors then press their argument further by pointing out that: 'The objective to be achieved is not a predetermined market structure but economic progress' and for this purpose 'other structures than the competitive one seem capable of assuring the realization of this objective'. They instance the case of a firm with some significant degree of monopoly power. If a competitive market structure were to be the only criterion of acceptability, the firm would be condemned, particularly if it was making abnormally high profits. They point out that such a static view may be wrong. Arguing on Schumpeterian lines they point out that the high profits stemming from the market power may be the means and inducement to innovative activity. Eventually other firms will be lured by the high profits, will emulate the innovation and drive down prices and profits to the benefit of the consumer. Market structures with elements of monopoly may therefore be more progressive than the conventional ones. 'What is blameworthy in a static situation becomes praiseworthy in a dynamic one.'

[30] EEC, *Conférence européenne Progrès technique et Marché commun* (1960), pp. 97–130.

Those who take this point of view doubt whether it is possible to create a logical anti-trust system by any abstract rules relating to 'desirable' and 'undesirable' economic structures. 'All laying down of rules, which are too general and too abstract, must therefore be avoided'. 'Agreement and concentrations must, in brief, be appraised according to their respective driving motives and not simply on the basis of conformity with the so-called competitive structure of the market'. 'It is thus not the form which must be condemned but the action or driving motive behind it'. The prohibition principle is therefore rejected in favour of a policy of preventing firms from following harmful policies. They do however recognize that firms which have some economic power may rest on their oars rather than innovate and may choose (or be in a position) to exploit the consumer over a long period. Because of this they propose a series of devices, other than the conventional competitive mechanism, for protecting the consumer. Briefly, their suggestions are as follows. First, the threat of nationalization can be a means of stimulating firms into activity, either because the firm is threatened with a take-over by the state or because the state can create enterprises to compete with private ones. Secondly, countervailing power can be exercised by buying firms. However, they recognize that, contrary to what Galbraith appears to believe, countervailing power does not automatically arise in response to economic power on the other side of the market. For example, where there is vertical integration—and they instance coal and steel as examples—no effective countervailing position exists. Because of this it might be necessary to confer upon the state and the EEC institutions the power to encourage the creation of countervailing power, partly by fiscal means[31] and also through their own purchasing machinery. They also refer to the co-operative movement, as exemplified in Sweden, as an effective source of consumer power.

Finally, one of the perennial criticisms of the principle of establishing and maintaining competitive market structures has been that it would prevent firms from growing to a size sufficient to compete with enterprises outside the Common Market, particularly in the US and the Eastern bloc. Such large enterprises might have considerable market power but only enterprises of

---

[31] They pointed out that the cascade tax favours vertical concentration whereas the added value tax as adopted in France is neutral in this respect.

such a size could reap the economies of scale and carry on the necessary amount of research and innovation. More recently this view has come much more to the fore, and in Chapter 8 we consider whether the need for larger enterprises might conflict with the anti-trust rules of the treaties.

6

Cartel Types in the Communities

IT will be readily admitted that cartels can in principle affect the process of integration. The purpose of this chapter is to illustrate in some detail the reality of this threat by analysing cartels into their main types and showing how their operation throws up quite unmistakable obstacles to it. It is also true to say that practices of large, dominant firms may conflict with the requirements of integration. It is, however, more convenient to reserve the discussion of these practices to Chapter 8 in which concentration policy is discussed specifically.

At the outset it must be stated that the following account is far from exhaustive and cannot claim to be much more than an impressionistic study. A comprehensive account of restrictive business practices is in fact impossible for two reasons. In the first place, although the EEC and ECSC authorities have established various mechanisms that involve the notification of restrictive practices, it is by no means certain that all the existing ones have in fact been notified. In particular, the more informal ones may have remained underground. Secondly, as opposed to the arrangements which exist in some European countries, notably Norway, Sweden, Denmark, and the UK, where cartel registers are kept which are open to public inspection, the EEC and ECSC systems do not provide such a facility.

It is, nevertheless, possible, by using a variety of sources of information, to provide a picture of some of the main kinds of restrictive business practice operated within the two Communities. When we come to discuss the actual implementation of the anti-trust rules of the two treaties, it will also be possible to indicate the apparent relative importance of the different categories.

Before discussing the main types of restrictive business practices that occur in the Communities four preliminary points may be noted. First, in the case of the EEC, only practices which are designed to (or do) prevent, restrict, or distort competition within the Common Market *and which affect inter-state trade* are covered by the anti-trust rules. In the ECSC, on the other hand, no such inter-state trade clause exists—all practices which directly or indirectly restrict or distort competition within the Common Market are covered by the rules. Because of this difference, the examples of practices involving Rome Treaty products have been confined to those which have some effect on inter-state trade. The many practices that are purely national in character which have come to light have, therefore, been ignored in this account.

Secondly, the practices selected are those which have been found to exist in the post-war period, and it cannot be guaranteed that they all still exist. Indeed, those which have been dealt with by the High Authority, the EEC Commission, or national authorities have presumably ceased to exist, at least in their original form.

Thirdly, it is not necessarily assumed that because certain defined types of practices exist, they are necessarily contrary to the treaties. Some of the practices cited may be justifiable, and, as we shall see later, both treaties provide 'gateways' for exemption from prohibition.

Fourthly, any systematic account of restrictive business practices inevitably runs up against problems of categorization. One of these is that although many cartel arrangements can be categorized exclusively under a particular heading, such as collective exclusive dealing or market sharing, sometimes they involve a number of ancillary restrictions. For example, collective exclusive dealing and a common price arrangement might be found together in one agreement. A neat division is impossible and the following sections on each of the main types of restrictive business practice inevitably involve some degree of overlap.

I. COMMON SELLING AND BUYING ORGANIZATIONS

Perhaps the most famous of these was GEORG (Gemeinschaftsorganisation Ruhrkohle GmbH), the Ruhr coal sales agency. In Germany the common sales agency, in all its variations, has been the traditional means of selling coal (and much else) over many years. As Diebold remarks in connexion with the High Authority's attempts to reform GEORG: 'You would look far to find a single voice of importance in Germany calling for a change. Owners, managers, union leaders, Socialists, politicians could all agree on this.'[1]

The sale of coal in the Ruhr has been under central control since 1893, when the Rheinische-Westfälische Kohlen-Syndikat AG (RWKS) was established with the aim of organizing the marketing of coal and stabilizing prices. The RWKS was a limited liability company whose stock was owned by the Ruhr mining companies. The syndicate determined the price at which coal would be sold. It also drew up sales quotas for the individual mining companies which were increased or decreased in line with changes in demand. Penalties were levied on companies that exceeded their quotas.

The market in Germany was divided into contested and un-contested areas. Contested areas consisted of export markets and those regions in Germany which were also served by other cartels. In the uncontested areas the RWKS had a monopoly and, as might be expected, prices there were higher than in the contested regions. A levy was, however, imposed upon sales in uncontested regions, the proceeds of which were used to compensate producers who sold in contested regions. In effect this meant that returns from selling a ton of coal were the same whether it was sold in a contested or uncontested area. It should be noted that the so-called contested regions were hardly competitive, since all coal, both that supplied by the cartels and that which was imported, was sold through the common sales agency Kohlenkontor.[2]

After the Second World War the RWKS was dissolved by the British Military Government, but the Allies then proceeded to establish another monopolistic organization, the Deutscher Kohlen-Verkauf (DKV), to control the marketing of all solid fuels in Western Germany. However, the Allies, as part of the decartelization programme, eventually replaced DKV by a new arrangement which was intended to be less monopolistic. Six coal sales organizations were created, together with a coordinating body, GEORG. The intention was that GEORG would

[1] Diebold, pp. 381–2.

[2] L. Lister, *Europe's Coal and Steel Community* (1960), pp. 256–8. Presumably the price of coal sold through Kohlenkontor, although a cartel price, was lower than the price in the uncontested areas.

provide statistical and technical services for the six agencies but would not control sales or prices. However, in practice, when the High Authority came to review the situation it discovered not the competitive market structure which had originally been envisaged, but a centralized selling mechanism operated through the medium of GEORG. It should be emphasized that in the ultimately crucial matter of price GEORG never exercised any control, since, during the period of its existence, coal prices were controlled at first by the German government and later by the High Authority. The continuation of price control by the High Authority was justified by the potential power of GEORG, which at that time controlled 50 per cent of total Community production. Also, as Liesner points out,[3] the high costs of the Belgian coal industry, and the relative isolation of the French industry from GEORG's market in Germany, further enhanced the market power which it could exert.

One of the main activities of GEORG was to allocate orders among companies when demand was low and supplies among consumers when it was high. It was also the medium through which an equalization scheme was operated which compensated high-cost mines in periods of low demand. GEORG also had a number of technical functions, one of which was to pool supplies of particular grades of coal, making sufficient quantities of any particular grade easily available. This latter function may have been beneficial, but, at the same time, the overall control which GEORG enjoyed allowed it to indulge in potentially less desirable practices, such as tie-in arrangements which enabled it to dispose of poorer grades of coal. GEORG's market power also enabled it to dictate terms concerning the qualifications of merchants. Liesner points out that GEORG imposed more restrictive terms of admission than had previously existed. Thus up to 1952 a merchant could buy directly from mining companies if he purchased a minimum of 6,000 tons per annum but GEORG raised this to 48,000 tons.[4]

The High Authority also found that the South German market was controlled by another common agency—the Oberrheinische Kohlenunion (OKU). This agency took the form of a joint stock company, the shares of which were held by coal-mining companies and by wholesalers (the latter in many cases

---

[3] Meade, Liesner & Wells, p. 240.   [4] Ibid. p. 411.

being owned by the mining companies). It was through this agency that the coal-mining firms of the Saar, Lorraine, Ruhr, and Aachen sold solid fuels in the South German market. Again OKU was in a position to influence prices, since in 1950 it controlled two-thirds of all solid fuels consumed in the South German market. OKU sold directly to consumers who took more than 30,000 tons per annum and to wholesalers who themselves dealt with the smaller consumers.

The other main private joint coal-selling agency was the Comptoir Belge des Charbons (COBECHAR), founded in 1934. This was the joint sales office of the Belgian collieries and sold only to certain classes of large-scale buyers and to big industrial consumers. Other sales were negotiated by the colliery companies themselves. (COBECHAR with few exceptions sold direct, but the mining companies had a choice of direct sales or sale to wholesalers and tended to prefer the latter.) On the face of it, the fact that colliery companies could negotiate their own terms for that part of their output not dealt with by COBECHAR suggests that the possibility existed that the agency prices and the company prices could differ. But in practice this was highly unlikely. In the first place most of the mining companies were members of COBECHAR and therefore might be expected to follow its prices. But, secondly, according to the High Authority, the ECSC Treaty prohibition on discrimination had led the colliery companies to follow the agency's schedules[5]—a rather convenient interpretation on the part of the mining companies.

The High Authority also had to deal with a number of small joint selling agencies in coal, coke, and briquettes. Thus the mining firms in Aachen sold hard coal, briquettes, and hard-coal coke through the Aachener Kohlen-Verkauf,[6] whilst those in Lower Saxony organized their sales of the same products through the Niedersächsischer Kohlen-Verkauf.[7] These were, however, relatively innocuous affairs, since the former controlled only 2·3 per cent and the latter 1 per cent of ECSC coal production. Brown-coal briquettes were also sold through the Helmstedter Braunkohlen-Verkauf GmbH.[8]

---

[5] ECSC, *4th Gen. Rep.* (1956), pp. 146–7.
[6] See High Authority Decision no. 32 of 1954 in *JO*, 6 July 1954, p. 434.
[7] See Decision no. 34 of 1954, ibid., p. 436.
[8] Decision no. 33 of 1954, ibid., p. 435.

By and large it is true to say that in the steel market, unlike the coal industry, common selling has not been a notable feature. It is true that the High Authority has authorized a number of common sales organizations in the steel industry. However, some of these involved enterprises under common financial control and such organizations could therefore be regarded as being one enterprise between whose constituent parts competition was unlikely.[9] There were two common sales organizations involving otherwise independent enterprises but as these arrangements also involved specialization agreements, they are dealt with below under that heading (pp. 108–9).

The device of the common sales agency is not, of course, confined to coal and steel but is also to be found in those industries which are subject to the jurisdiction of the Rome Treaty. A good example of this is the German Terrazzo Verkaufsgesellschaft. This was a syndicate through which three firms sold their tile production not only in Germany but also in other member states of the EEC. The syndicate was responsible for about 10 per cent of German production and about 50 per cent of German exports to the EEC. The arrangement required the members to do no independent selling but to turn over the whole of their production to the syndicate and to have no contact with the purchasers. The member firms, in collaboration with the management of the syndicate, arrived at uniform prices and discounts.[10]

A somewhat similar arrangement appears to exist in the case of the Holland–Exportgenossenschaft. This concerned small and medium-sized sawmills in Bavaria which, for the purposes of exporting wood products to Holland, had entered into a co-operative association.[11]

The essential features of these joint selling devices are therefore as follows. Where the membership is responsible for a preponderant part of the supply of a particular market, as was the case with GEORG, the power clearly exists to behave as a

---

[9] The common sales organizations are Ucosider (members of which are Cockerill-Ougrée, Rodange, Providence, and Aciéries et Minières de la Sambre), Ucometal (John Cockerill, Providence, S. A. Métallurgique de Sambre et Moselle) and Siderur (Ougrée-Marihaye, Rodange, Aciéries et Minières de la Sambre).

[10] BKA, *Jahresbericht* 1960 (1961), p. 60. See also R. M. Buxbaum, 'Antitrust Regulation within the European Economic Community', *Columbia Law R.*, lx (1961), p. 414.

[11] Ibid. p. 61.

classical textbook monopolist—supply can be restricted to bring about a desired price level. Where such preponderance does not exist, as was, for example, the case with Terrazzo, price rivalry is nevertheless completely eliminated between members. In the past such joint selling devices have also been able to practise price discrimination on a grand scale. As has also been shown, the big coal syndicates have been able to dictate terms respecting the admission to dealership and have used their power to operate tie-ins.[12]

2. HORIZONTAL PRICE AGREEMENTS

First, we may consider horizontal price agreements pure and simple between independent enterprises. Such agreements would normally lay down a schedule of prices which all adherents would charge, or regard as a minimum, in a particular market. So far few examples have come to light, although, as we shall see when discussing notifications of multilateral (as opposed to bilateral) agreements to the EEC Commission, it is clear that such agreements are, in percentage terms, extremely important. We shall see that price agreements are to be found in conjunction with, for example, market-sharing and collective exclusive-dealing arrangements. Also, as might be expected, price agreements have been a prominent feature of import and export cartels. The one example about which details have been published concerned dealing in iron and steel products. According to a report by the ECSC High Authority in 1962, a period of falling steel prices, a number of such dealers were discovered to be preparing agreements for the introduction of minimum prices in a part of the ECSC market. The dealers however abandoned the scheme when the legal position was brought to their attention.[13] Examples are available of price agreements in which enterprises in one member state respect the price levels charged by enterprises in another. The report of the United Kingdom Monopolies Commission

[12] For the sake of completeness it is necessary to mention the existence of three organizations for the joint allocation and/or buying of scrap. All three were at various times refused authorization by the High Authority. They were: Schrottvermittlungs GmbH, Düsseldorf (SVG); Consorzio Nazionale Approvvigionamento Materie Prime Siderurgiche S.p.A., Milan (Campsider); Westdeutsche Schrotteinkaufs-Vereinigung and Westdeutsche Schrotteinkaufsgesellschaft, GmbH (WSG).

[13] ECSC, *10th Gen. Rep.* (1962), p. 211.

provides evidence of two such arrangements. The first relates to electric wire and cable. Apparently the first international cartel in cable making was formed in 1907 and consisted of an agreement between British and German manufacturing groups. This was subsequently followed by agreements with other groups. In 1928 intensive competition in the sales of mains cable led to the formation of the International Cable Development Corporation, consisting of fifteen national groups (virtually all the European countries making cable) representing ninety manufacturers. This agreement continued up to the last war. Afterwards, in 1947, a meeting was held in Lausanne to consider reviving the system. The result was the Lausanne Arrangement. The basic feature of this arrangement was that: 'The Groups undertake reciprocally to urge their members to respect the home prices of a Producing Country by consulting this Producing Country before making an offer.'[14]

According to the Monopolies Commission Report of 1952, at that time the member groups included those of Belgium, France, the Netherlands, and Italy. Apparently, despite the achievement of this agreement, the intention of the parties to the Lausanne Arrangement was that it should only be regarded as an interim affair—the long-run aim was to conclude agreements between regional groups.

The second example is provided by copper and copper-based alloys. In 1946 an international conference of non-ferrous-metals manufacturers was held in Lausanne and was, among others, attended by representatives of Belgian and French firms. As a result the Lausanne Agreement, which was not limited in duration, came into effect immediately. Clause 6 of the agreement provided that the parties would observe each other's domestic delivered prices for all goods covered by the agreement —Belgian domestic prices were to apply in the case of the Netherlands.[15] (Apparently some concerns in Italy and Belgium outside the original agreement subsequently joined and then

[14] Monopolies and Restrictive Practices Commission, *Report on the Supply of Insulated Electric Wires and Cables* (1952), p. 53. A report of the French Commission Technique des Ententes in 1957 confirms the existence of a rigid international cartel in these products.

[15] According to C. D. Edwards, *Cartelization in Western Europe* (US Dept. of State, External Research Staff, Bureau of Intelligence and Research, 1964), p. 28, this agreement still appears to be in existence and is entered in the Swedish Cartel Register.

resigned.) Clause 8 provided that signatories would not sell in neutral markets at less than the prices embodied in the International Non-Ferrous Metals Price List which members of the agreement drew up. Originally neutral markets included Western Germany, Italy, and Luxembourg, although after 1952 Western Germany was removed from this classification. The fact that the Germans were not members of the original agreement proved to be a serious drawback, particularly in view of the revival of German competition discernible from 1949 onwards. However, by 1955, when the Monopolies Commission reported, there were signs that the German industry was considering entering into price agreements with foreign manufacturers.[16]

A more recent example has been unearthed by the French Commission Technique des Ententes. A report issued by the Commission in 1961 indicates the existence of an international cartel whose members include among others French and other Common Market producers of linoleum. One of the rules of the cartel was that members selling linoleum in France should align their prices on those offered by the French members.[17]

These three agreements were essentially formal in the sense that a written arrangement existed. In addition we have to consider the possibility that competition may be restricted by means of less formal arrangements, and steel seems to be a case in point. Although the High Authority of the ECSC has not authorized concerted practices with respect to steel prices, everything indicates that such practices do exist. According to Lister: 'In each country the steel firms discuss prices among themselves and negotiate collectively with their respective governments through their national trade associations.'[18]

Steel firms in smaller areas, such as the Saar and Luxembourg, follow the price changes in major producing areas. There appears to be no evidence of the kind of highly organized arrangements that existed in the inter-war period. Instead there is what has been called spontaneous coordination or self-discipline, which

[16] Monopolies and Restrictive Practices Commission, *Report on the Supply and Export of certain Semi-Manufactures of Copper and Copper-Based Alloys* (1955), pp. 59-65. See also Commission Technique des Ententes, *Rapport au Ministre chargé des affaires économiques pour l'année 1956* (1960), p. 21.

[17] Commission Technique des Ententes, *Rapport au Ministre chargé des affaires économiques pour les années 1960, 1961 et 1962* (1964), p. 25.

[18] Lister, p. 198.

manifests itself in the form of simultaneous and sometimes equi-proportionate increases in prices by all or most of the firms in a particular member state.

The existence of simultaneous and uniform increases in steel prices on national markets has in no small measure arisen from two factors. One has been the influence of the state in attempting to limit steel price increases. Realizing that this uniformity of action seems to contradict the letter and certainly the spirit of the Paris Treaty, the European Parliament has attacked the influence of governments in this field. In 1958 it observed that:

When the governments put pressure on the industry's representatives to keep prices from exceeding a fixed level, prices are naturally established at this level, uniformly and by agreement. This procedure not only leads to uniform prices but, what is more important, it stimulates the tendency to make agreements.[19]

The High Authority too has been aware of this national parallelism. In 1959 it stated that it had several times had occasion to note concerted practices whereby enterprises in the same area had made the same changes in their prices at the same time. The High Authority stated that: 'During the boom period these enterprises pleaded their Government's special representations to them not to raise their prices to the full extent of the increase in raw material prices and wages the object being to avoid a general rise in prices.' The High Authority apparently had 'repeatedly urged the Governments to refrain from encouraging collective decisions to raise or lower prices'.

The other main factor which had led to this behaviour, at least as far as France was concerned, had been the influence of planning. A perceptive commentator on the French planning system has alluded (in connexion with the French steel industry) to its effect in 'reducing the number of centres of initiative, increasing the importance of inter-firm connections and strengthening the pattern of co-operation at the expense of possible competition'.[20]

[19] European Parliamentary Assembly, Doc. no. 12, 1958, p. 30, quoted in Lister, pp. 230–1. This experience in the Six has been paralleled in the United Kingdom, where the maximum steel prices set by the state Iron and Steel Board have until quite recently been regarded as a minimum by the industry.

[20] J. Sheahan, *Promotion and Control of Industry in Post-War France* (1963), p. 87.

There is, however, no evidence to suggest that there is any formal coordination between the national groups respecting prices in the ECSC market. First of all, there is an absence of simultaneity in price changes. Secondly, the evidence which we discuss in detail in the chapter on steel pricing indicates that in periods of recession, when a restrictive arrangement would normally begin to be really effective in maintaining price levels, particular national groups did not hesitate to enter into vigorous price competition with other national groups and actual prices (as opposed to list prices) collapsed.

3. QUOTA AGREEMENTS

In 1965 the EEC Commission released details of a quota agreement which had been entered into by Belgian, German, and Dutch producers of silica—a material used in ceramics and in the manufacture of abrasives, soap, paint, and enamel. Under the terms of the first agreement six silica producers (four in Belgium, one in Germany, and one in the Netherlands) had between them fixed sales quotas in the Dutch market. There was also a second agreement under which four sales agents in the Netherlands dealt exclusively with these producers (unless they had no supplies available) and also fixed a common resale price. This agreement also provides for fines in the case of non-observance.[21]

The Commission Technique des Ententes reported in 1960 on an international cartel arrangement drawn up in 1956 between French and Belgian quarry owners supplying road-making materials in five Departments in Northern France— Nord, Pas-de-Calais, Somme, Oise, and Aisne. Apparently a global annual tonnage was arrived at each year which the parties collectively agreed to deliver in this geographical area. A third group of quarry owners agreed orally to accept a limitation on its deliveries equal to 25 per cent of the global figure.[22] The remaining 75 per cent was divided equally between the French and Belgian groups—the Belgians preferentially delivering in Nord and Pas-de-Calais and the French in the other three Departments. The agreement was buttressed by a system in which the

---

[21] EEC Official Spokesman, Doc. IP(65) 170, 5 Oct. 1965.

[22] None of the other contractual obligations of the cartel agreement were applicable to this group.

group in excess of its quota paid penalties to the group in arrears.[23]

4. MARKET-SHARING AGREEMENTS AND ARRANGEMENTS

The discussion here falls into very much the same pattern as that dealing with prices. On the one hand there are examples of market-sharing agreements which are formal in character in that they involve some kind of agreement written or oral. But there are also examples of arrangements which spring not from formal agreements but are a reflection of mutual awareness and a desire not to trespass on each other's territory.

A number of examples of the formal variety have come to light. Thus in 1961 the West German Federal Agency responsible for administering the cartel law, the Bundeskartellamt (BKA), at the request of the EEC Directorate General for Competition, took steps to ascertain whether a restrictive agreement existed in the trade in adhesive tape between Western Germany and the Netherlands. It transpired that, in 1954, a gentlemen's agreement had been concluded between the two groups of producers. The basis of the agreement was that the German producers would no longer supply the Dutch market, with the exception of one large consumer, while the Dutch for their part would keep out of the West German market.[24] There is also evidence of a market-sharing agreement in detergents ('Savon Noir') involving Belgian and Dutch firms. Under the agreement the Belgian parties were forbidden to sell their detergent either directly or indirectly in the Dutch market and Dutch producers entered into a reciprocal agreement. In order to buttress the agreement all parties also undertook, on pain of penalties, to prohibit any reselling by buyers which might prejudice the division of markets.[25] The packaging market provides yet a further example. Apparently an old Belgian firm (Tuberies Louis Julien SA) and a new post-war Dutch enterprise (Van Katwijk's Papier en Carton Verwerkende Industrien NV) had originally entered into detailed arrangements about the marketing of cardboard tubes. A dispute subsequently arose but

---

[23] Commission Technique des Ententes, *Rapport . . . 1956*, p. 14.
[24] BKA, *Jahresbericht 1961* (1962), p. 35.
[25] EEC Official Spokesman, Doc. IP(65) 148, 26 July *1956*.

was finally settled in 1952. The terms of the compromise were that the Belgian firm would not supply more than 20 per cent of total Dutch imports whilst the Dutch firm agreed not to supply the Belgian market at all, either directly or indirectly.[26]

The cement market also appears to have been subjected to international market-sharing arrangements. According to a somewhat cryptic account by C. D. Edwards, post-war international cement cartelization began with the Paris Agreement of 1950 and this was subsequently included in an agreement covering the Netherlands and Belgium in 1953 and a further one covering the Netherlands market in 1957. According to Edwards: 'The cartel pattern in cement involves allocation of markets to particular firms, production quotas, joint sales agencies, price fixing, uniform conditions of sale, lists of approved traders and efforts to exclude new enterprises.'[27] More recently the activities of the EEC Commission have provided definite evidence of a cartel in the cement industry involving fifty-three enterprises in Belgium, Western Germany, and the Netherlands. Apparently the parties to the agreement shared out the task of supplying the Dutch market with cement and cement clinker. They also agreed upon uniform prices and undertook not to erect plant in each other's country without obtaining the consent of the relevant parties to the agreement.[28]

There is a limited amount of evidence which suggests that market sharing has not been entirely absent in the steel industry. According to a report in 1958 (a period of recession in steel) an agreement was reached early in that year between steel producers in France, Belgium, and Luxembourg on the one hand and those in Western Germany on the other. Apparently at the request of the German steel group, producers in France, Belgium, and Luxembourg agreed to refrain from pressing their penetration of the South German market any further. In return the German steel group agreed to limit exports to third countries, accepting a quota for rounds and sections for the first quarter of 1958 which

---

[26] Decision of Arrondissements Rechtbank te Zutphen, Rol. nr 23/58, 11 July 1958 reported in *WuW*, Dec. 1958, pp. 779–82. There is also evidence of a market-sharing (and price) agreement between German and Dutch enterprises in a branch of the mining industry (BKA, *Jahresbericht 1960*, p. 61).

[27] Edwards, *Cartelization*, p. 30.

[28] EEC Official Spokesman, Doc. IP(66) 10, 24 Jan. 1966.

was one-third of the volume for the first quarter of 1957.[29] At that time rounds and sections constituted a large proportion of the exports of the Belgian and Luxembourg producers.

According to a report of the Commission Technique des Ententes in 1961 French producers of agricultural implements (scythes and sickles) were involved in a cartel with other Common Market producers by which the French producers were assigned a virtual monopoly of the French market, provided they abstained from exporting to the states of other cartel members. According to the Commission, customs data indicated that France did not import such implements apart from certain special models.[30]

As we have already seen, it is possible that enterprises may share up the market not by formal agreement but by a mutual reluctance to penetrate each other's territory. The production and sale of fertilizers appears to furnish a possible example of this. A report to the EEC Commission Directorate General for Agriculture by Professor Willi Albers in 1963[31] refers to the fact that, up to that point of time, there had only been an insignificant amount of inter-trading in fertilizers within the Six, while on the other hand EEC producers had largish export trades to third countries. This fact is quite intriguing when it is also realized that exports to third countries were being sold at very low prices, while prices within the Six were well above the world market level. Albers has argued that this phenomenon could be explained on the basis of oligopoly theory—that is, that each participant knows that an incursion into the territory of another would lead to damaging counter-measures. As a result a tacit arrangement develops in which each national group tends to confine its activity to its own national territory or third-country markets. Albers observes:

If importing dealers, in response to an enquiry they make to producers in another state about the possibility of importing supplies, receive the answer from the industry of this state that the entire production of the current fertilizer year has been sold out, and yet these same suppliers

---

[29] Lister, p. 244, see also *Financial Times*, 5 Feb. & 26 Mar. 1958.
[30] Commission Technique des Ententes, *Rapport. . .1960, 1961 et 1962*, p. 19.
[31] W. Albers, *Marktlage, Preise, und Preispolitik für Düngemittel in den EWG Ländern und ihre Bedeutung für die Produktionskosten der Landwirtschaft*, Doc. no. 7242/6/61–D, 1963.

are simultaneously exerting themselves to find outlets in third countries (developing countries), at very much more unfavourable prices for that part of their product that is in excess of domestic requirements, then this example illustrates strikingly just how strongly the industries respect the uncontested sales area of their competitors.[32]

Subsequent to Albers's main report, conditions changed in a way which he claims confirms his thesis that no cartel exists and that the trading pattern can be explained by reference to oligopoly theory. The change was that Belgian nitrogenous fertilizer producers made a sortie into the West German market. German wholesalers showed some interest in Belgian supplies because they were offered at a lower price than those of domestic producers. As a result nitrogenous fertilizer producers in the Ruhr struck back by founding a selling organization in Belgium (RUSTIBEL) independent of Belgian wholesalers. At the time of the Albers report a major clash had not developed, the relationship having stabilized itself—each country importing about 5 per cent of its domestic requirements from the other.

In Albers's view the existence of such a clash seems to indicate the lack of any rigid cartel arrangement. The two groups had in fact not allowed the competition to develop to serious proportions but had stabilized the interpenetration of markets at a relatively low level.

Albers's argument has much to commend it, although it must be pointed out that the process of deducing market structure from market behaviour is fraught with difficulties. Both a rigid cartel arrangement and a tacit respecting of territory could yield much the same behaviour in the market, although the emergence of competition in nitrates gives support to the Albers view. However, his arguments are not absolutely conclusive. Even the most rigid cartels do sometimes break down temporarily. Moreover, it is not beyond the bounds of possibility that the imminent cartel proceedings in Brussels could have led a cartel to decide that a modicum of competition would improve appearances considerably—although Albers's seems on balance the most reasonable explanation.

Some commentators have argued that parts of the fertilizer industry are indeed cartelized. Edwards, for example, states that,

[32] Ibid. p. 37.

according to a significant buyer of phosphates, European phosphate producers allocate markets, fix prices, suppress the cheapest sources of supply, and, with the help of their governments, keep out the cheaper American superphosphate. Although no evidence of price fixing is apparently available, 'Before the annual meeting of the associated producers . . . buyers cannot obtain quotations, whereas immediately after the meeting all producers quote a uniform price which prevails until the next meeting.'[33]

Edwards does not provide evidence that in the case of nitrates and potash there is any formal agreement to divide up the market but, as we shall see in the discussion of export cartels and suppression of sources of supply, some close and powerful links appear to exist between the producers of these products.

This discussion of the division of markets provides a convenient opportunity to refer briefly to exclusive dealership and the practice of export prohibition. In foreign trade it is quite common for a manufacturer, in order to promote the sale of his goods in a particular territory (the boundaries of which often coincide with those of a state), to grant a dealer the exclusive right to sell a particular good in that area. In addition, in order to protect such a dealer (and thus induce him to deal) a manufacturer may prohibit dealers in other countries from competitively exporting the product into the former dealers' territory. The effect of such an export ban is to eliminate all competition in the resale of the good by the dealers. Also a compartmentalization of the market ensues in which different dealer margins, and therefore ultimately different prices to the consumers, can persist. The possibility also exists that under this system the manufacturer can effectively discriminate in regard to prices as between dealers in different states.

5. COLLECTIVE EXCLUSIVE DEALING

One of the most interesting examples of this type of arrangement is provided by what has been called the Pottery Convention or 'Convention Faïence'.[34] This was a collective exclusive-dealing arrangement between Belgian dealers in (and layers of) wall and floor tiles and tile manufacturers in Belgium, the

---

[33] Edwards, *Cartelization*, p. 29.
[34] *JO*, 13 May 1964 and *Bull. EEC*, no. 5, May 1964, annexe II.

Netherlands, and Western Germany. The convention was signed in Brussels in 1958 between the Belgian trade association (Fédération Nationale des Patrons Carreleurs et Mosaïstes de Belgique and Union Professionnelle des Négociants en Carreaux de Pavement et de Revêtements) and ten tile manufacturers. By 1963 the manufacturers had increased to twenty-nine, whilst the recognized dealers numbered about 900. The object of the convention was stated to be to improve the normal distribution of convention goods, the promotion of their sale and correct laying and, on a higher plane, 'to strengthen goodwill between the interested parties'.

The basic features of the convention were as follows. Manufacturers agreed to deliver the convention products to approved customers only, that is, dealers and layers party to the agreement. Approved customers in return agreed not to buy or process goods which did not originate from manufacturers party to the agreement. (Approved customers who were not members of the two trade associations had to pay a surcharge on top of the normal purchase price.)

The exclusive dealing was tightly controlled. Apparently, approved customers could only be released from their exclusive-dealing obligation by the cartel and then only for goods that differed unmistakably from the products of those manufacturers party to the agreement. Manufacturers, too, could only be exempted from exclusive dealing by the cartel. Manufacturers who defaulted could be fined, and approved customers who did not fulfil their obligations could be temporarily or permanently removed from the approved list. New trade associations could only join the cartel with the unanimous consent of existing members, while new manufacturers could only join by unanimous consent of all manufacturers party to the agreement.

The second example concerns the supply of sand and gravel. The arrangement, which was dealt with by the EEC Commission in 1964, involved a number of enterprises in the building-materials industries in Belgium, the Netherlands, and Western Germany. Essentially it was an agreement providing for exclusivity in the sale and purchasing of sand and gravel. A number of producers had formed a group which had undertaken to deliver these two products exclusively to groups of dealers in Belgium and the Netherlands. The dealers had for their part agreed to obtain their supplies exclusively from these manufacturers. The agreement was supplemented by a territorial division of markets among dealers. Also the agreement stipulated that dealers' vehicles be used for transporting the materials and that appropriate prices be charged for the products. Suppliers outside the agreement could obtain permission to sell to dealer-members, but only on the basis of paying a specified charge per unit sold to supplier-members.[35]

The third example concerns the sale of water heaters in Belgium-Luxembourg. Under this arrangement manufacturers and importers of water heaters and dealers agreed to conduct business with each other exclusively. Manufacturers were barred from selling to outsiders in the BLEU and were required to prohibit the re-import of their products into Belgium or Luxembourg. Dealers were not allowed to procure supplies from outside manufacturers and importers or to export the goods concerned from Belgium (and presumably Luxembourg). This agreement was therefore different from the other two in that it contained a prohibition on re-import and export—a feature also to be found in the sole dealership arrangements discussed above. The agreement provided that prices of water heaters should be fixed by mutual agreement and the manufacturers agreed to maintain these prices, if necessary inflicting sanctions which could involve withholding supplies from recalcitrant dealers. Finally, the agreement not only limited the number of manufacturers and importers who could take part but also specified that three-fifths of them should possess Belgian nationality and have their main establishment in Belgium.[36]

It is probably worth noting that, in 1956, 850 cartels of national scope had been registered in the Netherlands and that they involved more than 100 collective exclusive-dealing arrangements. It is impossible to tell, without further details of actual contents, what proportion of the latter would restrict the flow of trade between the Netherlands and the rest of the EEC. Some of these, such as the Vacuum Cleaner and Gramophone Record Cartels, did include importers as well as Dutch manufacturers, so that the Dutch market could not be said to be completely sealed off. On the other hand, both these cartels only

[35] EEC Official Spokesman, Doc. IP (65) 65, 1 Apr. 1965.
[36] EEC Official Spokesman, Doc. IP (65) 136, 9 July 1965.

provided for the admittance of importers who had sole distribution rights. This condition clearly conflicts with the spirit of the Decision of the EEC Commission in the Grundig-Consten case (see below, pp. 170–8), which seeks to allow parallel imports by dealers who do not have such sole rights. These two cartels did in fact prevent retail traders, such as department stores, from obtaining supplies directly from manufacturers outside the Netherlands. The Dutch cartel authority however required this condition to be deleted.[37]

6. AGREEMENTS TO RESTRICT INVESTMENT

Rhine shipping provides an example of this kind of arrangement. It has been estimated that 85 per cent of all Rhine traffic is controlled by pools which are organized for different products. For example, one of the largest, the Kettwiger Pool, which is made up of German, French, Dutch, Belgian, and Swiss shipowners, controls the international transport of coal to Germany. Shipowners in five countries are also members of the Rheinschiffahrts-Konvention Getreide—a pool which controls all grain traffic on the Rhine. A commentator has recently stated that 'the establishment of international pools in Rhine shipping has led to uniform prices and concerted action, on an international plane, even though the industry is composed of such small units'.[38] He goes on to state that in 1958 a large proportion of the Rhine shipowners grouped together in pools agreed not to invest in any new vessels, with the exception of tankers, for one year.

7. SUPPRESSING AND WITHHOLDING SOURCES OF SUPPLY

The fertilizer industry is a particularly interesting example of this type of practice. According to Edwards,[39] the cheapest sources of phosphates in Europe and North Africa would, under

[37] P. Verloren van Themaat, 'Cartel Policy in the Netherlands', *Proceedings, International Conference on Control of Restrictive Business Practices* (Univ. of Chicago, 1960), p. 23; OECD, *Guide to Legislation on Restrictive Business Practices* vol. iv (1964), section 30, p. 5; Information made available by the Netherlands Ministry of Economic Affairs.

[38] B. T. Bayliss, *European Transport* (1965), p. 131.

[39] Edwards, *Cartelization*, p. 29.

normal circumstances, be a plant in Tunisia and one in Belgium. But apparently the Tunisian plant has been prevented from becoming a significant source of exports by its owners (who are the most important British and Dutch phosphate producers) and by the French government. The Belgian plant was acquired after the last war by producers of potash who, being also phosphate producers, have prevented the firm from competing with them.

8. REBATE ARRANGEMENTS

It is clear that agreements between potential competitors about the rebates they will offer on the sale of goods entering into interstate trade (Terrazzo was an example) can be such as to frustrate the beneficial effects of reducing tariff barriers. There are other forms of rebate arrangements which can be equally objectionable. For example, in 1961 the BKA issued a decision in connexion with a phosphate selling syndicate.[40] The syndicate operated an aggregated rebate system in which rebates were granted to consumers on the basis of the annual amount which they purchased from all its member firms. In principle it seems reasonable for a firm to accord a higher level of rebate to a particular customer if he purchases a large quantity per period of time, provided that the increased level of purchase leads to greater economies in production and provided the size of the rebate reflects that greater resulting efficiency. In practice it seems probable that the aggregated rebate system of the syndicate did not fulfil these ends. More to the point, however, such a system could be said to place outside manufacturers, and this includes enterprises in other member states, at a competitive disadvantage. For example, suppose the rebate system was graduated so that if a purchaser took 100 tons per annum from the syndicate, he would receive a 5 per cent aggregate rebate at the end of the year. Suppose that for annual purchases of 200, 300, and 400 tons he would receive 6, 7, and 8 per cent rebates respectively. Let us consider the case of a customer who has already taken 300 tons from the syndicate and is considering whether to take a further 100 tons from the syndicate or from a firm in another member state. The syndicate will only offer a rebate of 8 per cent but the outsider will have to reduce his price

[40] BKA, *Jahresbericht 1961*, p. 32.

by more than 8 per cent. That is to say the outsider, in order to secure the sale, would have to match the 8 per cent offered by the syndicate but would also have to compensate the customer for the 1 per cent he would forego on each 100 tons already bought from the syndicate. A rebate of 11 per cent would, however, only put the outsider on a par with the syndicate and a slight further cut would be necessary to tilt the balance in his favour. In other words the outside firm will be discriminated against in that it will have to accept a lower price than firms in the syndicate for the last 100 tons in our example. From an economic standpoint the outside firm might be more efficient but unless it was able to make the 11 per cent plus reduction it would lose the order to the less efficient syndicate members.

A similar practice by three German manufacturers of window and plate glass was objected to by the BKA on the grounds of the requirements of Article 85 and of those of the relevant section of the German Cartel Law. In this case the manufacturers, apart from charging identical prices and changing them simultaneously, also granted all wholesalers and processors turnover premia depending upon the volume of purchases which they made from flat glass manufacturers in Western Germany.[41]

Such aggregate rebate arrangements appear to be by no means uncommon in the EEC—a similar system was operated by a large number of German wallpaper manufacturers who had combined to form a 'union of interest'. This was objected to by the BKA on the basis of the German Cartel Law but not of Rome Treaty Article 85.[42] The BKA has also invalidated a similar rebate arrangement among five linoleum and synthetic-floor-cloth manufacturers.[43] Similar practices have come to light in the French nylon and linoleum industries in the course of investigations by the Commission Technique des Ententes.

9. SPECIALIZATION AND RATIONALIZATION AGREEMENTS

There are a number of examples of agreements between otherwise independent enterprises providing either for specialization or the more rational use of production capacity. In every case they relate to ECSC products.

[41] 'Re Fensterglas III', *Common Market Law Reports*, ii, pt. 8, 1963, p. 337; and BKA, *Jahresbericht 1960*, p. 92.

[42] OECD, *Guide to Legislation* (1964), ii. 5–6.   [43] Ibid.

The earliest example is an agreement, approved by the High Authority in 1954, between two iron and steel enterprises, the Compagnie des Forges d'Audincourt and the Société Lorraine-Escaut. Originally Audincourt had itself been making the special steel required to produce certain types of plate and sheet. However, because of the small tonnages which it produced, the process was relatively inefficient. Lorraine-Escaut was in a position to produce this steel more efficiently along with its other steel. An agreement was therefore entered into whereby Lorraine-Escaut alone would make the special steels and would guarantee delivery to Audincourt.[44] This is an example of a pure specialization agreement.

In some cases specialization has been combined with joint selling. For example, in 1961 the High Authority approved an agreement between two German iron and steel enterprises, Hüttenwerk Salzgitter-Drütte and Ilseder Hütte, Peine. Ilseder agreed to cease making certain flat products and tubes and Salzgitter undertook not to make certain sections and pilings. By concentrating on a narrower range, output of specific products in each plant would be increased, costs reduced, and prompter service rendered to customers. The agreement also provided for the joint selling of merchant bars—mainly through Ilseder's sales organization—and rules were laid down for the marketing of other products.[45]

As an example of a rationalization agreement, we may cite as an important development in this field the arrangement authorized by the High Authority in 1965 between Dortmund-Hörder-Hüttenunion, Hoesch AG, Hüttenwerk Oberhausen, and Mannesmann AG for the more efficient use of rolling capacity for rod, bars, and sections.[46] Under the agreement, which establishes the Stabund Formstahl-Kontor of Essen, they will continue to book orders separately but will distribute the orders among the mills in a manner calculated to produce the most economic production runs.[47]

---

[44] *JO*, no. 15, 1964.

[45] ECSC, *10th Gen. Rep.* (1962), p. 210.

[46] They collectively account for about 9 per cent of the Community's bar and rod capacity and 11 per cent of its section capacity.

[47] ECSC High Authority, *Rapid Information*, no. 49/65, 22 July 1965. See also OECD, *Ann. Rep. on Developments in the Field of Restrictive Business Practices* (1966), pp. 37–39.

10. IMPORT CARTELS

Agreements exist relating to imports from third countries but the only example that we can cite here concerns steel. In December 1962, at a time when the ECSC domestic market was passing through a period of severe price competition, particularly as a result of the appearance on the Community market of significant quantities of low-priced imported steel, an agreement was concluded between representatives of the ECSC steel industry and UK steel producers with a view to halting the downward movement of prices. Apparently, according to the British Iron and Steel Federation, the agreement, a reciprocal one, consisted of a 'ban on competition based on dumping, i.e. on offers at prices below both the home trade price of the exporter and the local price in the receiving area.'[48]

The agreement was not particularly successful, for the simple reason that although UK producers stood by the agreement, merchants selling British steel failed to play their part and undercut Community producers. (It is also interesting to note that the British government refused to give its assent to a formal antidumping agreement with the Six.) The producers of the Six also attempted to secure Japanese approval for a similar arrangement. Reports about the success of the approach are conflicting. One report suggests that the Japanese gave their assent. A meeting between ECSC and Japanese producers did indeed take place, but all the evidence suggests that the Japanese did not in fact enter into any such understanding.

11. EXPORT CARTELS

Broadly speaking export cartels do not fall foul of the antitrust rules of the Paris and Rome Treaties. Both sets of rules deal only with agreements which restrict competition within the Common Market.[49] For example, a price agreement between EEC producers when exporting to third countries would not be rele-

---

[48] British Iron and Steel Federation, *Steel R.*, no. 31, July 1963, p. 5.
[49] The inter-state trade effect is also necessary in the case of the Rome Treaty.

vant unless it could be proved to have some indirect restrictive effect in the Common Market itself.[50] The existence of agreements between producers in the various member states about exports to third countries does, however, provide suggestive, *though by no means conclusive,* evidence of the existence of agreements relating directly to trade within the Common Market itself. The fact that arrangements exist to enable producers to come together in organized discussion about their approach to third-country markets provides an excellent forum for discussions about the Community market. We have already seen an example of an agreement in the steel industry in which a freer hand in the South German market for one group was exchanged for a freer hand in third-country markets for another. For this reason we are including a selection of export cartel practices, although it must be added that no attempt has been made to collect together all the published examples.

Both of the main ECSC products have been subject to export cartels. The export of steel to third countries has been organized by means of the Entente à l'Exportation des Producteurs de l'Acier, or what is better known as the Brussels Entente. This was formed in 1953 and consisted of representatives of the main steel-producing groups in the ECSC. The basic function of the Entente was to operate a minimum-price system based upon a uniform basing point at Antwerp (the price at Antwerp also applied to exports routed through Dunkirk and Caen). The Entente was not always successful in controlling prices. For example, in the 1958 recession official minimum prices fell about 25 per cent in the twelve months to mid-1958, but apparently actual price cuts of up to 40–50 per cent had been operative. This inability to impose a rigid control of prices was due partly to reported undercutting by French producers and partly to the fact that some major exporters, such as the United Kingdom, were outside the scheme and were free to sell down in the depressed world market. On occasions the Entente has also operated export quotas.[51]

[50] Agreements between Community firms and firms in third countries which lead to an international allocation of export markets could however have a direct effect on competition in the Common Market and could fall foul of the Community anti-trust rules—see H. von der Groeben, 'Competition Policy in the Common Market', *Community Topics,* no. 19, 1965, p. 14.

[51] This account is based upon Lister, pp. 200–1 and 213–14.

5

In the case of coal the major example of a coal exporting cartel is provided by the Ruhr mining companies who have been permitted by the High Authority to maintain a common sales agency, the Ruhrkohlen-Exportgesellschaft, for exports to third countries.[52]

An arrangement exists between producers of steel tubes (an EEC product) in Western Europe in respect of exports to third countries. The European tube cartel was revived in 1956, apparently in the first instance for five years. One of the members of this agreement was Stewarts and Lloyds, and the fact that this company has (1966) discussions with European producers on exports suggests that some similar arrangement still continues. Under the 1956 agreement between the Longwy-Raty group in France and the Saar, Tubes de la Meuse in Belgium, Phoenix-Rheinrohr and Mannesmann in Western Germany, and Stewarts and Lloyds, quotas were allocated for the export of merchant tube (gas, water, and steam)—oilpipe being excluded. The German producers received 42 per cent of the export quota, the United Kingdom 33 per cent, and France, Belgium, and the Saar 25 per cent between them.[53]

Potash is another EEC product in which an export cartel appears to be operating. According to Edwards, an agreement in the Danish Register between German and French producers provides for maintenance of resale prices and includes the requirement that buyers may not deal in the product of other suppliers and may not re-export.[54]

Organizations which are presumably the same as those involved in the above agreement also control the sale of potash in the UK through the medium of Potash Ltd.[55] Potash Ltd has the sole selling rights in the UK for French, West German, and Spanish potash. As far as can be judged this organization is controlled by the Verkaufsgemeinschaft Deutscher Kaliwerke GmbH, the selling syndicate for potash mined in Western Germany, and Société Commerciale des Potasses d'Alsace, an organization which by

[52] *JO*, 13 Mar. 1956, p. 31.
[53] Lister, p. 199.
[54] Edwards, *Cartelization*, p. 30.
[55] European potash production has been cartelized for a considerable period of time. In 1926 a Franco-German cartel agreement was concluded, one of the main provisions being the reservation of home markets.

law holds the exclusive selling rights of potash mined in France.[56] The latter is referred to in our discussion of state monopolies.

The existence of a powerful and coordinated group of potash producers in Western Europe, and in the Six particularly, is partly indicated by the above evidence, but Edwards has also provided further relevant information. According to him, systematic efforts have been made to exclude independent supplies from the European market and to draw new suppliers into the sales organization. The activities of this cartel are such that they deserve a lengthy quotation. According to Edwards, these systematic efforts are evidenced

in the fact that a Belgian customer of a United States company informed its supplier that it must stop buying from the United States or forfeit discounts of $4\frac{1}{2}$ per cent plus $1.00 per ton. They are also evident in the relation of the Irish Sugar Company to the potash industry. Major incidents were as follows: (1) Immediately after the war Ireland received from an American agency in Paris an emergency allocation of 10,000 tons of Spanish potash, but Irish importers refused to buy it because the Spanish producers were not in the cartel. Because of this refusal the Irish Sugar Company entered the potash business and bought directly. In 1947 the Spanish producers told it that sales would be made thereafter through the London office of the cartel, Potash Ltd. Through diplomatic intervention it continued to obtain Spanish potash direct for a year but thereafter was again referred to the cartel. (2) When the company found an alternative source in East Germany, the cartel bought 250,000 tons of East German potash under an agreement that provided that East German producers would not export to other Western buyers. The agreement was subsequently evaded by barter deals. The cartel retaliated by trying to organise a boycott of Communist potash and induced certain dock unions to refuse to unload the product, but because of Communist sympathisers in the French and Italian labour movements, this effort was unsuccessful. The East German supply, however, varies unpredictably. (3) When Israel began to produce potash, the Irish Sugar Company bought direct from Israel. In 1959 the Israeli producers informed it that their sales to it were making their sales difficult elsewhere and that they would sell through the cartel. They are now doing so. (4) After Spanish private producers joined the cartel, the Spanish Government began to develop its own plant and

[56] The Monopolies Commission, *Report on the Supply of Chemical Fertilizers* (1959), pp. 73–77. The Commission is extremely obscure about the nature of the ownership and control of Potash Ltd, and the above statement must be regarded largely as a reasonable inference.

expressed interest in direct sale to the Irish company. In 1962 negotiations for direct sale were still in progress. However, in April 1963, when the Spanish Government plant had begun production, it informed the Irish company that 'a certain amount of potash' was available for export to Ireland and suggested that the cartel's London sales office be contacted for further negotiations. (5) An important Canadian source of potash has just been developed. Though Americans were originally involved in the development, they finally obtained no participation, and 50 per cent of the ownership was acquired by subsidiaries of two members of the cartel.[57]

Fertilizers also provide a further example of an export cartel, in this case dealing in nitrogenous fertilizers. This cartel, referred to as Nitrex, was founded in 1962 and originally included firms in Germany, Belgium, France, Italy, and the Netherlands as well as Norway, Switzerland, and Austria. Nominally a uniform price and discount is quoted.[58]

The final example relates to civil engineering and is provided by the Dutch Engineers' and Contractors' Association (DECA). This is made up of a group of four Dutch civil engineering contractors who act both on their own behalf and also on behalf of their associated companies registered in Western Germany, Belgium, and Italy. The Association maintains that it only deals with tenders for contracts outside the Six. Apparently a central office has been established and any contract of more than 1 million florins of which any member has knowledge has to be notified to it, so that the information can be passed on to all members in order that they should be able to co-operate in examining the details of the contract and preparing a possible tender. When a member intends to tender for a contract exceeding 2 million florins, it must declare its intention to the central office. This is then followed by a meeting of all who have made such a declaration. 'At the meeting the members have the possibility of deciding which firms are to tender and to carry out the work, and how the latter is to be distributed; a pool is formed.'[59]

---

[57] Edwards, *Cartelization*, pp. 29–30.
[58] According to Edwards, the cartel had not at the time of his investigation succeeded in stabilizing the price level. He notes that discounts were subject to negotiation and could be as much as 20 per cent.
[59] *JO*, 31 Oct. 1964.

12. LICENSING AGREEMENTS

The contents of licensing agreements, connected for example with patents, can conflict with the requirements of the treaties in so far as they provide, *inter alia*, for an undue amount of restraint of competitive activity on the part of the licensee. The BKA has ruled on one such licence agreement. The case concerned an exclusive licence granted under a patent for the production and sale of certain speed-cutter machines. The French licenser required the German licensee to promise among other things not to produce or sell competing items until three years after the termination of the agreement; to grant back to the licenser any improvement inventions—reserving to the licensee only the right to use the improvements.[60] This case is dealt with at greater length below (p. 159) in connexion with the Decisions of national cartel authorities, and a further example of the restrictive effects of a patent-licensing agreement is discussed in the section dealing with the Decisions of the EEC Commission (pp. 188–9).

One thing seems clear from the above account and it is this. It would be a great mistake to assume that international cartels are characteristic only of a depressed international economy such as existed in the inter-war years. Although we have not been able to draw upon the cartel notifications to the EEC Commission,[61] it seems reasonably clear from the evidence that we have been able to draw together that international cartels are a continuing feature of the international economy, at least in Western Europe. And it should be added that this is so despite the existence of full employment and rapid economic growth. With the reduction of trade barriers, cartel agreements at the national

---

[60] *WuW*, no. 9, 1959, p. 305, discussing BKA Decision re Geschwindeschneidemaschinen. See also Buxbaum, *Columbia Law R.*, lx (1961), p. 413.

[61] Not only this, but even information made available at the national level has sometimes been too scanty to be used in our account. For example, the French Technical Commission has indicated the existence of international cartels on metal barrels and agricultural equipment but without specifying their nature. It is perhaps also worth recalling that in certain industries, such as steel and automobiles, calls have on occasion been made by Community producers for some kind of international cartel arrangement. There is good reason to believe that these calls might have achieved results if there had been no international organization to keep a watching brief.

level lose some of their relevance and restrictive business arrangements have to be extended beyond national frontiers. For example, several of the international restrictive agreements exposed by the Commission Technique des Ententes, to which we have referred above, were either a direct response to the increased competition caused by trade liberalization under the Rome Treaty or were created in anticipation thereof.

There can be little doubt that those who have emphasized the importance of a vigorous anti-trust policy in making trade liberalization effective have not been guilty of exaggeration. It seems to us that there is much to be said for the proposition that trade liberalization without effective anti-trust action is, to a considerable degree, a meaningless exercise. This proposition has of course great relevance to other tariff-cutting ventures such as EFTA, the Kennedy Round, and the oft-discussed bridge between EFTA and the EEC.

7

Cartel Policy: Principles and Practice

I. THE EUROPEAN COAL AND STEEL COMMUNITY

THE Paris Treaty seeks to create competition not only within national coal-mining and steel-producing industries, but also between the national groups; and it seeks to achieve the latter by the removal of protective barriers such as customs duties. As the beneficial effects of dismantling such protection can be frustrated by cartel practices, a cartel policy is therefore necessary, and to this we now turn. The discussion of cases will be confined to the coal industry. Most of the cases concerning iron and steel have already been referred to in our discussion of types of cartel agreements—for example, specialization, joint sale, and rationalization arrangements. We have also referred to the proposed cartel arrangement between iron and steel dealers in 1961, which was terminated after warnings by the High Authority. In the scrap market the High Authority has had both to condemn formally and to warn. As an example of the former we can cite the Westdeutsche Schrotteinkaufsgesellschaft—an arrangement into which virtually all iron and steel enterprises had entered to buy scrap jointly. The High Authority refused to authorize the arrangement, because it gave the enterprises the power to determine prices of a substantial part of the scrap sold in the Community.[1] In 1960 the High Authority had to warn enterprises buying scrap of the practices forbidden by the treaty.[2] We have already drawn attention to the fact that at the national level there is evidence of concerted practices in respect of steel (and for that matter scrap) prices. The High Authority has been impeded in dealing with such cases by the difficulty of collecting evidence—it has, however, as we shall show below in discussing steel pricing, used its power to fine on at least one occasion. It is of course

---

[1] *JO*, 26 July 1955.
[2] ECSC, *9th Gen. Rep.* (1961), pp. 171–2.

clear that the activities of governments in connexion with steel prices have not helped the High Authority in its task of maintaining competition.

(a) The Anti-trust Rules

Article 65 of the Paris Treaty declares that all agreements among enterprises, all decisions of associations of enterprises, and all concerted practices tending either directly or indirectly to prevent, restrict, or distort the normal operation of competition within the Common Market are forbidden. This applies to the production of all coal and steel products listed in Annexe 1 of the treaty but, unlike the rest of the treaty, Articles 65 (and 66) also apply to enterprises engaged in distribution and sale—although it must be observed that the Article 60 prohibition on discrimination may, by virtue of Article 63 (a), be extended to first-hand dealers. The treaty singles out for particular mention those practices which tend to fix or determine prices; to restrict or control production, technical development or investment; to allocate markets, products, customers, or sources of supply. Prohibited agreements are void—that is to say, if a party to such an agreement were to depart from it, the other parties to it could not enforce it by resort to the courts.

However, as an exception to this general prohibition, the High Authority is required to authorize agreements which involve specialization in production or joint buying or selling, if it finds, and the three conditions are cumulative, (a) that such arrangements will substantially improve production or distribution; (b) that the practice is no more restrictive than is necessary to achieve this end; (c) that it does not give the participants the power to determine prices, or to control production or sale of a substantial part of the production in question in the Common Market.

As we shall see when we come to discuss the EEC cartel rules, there is a fairly close parallel between the rules of the Paris and Rome Treaties. Nevertheless there are some differences—the main ones being as follows. First, the EEC rules apply only to cartels affecting inter-state trade. Secondly, the emphasis in respect of authorization is different—the High Authority is *required* to authorize, but the ECC Commission *may* exempt, if the necessary conditions are fulfilled. Thirdly, exemption in the case of the EEC rules also requires that a fair share of the profit derived from the authorized agreement should accrue to consumers—the ECSC rules involve no such explicit requirement. Authorizations can be subjected to conditions and limited in duration. Renewal of authorizations is not automatic; it depends upon whether, for example, there has been a change in circumstances since the agreement was previously authorized.

In order to facilitate the making of decisions, the High Authority has been granted power to obtain all necessary information. It alone has the power to rule upon restrictive practices—subject, however, to the right of parties to agreements to appeal to the Court of Justice. In order to dissuade enterprises from operating void agreements or obtaining authorizations by supplying false information, the High Authority is empowered to impose fines and daily penalty payments.

(i) *The Joint Selling of Coal.* Before the Paris Treaty was signed it was realized that one of the big tests of the High Authority would lie in the field of cartels, of which the Ruhr joint selling agency GEORG was to be the most important. (It should perhaps be mentioned in connexion with GEORG that the trust-busters of the European integration movement could hardly have found a more difficult case to cut their teeth on—this was an industry in which cartelization was a tradition which received widespread support from trade unionists as well as employers. Any criticism of the High Authority should be seen against this background. It must be admitted that the task of creating competition is extremely difficult when the parties in question are entirely unconvinced of its merits. Had there been some independent spirits who could have been encouraged and assisted, the solution might have been easier. As it turned out, these were sadly lacking.) The Allies had established six selling agencies with a coordinating body, GEORG, but by the time the High Authority came to call for notification of cartels it was effectively GEORG, rather than the six supposedly independent agencies, which was selling Ruhr coal.

Although it did not actually control prices, since maxima were fixed by the German government and then by the High Authority, the power to do so was clearly there. Had the High Authority freed prices, GEORG could have raised them by restricting output. The High Authority could not therefore sit

5*

back and do nothing. Even a cursory glance at the treaty indicated that, as it stood, GEORG, which controlled 50 per cent of ECSC coal production and was responsible for 93 per cent of West German coal, was illegal. In case the High Authority did not act, the Dutch Government threatened to appeal to the European Court. However it is doubtful whether this was necessary since, however unpleasant and unpopular the fostering of competition may have been, it must have been apparent to the High Authority that it would hardly have had the moral authority to deal with the other joint selling agencies or the practices of nationalized or state-sponsored bodies if it had not first dealt with GEORG. Furthermore, a general failure to deal with cartels was bound to bring the European movement into disrepute in some circles, leaving it open to the criticism that it was conniving in the creation of a Europe of monopolies.

In 1953 the High Authority issued a Decision which in effect invited notification of all existing agreements, since it declared that the prohibition of Article 65 would take effect from 31 August of that year unless agreements were notified by that date. Among those who notified were the Ruhr mining companies.

The High Authority officials let it be known there were two ways to approach the problem posed by GEORG. One was flatly to prohibit it and leave it at that. Alternatively the High Authority could take a more positive role and sketch out the kind of framework within which the mining companies could organize sales without infringing the treaty. The High Authority opted for the second course—realistically it could hardly have done otherwise.

By 1956 the High Authority issued its Decisions[3] about the kind of sales organization which would be required if price ceilings were to be taken off. There were to be three joint selling agencies—they became known as Geitling, Präsident, and Mausegatt—not six, as had been decided by the Allies. On the face of it this was a climb down although it was defended by Franz Etzel, Vice-President of the High Authority, on the grounds that by reducing the number of agencies, and therefore increasing the size of each, they would be more independent. This point arose out of the fact that, in addition to the three sales agencies, there was to be a joint office which was to deal with those who wished to buy more than 50,000 metric tons per

[3] *JO*, 13 Mar. 1956.

annum. Each sales organization would balance orders among the constituent mining companies and the joint office would balance the large orders among the three agencies—one reason for balancing being to even out any unemployment. Etzel argued that:

With a larger number of less important sales organizations, the task and influence of the proposed coordinating body would be greater than with a smaller number of larger units. . . . These three autonomous sales organizations can by themselves, each in its own domain, largely regulate the balance of employment and the division of orders among types of coal necessary in a situation of excess, as well as equalizing supplies in a situation of shortage. In other words, three more important autonomous sales organizations could each develop for itself greater independence and more autonomy than six smaller sales organizations.[4]

Each agency represented a group of 14–19 coal-mining enterprises and produced about 15 million metric tons of coal and 5–6 million metric tons of coke per annum. An important ingredient of the arrangement was that the agencies were to be separate. Mining companies were to be members of only one agency and directors of one agency could not be directors of another.

The joint office, to which we have just referred, was administered by one representative from each agency. Apart from allocating orders between agencies, which were to be fulfilled on their terms and conditions, the joint office was the agency for operating compensatory assistance to high-cost mines in times of recession.

One thing is clear from this arrangement: no one, not even the High Authority, believed in establishing a system of free competition. Competition, if it was to exist, was to be a far cry from the atomistic variety of the textbooks and it was to be managed and hedged around with safeguards. In its Decision of 1956 the High Authority referred to the fact that free competition was not appropriate—in times of shortage it would lead to inequalities in supply to customers, in times of recession unemployment would be uneven in its incidence and this would lead to social tensions.

It seems to us that, from the point of view of objective economic analysis, the solution adopted by the High Authority was unsatisfactory and indeed it seems to find few supporters today. First, the High Authority, in authorizing a joint selling agency,

[4] *Common Assembly Debates*, 23 Nov. 1955, pp. 26–27, quoted by Diebold, p. 386.

had to be satisfied that a number of conditions were fulfilled. One was that it would lead to a substantial improvement in production or distribution and that the arrangement was no more restrictive than would be necessary to achieve these ends. The High Authority considered that 'joint sale permits a better distribution of fuel . . . having regard to the number of categories and grades of coal'.[5] It is true that a mining company might produce small quantities of several grades of coal, while orders might be big. But was it necessary for common selling to exist to overcome these difficulties? Surely merchants were capable of using a telephone to collect together a quantity of any particular grade, sufficient to meet a large order? Secondly, the High Authority justified the joint selling arrangement, together with the establishment of the joint office, on the grounds that it was necessary to provide for an evening-out of unemployment and an equitable allocation in times of scarcity. Did this constitute an improvement in production and distribution as referred to in Article 65? The High Authority evidently thought so, although others might consider that the article was referring to such things as reductions in the cost of production and distribution rather than questions of unemployment policy and rationing.

Be that as it may, it would probably have been more desirable if a more competitive structure had been introduced and the High Authority had at the same time undertaken to be ready and willing to use its powers to fix prices and allocate supplies and orders in times of over- or under-production. If the High Authority had undertaken this task there would have been less reason for establishing a cartel. There are, however, three other points which need to be made in relation to the problem of coping with unemployment and scarcity. The first is that at the time when the High Authority issued its Decision, there was a fuel scarcity which was expected to continue. This, at least in some degree, reduced the prospect of unemployment and social tensions. Secondly, it is questionable whether it is desirable to even out the utilization of productive capacity and unemployment. If less coal has to be produced, there is much to be said for producing it in the most efficient pits—this argument is all the stronger if the decline becomes permanent—which in fact it did later on. There is certainly much to be said against allowing the mining

[5] Ibid.

companies too much power in deciding how a contraction of output and employment should be dealt with. Thirdly, there was no guarantee that in times of scarcity the allocation of coal would be equitable.

The prospects for creating competition were bound to be slim. First, the High Authority was sanctioning the creation of an oligopoly—the possible implications of this for pricing are well known. Secondly, it is questionable whether there was much prospect of independence when the High Authority was agreeing to the creation of a joint office which would be run by representatives of the three agencies. This could be a permanent forum for the discussion of prices. Not only this, but the joint office, by virtue of its distribution of large orders, was in a position to bring those inclined to independent action, if any such existed, back into line. Thirdly, the arrangement failed to take account of proprietary relationships. Thus Lister has shown[6] that while no mining company was represented in more than one sales agency, proprietary groups were represented in two or even three of them. Sixty-six per cent of production in Geitling, 41 per cent in Präsident, and 85 per cent in Mausegatt had proprietary ties to firms in one of the other two agencies.

It is not surprising that by 1957 members of the Common Assembly were asking the High Authority about simultaneity in the price changes of the three agencies. Although the High Authority did not immediately concede the failure of the experiment, in 1959 when the 1956 authorizations were due to expire, it admitted that the agencies

concerning the sale of Ruhr coal have in their actual functioning frequently failed to comply with the authorizations granted; that the authorizations have not produced the result expected—in particular the three sales agencies have not developed an independent sales policy—and that, instead, a system of uniform sale which does not conform to the provisions of the Treaty has been established. . . .[7]

The High Authority decided to authorize the three agencies for one more year. In 1960 they again attempted to secure authorization but this time they proposed that Ruhr coal should be sold by one agency. It should at this point be noted that the mining companies were emboldened to make this request by virtue of the

[6] Lister, p. 261.   [7] *JO*, 7 Mar. 1959.

changed energy situation. Thus, as is shown in discussing energy policy in Chapter 10 (pp. 362–3) from 1957 to 1962 there was a general tendency for Ruhr coal prices to rise whilst on the other hand the price c.i.f. Rotterdam of imported crude oil fell quite markedly. As a result there has been a shift in energy consumption in the Community from coal to oil. Thus in 1955 75 per cent of Community internal primary-energy consumption (in terms of hard-coal equivalent) derived from coal and 16 per cent from oil. By 1964 the figures were approximately 43 and 40 per cent respectively. Despite the growth of absolute energy requirements, the falling percentage share of coal led to an absolute decline in Community coal production; and this affected the Ruhr, where production fell by 6 per cent between 1956 and 1964. The request for the authorization of one sales agency was turned down in February 1960. The sales agencies, on receipt of this news, telegraphed to the High Authority informing it that they were withdrawing their application and would submit another one. This they did in May 1960, but essentially their request was the same, namely that they wished to create a monopoly sales agency—the Ruhrkohlen-Verkaufsgesellschaft GmbH. The High Authority again refused authorization, pointing to the fact that the proposed agency's potential influence related to a substantial part of the products in question within the Common Market and thus the conditions for authorization laid down in Article 65 were not fulfilled.

The sales agencies therefore appealed to the Court of Justice, pending the judgment of which the three agencies were allowed to continue in existence. In 1962 the Court upheld the Decision of the High Authority.[8] It concurred with the Authority that such a single selling organization would have the power to fix prices at a level differing substantially from that which would be attained under conditions of competition. Such power could only be destroyed if external competition forced the proposed single selling organization to charge prices lower than those which would exist in its absence—a theoretical possibility which both the Court and the Authority denied. The Court went on to admit that both the coal and steel markets were oligopolistic and that a certain power to determine prices and a disposition on the part of

[8] Court of Justice of the European Communities, *Recueil de la Jurisprudence de la Cour*, viii (1962), pp. 165–222.

agencies to adapt their behaviour to that of their partners was inevitable. The task of the Community was to strive to limit this strategic margin and to safeguard the minimum of competition needed to achieve the objectives of the treaty. The Court then advanced the interesting notion that in considering the grant of authorization the criterion of a substantial part of the market should not be judged from the point of view of the percentage share of the market attained by the group in question, but by the relationship between that percentage and the percentage attained by other groups. An agreement could not be authorized if it had a disproportionate importance in the market. In short oligopoly is an established fact and policy must be directed to keeping a balance between oligopolists.

After this judgment, the High Authority decided, in 1963, in favour of two sales agencies—Geitling and Präsident. The companies in the previous three agencies were to be roughly equally divided between the two remaining ones and to be so regrouped: 'That legally separate companies in practice forming a combine will in future not be affiliated to different agencies but only to one.'[9] In short, action was at last being taken to deal with the problem of proprietary groups. Apparently the fact that two German state-owned mining companies were to be placed in separate agencies caused the High Authority some heart-searching since it appeared to consider it possible that the two would coordinate policy via the German government. The original arrangement was however allowed to remain. In addition various organizational links between the agencies were dissolved—the joint office for managing the common reserve stock, the standards committee which drew up common rules for the three agencies, the export company (to be replaced by two independent export companies), the joint financial arrangements carried out by the Ruhrkohlen-Treuhandgesellschaft were all abolished. Also interlocking directorates were prohibited as between the agencies and their regional offices and export companies, and as between these and the other joint organizations. All important decisions of the agencies' boards were to be reported to the High Authority— certain actions being prohibited without the latter's approval. Facilities were also provided to enable checks to be made upon

[9] ECSC, *12th Gen. Rep.* (1964), p. 177.

the agencies' compliance with the High Authority's requirements. The High Authority was determined to secure at least a
formal independence between the agencies.

The Dutch government appealed against the High Authority's
1963 reorganization. The appellant's case, summarized very
briefly, was based upon the proposition that the High Authority,
by imposing various obligations upon the two sales agencies,
such as the need to inform the Authority of certain decisions and
the need to seek approval before acting on them, indicated that it
was not convinced that the authorizations were in conformity
with Article 65 (2). The Dutch appeared to argue that a more
satisfactory structure would have emerged if three or four
agencies had been created. They pointed out that the similarity
in the structure of the two agencies excluded independent conduct, while oligopoly theory gave rise to doubts as to whether
two agencies would be likely to conduct their affairs independently. The Court rejected the appeal as unfounded on all the
main issues. It rejected the Dutch implication that the Authority
lacked conviction in its structural prescriptions, by pointing out
that the treaty granted the High Authority power to attach conditions to its authorizations. As for the degree of independence
likely to emerge from the reorganization, the Court's argument
has been summarized as follows:

The almost identical structure of the selling agencies places these two
bodies on an equal footing. In an oligopolistic market, comparable
economic power increases the equilibrium and independence of large
units. The coal market is such an oligopolistic market. Publication of
price scales and transport costs produces transparency of prices applied
by the various enterprises and, consequently, leads to considerable price
stability, even in truly competitive conditions. The immobility of prices
is not in itself undesirable, if it results from the play on the market of
the forces and strategies of independent economic units.[10]

There are two observations which need to be made about the
Court's judgments of 1962 and 1963. One is its assumption that
oligopoly or duopoly is a *fait accompli* in the coal industry. Is this
really correct? The equality of supplies argument for having
large selling units has disappeared now that coal is plentiful. Has
the evening out of unemployment argument much to commend

[10] OECD, *Ann. Rep. on Restrictive Business Practices* (Jan. 1965), pp. 54–55.

it? The post-war world has not witnessed the kind of fluctuations which would justify this kind of safeguard. The problem of the industry is rather one of slow decline in output, and, as Liesner points out,[11] what seems to be needed is an organization which will close down inefficient pits and concentrate output in the more efficient ones. There are signs that, as we indicate below in discussing energy policy, this may occur. On the question of productive and distributional efficiency, are the economies of scale such that the Ruhr can only support two agencies? Ruhr output in 1964 was higher than in 1952, yet we have witnessed a progressive whittling down in the number of agencies from six to three and now to two. The second observation concerns the notion of creating sales agencies of equal size. As we have indicated, the High Authority has abandoned any ideas about preventing bodies coming into existence which will have significant market power. Oligopoly is a *fait accompli*—the main aim now is to guarantee that the rivals are about equal in size, since this will be some guarantee of independence. Will they in fact be independent? Economic theory speaks with no absolute inevitability on this matter, although it would be reasonable to assume that, knowing the collusive background and in the light of the pricing rules which we discuss later, duopoly (in the Ruhr) is not likely to breed much independence.

We have already indicated that the coal industry has had to face a decline in demand in the face of competition from oil. This fact illustrates that a logical cartel policy should be conducted within the context of the energy market rather than just the coal market, and the Court of Justice has in fact said that the relevant market should be taken to be energy. The High Authority has been striving to reorient thinking on coal questions along these lines. Of course it is now quite obvious that coal cartels are no longer the problem that they were in the early days of the ECSC. Even the possibility of exploiting sales of coke to the iron and steel industry has failed in its objective since the latter has made successful efforts to utilize coke more efficiently.

We have devoted a considerable amount of space to GEORG because of the particular interest of that case. We will now briefly consider some of the other cases concerning joint selling of coal. In the case of the Oberrheinische Kohlenunion (OKU)—a cartel

---

[11] Meade, Liesner, & Wells, p. 47.

through which coal producers in the Ruhr, Aachen, Saar, and Lorraine sold coal in the south of Germany—the aim of the High Authority was to establish competition between the different suppliers of this market. The mining companies of the various regions owned the overwhelming majority of the shares of OKU and by this means were able to monopolize the distribution of solid fuel in South Germany. In 1957 the High Authority issued a Decision[12] which required the producers to withdraw from membership of OKU. Instead wholesalers were authorized to own shares in OKU, wholesalers controlled by Ruhr mining companies being, however, debarred from obtaining a controlling share of the votes. The basic idea was to create a body which was independent of the mining companies and whose members were free to draw supplies from any of the various regional coalfields, thus creating some competition. OKU was a purchasing organization buying solid fuels on behalf of wholesalers from coalfields designated by the latter. It had no monopoly of purchasing, since consumers buying more than 30,000 tons of coal annually, and first-hand wholesalers, could buy direct from mines or their agencies. OKU had no power to sell, nor had it the power to fix terms of sale. The impression which emerges is that, in the case of OKU, the High Authority has enjoyed some success in creating the competitive situation it originally intended.

In a number of other instances the High Authority has been able to authorize the joint sale of coal. This has notably been the case where the output of the agency has been small in relation to ECSC output and where some at least of the mining companies have been too small to carry out the selling function economically on an independent basis. Thus in 1954 the Aachener Kohlen-Verkauf (comprising mining companies in Aachen responsible for 2·3 per cent of ECSC coal output) and the Niedersächsischer Kohlen-Verkauf (comprising mining companies in Lower Saxony responsible for 1 per cent of this) were authorized by the High Authority.[13]

In Belgium, too, the High Authority has authorized centralized selling through the Comptoir Belge des Charbons (COBECHAR) for reasons very similar to those which were employed to justify the creation of three agencies in the Ruhr. COBECHAR fixes prices for all coal sales but only handles the orders of large

[12] *JO*, 10 Aug. 1957.   [13] Ibid. 6 July 1954.

customers. The smaller sales are handled by the mining companies. COBECHAR was empowered to equalize employment and the distribution of orders when there was a recession in the industry.[14]

2. THE EUROPEAN ECONOMIC COMMUNITY

(a) *The Anti-trust Rules*

The basic cartel provisions of the Rome Treaty are to be found in Article 85. Article 85 (1) prohibits a wide range of collusive practices and Article 85 (2) renders them null and void (that is to say non-enforceable in the Courts). But Article 85 (3) establishes a 'gateway' whereby otherwise prohibited practices may in fact be permitted. There is, therefore, an initial presumption against restrictive practices and a recognition that, in certain defined circumstances, they may be beneficial. This is the essence of the approach adopted under the Rome Treaty. Let us now consider the problems involved in this field.

What kind of practices are incompatible with the Common Market and prohibited? The treaty speaks of three general kinds: 'all agreements between undertakings, all decisions of associations of enterprises and all concerted practices'. These are of course exactly the ones specified in the Paris Treaty. The meaning of 'agreements' seems to be reasonably self-evident, although it must be added that the term should probably be taken to include not only contracts which are themselves enforceable at law but also those agreements whose sanctions are commercial in the sense that, for example, one of the parties may fear commercial retribution if he departs from it. The meaning of 'decisions of associations of enterprises' is probably best illustrated by the example of a firm which is a member of a trade association, and as such feels bound by a collective decision taken in accordance with the rules of that association. The concept of the concerted practice is wholly new to European lawyers and has been inspired by US anti-trust legislation. There is some obscurity about its actual meaning. It has been suggested that it relates to the common conduct by a number of firms which does not spring out of legal obligations (that is agreements) or out of a legal relationship (such as being a member of a trade association

14 *JO*, 18 Oct. 1956.

as discussed above). The example which has been cited is a recommendation to observe certain fixed prices.[15] It has been pointed out[16] that if the enterprises to whom recommendations have been made actually follow them out, this does not imply that the action is concerted, since they may have chosen to adopt that policy in any case. On the other hand a history of recommendations that are always followed out seems to indicate some understanding between the parties to the effect that they will be carried out.

It is important to note that the anti-trust rules refer to enterprises, and whatever their legal form—whether it be corporate body, partnership, or independent trader—they are included. The concept of an enterprise does, however, give rise to some legal difficulty. It would be unreasonable to expect a wholly-owned subsidiary to compete with the parent company and in this case common sense would treat the two as one enterprise. But the possibility exists that one company may have a limited participation of, say, 5 or 10 per cent in another. Such a participation would not unify the enterprises but clearly, at some higher level of participation, the situation would change and the two enterprises would in effect become one, and agreements between them could not be brought within the ambit of the anti-trust rules. Until cases actually arise it is impossible to say where this line is going to be drawn.[17] Article 90 requires that public undertakings and undertakings to which member states grant exclusive rights (nationalized industries are clearly covered by these two categories) shall not engage in practices contrary to Article 85. The same article also states that concerns entrusted with the management of services of a general economic interest or having the character of a fiscal monopoly shall be subject to the anti-trust rules 'in so far as the application of such rules does not obstruct the *de jure* or *de facto* fulfilment of the specific tasks entrusted to such concerns'. Some of the policy decisions in respect of state and fiscal monopolies were discussed earlier in Chapter 4.

[15] OECD, *Guide to Legislation*, vol. v, EEC 2.0, 1.

[16] F. Honig and others, *Cartel Law of the European Economic Community* (1963), pp. 10–11.

[17] V. Korah, 'Competition: Cartels and Monopolies', *Current Legal Problems*, 1963, pp. 142–3. This matter has been studied by the EEC Commission—see Mussard, *ICLQ*, Suppl. Publ. no. 4, (1962), p. 17.

It is also important to note that (unlike the UK Restrictive Trade Practices Act) the Treaty Rules apply to services as well as goods and in principle to agriculture and transport. The Rules do not apply to labour.[18]

Article 85 states that the kind of agreements, decisions of associations or enterprises, and concerted practices which fall under its prohibition are those which fulfil two conditions. First, they must be designed to or actually result in the prevention, restriction, or distortion of competition within the Common Market. Secondly, they must be likely to affect trade between member states.

It seems to us that prevention should be taken to cover the complete elimination of competition in a market, and restriction, some type of conduct which falls short of this, while distortion appears to refer, in this particular context, to a situation where, for example, competing firms are placed in unequal competitive conditions, possibly as a result of price discrimination by a supplier. The treaty provides a number of instances of prohibited practices, presumably because they are among the most objectionable. They are price fixing (vertical or horizontal); market sharing; limitation of production, investment or technical progress; discriminatory practices (if they result in a competitive disadvantage to the firm affected); and tie-in arrangements.

The phrase 'likely to affect trade between Member States' has given rise to considerable legal discussion—even to the extent of articles being written on the meaning of that single phrase.[19] The problem that arises is that the French term *affecter* translates as 'to affect' or 'to concern' whereas the words in the German, Italian, and Dutch texts all, in various degrees, are best rendered as 'affect adversely'. Again we shall avoid competing with legal commentators—it seems to us that there is much to be said for the German BKA view of the matter which is that: 'The protective object of Article 85 is injured or . . . at least endangered whenever a restrictive business practice diverts the flow of goods between Member States from its natural course.'[20] The emphasis here is on inter-state trade developing in a natural manner, that

---

[18] As Article 85 refers to enterprises.

[19] E. G. H. Coing, 'Interpretational Problems of Article 85', *New York Univ. Law R.*, xxxviii/3 (May 1963).

[20] BKA, *Jahresbericht 1961*, p. 62.

is, free from official and private interventions. We shall see later in this chapter in connexion with the Grundig-Consten case that this is very much the view taken by the EEC Commission.

What seems to be altogether more important from the point of view of economic analysis is the idea that only restrictions affecting inter-state trade fall within the scope of the anti-trust rules. The concept of inter-state trade could be interpreted narrowly to cover only practices which prescribe the terms and conditions of sale of goods actually passing over state boundaries. However, a wider interpretation is to be applied which will cover practices, which, although purely local, that is, confined to intra-state trade, nevertheless have an indirect effect on inter-state trade. An obvious example would be an exclusive-dealing agreement between manufacturers and retailers in one state, as it would have a definite effect on inter-state trade.

Of course, in a sense, the interdependence of economic forces could lead one to argue that any restraint in a member state will have results which will impinge on trade between states. In American terminology, intra-state restrictions have inter-state effects. However, it is not the intention of the Commission, on the basis of such logic, to attack every restriction in existence. A line will have to be drawn unless the Commission is to be submerged in a welter of cases. The Commission will in fact concentrate its attack on those restrictions which clearly impede the flow of inter-state trade. Where the line will actually be drawn will be revealed only by the cases the Commission deals with and the judgments handed down by the Court of Justice.

It is highly unlikely that the Commission will use the 'inter-state clause' in the same way as the US anti-trust authorities have done in cases such as that of the Lorain Journal Co.[21] This case involved a local monopoly by a newspaper in a single town. It was brought within the ambit of the Sherman Act by virtue of the fact that the activities of the paper involved transactions in inter-state commerce such as purchase of newsprint and sub-scriptions to nation-wide agency services: a very indirect effect indeed! There is a difference of emphasis in the case of the EEC which makes such an approach unlikely. Although the Sherman Act was an attempt to attack trade restraints in general, the Constitution required the insertion of the inter-state commerce

[21] *United States* v. *Lorain Journal Company* (Supreme Court, 1951).

clause which in practice is something of a hindrance. However, in the interest of fostering competition (which is something of an article of faith because it strikes at positions of unchecked power), the clause has been given a wide interpretation. In the EEC the aim is economic integration and political unity. Only those restraints which inhibit this process are likely to be attacked. The anti-trust rules are not likely to become a vehicle for a general and thorough rooting out of monopoly wherever it may exist.

Article 85 (3), which provides the possibility of exemption, deserves careful scrutiny. The prohibition of Article 85 (1) can be declared inapplicable if the restrictive practice in question helps to improve the production or distribution of goods or promotes technical or economic progress. It must also allow consumers 'a fair share of the resulting profit'—'profit' being used in the widest sense to cover not only a reduction of prices but also improvements in quality, and, according to rulings by the BKA and EEC Commission, quicker delivery and better customer service.[22] Two criteria must, however, be fulfilled. First, the practice must not involve any restrictions not indispensable to the achievement of the above objectives. Secondly, it must not enable the enterprises involved to *eliminate* competition in respect of a *substantial* part of the goods involved.

Where, may we ask, does this law stand comparatively in terms of severity?[23] There appear to be three main gradations of legal severity in this field. First, there is the *per se* prohibition, an approach which is characteristic of US anti-trust.[24] Thus in the case of agreements to fix a common price, as a result of the precedents set by a number of cases, among which the most important are *US* v. *Addystone Pipe and Tube Company* (1898) and *US* v. *Trenton Potteries Company* (1927), the situation may be said to be that, of itself, such a practice falls foul of Section 1 of

---

[22] *WuW*, 1959, p. 310. See also decisions by EEC Commission granting exemptions to sole-distribution agreements discussed below.

[23] It must be admitted that at this stage a judgment is difficult. Laws can be compared in terms of what they appear to imply *a priori* but since there is discretion in their interpretation, actual decisions would be a sounder basis for judgment. In the case of the EEC, however, more decisions than are at present available would be necessary to support any final judgment.

[24] Not uniquely of course, since the UK legislation flatly prohibits collective enforcement of resale prices.

the Sherman Act. The prosecution merely has to prove as a matter of fact that price fixing has occurred, and condemnation automatically follows. Broadly speaking it is true to say that the defence must confine itself to questions of whether or not an agreement exists, and the question of whether the agreement is beneficial or not is not really admissible evidence. Today not only price fixing but also market sharing, collective boycott, and collective exclusive dealing are regarded as illegal *per se*.

Secondly, there is *a priori* prohibition (or the assumption that certain classes of agreement are contrary to the public interest) with provision for exemption. This is clearly the approach adopted in the UK, where there is an initial presumption that horizontal agreements between two or more persons engaged in the production or supply of goods, relating to prices charged, quantities to be produced, and process of manufacture, and vertical agreements relating to individual resale price maintenance are against the public interest. Respondents have to prove through certain defined gateways that benefits exist which outweigh the presumed detriment. A somewhat similar approach is adopted in the West German 'Law against Restraints of Competition' which, following the *a priori* principle, declares in Section 1 that

Agreements made by enterprises or associations of enterprises for a common purpose and resolutions of associations of enterprises are invalid insofar as they are apt to influence, by restraints of competition, the production or the market conditions with respect to the trade in goods or commercial services.

But the law does provide that certain kinds of agreement, for example those relating to rationalization and those necessitated by a crisis, can be exempted. Similarly, in France, Article 59 *bis* of the Price Ordinance no. 45–1483 of 1945 (as subsequently supplemented and amended) declares that

every concerted action, convention, combine express or implied, or trade coalition in any form and upon any grounds whatsoever, which has the object or may have the effect of interfering with full competition by hindering the reduction of production costs or selling prices or by encouraging the artificial increase of prices, shall be prohibited.

However, Article 59 *ter* provides for the possibility of exemption if the promoters of an agreement can 'prove that its effect is to improve the market for their products or to ensure further economic progress by means of rationalization and specialization.'

Thirdly, there is prohibition of proved abuse only, where no prior presumption against agreements is made. This is sometimes described as the abuse principle and it is most clearly exemplified by the Belgian 'Act on Protection against the Abuse of Economic Power'. It is also the basis of the Netherlands Economic Competition Act of 1956, which continues the Dutch tradition of neutrality, restraints of competition being neither good nor bad in themselves, but being judged entirely on their individual results.

Clearly, as far as agreements are concerned, the EEC cartel rules fall into the second category. It could hardly be pretended that they fall into the first, although a number of American commentators seem to imply this or something very close to it. Thus Wilbur L. Fulgate has observed, quite rightly, that Article 85 (1) by virtue of its general prohibition is similar to Section 1 of the Sherman Act. He then goes on to note the exemption provision of Article 85 (3) and takes the view that this 'aligns article 85, paragraph 3, with the Sherman Act "rule of reason".'[25] This seems to be pressing the comparison a little too far. It seems to us that, in the matter of, for example, price agreements, the *per se* rules are clearly established in US anti-trust. Attempts to justify agreements on grounds of rationalization would hardly seem to fall within the category of matters in which the rule of reason might be applied. Moreover, Article 85 (3) admits of exemption being granted provided the agreement does not allow the enterprises concerned to *eliminate* competition (in respect of a substantial part of the goods concerned) and this seems to allow a significant degree of restriction. This seems to place Article 85 well outside the Sherman Act category.

In fact Article 85 strongly resembles the French Article 59 in three senses. First, it prescribes a general prohibition of agreements. Secondly, it provides among other things for exemption on grounds of rationalization. (In practice the French law provides one normally effective gateway, since the other ground for

[25] W. L. Fulgate, 'The Common Market and the United States Antitrust Laws', *New York Univ. Law R.*, xxxviii/3 (May 1963), p. 462.

exemption is a special one applicable in the case of agreements 'Arising out of the application of a legislative provision or regulation.') Thirdly, the Commission Technique des Ententes, which administers this law, has let it be known that agreements must not only profit their promoters but also 'to an important and equitable degree, their customers and the economy as a whole, which presupposes that a lowering of costs is accompanied by a reduction in retail prices'.[26]

(b) *The Implementing Regulations*

In order to make Article 85 an effective instrument, the Commission had to devise detailed implementing regulations—a requirement which was in any case stipulated by Article 87. The need for such regulations was intensified by the fact that not all the member states regarded Article 85 (and Article 86) as immediately applicable to all enterprises. The BKA did regard these articles as immediately binding and in fact ruled upon cartels from the beginning. On the other hand some other states regarded these articles merely as general principles which would only become applicable and binding when the necessary regulations had been produced. The Dutch, for example, seem to have taken this view. This point arose in connexion with the market-sharing agreement between the Dutch and Belgian cardboard-tube producers (see above pp. 99–100). In 1958 the Dutch party attempted to break out of its agreement with the Belgian enterprise by claiming that, by virtue of Article 85, it was freed from its contractual obligations. However, the Belgian party took the case to a Dutch court and succeeded in obtaining a favourable verdict upholding the agreement. The background to this finding was that following the entry into force of the Rome Treaty, there had been a considerable legal hiatus in the Netherlands on the subject of whether Articles 85 and 86 were or were not immediately valid and binding law. As a temporary resolution of the problem a transitional law was passed in the Dutch Parliament to the effect that all agreements and practices of dominant enterprises were to be regarded as valid as long as they had not been attacked by the competent authorities. Since the agreement

---

[26] M. Forsyth, 'Cartel policy and the Common Market', *Planning* (PEP), xxviii/464 (1962), pp. 223–4.

in question had not been attacked, the court therefore declared that it was valid.[27]

In 1962 Regulation 17 was adopted by the Council and with its promulgation these legal problems ceased to hold back the application of anti-trust policy.

(i) *Regulation 17.* This is a complicated, and in some degree obscure, legal document and we shall not attempt to compete with the legal commentators at this point either.[28] Rather we shall concentrate our account upon those aspects of this and subsequent regulations which are necessary to understand the mechanics of EEC anti-trust policy. It must be pointed out that there are differences of opinion between the leading commentators on the exact meaning and implications of Regulation 17 and so the present account is to be regarded as an interpretation only.

Article 1 declares that violations of Article 85 (1) (and Article 86) are prohibited, 'no prior decision to this effect being required'.

Two general problems then arise from this pronouncement. On the one hand, from the point of view of entrepreneurs, there is a need for legal certainty—that is to say they need to know whether their particular practice is or is not of the kind which is prohibited by Article 85. If it is prohibited they may require to know whether it can be exempted under the provisions of Article 85 (3). On the other hand, since it is necessary to attack agreements (or firms abusing a dominant position) which frustrate the steps taken to reduce trade barriers, the Commission needs to have machinery at its disposal for getting to grips with them.

In order to deal with the first problem, and in some degree the second, the Regulation provides for a notification system. At the request of enterprises or associations of enterprises the Commission may state that, according to the information it has received, there is no ground for it to intervene under Article 85 (1)

---

[27] *WuW*, Dec. 1958, pp. 779–82.
[28] Those who wish to delve deeper should consult Honig and others, *Cartel Law;* Junckerstorff; OECD, *Guide to Legislation*; A. Campbell and D. Thompson, *Common Market Law Texts and Commentaries, First Supplement* (*1963*); EEC Commission, *Guide pratique concernant les Articles 85 et 86 du traité instituant la CEE et leurs réglements d'application*, Document 2383–2/IV/ 62–F (1962). We attempted an early interpretation (see McLachlan & Swann), 'Competition Policy in the Common Market', *Econ. J.*, lxxiii (Mar. 1963).

(or Article 86) in respect of a practice or class of practices—this is referred to as the granting of a 'negative clearance certificate'.

The notification system also applies to enterprises that wish to apply for exemption under Article 85 (3).[29] The actual nature of the notification arrangements depends, first, upon whether the practices are 'old cartels', that is to say those which were in existence on 13 March 1962 when Regulation 17 became operative, or 'new cartels', that is, those which were formed after that date. Secondly, it depends upon whether the cartels belong to a specially designated category regarded as being of less immediate importance from the point of view of the development of the Common Market (we shall call these the 'secondary category'), or fall outside that class (the 'main category').

Old Cartels. According to the Regulation these had to be notified to the Commission on or before 31 October 1962[30] except for the special category which was defined as

(a) agreements etc. where enterprises in only one member state take part and which involve neither imports nor exports. (The word 'involves' is to be interpreted strictly to mean directly involve.)
(b) agreements etc. involving only two enterprises and the sole effect is (i) to restrict the freedom of the party receiving the goods to fix price or other conditions of trading on resale; (ii) to impose restraint upon the exercise of the right of an assignee or user of industrial property rights;
(c) agreements etc. whose sole object is (i) the development or uniform application of standards and types (ii) joint research to improve techniques, the results being accessible to all parties.

It should be emphasized that, despite several statements to the contrary, notification is not compulsory. But unless an agreement is notified the Commission cannot grant exemption. When an agreement is notified inside the time limit it is temporarily valid until the Commission rules upon it. When the Commission declares that an agreement cannot be exempted it becomes retroactively invalid to 13 March 1962. Fines and penalties cannot be levied if the parties to the agreement have been operating it up to the date of the Commission's adverse decision, but they can be levied if the parties continue thereafter to operate the

---

[29] Regulations 27 & 153 of 1962 prescribed forms for notification.
[30] Originally this was 31 July 1962.

agreement. If on the other hand the agreement is exempted, it becomes retroactively valid to 13 March 1962. In granting exemption the Commission can attach a time period to it and add stipulations about the future conduct of the parties. The existence of a time period involves the parties in renewing the application for exemption when the period in question has elapsed. The Commission can revoke its exemption if conditions essential to its Decision change, if its stipulations are infringed, and so forth.

Once the Commission has declared that exemption cannot be granted the continued operation of the agreement leaves the parties open to fines. The Commission is empowered to impose upon enterprises or associations thereof fines of from $1,000 to $1 million—the latter can be increased to 10 per cent of the turnover of the preceding business year of each enterprise involved in the agreement. Alternatively the Commission can impose daily penalties of from $50 to $1,000 per day's delay in conforming to a Decision.

Those agreements which have not been notified at all are retroactively invalid to 13 March 1962—even if the conditions necessary for exemption exist, they cannot be exempted and financial penalties can be levied. It appears, however, that if such an unnotified agreement is caught by the Commission and is then notified, an exemption can at best be retroactive to the date of notification—from 13 March 1962 until then it is invalid;—and this would seem to involve the possibility of a financial penalty. If the agreement is not exempted, its invalidity must be retroactive to 13 March 1962—again financial penalties seem possible.

It is fairly clear from all this that there was a strong incentive to notify within the time limit set. But there is a further point in favour of timely notification. Article 7 contains a special provision in respect of old cartels. It declares that where they were notified *within the time limit* but do not satisfy the requirements for exemption, nevertheless the prohibition can be lifted with retroactive effect if the parties discontinue the agreement or modify it in such a way as (*a*) to avoid the prohibition of Article 85 (1), or (*b*) to obtain exemption.[31]

[31] This also applied to the special category of less harmful agreements. Originally the time limit for their notification if they were to enjoy the benefits of Art. 7 (1) was before 1 Jan. 1964 but was later extended to 1 Jan. 1967.

The position with respect to the special category of cartels is not too clear. The Regulation says they 'may' be notified. Although notification may not be compulsory it is necessary to notify before 1 January 1967 in order to be entitled to the benefits of Article 7 (1).

New cartels—that is, those which came into effect after 13 March 1962 (other than the special category)—must be notified if the parties wish to claim exemption. Notification is not compulsory, but again it leads to temporary validity until the Commission pronounces. If the Commission exempts[32] the agreement it is valid from the date of notification—if it is not exempted it is retroactively void from the date of the formation of the agreement. It therefore follows that enterprises who form new agreements should notify them immediately. In the first place, the operation of an unnotified agreement leads to automatic invalidity and possible financial penalties. Secondly, a notified agreement at best can only be exempted retroactively to the date of notification; and if this is after the date of formation, the period in between is one of invalidity which must presumably be subject to financial penalties. If the Commission decides against exemption, then, of course, the continued operation of the agreement leaves the parties open to fines or penalties.

In the case of the special category of cartels, again these 'may' be notified.

Clearly the notification system allows the Commission to get to grips with many of the cartel practices which need to be scrutinized. But the possibility exists that agreements which are highly unlikely to be exempted may not be notified. In other words, it is not unreasonable to assume that in some degree the most pernicious agreements will not be notified and that only the more innocuous ones will be revealed to the Commission. To deal with unnotified arrangements two other procedures have therefore been provided. The first allows the Commission acting on its own initiative, or on request, to attack infringements of the anti-trust rules and to issue Decisions obliging the parties to desist. Requests for action may be made by member states or by natural or legal persons. Use of this channel of information has already begun to yield results. For example the Pottery Convention

---

[32] The stipulations and time period attachable to exemptions, as discussed above, apply here too.

appears to have come to the notice of the Commission through a written question raised by a member of the European Parliament.[33] The exclusive-dealing arrangement between Belgian, German, and Dutch enterprises supplying sand and gravel was brought to the attention of the Commission as a result of a formal complaint lodged by an outside dealer.[34] As might be expected, national cartel authorities have forwarded information about international cartel practices which have come to light in the process of investigating national arrangements. For example, in 1961 the Commission Technique des Ententes in its report on the restrictive practices of French scythe and sickle makers drew attention to the existence of an international cartel arrangement in this field and suggested that details be forwarded to the EEC Commission.[35] It is worth noting that before making a Decision the Commission may attempt to induce the cartel members to make their practices acceptable by addressing Recommendations to them—a form of 'earstroking' with which students of UK monopoly policy are familiar.

The other procedure involves the Commission making inquiries into economic sectors. If the trend of trade, in terms of prices, volume, or whatever, between member states is such as to suggest that restrictions of some kind are being applied, the Commission has the power to conduct a general inquiry in that sector. In 1965 the Commission decided to make use of this provision. A general inquiry was set on foot in the margarine sector, the reason given being that despite substantial price differences between the member states, trade between them in this product had lagged strikingly behind the general development of trade in other products. The inquiry was to extend not only into manufacture and trade but also into differences in member states' laws and regulations regarding the composition and packaging of margarine and rules on prices.[36]

In order to assist the Commission in making Decisions and Recommendations the Regulation confers upon the Commission

---

[33] *JO*, 22 Sept. 1959.
[34] EEC Official Spokesman, Doc. IP(65)65, 1 Apr. 1965.
[35] Commission Technique des Ententes, *Rapport . . . 1960, 1961 et 1962*, p. 19.
[36] EEC Official Spokesman, Doc. IP(65)118, 24 June 1965. (Belgian and German prices were about twice the Dutch level and two and a half times the French level.)

considerable powers to obtain the necessary information. The Commission is empowered to seek necessary information from member-state governments and their competent authorities as well as enterprises and associations thereof. If the information requested from enterprises is not forthcoming or is incomplete, the Commission can request the information by means of a Decision. The Commission's staff can examine the books and business documents of enterprises and can make copies of them, and can ask for oral explanations on the spot, and so forth. Enterprises can be obliged to supply complete and truthful information by means of financial penalties.

Before the Commission takes a Decision about such things as negative clearance or exemption from prohibition, an opportunity has to be given to the parties to agreements to express their views. It is possible for other natural or legal persons who have a 'sufficient' interest to be heard also.

What is the relationship of the Commission to the cartel authorities in the member states? A Consultative Committee on Cartels and Monopolies, consisting of one official qualified in the field of anti-trust from each member state, has been created. The Commission must consult this committee before taking action in respect of infringements of Articles 85 and 86 or negative clearances and exemptions. It is interesting to note that the competence of national cartel authorities to apply the anti-trust rules is severely circumscribed. Only the Commission can grant exemptions. The national authorities can prohibit, but even this power is limited, for, broadly speaking, it is true to say that once the Commission has initiated proceedings in connexion with a cartel, the national authority ceases to be competent to act.

Finally, it is important to note that the decisions of the Commission are subject to review by the Court of Justice.

(ii) The Volume and Type of Notifications. Up to 31 March 1966 the Commission had received 38,154 notifications, applications, and complaints—the actual number of complaints under Article 3 of Regulation 17 being 109.[37] Unfortunately no data are available about the breakdown of this total into the main types of agreement and for this purpose it is necessary to go back

[37] EEC, *9th Gen. Rep.* (1965), (French, mimeo.), p. 51.

to 1964. However, as, according to the Commission, the breakdown since 1964 has not changed to any significant extent, there is no great disadvantage in using the 1964 data.

Up to 31 March 1964 the Commission had received about 37,000 notifications, applications, and complaints—the number of complaints was 48. At that date 556 of the total of notifications and applications were of a type which involved more than two enterprises. These would therefore cover multipartite horizontal restrictions such as price fixing, market sharing, &c., and multipartite vertical restrictions such as collective exclusive dealing. By subtraction it follows that about 36,396 notifications and applications were bipartite in character, 81 per cent (approximately 29,480) were concerned with exclusive agency, 16 per cent (approximately 5,823) were connected with licensing contracts, and 3 per cent (approximately 1,093) were miscellaneous in character. Of the approximately 29,480 cases of exclusive agency 12,000 were of the simple exclusive-dealing variety. These latter are either arrangements whereby a manufacturer makes an *independent trader* a sole dealer in his goods in a particular area, or where such a dealer agrees to buy certain goods from that manufacturer only, or a combination of both. The arrangement must not, however, contain certain types of restriction, as for example a territorial restriction which would prevent consumers in any particular territory from obtaining the manufacturer's product from another sole dealer outside that territory.[38]

Some data are available about the breakdown of the grand total of notifications by the type of product covered by the agreement (as opposed to the form of activity in which the participants in the agreement are engaged)—this is shown in Table 1 (p. 144).

The majority of the agreements in Table 1 are of the exclusive-dealing variety. But we show in Table 2 (p. 145) the data relating to multilateral agreements, which, from the point of view of the development of competition between producers in the various member stages, may well be much the more important.

It would be interesting to know which sectors of the interstate trade are the most cartelized. Table 2 provides data about the percentage of total restrictions in six industrial product groups—unfortunately the product categories are so vague that a

---

[38] This data on notifications is from EEC, *7th Gen. Rep.* (1964), p. 66.

6

TABLE I

Notifications and Complaints to the EEC Commission
Analysed by Type of Product Covered

Product	% of total notifications and complaints
Metals	69·0
of which machines, apparatus & mechanical equipment	40·7
Optical, cinematographic, precision, mechanical, surgical, sound recording & reproducing equipment, & watches & clocks	11·7
Electrical machinery & equipment	4·8
Motor vehicle industry	2·8
Other metal products	9·0
Chemicals	14·7
of which pharmaceuticals	5·7
Plastics & rubber	2·9
Perfumery & cosmetics	2·6
Other chemical products	3·5
Agricultural products & foodstuffs	10·0
Building materials	1·5
Textiles	1·2
Paper & graphic arts	1·0
Leather goods	0·3
Misc. (mainly glass, toys, furniture)	2·2
	100·0

Source: Based upon EEC, *7th Gen. Rep.* (1964), p. 67.

comparison of percentage of total restrictions with the percentage of total inter-state trade in that product group is impossible. The fact which does stand out is that metals and chemicals between them (probably as defined in Table 1) are involved in 50 per cent of all the restrictions and 55 per cent of all the agreements.

Restrictions and Multipartite Agreements Reported to the EEC Commission

	Metal	Chemical	Textile	Food	Construction materials	Paper	Miscellaneous	Insurance	Banking	Dept stores & chains	Miscellaneous	Total of restrictions	% of grand total of restrictions by type
Prices	44	27	14	13	13	16	31	1	8	3	3	173	14·7
Discounts	14	2	9	5	2	12	7	—	—	1	1	53	4·5
Conditions of sale	28	13	16	8	14	14	21	5	8	3	7	137	11·6
Control of production	22	12	4	5	3	—	15	—	1	3	—	64	5·4
Control of sale	23	24	3	3	8	7	20	—	—	3	2	93	7·9
Allocation of territorial markets	15	5	—	2	5	2	3	—	—	—	1	33	2·8
Quotas	23	10	4	5	11	2	20	—	—	—	2	77	6·5
Division of sale & purchase	8	17	3	2	14	3	8	—	—	4	1	60	5·1
Technical co-operation	25	3	2	4	—	—	5	1	—	1	2	43	3·6
Normalization, joint research & publicity	39	11	12	3	3	10	5	2	8	9	16	118	10·0
Export & import	38	23	14	4	10	4	22	—	—	—	—	115	9·8
Collective exclusive dealing	35	9	2	1	3	1	6	—	—	—	—	57	4·8
Multilateral licensing	101	25	6	7	1	1	11	—	—	3	1	156	13·2
Total of restrictions by product or service	415	181	89	62	87	72	174	9	24	30	36	Grand total of restrictions 1,179	
% of grand total of restrictions	35·2	15·4	7·5	5·3	7·4	6·1	14·8	0·76	2·0	2·5	3·1		
Total of agreements by product or service	203	70	37	23	31	24	51	6	8	13	27	Grand total of agreements 493	
% of grand total of agreements	41·1	14·2	7·5	4·7	6·3	4·9	10·3	1·2	1·6	2·6	5·5		

Source: Edwards, *Cartelization*, table v, p. 26.

Table 2 is more helpful in indicating the percentage importance of the various kinds of restrictions. Restrictions relating to price (14·7 per cent) are the most important—this would be more pronounced if discount restrictions were taken into account. It is difficult to say whether this figure is higher or lower than might have been expected. Tentatively, however, we would be inclined to say that it is on the low side. Our only standard of comparison is data, provided by C. D. Edwards, of international restrictions reported to the cartel authorities of Western Germany, the UK, Denmark, Sweden, and Norway in 1963. This shows that 30 per cent of the total restrictions so reported concerned prices.[39] By this standard the EEC percentage is on the low side. The figure of 2·8 per cent for territorial allocation of markets must be judged to be remarkably low, considering that the Edwards data just referred to gives a figure of 26 per cent and commentators are generally agreed that this practice is the one most frequently adopted by international cartels.[40]

The value of the breakdown in Table 2 depends upon the degree to which enterprises have felt obliged to notify their practices. According to Edwards, a leading Swiss trade association advised its members not to notify and believes its advice was widely followed. He also indicates that numerous enterprises with which he had had private conversations had indicated that for a variety of reasons they did not notify. Responsible officials of the Commission and member states have variously estimated the proportion of relevant agreements which were notified as lying between 5 and 50 per cent. The variation indicates that these are little more than subjective impressions, but the fact that the most optimistic of them could not conceive of more than half being in the net is significant. Unfortunately there is no objective basis for estimating how many ought to be notified.

In Table 3 (p. 147) we also provide data showing the breakdown of parties to notifications by country. On the face of it the Italian notification figure appears to be on the low side. Since most notifications concern export distribution agreements, one way to establish whether or not Italian notifications are relatively low would be to compare the ratio of Italian notifications to

---

[39] Edwards, *Cartelization*, table iv, p. 21.
[40] See GATT, *Restrictive Business Practices* (1959), p. 27, and UN, *International Cartels* (1947), p. 15.

Italian exports to the EEC with the ratios of other EEC states. Such a comparison does not confirm our initial impression.

TABLE 3

Breakdown of Parties to Notifications by Country

	% of total notifications on Forms A, B and C*	% of total notifications on Form B1†
France	18·7	15·2
Western Germany	25·0	24·6
Italy	9·5	10·3
Belgium	9·0	11·2
The Netherlands	8·6	10·9
Luxembourg	1·1	0·8
United Kingdom	8·8	10·1
Switzerland	4·4	3·3
Other European third countries	6·4	6·1
US & Canada	6·6	5·8
Other non-European third countries	1·9	1·7
	100·0	100·0

* Form A for negative clearances; Form B for exemptions; Form C for complaints.

† Form B1 for notification of simple exclusive-dealing arrangements.

Source: OECD, *Ann. Rep. on Developments in the Field of Restrictive Business Practices* (1965), p. 38.

The impression which emerges, and inevitably it is highly subjective, is that there has been a significant amount of concealment. We base our conclusion on two facts. The first is that responsible officials, none of whom have any incentive to underestimate the effectiveness of their own work, do not lay claim to more than a 50 per cent catch. The second is that notification of certain types of cartel practices—particularly those relating to territorial market sharing—have fallen below what might have been expected. We take this to mean that the participants in the practices of this kind felt that because of their very nature they would be struck down by the Commission. Because of this it was politic not to notify them—they could of course have abandoned them, but we feel that the participants might well have chosen to wait and see how the EEC anti-trust policy developed before taking such a drastic step.

(iii) *Subsequent Regulations.* Several anti-trust regulations have subsequently been issued and we shall briefly discuss their content. Regulation 27 of 1962 dealt with the relationship of the anti-trust rules to production of and trade in agricultural produce. The main burden of this Regulation was that Article 85 (1) would be applicable to agreements, &c. in the trade or production of agricultural products listed in Annexe II of the treaty. But it would not apply to practices which were an integral part of a national market organization or were necessary for the attainment of the objectives of the Common Agricultural Policy set out in Article 39. By virtue of Regulation 141 of 1962 Regulation 17 was declared inapplicable to transport until at least 31 December 1965. (In 1965 Regulation 165 extended this inapplicability to 31 December 1967.) In 1963 Regulation 99 was issued providing machinery for allowing the parties to an agreement, or others who have a sufficient interest, to be heard before the Commission prior to a decision being taken. This process takes place before a reference to the Consultative Committee. The parties entitled to be heard by the Commission can appear in person or can be represented by those entitled by law, or by the rules of their articles of association, to represent them. If they appear in person they can be assisted by members of the bar or by professors entitled to appear before the Court of Justice of the European Communities. Finally, in 1965 the Council of Ministers gave their approval to a Regulation authorizing the Commission to grant block exemptions to certain classes of agreement. This was a very necessary step if the Commission was to be able to get to grips with the very large number of notifications, particularly those of a bilateral nature. The Commission had originally hoped for a Regulation covering a wide variety of agreements but the Council of Ministers limited its scope to exclusive dealing and licensing agreements. Subsequently the Italian government, which had originally opposed the block exemption Regulation in Council, but had been overruled by a majority decision, appealed to the Court of Justice to annul the Council's decision. One of the main pleas of the Italian government was that Article 85, unlike Article 86, did not apply to vertical agreements—that is to say agreements between parties who are at different stages in the economic process. The Court rejected this plea by ruling that nothing in Articles 85 and 86 established a distinction between enterprises operating at the same stage and enterprises operating at different stages in the circuit from producer to consumer. It therefore followed that a vertical agreement, if it fulfilled the tests relating to restrictions upon competition and inter-state trade, would be caught by the ban of Article 85 (1). The Italian government also submitted that the Council had been guilty of wrongful legal procedure in that the latter had ruled on Article 85 (3) exemptions without first having specified the extent of the Article 85 (1) prohibition. As a result the Council was guilty of acting as though everything not authorized is banned. In reply the Court held that the Council could by regulation apply to a category of agreements the exemption provided for in Article 85 (3) without entailing the prohibition of agreements which were not specifically exempted. The Italian plea failed and the block exemption Regulation was upheld.[41] In August 1966 the Commission published a draft of a proposed Regulation to exempt sole buying and sole selling agreements, as well as agreements involving both these elements. One of the most important conditions for exemption is that territorial protection must not exist. The Regulation was subsequently adopted.[42]

(iv) *Industrial Property.* Let us consider *patents and patent licences* first. In all the member states an inventor of a new product or process can obtain a patent conferring upon him a monopoly of that product or process for a period of years. He can also license others, usually for a fee, to use that process or produce that product and can impose conditions upon the licensee. Such conditions can restrict the competitive activity of the licensee, and the problem which arises is whether such restrictions fall within the purview of Article 85 (1) (or Article 86) or not. A number of commentators have, with varying

---

[41] EEC Official Spokesman, Doc. P-44, July 1966.
[42] *JO*, 26 Aug. 1966 and 25 Mar. 1967.

emphasis, stated that patents (and indeed all forms of industrial property) cannot be interfered with by Articles 85 or 86. This position has been defended by reference to Article 36 of the Rome Treaty, which states that the prohibition of quantitative restrictions on imports embodied in Articles 30–34 shall not preclude restrictions of imports on the grounds of protection of industrial and commercial property. However, this is a wild overestimation of the implications of Article 36 and the Director-General of Competition in the EEC Commission has explicitly stated that Article 36 has no significance in the interpretation of Article 85—the meaning of Article 36 merely being that the absolute prohibition of imports contained in Articles 30–34 did not make it possible for a patent holder to prevent the import of the product in question by imitators.[43]

In 1962 the Commission issued an Announcement specifying the kind of clauses in patent licence contracts which in its opinion are not covered by the prohibition of Article 85 (1).[44]

[43] P. Verloren van Themaat, 'Article 36 in relation to Article 85 and Patent Licencing Agreements', *Common Market Law R.*, i/4 (Mar. 1964), pp. 428–30.

[44] These include

'A. Obligations imposed on the licensee which have as their object:
  1. the limitation to certain of the forms of exploitation of the invention which are provided for by patent law (manufacture, use, sale);
  2. the limitation:
     (a) of the manufacture of the patented product,
     (b) of the use of the patented process,
     to certain technical applications;
  3. the limitation of the quantity of products to be manufactured or of the number of acts constituting exploitation;
  4. the limitation of exploitation:
     (a) in time
        (a licence of shorter duration than the patent),
     (b) in space
        (a regional licence for part of the territory for which the patent is granted, or a licence limited to one place of exploitation or to a specific factory),
     (c) with regard to the person
        (limitation of the licensee's power of disposal, e.g. prohibiting him for assigning the licence or from granting sub-licenses);
B. Obligations whereby the licensee has to mark the product with an indication of the patent;
C. Quality standards or obligations to procure supplies of certain products imposed on the licensee—in so far as they are indispensable for the technically perfect exploitations of the patent;
D. Undertakings concerning the disclosure of experience gained in exploiting the invention or the grant of licences for inventions in the field of perfection or application; this however applies to undertakings

It should be noted that in this Announcement the Commission was not saying that Article 85 (1) was not applicable to the clauses specified but that in its opinion they did not prevent, restrict, or distort competition within the Common Market and did not unfavourably influence trade between states. Clearly this Announcement does not cover all the types of restriction to be found in patent licences, and in particular it does not refer to the more important of them. For example, a licence agreement might require the licensee to charge a particular price for a patented product, or to purchase material used in producing the patented product from the licenser, to refrain from producing or distributing goods competing with those of the licenser. It would appear that such clauses also come within the purview of Article 85 (1). Two points arise here. One is that, in so far as this interpretation is correct, although patents and patent licences are granted under municipal law, the Community law in the shape of Articles 85 (and 86) apparently supervenes. Secondly, it must be presumed that the Commission, in appraising clauses in patent licences (other than those listed in the Announcement), will have to set against their restrictive effect the fact that the patent is intended as a form of protection for the patentee and he is presumably entitled to some protection from the competition emanating from his licensees. It is questionable whether licences would be forthcoming—and new technologies diffused—if patentees could not be guaranteed some protection. In other words, the Commission will have to decide what restrictions can reasonably be imposed on licensees and what restrictions go beyond acceptable limits.

Industrial Property in the Common Market. The subject of patent licensing leads on to the whole question of industrial property in the form of *patents, trade marks, designs and models.* These property rights do create great problems for those who seek to create a truly common market. For example, the inventor of a new product can apply for a patent in each of the member states

---

entered into by the licensee only if those undertakings are not exclusive and if the licensor has entered into similar undertakings;
E. Undertakings on the part of the licensor:
  1. not to authorize anyone else to exploit the invention;
  2. not to exploit the invention himself.' (*JO*, 24 Dec. 1962.)
6*

and therefore can enjoy a temporary monopoly of the production or supply of that product in each state. This would enable him (or his licensees) to set different prices for the same product in the various markets. The patentee (or his licensees) would of course be legally entitled to prevent supplies from percolating in from markets where prices were lower. Such compartmentaliza- tion of the Common Market is equally possible through the agency of trade marks, with the added problem that the latter are easier to obtain than patents.

In 1959 the governments of the member states decided, in collaboration with the EEC Commission, to investigate the possibility of harmonizing their legislations relating to industrial property. The idea was to prepare three conventions relating to patents, trade marks and designs and models, and three working groups were formed. The word harmonization is perhaps mis- leading in this context, since it was not proposed that the national laws should themselves be brought into line but that a common European law in these fields should coexist with the national laws.

The draft of a possible convention on patent law was published in 1962. We shall not attempt to describe the content in detail[45] but will confine ourselves to mentioning features which are immediately relevant to competition policy.

The draft convention provides the opportunity for an inventor to obtain a Community patent whose protection would extend over the whole territory of the EEC, the implication of this being that the compartmentalization of the Common Market, which can arise under the national patent system, would be ruled out. Once a patentee had placed a patented product on the market of a member state, he could not avail himself of the patent in order to prevent the circulation of these products in other states. Price differences would therefore be eliminated by importers shifting supplies from low- to high-price markets.

The Community patent would not provide an automatic solution to the compartmentalization problem since an inventor could still avail himself of the national patent system. However, it would appear that the long-term aim of the convention is to replace national by Community law—but there is no automatic requirement to this effect.

[45] A copy of the draft together with a commentary is to be found in G. Oudemans, *The Draft European Patent Convention* (1963).

The patent convention has unfortunately run into political difficulties and no agreement has been reached in Council upon it. Apparently the source of the difficulty is the conflict between two schools of thought.[46] On the one hand the Commission proposes a patent convention concluded exclusively between the Six. Provisions would however exist by which non-members of the Community could be associated. In the latter case the Community patent would be valid not only over the whole territory of the Six but also in those non-member countries who accepted a Community patent as a national patent. On the other hand it has been suggested that an international patent agreement should be drawn up between as many states as possible. The arrangement would consist of a unified system for granting patents, not in the form of a single patent but as a series of national patents. This proposal has been supported by the Netherlands and, outside the Community, by the UK and its EFTA partners. Under this arrangement the latter would be able to participate on all fours with Community countries. The EEC states would of course be free to draw up a second convention under which national patents would be combined into a single patent valid over the whole territory of the EEC.

In 1965 it was reported that a first version of a preliminary draft convention relating to a European trade-mark law was complete and that work on a European model and design law was to be resumed.[47]

3. THE DECISIONS AND JUDGMENTS OF NATIONAL AUTHORITIES UNDER THE ROME TREATY

(a) *West Germany: The BKA and Courts*
Before reviewing the national decisions it is necessary to note that up to the time when Regulation 17 became operative, the national authorities, in dealing with cartels which were *prima facie* violating Article 85, did in fact in all or virtually all cases apply concurrently national and EEC law.

In 1963 the BKA in its Annual Report gave an account of its activities in respect of Articles 85 and 86 from the entry into force

---

[46] See J-C. Soum, 'Why a Community Patent', *European Community*, no. 11, Nov. 1965, pp. 8–9.
[47] EEC, *8th Gen. Rep.* (1965), p. 105.

of the Rome Treaty until the promulgation of Regulation 17—
thereafter the BKA began to take a less active role. During this
period it expressed its opinion in 22 formal Decisions on the
compatibility of restrictive agreements with Article 85. Of these
17 were cartel agreements and 5 licensing agreements. In 11 of
the Decisions no conflict with Article 85 was found. In the
remaining cases, where a conflict was found, action was taken and
brief details of 10 of the actions are contained in Table 4 (p. 155).

Apart from issuing formal Decisions, the BKA has also
operated on an informal basis by inducing members of cartels
either to abandon them or to bring about suitable modifications.
Unfortunately the reports of the BKA are not as detailed as
could be desired, particularly in respect of its informal activities.
Below we present such information as is available about some of
the formal and informal decisions.

(i) *Common Sales Syndicates.* Details of the Terrazzo case were
given earlier. It will be remembered that by this arrangement
three German producers conducted both their domestic and
export sales by means of a joint syndicate. The arrangement
provided for the setting of uniform prices and discounts for the
products of the three members. The BKA considered that the
agreement was such as to affect adversely trade between member
states and to constitute a restriction upon competition within
the Common Market, because consumers throughout the Community faced one selling agency, rather than the three separate
firms, and because the exports of the syndicate amounted to
almost one-half of total German exports of this product to
Common Market countries. *Prima facie* therefore the agreement
was violating Article 85 of the treaty. However, afterconsulta-
tion with the Brussels Commission, the BKA ruled that the
exemption of Article 85 (3) applied. In granting its exemption
the Federal Cartel Office took into account the following
circumstances that were relevant to Article 85 (3):

It could be ascertained that the cartel agreement contributes to an
improvement in production in that the individual member of the cartel
is enabled, by the common selling agency, to produce only such types
as are best made from the material of its quarries, and is no longer
obliged to produce the whole range of Terrazzo products irrespective
of its own resources. The specialization of types made possible by the

TABLE 4

Brief Summary of Action taken by the BKA re Agreements in Conflict with Article 85, 1958–62.

Practice	*Action taken*
Rebate cartels (2 cases)	In one case the cartel was ordered to extend its aggregated rebates to purchases made from outsiders in other member states. In another case it was not necessary to condemn the cartel formally from the standpoint of Article 85 as it could be attacked under the provisions of the German cartel law.
Export cartels (2 cases)	One cartel was designed to cover the territory of member states of the EEC but was approved provided it was made to apply to third countries only. The other was concerned primarily with sales to one of the EEC states and was considered contrary to Article 85 (1). It was permitted for a limited period to allow the objectionable features to be dismantled and it was then further permitted on the understanding that it would cease to be effective if not notified to the EEC Commission or if any subsequent resolution was practised before being notified to that body.
One cartel & 3 licence agreements	Were considered in conflict with Article 85 (1) but granted exemption under Article 85 (3).
Two licence agreements	Their compatibility with Article 85 (1) was left open but, as a precaution, a declaration under Article 85 (3) was made.

Source: BKA, *Jahresbericht 1962* (1963), p. 75.

cartel agreement and the concentration of production in the case of large orders lead furthermore to an improvement of distribution. The foreign consumers share in the 'profit resulting' because, as a result of the obligations of the participating enterprises, they obtain the advantages of production superior in types and qualities, and at appropriate times, and they can give large orders through the syndicate at favourable rates of freight which could not be offered by the separate firms. The improvement in the production and distribution of goods and the participation of users in the profit resulting could not be achieved without a limitation on competition in the sense defined in Article 85 (1) of the Rome Treaty or by a weaker limitation of competition than that adopted in the actual agreement. In conclusion, the agreement does not admit the possibility of eliminating competition in respect of a substantial amount of the product in question, as other German and foreign enterprises, as well as the syndicate, sell in the other countries of the Common Market.[48]

The BKA instanced as specific benefits certain gains to consumers—for example that Belgian consumers enjoyed a lower price because of the larger deliveries made by the syndicate and that Dutch consumers benefited from cheaper water freights.

In the case of another common sales syndicate—the Ruhrstickstoff (nitrogen) Syndicate—the Decision of the BKA was that it did not violate Article 85 (1) since it exported only 'relatively insignificant quantities' of the good in question to the member states.[49]

(ii) *Market Sharing*. In the case of the market-sharing arrangement between German and Dutch enterprises engaged in producing adhesive tape (which we have already dealt with in Chapter 6, at the instigation of the BKA the German association of producers informed its Dutch opposite number that the agreement was in conflict with Article 85. The German association also informed its members to the like effect.[50]

---

[48] BKA, *Jahresbericht 1960*, p. 60. The foreign enterprises with which the syndicate competed included French, Italian, Swiss, Spanish, and Hungarian terrazzo producers. It is also relevant to note that the BKA exempted the syndicate under Section 5 of the German cartel law which relates to rationalization cartels.

[49] J. Bieberstein, 'The German Cartel Law and its Administration; Role of the Federal Cartel Office in relation to the EEC Anti-Trust Provisions', *ICLQ*, xii (1963), p. 883.

[50] BKA, *Jahresbericht 1961*, p. 37.

The BKA Report for 1960 refers to the fact that it had received notification of a market-sharing (and price) agreement between German and Dutch enterprises in a branch of the mining industry. The BKA maintained that the agreement infringed both Article 85 (1) and Section 1 of the German Cartel Law. It therefore ordered the German enterprises to take no further part in the practices, and this order was obeyed. It also requested the EEC Commission to take steps to ensure suitable action by the Dutch concern involved in the agreement.[51]

(iii) *Rebate Cartels.* The fact that aggregated rebate cartels can be operated in a way which violates Article 85 (1) has been discussed above in the account of cartel practices. The BKA has considered two such arrangements under this heading—one concerning window-glass manufacturers, the other producers of phosphates.

In 1960 objection was raised by the BKA to an aggregated rebate cartel involving three West German manufacturers of window and plate glass—the objection being upheld by an appeal section of the same body. The facts were that in 1959 these three manufacturers had agreed to grant to wholesale distributors and processors of flat glass a storage premium of 5 per cent in respect of window glass, and a turnover premium which was based upon the individual wholesaler's or processor's aggregate purchases during the year from all window-glass manufacturers in the Federal Republic. The turnover premium had to be calculated on a progressive scale of from 1 to 4 per cent for quantities of from 70,000 to 250,000 or more square metres. In 1961 they agreed to a turnover premium for plate glass—the scale in this case was from 2·5 to 10 per cent for quantities of from 450 to 5,300 or more square metres.[52]

This case was considered by the BKA under the concurrent jurisdiction of the German Cartel Law (Section 3 of which exempts rebate cartels from the automatic prohibition of Section 1, but Sections 3 and 12 also provide grounds upon which the BKA can declare such a cartel invalid) and Article 85. The BKA attacked the cartel on two grounds. First, on the basis of the German law it maintained that there was a marked lack of

---

[51] BKA, *Jahresbericht 1960*, p. 61.
[52] 'Re Fensterglas III', *Common Market Law Reports*, ii, pt. 8 (1963), p. 337.

competition between these three manufacturers who, with unimportant exceptions, were the only German suppliers. They all charged identical prices for identical products, and prices were changed simultaneously and in identical proportions—this kind of behaviour had been evident since 1948. Even preferences arising from proximity to consumers had been eliminated as the prices charged by the cartel were equal to delivered prices inclusive of freight charges. The BKA therefore refused to validate the cartel, arguing that if a rebate cartel was such that its existence excluded the last element of effective competition or so weakened competition that it could no longer exercise its guiding function, then the cartel was contrary to the German law and was abusive. The BKA also objected to the cartel on the grounds that it did not take into account consumers' purchases from manufacturers outside Germany—this was an offence within the meaning of Article 85 (1). The three enterprises however appealed to the Kammergericht in Berlin, which set aside the BKA Decision. This judgment rejected the BKA's view of the effect of forbidding the rebate agreement—the Court appears to have argued that, given the oligopolistic nature of the market, competition in rebates was as unlikely as competition in prices. The objections to the application of Article 85 (1) were largely procedural. The Kammergericht argued that the rebate arrangement might fall under the ban of Article 85 but the contents of Regulation 17 prevented, at least for the time being, both the BKA and the Court from objecting on the basis of Article 85. The Court also observed that the enterprises involved had offered to include customers' purchases from outside manufacturers in the EEC in the calculation of rebates. The Court took the view that this fact also precluded action under Article 85 but, as reported, it observed that:

After an unsuccessful request for the inclusion of purchases from EEC outsiders in the calculation of the aggregate turnover, the Federal Cartel Office would be at liberty, given the right conditions, to invalidate the rebate resolutions under Article 12 (1) (i), G.W.B. in conjunction with Article 85 (1) of the EEC Treaty.[53]

[53] Ibid. p. 345. (Art. 12 (1) (i) permits invalidation of a rebate cartel if 'The agreements and resolutions or the method of their execution constitute an abuse of the market position obtained as a result of the exemption from Section 1'.) GWB is an abbreviation for Gesetz gegen Wettbewerbsbechränkungen which is usually referred to as the German Cartel Law.

In the case of the phosphate manufacturers organized in the Thomas-phosphate Syndicate the BKA in its Decision of 1962 took the view that its aggregating system was violative of Article 85 (1) because in calculating rebates it did not take into account purchases from domestic and other EEC producers outside the cartel.[54]

(iv) *Licensing Agreements*. That licensing agreements will generally tend to include clauses involving restrictions of competition which Article 85 seeks to prevent is to a degree unavoidable. It is a common feature of patent practice in many advanced industrial countries that patent owners in return for licensing others to produce patented goods or employ patented processes can exert, as a reward or inducement for granting a licence, some control over the competitive behaviour of those whom they license. Nevertheless it is also clear that licence agreements may contain clauses which are more restrictive than is reasonably necessary to reward the licenser and these restrictions may be such as to violate Article 85 (1).

The BKA has dealt with several cases which fall into this general category of practice. In one case a French firm licensed a German manufacturer to produce its patented speed-cutting machines. The French licenser required the German licensee not to produce or sell competing items until three years after the termination of the agreement; to grant back to the licenser any improvement inventions—reserving to the licensee only the right to use the improvements; and to mark the goods conspicuously with the name and patent markings of the licenser. This agreement was considered under both Section 20 of the German Cartel Law (which deals with licensing agreements) and Article 85. The BKA objected to the arrangement on two counts. It insisted in connexion with the first condition that the prohibition on the sale of competing goods should be narrowed down and should only apply to goods produced by the particular licensed method. In respect of the second provision the BKA required that it should cover improvement inventions only and not independent parallel inventions. The BKA then considered that the agreement could be exempted under Article 23 (3) of the German Cartel Law. The exemption was accorded on the grounds of the economic and technical investment of the licenser in his patents—the result of twenty years of activity in this field. The grant back of improvements (subject however to the licensee's right to use them) and the restriction of competition for a limited period were necessary to induce the licenser to grant a licence. The BKA also considered Article 85 applicable, a restriction of competition under Article 85 1(b) and an effect on trade between states were both deemed to exist. However, the conditions necessary for exemption under Article 85 (3) were considered to be present. The justification for exemption 'was found in the marketing of a new product, advanced technological progress, decreased prices, and improvements in quality, thus, giving consumers sufficient advantage'.[55] The restraints in the licence had been narrowed down by the BKA and were no more than was necessary to induce the licenser to grant the licence—that is to say the conditions of Article 85 (3) were fulfilled. The fact that the licensee did not enjoy a dominant market position meant that competition was not eliminated in a way which failed to fulfil the requirements of Article 85 3(b).[56]

In the case of another licence agreement, the BKA decided against the arrangement on the grounds that it was an Article 85 1 (b) offence. This Decision involved a licensing agreement concerning trade secrets in which a German licensee was to be restricted from manufacturing certain goods, which were the subject of the agreement, in the Netherlands or exporting them thereto, even after the technical 'know-how' had become apparent.[57]

(v) *Export Cartels.* The general prohibition of Section 1 of the German Cartel Law does not apply to export agreements and broadly speaking upon application the BKA is required to approve them. However, in granting its approval, the BKA has always paid attention to the compatibility of the agreements with Article 85. Thus in one case a cartel was only granted permission under Section 6 (2) of the German Cartel Law on the understanding that the territorial scope of the cartel did not include

[55] Buxbaum, *Columbia Law R.*, lx (1961), pp. 413–14.
[56] Ibid.
[57] Bieberstein, *ICLQ*, xii (1963), p. 881.

the EEC, and the BKA has generally not been satisfied merely by a statement by the participants that their cartel only applied to countries outside the EEC. In the case of another export cartel arrangement involving twenty-one enterprises, which took the form of a skeleton contract, permission to operate it was not limited to countries outside the EEC, but the BKA required that both the agreement and any resolutions referring to exports to EEC countries passed prior to Regulation 17 be notified to the EEC Commission within the specified time limit if the agreement was not to lose its validity. Resolutions, referring to exports to the EEC, passed subsequently to Regulation 17 were not to be put into effect before being notified to the Commission.[58]

(vi) *Re-export Prohibitions in Bilateral Vertical Agreements.* The BKA has had to give an opinion in connexion with questions of this kind arising from a case in the German courts concerning Braun electric razors. Braun normally required German wholesalers to sign an undertaking that they would resell the razors only to dealers specializing in the electric appliance trade who were to resell them at retail prices stipulated by Braun. The case arose out of the action of a German wholesaler who sold the razors retail at DM56 instead of DM70 as stipulated by Braun. Braun suspended deliveries to the wholesaler but the latter was able to obtain supplies from dealers in other EEC states, to sell below the stipulated price, and in so doing to make what it regarded as a satisfactory profit margin of 20 per cent on the resale price. Braun took the matter to the Landesgericht (Court of First Instance) at Frankfurt and obtained an injunction, requiring the wholesaler to cease selling the razors retail and below the stipulated price, together with damages. This judgment was appealed against by the wholesalers to the Oberlandesgericht (Superior Court) Frankfurt. Basically the case of the wholesaler was that Braun imposed upon foreign dealers a prohibition against re-exporting the razor, for example to Germany. The wholesaler maintained that this was contrary to Article 85 and asked the Court either to set aside the earlier judgment, or in the alternative to amend the judgment so as to permit the retail sale of Braun dry razors in general, and the

---

[58] Detail on export cartels from Bieberstein, *ICLQ*, xii (1963), p. 883.

retail sale of Braun-Combi dry razors in particular, *where the appliances had been re-imported from another country in the European Economic Community*. The BKA was called upon to express its opinion in writing.[59] It observed that in the branch of the industry to which the case applied, it was usual to conduct exports to other members of the EEC by means of sole importers and to impose re-export prohibitions on foreign customers. The case was therefore intimately bound up with sole agency and associated export prohibitions. The BKA stated that, in consultation with the EEC Commission and cartel experts of other member states, it had come to the conclusion that this form of export prohibition was to be regarded as a violation of Article 85 (1). In this particular case the BKA concluded that the share of the product in question in total German exports of electric razors was so considerable that the restriction imposed upon foreign buyers adversely affected inter-state trade. It went on to point out that the adverse effect resulted from the fact that all German manufacturers of the product imposed similar prohibitions. As a result the German market was sealed off from the rest of the EEC, and this made it possible for German producers to maintain a higher price in the German market than in other EEC countries. The abolition of the prohibition would on the other hand approximate prices in the various national markets and contribute to a common market.

The Oberlandesgericht in its judgment stated that the export prohibition was a breach of Article 85 (1) and was void by reason of Article 85 (2). Braun, however, appealed to the Bundesgerichtshof (the German Supreme Court) which, on the basis of technical argument about the entry into force of Regulation 17 and in the light of the judgment of the European Court in the Bosch case, considered the export prohibition, as part of an old cartel which had been notified, provisionally valid. The final decision about the practice was therefore left to the EEC Commission.[60] As we shall see below, in connexion with the Grundig–Consten case, the Commission subsequently delivered a Decision about the territorial protection conferred upon sole distributors by export prohibitions.

---

[59] BKA, *Jahresbericht 1960*, p. 61.
[60] See 'Re "Braun" Electric Razors', *Common Market Law Reports*, iii, pt. 9, Mar. 1964, pp. 59–83.

(b) France: The Commission Technique des Ententes

In 1960 the Commission Technique des Ententes was asked by the French Secretary of State for Internal Commerce to consider an agreement between French and Belgian stone-quarry companies producing road-construction materials—the relevant law being Article 59 of the Decree No. 45–1483 of 1945 and Article 85.

The agreement was concluded in 1956 between Belgian quarry firms who had formed a common organization—the Union Commerciale du Porphyre—and the French quarry firms, Société Anonyme Pagnac-Limousin, Société Anonyme des Carrières de L'Ouest, and Société Anonyme des Carrières de la Meilleraie. Under the terms of the agreement the two sides agreed to share by halves the supply of hard-ground rock in the five Departments in the north of France—Nord, Pas-de-Calais, Aisne, Oise, and Somme, the Belgians having a preference in the first two Departments and the French in the other three. The two groups also entered into a verbal agreement with a group of local quarry enterprises—the Carrières de l'Avesnois—guaranteeing them 25 per cent of the general tonnage of road-construction materials delivered in the zone. This latter arrangement carried none of the agreement's contractual obligations.

The agreement had in fact a dual aspect. First, it involved a territorial allocation of markets which appears to have been scrupulously respected. In addition, a sales quota seems to be implied since the report of the Technical Commission referred to the fact that 'respect for the division of the market is guaranteed by the control of tonnage delivered in the zone of the agreement and by a method of penalties paid by groups exceeding sales allowance to groups falling below'. At first sight it appears curious that a quota arrangement should be necessary, since if any group overstocked its part of the market the consequences would appear to rebound to its disadvantage alone. However, once it is recognized that there would be merchants, outside the agreement, who might shift supplies from the overstocked territory to the relatively understocked one, it is not difficult to see why the protection afforded by a limitation on deliveries into each zone was felt to be necessary by both parties.

It is also worth noting that the Belgian producers enjoyed the benefit of a special through rail rate to Nord and Pas-de-Calais as opposed to the more normal and disadvantageous broken freight rate as calculated for cross-frontier journeys. The French producers, in order to remain competitive in the area adjacent to the 'contractual frontier', practised an equal delivered price system whereby consumers close to the quarries subsidized those close to the 'frontier'.

The Technical Commission considered that the geographical and quantitative restrictions in the agreement placed an obstacle in the way of the normal play of competition as defined in Article 85 and in Article 59 of the French law. The Technical Commission also singled out for criticism the equalization of delivered prices on the grounds that it distorted the working of the price mechanism and imposed an excessive burden on consumers close to the quarries.

On the other hand the Technical Commission noted that from 1956 to 1960 prices had remained virtually stable, so that relatively speaking the cost of road-making materials had fallen over the period. It was however difficult to know to what extent this could be ascribed to the workings of the agreement, since there had been no co-ordination of investments between the members, who had in fact remained virtually independent. On the other hand the guaranteeing of a market might have had the effect of inducing the enterprises to undertake a more ambitious programme of investment. The Technical Commission also noted that the market power of the parties to the agreement was limited by virtue of the fact that it did not cover all producers or all forms of road-making material.

However, the Technical Commission did not advise the Secretary of State to condemn the agreement. Instead it proposed that in terms of membership and material covered, it should remain limited in scope and that the signatories should introduce greater flexibility into the division of the market.

The Technical Commission's reasons for not recommending the establishment of free competition appear to have been as follows. The French producers had good reason to fear Belgian competition. The Belgian producers had traditionally held a a powerful position in the market in the north of France. They undoubtedly were technologically well in advance of their rivals and geographically they were well placed to tap the French market. From the French point of view the agreement was essentially defensive and without it, particularly after trade liberalization, the incursion of the Belgians would almost certainly have been even greater. From other points of view the Technical Commission also envisaged an uneven struggle—if the powerful semi-monopolistic Union de Porphyre was given a free hand it could dominate a wider market; the Technical Commission did not say how but presumably its financial resources and size would enable it to discriminate very effectively. The Commission also seemed to feel that a spate of competition would lead to the Belgian group taking over French enterprises and that this would mean even less competition than already existed.

But the motive which really led the Commission to decide not to recommend any substantial change in the *status quo* was the fact that it felt that any action on its part would not necessarily be paralleled by action on the part of the Belgian authorities. Reference has already been made to the fact that the Belgian producers enjoyed the advantage of special rail freight rates. The Commission also indicated that there were other features of the situation over which it had no control. It hinted darkly that the provision of materials for public authorities in Belgium had in the past been regulated in a way which indicated that, if a competitive solution were to be adopted, those French quarries which were well placed to tap the Belgian market would in fact find their sales outlet limited.[61] It also indicated that the transport of French materials into Belgium would take place under discriminatory conditions. In fact the Technical Commission felt that free competition would

have the likely effect, while doing away with the Belgian clientele for French producers, of yielding part of the national (i.e. French) market to foreign products, under the benefit of restrictive practices and discriminatory measures which are illegal both in French law and under the Treaty of Rome.

The French Secretary of State therefore excused himself from making a decision on two grounds. First, Regulation 17 had been promulgated—this he said took the power to exempt away from the national authorities. (This was true, although it did not take

[61] Whether the Commission was referring to the entrenched position of the Belgian group, which would enable it to exclude outside competition or whether it was referring to a preference for Belgian supplies on the part of the public authorities is not clear.

away the power to prohibit.) Secondly, he maintained that a solution could only be found on the Community plane—that is by a body which could ensure some equality of action.[62] This case raises a number of interesting points. Above all it illustrates the wisdom of creating a body, such as the Common Market Commission, endowed with supranational anti-trust powers. Without such a body action in respect of international cartels would be minimal. One member state is unlikely to take action independently of another. The state which is likely to lose, in this case the French, is likely to prefer inaction, whereas the Belgians, because of their geographical position and technical efficiency, should to that extent be allowed increasingly to penetrate the French market. The second point is that this case illustrates the unity of competition policy—that is to say that ultimately a rational competition policy must embrace not only the familiar problems of anti-trust but also distortions arising in transport policy and possibly in government procurement policy.

4. THE DECISIONS OF THE COMMISSION AND THE JUDGMENTS OF THE COURT OF JUSTICE UNDER THE ROME TREATY

Before proceeding to discuss the actual anti-trust Decisions, an outline of the action taken by the Commission is presented in Table 5 (p. 167). This indicates that in January 1966 the Commission was in process of instituting 55 procedures in connexion with various types of cartel agreements—in addition it had since 31 August 1964 concluded procedures in six cases.[63] The table shows the procedures broken down by industry. On the right of the table is shown the channel through which the procedures were instituted. In connexion with the latter it should be emphasized that, in addition to notifications, applications, and complaints, a growing body of procedures arise from *ex-officio* actions by the Commission. It should also be noted that the fact

[62] See Commission Technique des Ententes, *Rapport . . . 1960, 1961 et 1962*, pp. 14–16.
[63] These were the Grundig–Consten, the Dutch Engineers and Contractors, the DRU–Blondel and the Hummel–Isbecque agreements. Agreements were also terminated in the chemical-pharmaceutical and construction sectors. Some procedures were terminated before August 1964, see the discussion of cases below and *Bull. EEC*, no. 9/10, 1964, p. 31.

TABLE 5

Cartel Procedures of the EEC Commission–August 1964–January 1966

Branch of industry	Procedures in progress at 31.8.64	Procedures initiated since 31.8.64	Procedures concluded since 31.8.64	Procedures in progress Jan. 1966	Channels through which procedures were instituted		
					Notifications & applications	Complaints	Cases taken up ex-officio
Chemicals & pharmaceuticals	6	–	1	5	11	1	–
Fertilizers	6	1	–	7	20	13	–
Plastics & rubber	2	2	–	2	6	1	–
Electronic equipment	5	3	1	6	26	5	1
Precision instruments, optics	4	1	–	4	13	4	–
Domestic articles & appliances, non-electric	1	1	1	1	1	1	–
Motor vehicles	2	–	1	1	2	–	–
Machine tools & other machines	1	1	–	2	8	–	–
Metal products, tools, & mechanical accessories	1	2	–	1	14	2	–
Building materials	3	2	–	4	14	–	–
Beverages	2	2	–	4	13	6	–
Textiles	3	–	–	3	2	2	–
Services	4	1	–	5	15	1	–
Commerce	2	1	–	2	17	1	–
Leather goods, shoes	1	–	–	1	1	–	–
Paper, cardboard, graphic arts	5	1	–	5	12	1	–
Furniture, toys	1	–	–	1	1	–	–
Construction	2	–	2	1	6	–	–

Source: Bull. EEC., no. 6, June 1965, p. 15; no. 11, Nov. 1965, pp. 10–11; no. 1, 1966, pp. 9–10.

that only 55 procedures were in process in January 1966 underestimates the amount of anti-trust activity then being undertaken. These were formal actions but in fact on 31 March 1966 the Commission was reported as being involved in 606 '*affaires*'.[64] The difference between the two figures arises almost wholly from the fact that at any moment in time the Commission will be investigating particular cases to see whether action is called for as well as being engaged in formal actions.

(a) Sole or Exclusive Selling Contracts.

This type of agreement has already been touched upon in our discussion of cartel types and again in our account of the work of the BKA. So far however we have not analysed in any detail the nature of sole or exclusive agency contracts, and as a result we have not yet indicated the ambiguity of the term from the point of view of EEC anti-trust policy. As we indicated earlier the term refers to a situation in which, for example, a manufacturer appoints a sole seller and agrees to supply his goods in a particular territory to that seller only. The seller might additionally or alternatively agree to purchase and supply only the manufacturer's goods in that territory. The seller may be one who merely acts on behalf of his principal (the manufacturer), enters into contracts on his behalf, and is subject to his instructions. In this sense he is not an independent trader and may properly be called an agent. On the other hand, there are sole sellers, to distinguish them they are sometimes called sole distributors, who are independent traders who trade and resell for their own account. The view of the EEC Commission is that the former type of arrangement does not fall within the purview of Article 85 (1)—whereas the second does. In practice these two types are only two of many varieties, and it was necessary for the Commission to draw a line of distinction based on economic criteria between the arrangements which are and which are not relevant to Article 85 (1). In order to assist enterprises in deciding where they stand, the Commission in 1962 issued its *Announcement on Exclusive Agency Contracts Made With Commercial Agents*.[65] The Announcement indicated that the characteristic of the agent not covered by Article 85 (1) was that

---

[64] EEC, *9th Gen. Rep.* (1966) (French mimeo), p. 54.
[65] See *Board of Trade J.*, 11 Jan. 1963, p. 121.

he should neither undertake nor engage in activities proper to an independent trader in the course of commercial operations. The Commission regards as the decisive criterion, which distinguishes the commercial agent from the independent trader, the agreement—express or implied—which deals with responsibility for the financial risks bound up with the sale or with the performance of the contract. Thus the Commission's assessment is not governed by the way the 'representative' is described. Except for the usual *del credere* guarantee, a commercial agent must not, by the nature of his functions, assume any risk resulting from the transaction. If he does assume such risks his function becomes economically akin to that of an independent trader and he must therefore be treated as such for the purposes of the rules of competition.

The Commission considered that an independent trader was most likely to be involved where the contracting party 'is required to keep or does in fact keep, as his own property, a considerable stock of the products covered by the contract', or 'is required to organise, maintain or ensure at his own expense a substantial service to customers free of charge, or does in fact organise, maintain or ensure such a service', or 'can determine or does in fact determine prices or terms of business'.

The Commission takes the view that sole or exclusive agency contracts with commercial agents, as opposed to independent traders, do not fulfil the conditions for a prohibition under Article 85 (1) since they do not have as their object the prevention, restriction, or distortion of competition in the Common Market. The commercial agent merely performs the auxiliary function of seeking customers on behalf of the other party to the contract (that is, the manufacturer) who himself does the selling. In effect the Commission appears to be arguing that the agent is really an extension of the manufacturing firm and as such it would be unreasonable to regard the arrangement as akin to a restrictive agreement freely entered into between independent enterprises. The Announcement, however, indicated that, in the case of contracts with independent traders, the possibility that Article 85 (1) could be applicable could not be ruled out. Here there was, for example, a limitation of supply where the vendor undertook to supply the product to one purchaser only for resale. Whether the restriction would be liable to affect inter-state trade would depend upon the circumstances of the case.

It now remains to consider the approach of the Commission

and Court of Justice to sole distributorships—that is where an independent trader is involved.[66] In 1962 the Court had an opportunity to indicate the legal position when it considered the Bosch case. The facts of the case were as follows. Van Rijn, a Dutch company, had been granted the sole and exclusive right by Bosch, a German company, to import the latter's products into the Netherlands. Moreover Bosch, in order to safeguard the exclusive selling right of Van Rijn, made an agreement with all purchasers of its products that those products should not be exported, directly or indirectly, to foreign countries. In 1959 and 1960 a Dutch importer, de Geus, imported Bosch refrigerators into the Netherlands—the latter having been bought from Bosch's distributors in Germany (who had agreed not to be involved in any such transaction). Bosch and Van Rijn therefore brought an action against de Geus in the Court of Rotterdam seeking both to restrain de Geus and to exact damages. De Geus claimed that the exclusive contract in question was void by virtue of Article 85 (2) but the Rotterdam Court rejected this contention. De Geus appealed to the Court of Appeal at The Hague which held that since this was a question of interpreting the Rome Treaty it should be referred to the Court of Justice of the European Communities. Unfortunately the judgment of the latter[67] proved to be something of a damp squib since, whatever light it may have thrown on other areas of uncertainty, it confined itself to a statement to the effect that it was not impossible that export prohibitions of the type in question fell within the definition contained in Article 85 (1) and in particular within the wording 'agreements . . . likely to affect adversely trade between Member States'.

In 1964, however, the Commission took an important step on the road to building up Community case law in this field by prohibiting the Grundig–Consten sole distribution agreement—this was the first time it had exercised its power of formal prohibition. The background to this case is dissimilar to that just described. Grundig had appointed the Consten company of Paris sole distributor of Grundig receivers, recorders, dictating

[66] It is probably worth reminding the reader at this point that such contracts are notifiable, that the simple variety are notifiable on a special form B1, and that the Commission has the power to exempt whole classes of exclusive agency contracts.

[67] Cour de Justice des Communautés Européennes, *Recueil de la Jurisprudence de la Cour*, viii (1962), pp. 115–42.

machines, and television equipment in France and, in addition—
and this was to prove of the highest importance—Grundig had
granted Consten absolute territorial protection by imposing an
export ban on all its dealers in other countries. In addition,
Grundig and Consten had signed a supplementary agreement
covering the use of a special trade mark 'Gint' in France, the
purpose of which was also to hinder the importation by firms
other than Consten of Grundig products. Consten for its part
undertook not to deal in the same or similar goods of other
manufacturers. It transpired that a rival firm, UNEF of Paris,
managed to obtain Grundig products from German wholesalers,
to import them into France, and resell at more favourable prices
than those asked by Consten. Several traders in the Consten
chain complained about the activities of UNEF. By 1961 UNEF
was responsible for about 10 per cent of Grundig sales in France.
Consten sought to uphold its claim to exclusive distributorship
by taking action against UNEF in the Paris Court of Appeal
on the grounds of unfair competition. The French Court,
however, reserved judgment pending a Decision by the EEC
Commission on the compatibility of this type of arrangement
with Article 85 of the Rome Treaty.[68]

The Commission in its reasoned prohibitory Decision[69]
observed that the result of the agreement was a considerable
difference in the prices of the agreement goods in Germany and
France—a difference which could not be explained solely by
reference to customs duties or fiscal disparities. In 1962 the
actual catalogue price (less 'discounts') of a particular type
of Grundig recorder was 23 per cent higher in France than
Germany—after deduction of customs duties and taxes the
difference was 44 per cent. The Commission was also able to
show that since Grundig's ex-works prices were the same to
German wholesalers as to Consten, and since retail margins were
in absolute terms the same in both countries, the major part of the
difference in prices was to be ascribed to differences in the
margins of the wholesaler, that is, Consten's stage of the
distributive chain.

---

[68] OECD, *Ann. Rep. Restrictive Business Practices* (1965), p. 41.
[69] Decision by the Commission of 23 Sept. 1964 concerning procedure
under Article 85 of the Treaty (IV-A/00004–03344 'Grundig–Consten')—
JO, 20 Oct. 1964.

The Commission first maintained that the arrangement restricted competition, since the sole distributorship, coupled with the absolute territorial protection given by the export ban, effectively placed Consten in a monopoly position at its stage in the distribution process. In the words of the Commission: 'Competition at the distribution stage, in particular between wholesalers distributing articles of the same brand, is therefore especially important. That conclusion is all the more valid as distribution costs account for a considerable part of the total cost.'[70] Secondly, the Commission maintained that the agreement was liable to affect trade between the member states. It pointed out that the agreement prevented firms in France other than Consten from importing Grundig's products: 'The importance of that prevention is shown by the steps, both legal and extra-legal, undertaken by Consten and Grundig against the parallel importers and exporters, particularly against UNEF and their suppliers.'[71] As a consequence the integration of national markets into a common market was impeded if not prevented— an effect clearly shown by the differences in prices, particularly between France and Germany. Also the agreement concerning the registration of the trade mark 'Gint' was conducive to the isolation of the national markets. It had been contended that the agreement did not affect inter-state trade since, during its currency, Franco-German trade in Grundig products had increased considerably. The Commission rejected this contention; and the actual words used are worth quoting, as they indicate how the Commission construes the meaning of the treaty on this subject.

However, no weight can be given to that objection, since, for the implementation of Article 85 paragraph 1, it is enough for a restriction of competition within the meaning of Article 85 paragraph 1 to cause trade between Member States to develop under other conditions than it would have done without that restriction and for its influence on market conditions to be of some importance.[72]

The agreement having fulfilled the conditions for prohibition, the question then arose as to whether the benefits of Article 85 (3) could be accorded. The Commission was prepared to concede

---

[70] *JO*, 20 Oct. 1964, p. 5.   [71] Ibid.   [72] Ibid.

as a hypothesis that the agreement contributed to the improvement in the production or distribution of goods—its willingness to accept this proposition was based not upon its self-evident truth but upon the fact that it felt that it would be able to prove that the other conditions of Article 85 (3), which were indispensable for an exemption to be accorded, were not fulfilled. In the first place it was necessary that the agreement should allow consumers a fair share of the resulting profit. The Commission argued that this condition was not fulfilled, basing its case upon the fact that the difference in prices between France and Germany indicated a lack of competition in the former at the level at which Consten operated. This prevented the beneficial effects of competition in the form of reduced margins from being passed on to consumers. It was true that competition had not been entirely frustrated, due to UNEF, but it was still insufficient.

But the main reason why exemption could not be granted lay in the fact that Article 85 (3) required that the restrictions imposed be no more than necessary to secure the improvement in production or distribution. In the view of the Commission the absolute territorial protection was not necessary to secure the advantages claimed for it.

Grundig and Consten claimed that the sole distribution system was an indispensable distributional device. The Commission replied that it did not see why all the supposed advantages of employing a sole distributor and conducting exports through him could not be enjoyed without the addition of absolute territorial protection. The reason why, in the case in question, the sole distributor had been circumvented was that Consten's margin was too high, and this had created a profitable opening for imports by third parties. If Consten's margins were the same as those of wholesalers in Germany, no trader in France would find it worth while tackling the difficulties involved in importing. The Commission was really arguing that provided margins were comparable as between Consten and the German wholesalers, trade would flow into France through the sole distributor. (If the margins deviated significantly, competitive activities of enterprises such as UNEF would tend to bring them into line.)

Grundig and Consten argued in defence of sole distributorships that they enabled the distributor to make forecasts which allowed the producer to adapt his production to demand. The Commission countered by saying that absolute territorial protection was not a necessary condition for such a function to be performed. It pointed out that German wholesalers who did not have absolute territorial protection were not apparently impeded in their forecasting. It must be presumed that the Commission had factual evidence on this point. The Commission also argued that if absolute territorial protection were to be abolished and supplies were to enter France through German wholesalers, then this type of sale would be included in the German wholesalers' forecasts.

Grundig and Consten also referred to the importance of the guarantee and after-sales service which the sole distributor provided and which, if not provided adequately, would lead to a fall in sales. The implication of this argument would appear to be that other unofficial importers would neglect to provide these services, and, therefore, damage the reputation of the goods, and would rely upon Consten's services instead of providing their own. The Commission's reply was that guarantee services were the responsibility of the supplier, so other suppliers could not load it on to Consten. In any case if absolute territorial protection were abolished and other enterprises began to import, then Grundig could assist them to provide the guarantee service. As for after-sales service, there was no reason to believe that other suppliers would not provide it—competition would force them to do so. Since in any case customers had to bear the cost of such after-sales service, even if they approached Consten to provide it, this was not an unprofitable proposition. In any case the relevance of the costs of a guarantee and after-sales service were easily exaggerated—they accounted for only 1·18 per cent of Consten's turnover in 1963.

The argument was advanced that parallel imports would reduce the sole distributor's margin to such an extent that he would not be able to cover the publicity costs which he is normally required to bear. This was rejected by pointing out that such an argument tended to exaggerate the size of the publicity cost borne by Consten—it was 1·9 per cent of the latter's turnover in 1963.

Finally, as it had been shown that the agreement failed to satisfy the condition that it be no more restrictive than necessary to secure the alleged improvement of production and distribution, the Commission therefore did not consider itself called upon to consider whether the agreement made it possible to eliminate competition in respect of a substantial part of the product in question.

This Decision provoked Grundig and Consten to appeal to the Court of Justice. In this they were joined by the German and Italian governments. The Commission for its part enjoyed the support of UNEF and another company—Leissner. In July 1966 the Court delivered its verdict, which can be described as a triumph for the Commission. The Court upheld the latter's Decision—the only reverse the Commission suffered was the quashing of the original Decision in so far as it applied to the whole of the agreement rather than to the offending clauses. Parenthetically it should be added that the Court's judgment must have come as a considerable relief to the Commission, because the Advocate-General, in his summing up, had come out in favour of Grundig and Consten. The familiar Italian plea that Article 85 only applies to horizontal agreements was once again dismissed by the Court. The plaintiffs claimed, and in this they were joined by the German government, that the Commission had not shown that, in the absence of the agreement, inter-state trade would have been greater. The Commission countered by arguing that the stipulations of Article 85 (1) were met if such trade took place under conditions other than those which would exist in the absence of the agreement. In the Court's view the crux of the matter was whether the agreement was liable to threaten, directly or indirectly, actually or potentially, the freedom of trade in a way which impeded the attainment of a single market. It felt that the re-export prohibition patently did constitute such an impediment and therefore the plea failed.[73]

What then are the implications of the Commission's Decision in the Grundig–Consten case? It certainly does not undermine the position of all sole distribution agreements. The fact which brought the downfall of this particular arrangement was its inclusion of measures designed to give absolute territorial protection which could not be justified as being necessary to secure the advantages held to flow from the sole-concessionaire agreement.

[73] EEC Official Spokesman, Doc. P-44, July 1966.

The fact that sole-concessionaire agreements without territorial protection are likely to be accorded more favourable treatment is illustrated by the Commission's judgments in two recent cases—these are the Diepenbrock and Riegers–Blondel[74] and Hummel–Isbecque[75] exclusive-dealing agreements. In the first agreement Diepenbrock and Riegers N.V. ('DRU') of Ulft, Netherlands, a producer of household equipment in enamelled iron, granted Établissements Blondel SA of Paris sole selling rights for these products in France. The Commission's view was that the agreement had as its object the restriction of competition in the sense of Article 85 (1) and it was liable to affect inter-state trade. The Commission maintained that a restriction existed in that only Blondel could obtain supplies directly, other importers being denied this privilege. The economic significance of this type of arrangement was as follows. The Commission recognized that there was competition at the production stage in respect of the goods covered by the agreement, but it implied that in France, at the distribution stage in question, this agreement would create a monopoly if territorial protection was also conferred. Given the differentiation of products and the preference built up for DRU goods, Blondel would enjoy a significant degree of market power and could as a result raise the price of DRU goods above those charged by other sole distributors of similar household goods.[76] However, the fact that in this case territorial protection had not been conferred meant that parallel imports were possible, which would prevent Blondel from being able to exert any significant degree of market power. Indeed, the Commission observed that in practice prices in France and the Netherlands were not dissimilar, and Blondel had in fact reduced its commercial margin.

The Commission considered that an exemption under Article 85 (3) was applicable—this being the first case of an exemption being accorded by the Commission.[77] The basis of its Decision

[74] Decision by the Commission of 8 July 1965, concerning procedure under Art. 85 of the Treaty (IV/A–03036 DRU–Blondel), *JO*, 17 July 1965.

[75] Decision by the Commission of 17 September 1965 concerning procedure under Art. 85 of the Treaty (IV/A–02702 Hummel–Isbecque), ibid. 23 Sept. 1965.

[76] If the goods sold by sole distributors were homogeneous the danger from territorial protection would seem to be less.

[77] This was retroactively granted and would extend forward for five years.

was that exclusive selling improves the distribution of goods—a view which is highly significant. The Commission argues that sole distribution makes exporting easier than would be the case if the exporters had to have a multiplicity of contracts with traders, and the concentration of sales enables the manufacturer to obtain a better overall view of market developments.

In addition, the Commission argued that consumers would be given an equitable share in the benefits resulting from such an improvement in distribution because French consumers could obtain goods quickly and easily through a firm enjoying sole selling rights. Furthermore the restrictions involved were no more than necessary to secure the advantages, and the elimination-of-competition aspect of Article 85 (3) was covered by the fact that there was no territorial protection and DRU goods competed with those of other manufacturers on the French market.

The Hummel–Isbecque arrangement was broadly similar— Ludwig Hummel of Heitersheim (Baden) produced tractors and appointed the Belgian firm of Edmond Isbecque of Brussels sole selling rights in Belgium, but gave no undertaking to prevent indirect deliveries into the Belgian market. Again, the Decision held that the agreement fell within the ban on cartels but could nevertheless be approved. The agreement was favourably viewed because, unlike the Grundig–Consten arrangement, it did not contain clauses such as export bans which separated off the markets of member states. This in itself constitutes a condition making it less harmful rather than a positive reason for conferring exemption. The Commission's grant of exemption was actually based upon the fact that sole selling improved distribution—the argument being the same as that employed in the case of the Diepenbrock–Blondel agreement. Also Isbecque performed a valuable function in the selling process. According to a Commission statement:

Isbecque arranges to demonstrate and service the technically complex and relatively expensive products which it imports from Hummel, and keeps a stock of spare parts. As the accessories manufactured by Hummel are not all suitable for soil and working conditions in Belgium, Isbecque has suitable accessories made, in particular ploughs, cultivators and harrows.[78]

[78] EEC Official Spokesman, Doc. IQ (65) 161, 23 Sept. 1965.

These particular functions carried out by Isbecque, particularly the latter, were probably regarded by the Commission as assisting the penetration of the Belgian market by the German firm, and as such the sole distributorship was a reasonable reward or inducement to concede to Isbecque. In 1966 the Commission also exempted a somewhat similar but reciprocal exclusive-dealing agreement in the protective footwear trade.[79]

Just prior to the Grundig–Consten judgment the Court of Justice delivered a ruling on a sole-distribution agreement between the German firm Maschinenbau Ulm and the French firm Société Technique Minière. The importance of the case arises from the interpretation given to Article 85 (1), but it is convenient to discuss it here because the background to the case forms the subject-matter of this section. The agreement, which concerned grading machines, did not involve territorial protection—the French firm could sell to concession holders in other member states or import from them. The case arose because the French firm broke a contract to take a specific quantity of the machines. The commercial court (Tribunal de Commerce) of the Seine found that Technique Minière had defaulted, and it was this that provoked the latter to appeal against the judgment on the grounds that the contract was null and void by virtue of Article 85.

In dealing with this matter the Paris Court of Appeal encountered a number of difficult legal points and it turned to the Court of Justice for a preliminary ruling on the position of exclusive-dealing agreements, without absolute territorial protection, in relation to Article 85. The EEC Commission was inevitably involved, and the interest of the case resides in what the Commission pleaded and how far the Court was prepared to go in accepting its pleadings. The Commission maintained that a sole-distribution agreement was a restraint of competition of the kind referred to in Article 85 (1), in that there was a limitation upon the freedom of action of one or more parties. The producer agrees to sell to one concessionaire only. The concessionaire may agree to buy from that producer only. Dealers can get supplies from only one concessionaire. The Commission agreed that the

---

[79] Decision by the Commission of 17 Dec. 1965 concerning procedure under Article 85 of the Treaty (IV), A-22491 'Maison Jallatte SA–Hans Voss KG', in *JO*, 6 Jan. 1966.

restriction had to be a 'perceptible' one—in this case it was up to the Paris Court to decide whether there really was a perceptible restriction. Also the Commission agreed that some effect on trade must be present—the effect should be of 'some importance'.

The reply of the Court of Justice was in effect this. The Commission was saying that in the case of sole-distribution agreements of the kind in question there was a presumption of illegality. But in the Court's view no category of agreements as determined by its legal character is automatically banned by Article 85 (1). Only individual agreements, by virtue of the specific *de facto* economic situation, or as a result of clauses in the agreement, can be said to be inconsistent with the Common Market.[80]

The Commission appears to have been trying to obtain the approval of the Court to a sweeping interpretation of Article 85 (1) to the effect that all agreements of the kind in question are automatically restrictive. At the risk of some exaggeration it may not be unfair to say that the Commission was looking for a block ban to complement its block exemption powers. That the Commission, had it been successful, would have been generous in according exemption is not in doubt—the cases above indicate this. But the freedom of action given to the Commission would have been considerable—it could then concentrate its attention on the problem of according exemption, safe in the knowledge that this type of agreement was universally restrictive. What the Court did was to tilt the balance the other way. There is no automatic presumption of illegality—the onus is on the Commission to prove it in each case.

In order to stress the need for individual treatment, the Court observed that under certain circumstances a sole-distribution agreement might be necessary to enable a firm to penetrate a new market. Thus this type of agreement might be seen as aiding rather than frustrating the creation of a single market. This judgment must be regarded as something of a reversal for the Commission in that it makes the prohibition of agreements more burdensome.

(b) Other Distribution Agreements

At this point it is convenient to discuss two other distribution

[80] EEC Official Spokesman, Doc. P-40, July 1966.

agreements—the first between a US enterprise, Bendix, and a
Belgian distributor, Anciens Établissements Martens et Straet,
covering the distribution of brakes, servo-brakes, and accessories
produced by the former. Bendix granted the distribution
concession to Mertens and Straet but defined no sales territory,
reserving the rights to appoint other distributors in Belgium and
to sell directly. The agreement did not prohibit Martens and
Straet from selling products made by Bendix's competitors. The
Commission observed that the treaty was applicable to all
agreements which restricted competition and affected inter-
state trade. Even if one of the parties to the agreement, in this
case the firm granting the concession, lay outside the Common
Market, Article 85 still applied because the agreement produced
effects within the Common Market. However, on examination
the Commission granted a negative clearance.[81] It maintained
that the provisions of the agreement did not prevent, restrict,
or distort competition since Bendix had not undertaken to
reserve the supply of products in question to Martens and
Straet. Bendix reserved the right to appoint other suppliers in
Belgium or to supply that market itself. In other words, Martens
and Straet were not sole distributors, still less were they given
absolute territorial protection—because of this the Commission
declared that it had no grounds to intervene in the arrangement.

The other agreement was between the French limited company Grosfilex, which produces household and hygienic pro-
ducts in artificial textiles, and the Swiss firm Établissements
Fillistorf of Zürich. The latter was authorized to distribute the
Grosfilex products in Switzerland only. Fillistorf agreed not to
make or sell any articles which might compete with the Grosfilex products. Grosfilex also undertook to sell only through
Fillistorf and to prevent sales by third parties in Switzerland.
The Commission granted this agreement a negative clearance.
The basis of this Decision was as follows. Fillistorf's sole
distribution and the territorial protection afforded to it, together
with its agreement not to produce or sell competing items, did
involve a restriction of competition, but this was in Switzerland
and not within the Common Market as required by Article 85 (1).

[81] Decision by the Commission of 1 June 1964 on an application for negative
clearance submitted in accordance with Article 2 of Regulation no. 17 (IV-A/12,
868) in *JO*, 10 June 1964.

However, since the agreement did prohibit Fillistorf from selling Grosfilex goods in the Common Market, a restriction of competition in the EEC within the meaning of Article 85 (1) might exist. The Commission, however, decided that since Grosfilex goods entering the EEC from Switzerland would have to bear the relevant customs duty, this would prevent them from entering anyway, particularly as there was no reason to believe that Grossfilex's prices on the Swiss market were any lower than those quoted on the Common Market.[82]

(c) Collective Exclusive Dealing.

The Pottery Convention is one of the most interesting Recommendations (the only one at the time of writing) in this field and the one about which most information is available. It will be remembered from our previous account of it that this was an arrangement between Belgian dealers in, and layers of, wall and floor tiles, and tile manufacturers in Belgium, the Netherlands, and Germany. Basically the manufacturers could only deliver to approved customers party to the agreement, and the latter were not to purchase goods from outside manufacturers. New trade associations of dealers and layers could only join by the unanimous consent of existing members, and new manufacturers could only join by unanimous consent of the manufacturers already party to the agreement.

The Commission had started *ex-officio* proceedings before Regulation 17 came into force. Subsequently, the members of the cartel requested the Commission to grant a negative clearance, but, wisely realizing that this request might be dismissed, also notified the cartel with a view to obtaining an exemption. In its Recommendation to the cartel the Commission declared that it was unable to say that there were no grounds for it to intervene. On the contrary, the conditions necessary for Article 85 (1) to be applicable clearly existed, and, furthermore, the conditions necessary for an exemption under Article 85 (3) were not fulfilled.[83]

The Commission's approach was first to establish the existence

---

[82] Decision by the Commission of 11 March 1964 on an application for negative clearance submitted in accordance with Article 2 of Regulation No. 17 made by the Council (IV/A-00061) (64/233/CEE), ibid. Apr. 9 1964.

[83] *Bull. EEC*, no. 5, May 1964, Annexe II.

of a restriction within the meaning of Article 85 (1). It alleged that the agreement excluded approved customers from outside sources of supply. If a dealer wished to acquire goods produced by a manufacturer party to the agreement it was necessary to seek the status of an approved customer. Once he became such an approved customer, he was forced to buy exclusively from agreement manufacturers, and even consumers having goods processed by an approved customer were forced to confine their choice to the products of agreement manufacturers. The Commission also observed that if a dealer or layer applied for membership of the Pottery Convention he had no appeal if his request was refused (or if, having become an approved customer he was subsequently thrown out). General contractors and independent dealers and layers who were both outside the agreement were inevitably restricted in their source of supply. They were in fact cut off from direct contact with 29 important suppliers: 4 in Belgium, 24 in other Common Market countries, and 1 in the UK. Inevitably the agreement also restricted manufacturers outside the agreement since these were barred from selling to approved customers. Basically their competition was impeded since the agreement split the Belgian market into two self-contained parts—agreement manufacturers had the approved customers reserved for themselves, while outside manufacturers were confined to selling to independent dealers and layers and general contractors.

The representative of the cartel put the point to the Commission that manufacturers outside the cartel could join the convention, but the Commission retorted that such an admission would need unanimous approval by the manufacturers party to the agreement—the implication being that there was no guarantee that the approval would necessarily be forthcoming. In any case it was quite unreasonable to expect manufacturers who wished to sell freely in the Belgian market to have to conform to the requirements of such an agreement before being allowed to do so. The Commission also observed that if all outside manufacturers did join the cartel, the independent dealers (and layers) and general contractors would have their ability to import entirely taken away.

The existence of the restrictions having been proved, the existence of an effect on inter-state trade was easily demonstrated.

Manufacturers in EEC states other than Belgium who were not party to the agreement were barred from dealing with the Belgian dealers and layers party to the agreement.

In order to benefit from Article 85 (3) the agreement had to be such as to improve the production or distribution of goods or to promote technical or economic progress. The Commission therefore considered the agreement under this head. One of the aims of the agreement was to further the satisfactory processing of products in order to prevent a decline in sales. The Commission observed, however, that at most the agreement could only incidentally achieve this end. The agreement did not go far towards establishing the professional qualifications of approved customers: 'the agreement contains no clauses which could directly and decisively promote the correct processing of the goods in question, such as requirements relating to the occupational qualifications of the workers or technical provisions on the treatment of the products'.[84] Nor did it prevent processing by unskilled hands since approved dealers could sell the products to any willing buyer without supervising the use to which they were put. Moreover general contractors were outside the agreement, and their position in the building industry argued that they were not necessarily incapable of handling the products properly.

Another aim of the agreement was to improve the distribution and sale of the products, but the Commission could find no evidence of the alleged special-sales network having been set up. It could not be pretended that sales were made easier just because the manufacturer received lists of regular purchasers—any producer could have such a list compiled at a moderate price.

The cartel representative also maintained that distribution had been improved because the agreement had banned the indiscriminate selling by manufacturers which had led to faulty processing and, therefore, to a decline in the use of the products. The Commission responded by pointing out that the agreement did not make it more probable that the product would be processed by skilled workers. Nor was there any sign of a decline in the use of the product—between 1957 and 1960 the use of the product in building had run parallel with the use of other more important building materials.

It was also argued by the representative of the cartel that the

[84] *Bull. EEC*, no. 5, May 1964, Annexe II, p. 50.

7*

obligation on approved dealers to maintain a minimum stock helped to improve distribution. But at this point the Commission indicated that there was no reason to pursue the analysis any further. Even if the Commission accepted the proposition that the agreement improved distribution or contributed to technical or economic progress by promoting correct processing, and even if a fair share of the benefit was passed on to consumers, yet exemption could not be accorded because the agreement imposed upon manufacturers and approved dealers restrictions which were not indispensable to these aims. The reciprocal exclusive-dealing clauses were not necessary to attain these ends. Thus, for example, if a minimum stock was vital, it would be up to the manufacturer to encourage a minimum stockholding by supplying only those dealers who kept such a stock. It was not clear why the obligation of approved dealers to buy only from agreement manufacturers was indispensable for the maintenance of minimum stocks. In the opinion of the Commission all the objects of the agreement could be attained without forbidding approved dealers from buying or processing the products of non-member manufacturers—and the same applied to the member manufacturers' obligation to supply only approved dealers: 'For these purposes it would be sufficient for member manufacturers to sell only to customers who possess certain qualifications and satisfy certain objective requirements, such as the maintenance of a minimum stock.'[85]

The Commission therefore refused exemption, recommending the cartel members to remove from the agreement the obligation on approved customers to buy only the products of cartel manufacturers and the obligation on cartel manufacturers to supply the agreement goods only to approved dealers. If this were done the Commission would be prepared to consider the agreement under Article 7 of Regulation 17.[86] Subsequently the parties to the Pottery Convention amended their agreement and submitted it

[85] *Bull. EEC*, no. 5, May 1964, Annexe II, p. 52.

[86] i.e. 'Where agreements, decisions and concerted practices already in existence when the present Regulation comes into force, and of which the Commission has been notified before August 1, 1962, do not meet the requirements of Article 85 (3) of the Treaty, and where the undertakings and associations of undertakings concerned put an end to them or modify them so that they are no longer prohibited by Article 85 (1) or so that they then meet the requirements of Article 85 (3) the prohibition laid down in Article 85 (1) shall apply only for a period fixed by the Commission.'

to the Commission, asking for a grant of a negative clearance.[87] This case has not yet been concluded.

In 1965 the Commission also dealt with two other exclusive-dealing arrangements—one covering water heaters, the other sand and gravel. The details of both these agreements have been presented in the previous chapter and we shall not repeat them here. In the case of the water-heater agreement the Commission informed the parties to it that the agreement notified to it fell under the ban of Article 85 (1) and did not qualify for exemption under Article 85 (3). As a result of the Commission's communication the parties to the agreement then lost the protection from fines enjoyed by virtue of notification.[88] In the case of the sand and gravel arrangement, the Commission issued a similar communication to the one above and similar legal consequences followed. The enterprises subsequently informed the Commission that they had either dissolved the restrictions or changed relevant clauses. This meant that the provisions for collective exclusive sales or purchase of the products concerned, the provisions on area protection and market sharing, the restrictions on the utilization of vehicles, and the rules on agreed prices had all been withdrawn.[89]

(d) Market Sharing

The market-sharing agreement between Dutch and Belgian enterprises concerning the detergent 'Savon Noir', whereby each was forbidden to sell their products directly or indirectly on the domestic market of the other, was also in 1965 declared prohibited, exemption not being warranted. As a result the firms dissolved the agreement.[90]

(e) Quota Agreements

In 1965 the Commission also declared that the quota agreement between four Belgian enterprises, one German one, and one Dutch one selling silica in the Dutch market, did not warrant exemption. Likewise, two other ancillary restrictions, one requiring four sales agents to deal only with the above suppliers (except

---

[87] Notice pursuant to Article 19 (3) of Regulation no. 17 (1) concerning notification no. IV/A-00010 (64/290/CEE), *JO*, 5 June 1964.
[88] EEC Official Spokesman, Doc. IP (65) 136, 9 July 1965.
[89] EEC Official Spokesman, Doc. IP (65) 65, 1 April 1965.
[90] EEC Official Spokesman, Doc. (65) 148, 26 July 1965.

in exceptional circumstances) and the other involving the fixing of a common price by the agents, were also refused exemption. After this declaration by the Commission immunity from fines was terminated.[91]

In 1966 EEC anti-trust policy took a significant step forward when the Commission made public its findings on a major cartel involving fifty-three cement-producing enterprises. The notified agreement involved the application of quotas in supplying the Dutch market, but was buttressed by agreements respecting uniform prices and sales conditions and consultations prior to the establishment of a new plant in the territory of parties to the agreement. The Commission has declared that the agreement falls under the ban of Article 85 (1), as it is prejudicial to trade in cement and cement clinker between the Netherlands and Belgium and Germany and as it restricts competition in the Dutch market. The Commission has found no grounds for exemption and as a result the continuance of the agreement could lead to fines being imposed.[92] Subsequently the parties to the agreement appealed to the Court of Justice for an annulment of the Communication. The Court upheld the appeal although this was on procedural grounds and did not legalize the cartel.

(f) *Export Cartels*

The Commission has so far only issued one Decision in this field—this concerned the Dutch Engineers' and Contractors' Association which dealt with civil engineering contracts outside the Common Market and the French Associated Territories (the rules of competition apply to the latter). The contractors party to the agreement formed a pool for contracts worth more than 2 million florins, and decided who was to tender, how the work was to be carried out, and how it was to be distributed. The existence of a restriction of competition seems self-evident, but it is not a restriction of competition within the Common Market, and since the Commission was not aware that this co-operation had any effects on competition there, it felt obliged to declare that it had no cause to intervene.[93]

[91] EEC Official Spokesman, Doc. IP (65) 170, 5 Oct. 1965.
[92] EEC Official Spokesman, Doc. IP (66) 10, 24 Jan. 1966.
[93] Decision by the Commission of 22 Oct. 1964, on an application for negative clearance submitted in accordance with Article 2 of Regulation No. 17 made by Council (IV/A–00071), *JO*, 31 Oct. 1965.

(g) Trade Marks and Patents

The first case in this field examined by the Commission concerned the sales in 1961 by the French enterprise Nicholas Frères of the brand name Vitapointe, together with patents, trade marks and designs, to the British firm Vitapro, for use in countries outside the Common Market (Nicholas had acquired the Vitapointe business). The sale was contingent upon two conditions being observed. First, that Vitapro would not for a period of five years manufacture or sell its own hairdressing products in the Common Market. Secondly, without time-limit, it would not use the trade mark Vitapointe in the Common Market. The Commission granted the agreement negative clearance. In respect of the first condition the Commission observed that the agreement not to compete would expire in 1966, and in any case the ban did not apply to products which the British firm purchased from third parties or which it produced and sold under licence from third parties. With respect to the second point, the division of rights in respect of the trade mark was such that the Common Market was not divided into zones, and the absence of an independent British competitor selling under the name Vitapointe would not substantially affect competition, in view of the fact that there were a large number of other independent sellers of this type of product and Nicholas was not amongst the largest of them.[94]

(h) Rebate Cartels

In January 1966 the Commission revealed that a rebate agreement between all the rubber and plastics manufacturers in one member state, which had been notified to it, fell under the ban of Article 85 (1) and could not be exempted. The essence of the agreement was that, in computing the collective rebate allowed to dealers established in the state in question, only purchases from the parties to the agreement were taken into account. The Commission held that this arrangement, which appears to be similar to those discussed in Chapter 6, artificially protected the national market from outside offers. The Commision also took into account the fact that as between the parties to the agreement there was no

[94] Decision by the Commission of 30 July 1964 on an application for negative clearance submitted in accordance with Article 2 of Regulation 17 made by the Council (IV/A 00095) (64/502/CEE), *JO*, 26 Aug. 1964.

competition in respect of prices or other terms of sale. A final decision was to be made after the enterprises had had an opportunity to express their opinion on the Commission's findings.[95]

(i) Common Resale Prices

In January 1966 the Commission also announced that it was engaged in a case concerning the sale of both home-produced and imported pesticides in one member state. The main clause of the agreement involved the fixing of identical resale prices for home-produced and imported products and the application of uniform terms of sale. In addition, the agreement provided for collective boycott of dealers who did not observe the general terms of sale. The Commission found that the agreement substantially reduced the sales openings for supplies from other member states and that it therefore fell under the ban of Article 85 (1). The case came to the attention of the Commission by means of a complaint and, since the agreement had not been notified, exemption could not be considered until notification had taken place.[96]

5. THE COMMISSION'S INFORMAL PROCEDURES

The preceding discussion has for the most part been concerned with the formal procedure of issuing Decisions and Communications. But in addition the Commission relies on informal negotiation, and on occasions this is sufficient to secure either the total abandonment of an agreement or the suppression of offending clauses. This is a feature of the Commission's work which tends to be neglected because little information is made available about the cases concerned. Nevertheless it is an aspect of EEC cartel policy which needs to be taken account of in any balanced assessment.

During the year ending June 1966 the Commission obtained satisfaction in eight cases. One dealt with restrictions arising in connexion with patent licensing. The case arose out of a complaint by a French plastics manufacturer against two of its Common Market competitors—one French and one German. They had exchanged licences in respect of these patents together with the right to grant sub-licences. Such licences, however, were only to be granted if the sub-licensees bought from the licensers

[95] *Bull. EEC*, no. 1, Jan. 1966.   [96] Ibid. pp. 10–11.

certain non-patented products used in the patented process. If certain other products were purchased from the licenser the licence fee was waived, but if not, it had to be paid. The effect of all this was to force or induce sub-licensees to obtain supplies from the licensers, and to this extent the market was foreclosed to other producers. The complainant, presumably following the Commission's patent-licensing Announcement of 1962, objected that the obligation to obtain from the licensers non-patented products which were not essential to the technically-perfect exploitation of the patent monopoly was in fact an unwarranted extension of that monopoly. However, before the Commission could issue an adverse Decision, the two firms announced, in 1966, that they had abandoned the clauses complained of.[97]

Two of the cases concerned price fixing. One involved four German manufacturers of industrial plant who notified each other of all foreign inquiries and drew up a table of export prices involving a minimum-price agreement. The other related to an agreement in the paper industry which involved quotas for the Dutch market and a mutual respecting of domestic price levels. Another agreement involved a Swiss machine manufacturer who required absolute territorial protection in his sole-selling contracts. Yet another agreement related to the granting of trade secrets in the production of paint and incorporated an export prohibition. The final three agreements involved common sales organizations; one was between two French manufacturers of spare parts for cars, another concerned firms involved in the production of nuclear plant, and the third related to four manufacturers of medicines for export.[98]

6. A PROVISIONAL APPRAISAL

Any attempt at this stage to consider the impact of Article 85 must take the form of a tentative interim assessment. Too little time has elapsed since Regulation 17 was promulgated and there are too few cases upon which to base any firm judgment.

Article 85 itself must be judged to be reasonably rigorous. It

[97] EEC, Official Spokesman, Doc. IP (66) 10, 24 Jan. 1966.
[98] The source for all these cases (except that relating to patent licensing) is EEC, *9th Gen. Rep.* (1966, mimeo. French), p. 59. Earlier examples of informal procedures leading to termination of agreements are to be found for example, in *Bull. EEC*, no. 9/10, 1964, p. 31; no. 11, 1965, p. 11; no. 1, 1966, p. 10.

prohibits *a priori*, although it provides the possibility of exemption. Those who admire the *per se* approach will find this latter aspect disappointing. However, this is not the point at which to develop a lengthy discussion of the relative merits of the *per se* approach as opposed to that which provides for 'good trusts'. It seems to us that although the *per se* approach is sometimes highly regarded because of its patent rigour, economically speaking it is questionable whether it is logical. There clearly seem to be situations in which exemption can be beneficially accorded— for example specialization or standardization agreements which can increase productivity but which do not significantly lessen the degree of competition. It seems reasonable, if we accept Scitovsky's view that West European productivity is low because of, among other things, excessive product differentiation, that such agreements may have much to commend them. It has of course been argued that one advantage of the *per se* rule is that it obviates the need for anti-trust bodies to make extremely complex economic judgments which involve forecasting the effect of, for example, abrogating an agreement. This point has been made in respect of the UK Restrictive Practices Act where a court of law has the task of implementing cartel policy. The problem of assessment in the UK is made more difficult by the fact that there are seven separate 'gateways' involving consideration of the effects of agreements on various economic phenomena such as employment and exports. In the EEC there is basically only one gateway (although it is fairly broad). This at least limits the range of issues to be considered and therefore makes the task of assessment easier. Furthermore the initial administrative procedure of the EEC avoids too much reliance being placed upon the opinion of judges, who may have little expertise in economic matters.

The conditions which must be satisfied in order to gain exemption are quite rigorous, when considered together. An agreement must improve production or distribution or further technical or economic progress. But the interest of consumers is taken into account—they must have a fair share of the profit. The agreement must be no more restrictive than necessary and must not allow the elimination of competition in respect of a substantial part of the products in question. This is a fairly rigorous test and, as we have tried to indicate by discussing at length the stage-by-stage reasoning of the Commission in cases such as the Pottery Convention and the Grundig–Consten agreement, the Commission demands that all these conditions shall be satisfied. The Commission appears to apply a rigorous standard in judging cartels and the impression which emerges is that cartels will not find exemption easily come by.

How adequate is the machinery of enforcement provided by Regulation 17? The centralizing of the power to exempt and grant negative clearance in the hands of the Commission is undoubtedly a prime feature of that Regulation. Had this power been divided between the Commission and the national authorities—still worse had it been left in the hands of the latter—the consequences would in all probability have been disastrous. Not only would there have been conflicting decisions, which would have discredited the idea of a Common Market, but there would have been a temptation for national authorities either to take a lenient view of, or cast a blind eye in the direction of, their own cartels—particularly ones which could, for example, exploit consumers in other member states and improve the balance of payments. It is our very clear impression that anti-trust powers are most likely to foster the process of economic integration when they are vested in a body with supranational power which can decide cases on the basis of the requirements of the integration process rather than particular national interests.

The centralizing of the power to exempt does cut down the chances of conflicting decisions, but it is probably worth noting that it does not rule them out entirely. P. Verloren van Themaat has pointed out[99] that unequal treatment of agreements could arise if a national authority forbade an agreement upheld by the Commission. This is no great threat at the moment and probably never will be, but if it was it would point to the need for harmonization of national legislation.

The enforcement process is likely to be somewhat weakened by the absence of national cartel bodies in Italy and Luxembourg. The usefulness of such bodies has already been illustrated by the passing to the EEC Commission of information about international arrangements which has emerged in the course of national anti-trust actions.

[99] 'The Antitrust Policy of the European Economic Community', *ICLQ*, Suppl. Publ. no. 6 (1963), p. 24.

Progress in dealing with the cartel problem has been slow and at the time of writing only just over a dozen Decisions and Communications have emanated from the Commission directly during the four years which have elapsed since Regulation 17 was promulgated. (We should not of course ignore informal procedures.) The reasons for the delay are fourfold. The first is the sheer volume of notifications which the Commission has had to sort out. Secondly, the Council of Ministers has not been willing to make extra staff available in the numbers required by the Commission. Apparently all the governments have in some degree been responsible for this situation. Thirdly, the Commission has had to tread cautiously. Its initial Decisions have had to be formulated with great care because they constitute precedents for the future, and in addition a reversal by the Court of Justice could be damaging. It is at first sight a little surprising that the Commission has chosen to spend so much of its time in dealing with various forms of distribution agreement—all the early Decisions dealt with this topic. The question naturally arises, has the Commission misallocated its time and scarce resources? Would it have been better to concentrate on cartels which suppress inter-state competition completely rather than those which merely limit competition at the dealer stage? Might it have been better to have suspended notification of distribution agreements until much later? It is difficult to answer these questions, but it seems likely that however desirable it may have been to delay consideration of distribution agreements, events may have forced the Commission to adopt its present course. The Commission was bound to consider the possibility that sole distribution agreements, broadly defined, could offend against Article 85. Once it was generally known in business circles that this possibility existed, it was natural that businessmen (and the Commission) should wish to have some speedy decisions in a field which affects so much of inter-state trade. It also seems likely that cases pending in the courts forced the Commission to reach decisions quickly. But the main reason why so little has been heard about the major cartels is quite simply that the length of time that it takes to prepare a case and reach a Decision on a full-scale horizontal cartel is much greater than in the case of a distribution agreement.

There is, however, hope that more rapid progress will now be made. In the first place the examination of important horizontal cartels is now nearing completion and Decisions on them may be expected to start appearing in the near future. Secondly, the Commission has made up its mind about a number of different types of distribution arrangement and the block exemption power should enable it to clear many of the bilateral agreements away, thus making room for an attack on other types of restrictive business practice.

In conclusion it is worth noting that the mere existence of Article 85 is likely to assist in generating more competition. The fact that agreements which are contrary to that article cannot be enforced in a court is of considerable significance. A firm which wishes to break out of an agreement, or wishes to circumvent an agreement to which it is not a party, can now do so if it knows or expects that the agreement cannot be enforced. We have already seen in the Dutch–Belgian cartel relating to cardboard tubes and in those of De Geus–Van Rijn and Grundig–Consten that some firms want to break loose from restrictive agreements and others want to make inroads into monopolistic positions supported by the law. This fact must encourage the Commission in its attempts to create a greater degree of competition. Clearly it is the task of the Commission to clear the way for such independent spirits and potential competitors. In this respect its task may be easier than that which faced the High Authority in dealing with GEORG. It would certainly be a great mistake to assume, as some have done,[100] that the failure of the High Authority in that particular instance was an omen for the future of the EEC.

There are three final observations which we wish to make. Firstly, it is to be hoped that, as provided in Regulation 17, the Commission will issue periodic reports on its cartel policy, and that these will not be confined to generalities but will give in detail the reasoning and facts behind its findings in particular cases. Although the Commission may not wish for its Decisions to be appealed against to the Court of Justice, commentators would derive much benefit from this—particularly if it occurred in the case of a major cartel—since the Court's proceedings are published. Secondly, experience has shown that the

---

[100] W. Pickles, *Not With Europe: the Political Case for Staying Out* (1962), p. 18.

abandonment of formal price agreements can give rise to information agreements[101] in which there is no explicit agreement about prices but only an agreement to make information available. Again the banning of a formal division of markets could be followed by a mutual respecting of territories. In such circumstances it would prove difficult, if not impossible, to persuade entrepreneurs to make sorties into each other's territories if they were convinced that life would be more pleasant if they kept out of each other's way. Thirdly, however, when more cartel agreements have been dealt with, the possibility of empirically testing the effectiveness of EEC anti-trust policy, by observing the course of trade and prices, will present itself. It should then be possible to decide whether formal cartels are in fact being replaced by other devices and, if so, how policy should be adapted to deal with that situation.

[101] For an analysis of the economic impact of information agreements see D. P. O'Brien and D. Swann, 'Information Agreements—A Problem in Search of a Policy', *The Manchester School*, Sept. 1966, pp. 285–306 and a forthcoming article by the same authors entitled 'Information Agreements: A Further Contribution', ibid.

8

Concentration and Market Domination

I. THE GENERAL ATTITUDES OF THE TREATIES

A BRIEF comparison between the main principles of anti-trust in the US and the Communities, shows the general nature of the latter in a revealing light.

Since the days of the Sherman Act it has been customary to divide anti-trust problems into two main categories—those arising from various types of agreements between otherwise independent enterprises, and those arising from the practices of individual enterprises that are in themselves large enough to exercise considerable economic power. This is the general distinction that we are following here. As opposed to the comparatively straightforward principle of *per se* prohibition embodied in both parts of the Sherman Act, however, the approach followed in the Community is selective. As we have seen, the policy with regard to cartels in both the ECSC and EEC, while it is based upon a prohibition principle (that is, it involves an initial presumption against them), simultaneously assumes that they may be beneficial in certain circumstances. In other words, in its endeavours to promote economic and technical progress, the Community has been quite prepared to accept some diminution of competition. This is in marked contrast to the approach in American law which, because it does not involve any assumption that cartels can ever have any beneficial effects, does not burden either judges or administrators with the awkward (some would say impossible) task of weighing the relative advantages of maintaining competition or promoting technical progress or some other desirable goals.

There is, however, a definite similarity between the American approach to mergers and that adopted in the ECSC to concentrations. Both systems attack mergers that substantially reduce competition without allowing the question of their effects on technical efficiency to be so much as raised. This is in remarkable contrast with the approach of the Rome Treaty which embodies a highly permissive attitude to mergers and contents itself merely with a prohibition of the abuse of market power.

Thus, American anti-trust is reasonably consistent towards both cartels and unified monopolies: broadly speaking, the former are regarded as bad and unnecessary, the latter as bad but on occasions perhaps inevitable. The ECSC and EEC, on the other hand, adopt much milder but mutually consistent approaches to cartels in the sense that both make provision on broadly similar lines for exempting some cartels from the general prohibition, but have very different emphases in their policies towards concentrations of economic power.

Why should there be this marked difference of emphasis as between ECSC and EEC in this branch of anti-trust? Very broadly the answer is that those who were most responsible for the Paris Treaty were obsessed by the dangers of economic power and constructed an elaborate apparatus to deal with the problem. (Article 66 dealing with concentrations is the longest in the whole treaty.) It is particularly important to realize that at the time the treaty was being negotiated the US was an occupying power in West Germany. American influence on the drafting of the treaty was therefore bound to be considerable. In particular the US policy of trust busting, not only at home but in Western Germany, was reflected in the content of Article 66. But by the time the Rome Treaty was signed the opposite fear was beginning to be felt: that the scale of European business was too small to take full advantage of the large market being created. The path to concentration was therefore left almost entirely clear. An additional reason might also have been that by the time that the Rome Treaty was negotiated, the opinions of German industry could no longer be ignored.

Which approach was right? Were both right in the circumstances? What is 'right' in this context? In other words, do the policies of the ECSC and EEC present a satisfactory compromise between principle and feasibility in this branch of anti-trust? And do the aims of anti-trust conflict with other important goals—technical progress for example?

2. THE EXPERIENCE OF ECSC

The concentration provisions of the ECSC were worked out economically as an integral part of a régime intended to foster competitive market conduct, and, more significantly, as a political means for ensuring the continuation of a measure of supranational control over the Ruhr. As Article 66 was designed to serve an important political purpose as well as an economic one, it is not surprising to find that its provisions are detailed and far-reaching.

(a) Responsibilities and Powers of the High Authority

The fundamental task of the High Authority in this field is to prevent any further concentration in the coal or steel markets that could significantly reduce competition in them. Concentration in this context includes mainly mergers, take-overs, and acquisition of majority holdings. It is well known that German industries, especially coal and steel, were highly concentrated in pre-war years, and that these concentrations were not without influence on the course of political events in that country. After the war, Allied deconcentration measures broke up a number of the leading firms into smaller independent units. Thus whereas in 1937 the Vereinigte Stahlwerke group produced 40 per cent of German (Reich) crude steel output, the largest successor enterprise of the former VS complex, August Thyssen Hütte, accounted for only about 10 per cent of German (Federal) output after deconcentration. This was the kind of situation that the High Authority inherited when it began to take up its responsibilities in 1953 and which it was expected to preserve in substance by the application of Article 66.

To help the High Authority in this task, coal and steel enterprises are required to obtain its prior approval before entering into any form of concentration. The High Authority has laid down what kind of transaction it regards as constituting control of an enterprise. It may be noted that besides the usual category of amalgamations, mergers, acquisitions of shareholdings, and so forth, the term concentration is now held to cover the case of joint enterprises—that is, where two or more enterprises, although not in any way organically linked to each other, contribute jointly to the establishment of a third enterprise. In such case each of the joint owners is considered to be concentrated with the joint enterprise for the purpose of Article 66. To avoid wasting time with insignificant cases the High Authority has established a minimum size of transaction below which authorization is not required. On the other hand, to minimize the risk of significant concentrations occurring secretly, for example by the gradual acquisition of shares through nominees over a period, the High Authority is empowered to obtain information on matters that appear to have a bearing on concentrations. Apart from concentrations occurring within the coal and steel industries themselves, these provisions also apply to concentrations between coal and steel enterprises and between such firms and those outside the coal and steel sectors—although in the latter case the High Authority is obliged to consult with the government concerned before coming to any decision. In all cases authorization might be made subject to specific conditions.

If an authorizable concentration occurs without in fact having been authorized, then the High Authority will impose a fine upon the enterprise concerned. If this is not paid, then the concentration becomes illegal. If a non-authorizable concentration occurs, then the High Authority can order divestiture and, if necessary, safeguard the interests of competing enterprises, presumably by fixing prices and delivery terms for the concentration.

It is, of course, possible that a concentration of economic power can occur other than as a result of ordinary mergers and the like. The two most important ways in which this might happen would be by nationalization or by the growth of a firm as a result of markedly superior efficiency. These possibilities appear to have been considered only at a rather late stage in the evolution of the Paris Treaty, in spite of the fact that the Charbonnages de France and its associated monopoly for importing coal into France, ATIC, had already been in existence for some time. Nationalization, being a major political act, does not require authorization by the High Authority, and a position of market power achieved as a result of superior efficiency can hardly be held of itself to be in any way blameworthy. None the less nationalized industries or large dominant private firms might resort to practices that are in themselves objectionable. The treaty therefore gives the High Authority power to control the conduct of market-dominating enterprises in the event of an abuse of market power.

(b) The Criteria for Authorization

Having been notified of a proposed concentration, the High Authority is required by the treaty to allow it to proceed provided that certain effects will *not* result. These negative criteria are that the concentration will not have power in the field of ECSC products:

to influence prices, to control or restrain production or marketing, or to impair the maintenance of effective competition in a substantial part of the market for such products; or

to evade the rules of competition resulting from the application of the present Treaty, particularly by establishing an artificially privileged position involving a material advantage in access to supply or markets.[1]

The first condition is largely aimed at preventing the emergence by the process of horizontal integration of any enterprise large enough to have a decisive influence on the markets in which it operates—we discuss subsequently some of the ways in which such an influence could be exerted in practice. If this occurred the prospects for competitive pricing would be greatly reduced. The second condition recognizes that under certain circumstances the survival or success of a coal or steel enterprise may be affected by its relationship with raw-material suppliers or markets. For example, in a period of coal shortage such as prevailed for many years after the war, steel producers found vertical integration with coal mines an important method of ensuring regularity of supplies. In such circumstances the technical efficiency of the steel producer might count for less than his proprietary link with the coalmine. This could lead to a maldistribution of resources if other more efficient steel producers were prevented from expanding for lack of coal supplies.

The criteria for authorization, therefore, amount to assessing the effects of a proposed merger on competition. On the other hand it is not necessary for the enterprises proposing to merge to demonstrate that the concentration will have any beneficial effects either for themselves or for the rest of the economy. This would appear to follow from the absence in Article 66 of any

[1] *Paris Treaty*, Art. 66 (2).

clause comparable to the technical 'gateway' established for cartels under Article 65 (2). But one of the main aims of the ECSC as laid down in Article 2 is the improvement of productivity, and for this basic reason the High Authority must at least take a general interest in the technical effects of a proposed merger. It would seem, however, that the only circumstance in which these considerations can be given any weight—and then not very much—is when an element of doubt exists under the negative criteria, and the High Authority must therefore exercise discretion. In all cases, to avoid any possibility of discrimination, and to the extent that it is necessary 'to avoid or correct the disadvantages resulting from an inequality in the conditions of competition', the High Authority is required to take the size of similar existing enterprises into account before ruling upon a proposed concentration.

Concentrations divide naturally into two main categories. First, there are horizontal integrations, for example the merger of two coalmining enterprises or two steel producers. Secondly, there are vertical integrations such as the acquisition by a steel producer of a coal or iron-ore mine or a merchanting or manufacturing enterprise (the former cases would be backward integration from the point of view of the steel producer, the latter forward integration). To some extent, of course, the two categories inevitably overlap, as, for example, when a steel producer that is already part of a vertical concentration merges with another steel producer, or perhaps when a joint enterprise is established.

Some idea of how active the High Authority has been in the field of concentrations may be gained from Table 1, which analyses the total number of concentrations that have been authorized from 1952 through 1964.

In this table mixed cases have been grouped under what seemed the most important heading for the particular transaction concerned. The table also subdivides horizontal and vertical concentrations according to the detailed nature of the individual concentration concerned.

For the first five years of the Community's existence most practical applications of Article 66 related to concentrations brought about by vertical integration, as German enterprises attempted to re-establish some of the links that had formerly

TABLE I

Analysis of Concentrations Authorized, 1952 through 1964

Horizontal			
Coal/coal	Steel/steel	Steel/special steel	Mcht/mcht
5	16	4	3

Vertical						
Steel/ coal	Steel/ ore	Steel/ scrap	Steel/ mfg	Steel/ mcht	Coal/ mcht	Mcht/ mfg
8	1	3	27	11	3	1

Sources: ECSC, 12th Gen. Rep. (1964), pp. 196–202; and 13th Gen. Rep. (1965), pp. 186–99 (German).

brought coal and iron mining, steel production, and engineering under unified control in one *Konzern*. This first series of mergers does not appear to have raised any major problems in the field of competition policy, as in no cases did the enterprises involved gain a sufficiently great advantage in access to supplies or markets to give them an artificially privileged position *vis-à-vis* other enterprises in the Community. The Decisions of the High Authority allowing all these concentrations to proceed were supported by the Market Committee of the Common Assembly and by the Common Assembly itself.[2] But since 1958 requests for authorization under Article 66 have raised difficult problems relating to both vertical and horizontal concentrations, and German enterprises have again been the ones mainly involved.

In the following sections we consider some examples of the problems that have confronted the High Authority in dealing with this latter series of more controversial concentrations,

(c) Vertical Concentrations

The first application for the authorization of a vertical concentration that raised difficulties was the request by August Thyssen Hütte (ATH) to take over the important steel merchanting enterprise Handelsunion. As the latter was the sales outlet for

[2] Richard A. Hamburger, 'Coal and Steel Community: Rules for a Competitive Market and their Applications', in J. P. Miller, ed., *Competition, Cartels, and their Regulation* (1962), p. 376.

a number of steel producers, especially ATH itself and Dort-mund-Hörder-Hüttenunion and its subsidiary Hüttenwerke Siegerland, the acquisition of Handelsunion by ATH would have left Dortmund with no alternative selling arrangements, or rather, would have put its selling arrangements in the hands of a competitor. This would inevitably have restricted competition either by jeopardizing the sales outlets available to Dortmund or by influencing the decisions of the latter in a way favourable to ATH. The latter possibility of restriction was probably remote, as Dortmund was itself a subsidiary of the nationalized Dutch steel producer Hoogovens, and presumably would not, therefore, acquiesce willingly in any situation in which it was forced to play a minor role. The High Authority therefore only allowed ATH to take over Handelsunion as part of a wider rearrangement of steel merchanting as a result of which Dortmund acquired control of another merchant firm, Establech, and undertook to scale down its sales through Handelsunion to a level comparable to the usual rate for German producers selling through indepen-dent dealers. The independence of ATH and Dortmund thus brought about was further enforced by the requirements that ATH should dispose of its minority holding in Siegerland, a subsidiary of Dortmund. An interesting feature of the arrange-ments was that ATH was also required, as the new controlling interest in Handelsunion, to be responsible for the implementa-tion of the arrangements in so far as they affected that company, that is, mainly the scaling down of deliveries from Dortmund in the agreed manner.[3]

(d) Horizontal Concentrations

One of the most important purposes of the Community's policy on concentrations is to prevent the growth by any form of amalgamation of enterprises large enough to dominate the

[3] A further important aspect of this concentration between ATH and Handelsunion was the fact that ATH was simultaneously proposing to increase its shareholding in Stahlwerke Rasselstein to 50 per cent, the merchanting firm of Otto Wolff holding the remaining 50 per cent. ATH was allowed to increase its shareholding in Rasselstein only on condition that this holding did not exceed 50 per cent and that Otto Wolff should continue as before to market all Rasselstein production, this to minimize the risk of any joint type of action between ATH and Otto Wolff (ECSC, *10th Gen. Rep.* (1962), pp. 212–14). This type of problem is discussed more fully in a later section of this chapter dealing with Joint Ventures.

markets in which they operate. Market domination would occur when a firm, by being responsible for a significant proportion of total supply in the market, could, by adjusting the quantity that it supplies, have a significant influence upon the price of all supplies in the market. Alternatively, it could imply a situation of price leadership, which would in practice probably also be based upon much the same type of concentrated industrial structure. If this situation arises, then prices tend to be determined fundamentally by the policy of the dominant enterprise rather than by neutral market forces. In such cases prices will probably be higher than they would have been under a competitive régime, will tend to be inflexible, profits and/or costs are likely to be higher, and excess capacity more in evidence. Many economists would cite the experience of the US steel industry to show that these fears are by no means unjustified. The policy of the High Authority in this field is therefore to prevent firms growing relative to other firms by the process of amalgamation to such an extent that they become dominant in the sense that they can influence prices in either of the ways described above. The basic problem involved in assessing the effects of a proposed horizontal concentration is, therefore, to ascertain whether it would achieve a degree of size that would result in market domination. To do this it is necessary to be able to measure size, and—the kernel of the problem—to demarcate the economic area—the 'relevant market'—within which the concentration would operate and in relation to which its own size ought, therefore, to be judged. There is no completely precise way of doing this, but it is possible to approach the problem from a number of directions that together reduce much of the dubiety inherent in the situation. Fortunately, in many cases that the Community has had to contend with, the possibility of market domination could be dismissed by any reasonable quantitative standard. But a few cases, especially some very recent ones, have revealed the underlying problems in a particularly acute form.

The simplest way of assessing the relative size of any concentration would be to express its production of crude steel as a percentage of total Community crude steel production. By this standard one could say, for example, that the important Cockerill/Ougrée-Marihaye merger in Belgium in 1955 covered a mere 4 per cent of Community production. Judged in this way this merger could not possibly have been regarded as market dominating. But in 1955 and, to an appreciable extent, even now, the national markets have far from lost their individual identities, and, considered in relation to Belgian production alone, the merger involved about 34 per cent of production. Could the possibility of a significant influence upon price in the Belgian market be completely ignored? If the Belgian market was in fact the relevant market rather than the Community market, then in accepting a 34 per cent share as compatible with competition, the High Authority has shown itself distinctly more generous than the US Supreme Court which recently ruled: 'Without attempting to specify the smallest market share which would still be considered to threaten undue concentration, we are clear that 30 per cent presents that threat'.[4]

Clearly the boundaries of the national markets and the boundaries of the Common Market represent two quite different standards, and both are in principle equally unreliable as guides to a delineation of the relevant market in the geographical sense that is required for the purpose of Article 66. Furthermore production of crude steel is of doubtful relevance as crude steel does not itself appear in the market: here the appropriate data would really have to relate to output of particular products. Geographically, the relevant market is that area in which most of the products of the concentration are sold, and it is quite likely to include parts of several member states. In spite of the obvious importance of transport costs for goods such as steel, it is also likely to be a widening geographical area as the more effective interpenetration of markets and the necessity to spread the increasing fixed costs of large new capital schemes will both work to widen the horizons of the individual firm. Indeed, in the not too distant future the geographically relevant market may well correspond more closely with the boundaries of the Common Market itself, as larger and larger plants are brought into operation. Having identified this geographical area for any particular proposed concentration, the next problem is then to decide whether other enterprises sell a sufficient volume of output in this area to constitute genuine competition. It is at this stage that there arises the classical problem in this branch of anti-trust: defining the relevant market by product. To analyse

[4] *United States* v. *Philadelphia National Bank*, 374 US 321 (1963).

this side of the problem it is necessary to bear in mind that competition can occur not only between the firms constituting the industry, but also between these firms and producers in other industries that make largely similar products. Defining the relevant market by product involves ascertaining where there is a marked discontinuity in the chain of substitution, that is where the cross-elasticity of demand between the product made by the concentration and the production of other enterprises, perhaps in other industries, becomes very low. It will be recalled that in the *Cellophane Case* in the US, Du Pont's control over a large part of cellophane production was held not to constitute market domination in view of the considerable competition existing between cellophane and other flexible packaging materials over which Du Pont had no control.[5]

It would seem that the High Authority has now abandoned the excessively simplified approach that it apparently adopted in relation to the Cockerill/Ougrée merger. In certain recent cases it seems to have made considerable endeavours to assess the question of dominance in the sophisticated way that is required by the complexity of the problem. This can be seen from the way in which it finally dealt with one particularly important horizontal merger, that between August Thyssen Hütte and Phoenix-Rheinrohr, and how it has analysed the problems posed by the creation of joint enterprises.

(i) *The ATH-Phoenix-Rheinrohr Case.* The ATH-Phoenix case has come to occupy a unique position as a *cause célèbre* in the history of the ECSC's anti-trust policy. ATH first requested authorization of its plan to obtain control of Phoenix-Rheinrohr in 1958. This would have brought about 6 million tons of crude steel capacity under unified control and constituted by far the largest enterprise in the Community. In its examination of this request, the High Authority appears to have concluded that, while market domination would not occur, there would, however, have been inevitably a marked hardening of a market structure that was already highly oligopolistic. This was regarded as undesirable and authorization was therefore made subject to the acceptance of certain conditions. These related mainly to the elimination of

United States v. E. I. Du Pont de Nemours and Company, 1956.

certain proprietary and supply connexions between the concentrated enterprise and other firms—this with the obvious intention of preserving the complete independence of the competitors outside the concentration. These conditions were acceptable to ATH. But a further condition—that the High Authority should control the investments of the new group to prevent it acquiring dominant market power in the future—was unacceptable and caused ATH to withdraw its request in 1960.

It had, of course, been widely known for a long time that these two successors of the former Vereinigte Stahlwerke complex were already closely connected by personal links, the octogenarian Frau Thyssen, the widow of Fritz Thyssen, holding 52 per cent of the capital of Phoenix-Rheinrohr, and her two daughters holding together about 40 per cent of the capital of ATH. It could reasonably be assumed that on the death of Frau Thyssen her holding in Phoenix-Rheinrohr would be inherited by her daughters and that a high degree of proprietary concentration between ATH and Phoenix-Rheinrohr would be brought about automatically by this inheritance. If this had occurred and the High Authority had still maintained its unacceptable condition for the authorization of the concentration, the possibility of divestiture would have had to be considered. Such a divestiture, the first in the ECSC, would probably have been bitterly contested in national courts and in the Community's Court of Justice, and a victory for the High Authority would simply have unloaded further politically embarrassing steel assets on to the German market alongside those of the Krupp Rheinhausen Steelworks that had for so long proved unsaleable. It was even conceivable that potential purchasers of the assets, if any could be found, might include some highly inappropriate names—other steel firms, for example.

This daunting complex of possibilities was, however, conveniently avoided when ATH submitted a second request for authorization in 1962. This time the High Authority was able to authorize the concentration without imposing unacceptable conditions, and it was finally settled in 1963.

Why was the authorization granted at the second request? There are probably two main reasons (apart from the probability that the High Authority was anxious to get itself off the hook). The first is that by 1962 the High Authority had already authorized one other concentration[6] that was not dissimilar in size to the ATH-Phoenix complex and had become aware that Italsider's expansion plans would result in that enterprise too achieving major proportions. In accordance with the general principle of non-discrimination, which is also given a specific connotation in Article 66, the High Authority was therefore compelled to judge the ATH-Phoenix case in the light of these new events. The second reason was that the High Authority appeared to have had second thoughts about the wisdom of the controversial condition that had prevented the concentration going through on the first occasion—the condition that the group's expansion projects be made the subject of a High Authority veto. This would certainly seem to be the most reasonable construction to place upon the High Authority's answer to a question on this subject raised in the European Parliament. In 1960 the High Authority had stated that it was 'of the opinion that control over investments does not constitute, in principle, a condition which is appropriate to the objectives laid down in Article 66'.[7]

Apart from reversing the position on investment controls as a technique of anti-trust taken in the ATH-Phoenix case, this view would appear to cast doubts upon an earlier decision by the High Authority concerning Krupp's acquisition of the Bochumer Verein. In this case the High Authority had taken the view that affiliation with Krupps would give the Bochumer Verein access to such considerable sources of finance that its growth might threaten market domination. Although the *Seventh General Report* simply remarked cryptically that the High Authority would 'keep a special check on all capital schemes embarked upon in future in the steel sector by the enterprises in question',[8] it is clear that this could only be a meaningful exercise if it implied the possibility of actual control by the High Authority.

In finally authorizing the ATH-Phoenix concentration in 1963, the High Authority distinguished between the markets for finished rolled products, except flat products, on the one hand and those for flat products on the other. Inspection of the delivery statistics of the enterprises led the High Authority to regard the

---

[6] This was the joint venture SIDMAR (see below, pp. 209–11).
[7] *JO*, 27 July 1960.   [8] ECSC, *7th Gen. Rep.* (1959), p. 159.
8

German national market as the relevant market in the first case and the northern industrial triangle (defined for statistical simplification as the Common Market minus Italy) as the relevant market in the second case.[9] The High Authority took the view that in each case there were sufficient independent enterprises competing in the same markets to constitute an effective check on the new concentration, provided that no connexions were allowed to exist that might reduce the independence of the concentration and its competitors. To ensure this independence the High Authority therefore authorized the concentration on two conditions. First, it required that an existing long-term delivery contract between one of the enterprises in the concentration and an enterprise belonging to another group should be reduced in tonnage terms and limited in duration. Secondly, no interlocking directorates were to be permitted between the ATH-Phoenix group and any other enterprise engaged in the production or marketing of steel.[10]

(ii) *Joint Ventures*. Joint ventures—the establishment of new enterprises with capital provided by several existing ones—have recently been responsible not only for some of the most important developments in the ECSC steel industry, but also for the emergence of a new range of problems in the field of concentration policy. Substantially similar problems are also posed by the joint control of an existing enterprise by two or more other ones. Indeed, as we have seen, it was in connexion with the joint control of an existing enterprise that this new range of problems was first posed. This occurred in 1961 when ATH increased its shareholding in Stahlwerke Rasselstein to 50 per cent and thereby became in some degree connected with the Otto Wolff group.[11] In this case the High Authority had had to consider whether this relationship between ATH and Otto Wolff, based upon their joint ownership of Stahlwerke Rasselstein, would lead indirectly to a diminution of competition between the two groups. The High Authority authorized this concentration only on condition that the existing arrangements under which Otto Wolff distri-

---

[9] 'Die Politik der Hohen Behörde bei Kartellen und Zusammenschlüssen', *Bull. ECSC*, no. 47, 1964, p. 37.
[10] ECSC, *12th Gen. Rep.* (1964), p. 183.
[11] See above, n.3.

buted all Rasselstein's production should be maintained. In other words, ATH's increased participation in Rasselstein was only acceptable as long as it remained comparatively passive. Whether competition between the two groups was in fact maintained by this device is not so doubtful as whether there was very much competition between them in the first place—indeed it would not be altogether surprising if further links were established between the two groups in the future. If the relationship between these two groups is rather ambivalent at the present time, it becomes all the more important that the really effective competition provided by other national groups and, even more, by enterprises from the other member states, should not be jeopardized. It is primarily for this type of reason—the maintenance of effective competition between independent groups— that the High Authority's treatment of the anti-trust problems raised by certain joint ventures is of considerable significance for competition policy. The questions involved in such cases are best considered by referring to two of the leading cases, those of the Sidérurgie Maritime (SIDMAR) and Société Mosellane de Sidérurgie (SOMOSID).

(iii) *SIDMAR*. In 1962 the High Authority authorized the joint foundation of SIDMAR by the following important enterprises: Cockerill-Ougrée, Forges de la Providence, Société Générale de Belgique, Compagnie Financière et Industrielle (Belgium); ARBED (Luxembourg); Schneider & Cie, Société Métallurgique de Knutange, Société Minière de Droitaumont-Bruville (France).

The size of the new concentration (which is in fact one of the most important parts of a scheme to revitalize Ghent as a port) may be judged from the following facts. Port facilities have been provided to handle ore carriers of up to 60,000 tons, and ore-preparation plants have been completed on a corresponding scale. The main part of the plant consists of two large-capacity blast furnaces, three LD oxygen steelworks, a slabbing mill, a continuous hot-strip-rolling mill, and a tandem cold-rolling mill. In the early stages annual output was expected to be about 1·5 million tons, but this was scheduled to grow in a few years to over 6 million tons. The whole complex is a major integrated works that will make 'a noticeable difference to the position as regards flat products, particularly hot-rolled wide strip and cold-reduced sheet'.[12]

What were the implications of this joint venture under Article 66? First, the High Authority decided that a concentration existed in the sense that each participant in the new firm would to some degree be concentrated with it, although this in no way necessarily implied concentration between the participants themselves. But when, as in this case, the participating enterprises produced the same type of products as the joint enterprise, it would be reasonable to assume that in taking important decisions concerning, for example, the prices to be charged by the latter, they would simultaneously take into account their own price policies, and that the price policies thus followed by each of the promoters would, therefore, be far from independent. For competition purposes the joint enterprise and its promoters could be regarded as an almost homogeneous economic group and the question therefore arose as to whether that group would dominate the market. The relevant geographical market for flats suggested by the likely sales territories of such a large integrated concern in that location was taken to be the northern industrial triangle of the Community consisting of the Ruhr, the Netherlands, Belgium, Northern France, Lorraine, the Saar, and Luxembourg. Indeed, while technical progress is making for a more and more oligopolistic structure in the steel market, the need to spread the overheads of the largest integrated plants encourages producers to look farther and farther into the erstwhile territories of rival groups for their markets. Because of this, competition is being maintained, and it may even be growing keener in spite of the reduction in the number of completely independent producers.

What, therefore, is of major importance in these circumstances is to make sure that these various separate groups of enterprises do not develop interconnexions that might have an anti-competitive effect. It was for this reason that in authorizing the establishment of SIDMAR the High Authority had to insist that a connexion between one of the enterprises in the SIDMAR group, Forges de la Providence, and an enterprise in another French group producing flats, USINOR, should be terminated.

It is clear from the foregoing account of the problems of group control that the effects of a joint enterprise on competition can

[12] ECSC, *11th Gen. Rep.* (1963), p. 321.

only be estimated if the production programme of the new concern is known in advance. If, for example, the sponsors of a proposed joint enterprise were collectively in a dominant position with regard to any particular product, and this was also to be produced by the joint enterprises, the reduction in competition between them consequent on their control of the pricing policy of the new concern would probably make such a joint venture inadmissible under the treaty. In authorizing SIDMAR the High Authority therefore laid down as a second condition that its production programme should be limited to the range of products specified in the original application. As long as production by SIDMAR was in fact limited to these products, the High Authority would impose no limits to the growth of the new firm (i.e. the policy followed earlier with regard to the concentration between Krupp and the Bochumer Verein and the first ATH-Phoenix application was disavowed). But if new lines were to be added to the range of products, this would raise a further series of questions for competition and authorization for such developments would have to be sought again.

(iv) *SOMOSID.* In 1963 the High Authority was asked to authorize a concentration between the Société Métallurgique de Knutange and the Union de Consommateurs de Produits Métallurgiques et Industriels, the concentration to be effected by the creation of a new company, the Société Mosellane de Sidérurgie (SOMOSID), jointly owned by the two concerns mentioned. The two plants were situated close to each other and would be extended and run as one with total production of about 2 million tons per year—a size comparable to that of many other enterprises in the Community and not of itself likely to cause any problems for competition.

The anti-trust problems involved in the concentration may be appreciated more easily by referring to Diagram 1 (p. 212), which sets out the main proprietary connexions between the various enterprises directly and indirectly involved in the case. These are explained further in the text below.

The problems for anti-trust arose basically because Knutange was not itself an independent enterprise—it was in fact controlled by Schneider, and other shares were also held by de Wendel and Denain-Anzin. Again, Union's shareholders included certain

DIAGRAM I

Proprietary Connexions in the SOMOSID Case

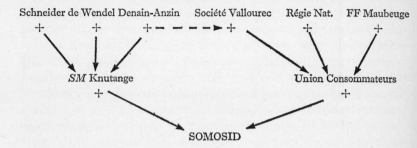

firms such as the Régie Nationale des Usines Renault and Fabrique de Fer de Maubeuge having controlling interests in iron and steel enterprises, and the Société Vallourec in which Denain-Anzin were the main shareholders. In their original application for authorization each of these participants in Knutange and Union wished to appoint a member of the Board of Directors of SOMOSID.

The essence of the problem as seen by the High Authority is set out clearly in the following quotation:

If the Somosid concentration had been allowed to entail close and sustained co-operation among the Schneider, Denain-Anzin and de Wendel groups, the results very definitely would have affected a substantial part of the relevant market, and hence been liable 'to give to the interested enterprises the power to prevent the maintenance of effective competition and/or to evade the rules of competition' (Article 66 of the Treaty).[13]

The High Authority appears to have considered that the prevention of 'close and sustained co-operation' between the three important groups mentioned in the quotation could be effected by excluding representatives of the last two from directorships of SOMOSID and by placing a similar ban upon any director nominated by Société Vallourec who was at the same time a representative of the Denain-Anzin interests in that firm.

[13] ECSC, *12th Gen. Rep.* (1964), p. 185.

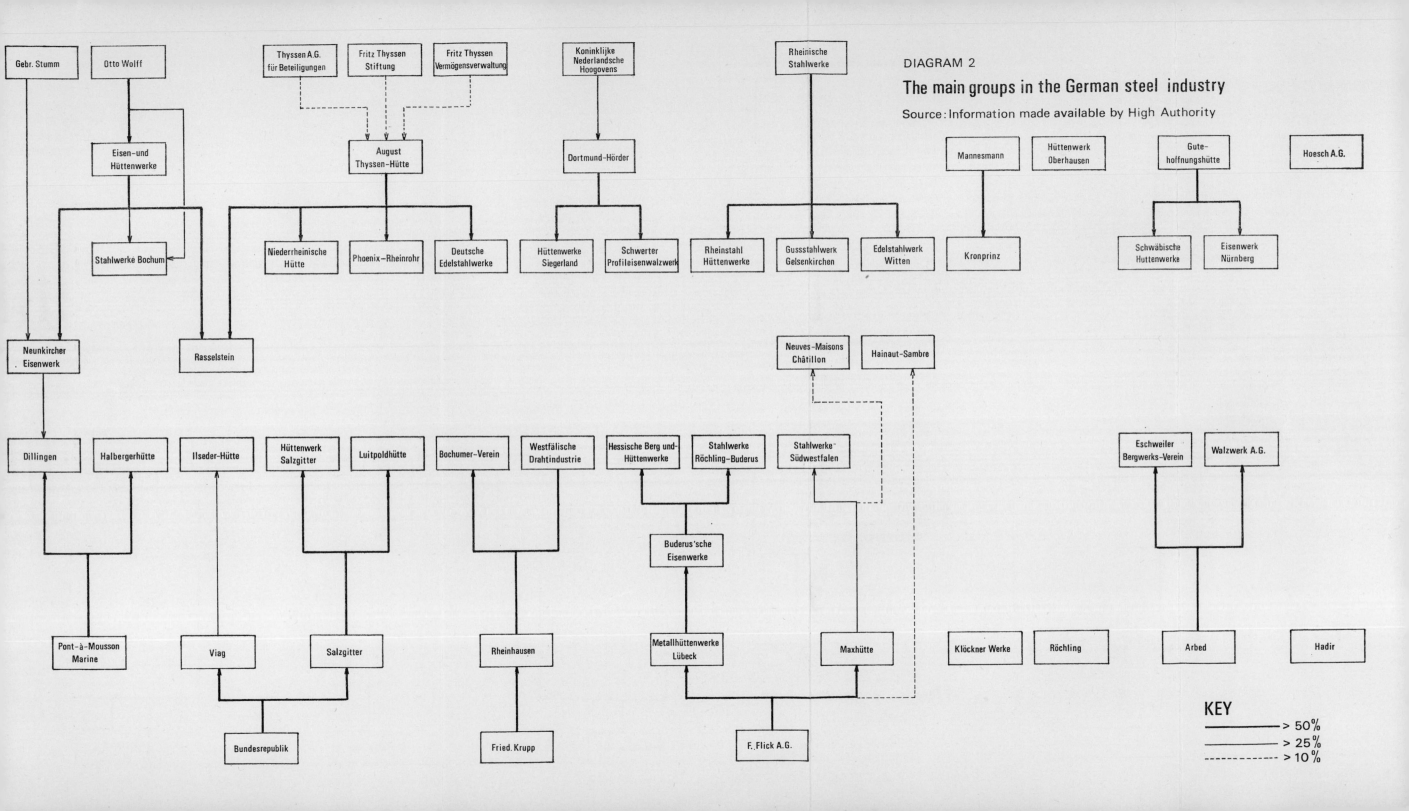

DIAGRAM 2

The main groups in the German steel industry

Source: Information made available by High Authority

KEY

——————— > 50%

————— > 25%

- - - - - - - > 10%

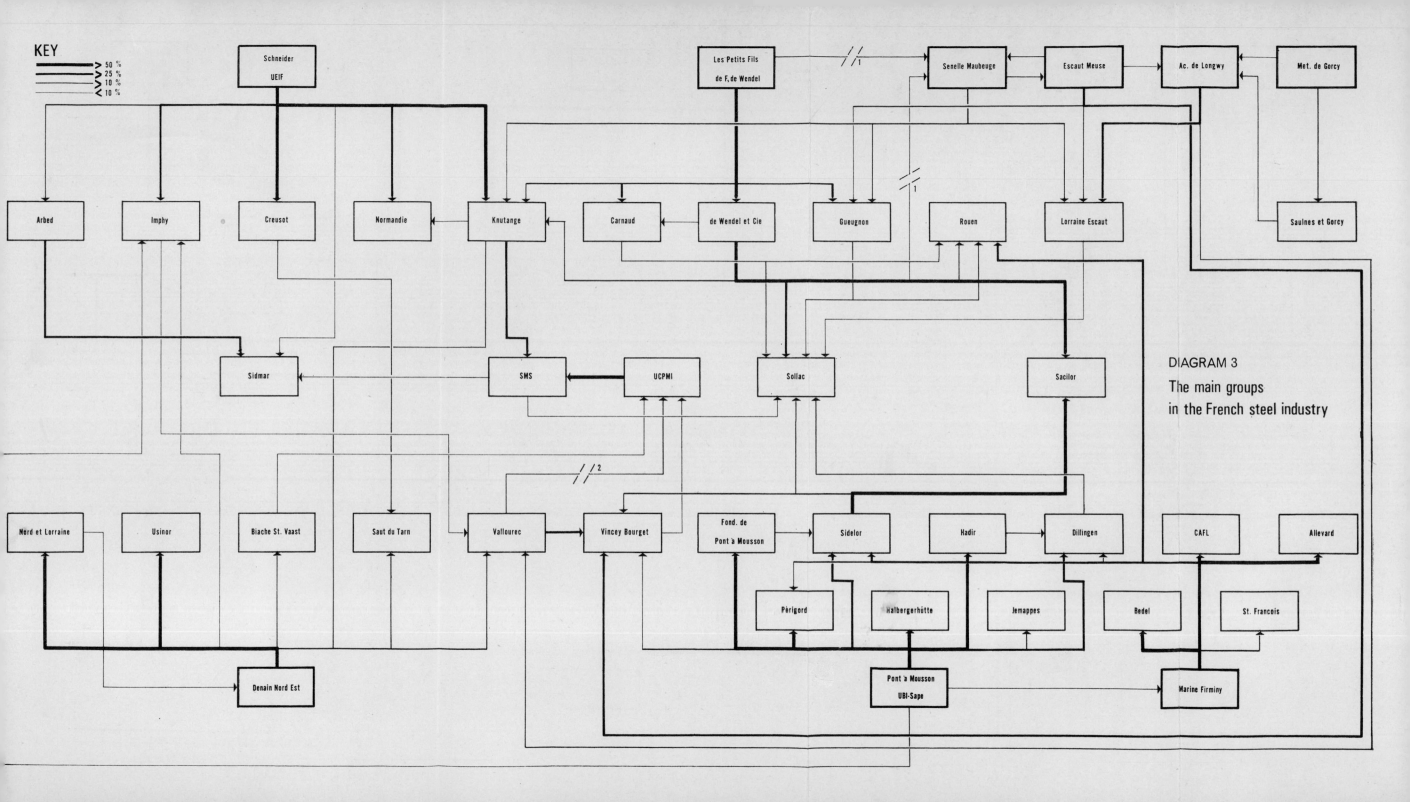

KEY
> 50 %
> 25 %
10 %
< 10 %

DIAGRAM 3
The main groups
in the French steel industry

Schneider
UEIF

Les Petits Fils
de F. de Wendel

Senelle Maubeuge

Escaut Meuse

Ac. de Longwy

Met. de Gorcy

Arbed

Imphy

Creusot

Normandie

Knutange

Carnaud

de Wendel et Cie

Gueugnon

Rouen

Lorraine Escaut

Saulnes et Gorcy

Sidmar

SMS

UCPMI

Sollac

Sacilor

Nord et Lorraine

Usinor

Biache St. Vaast

Saut du Tarn

Vallourec

Vincey Bourget

Fond. de
Pont à Mousson

Sidelor

Hadir

Dillingen

CAFL

Allevard

Pèrigord

Halbergerhütte

Jemappes

Bedel

St. Francois

Denain Nord Est

Pont à Mousson
UBI-Sape

Marine Firminy

Just how effective this solution is, it is difficult to say precisely. There is perhaps no more intractable range of problems in antitrust than those posed by oligopoly, and within that category the problems least amenable to analytical assessment but most likely to give rise to the deepest misgivings are caused by proprietary and personal interconnexions between ostensibly independent enterprises. In this particular case it could be argued that the High Authority's solution was a classic case of shutting the stable door, for the real cause of the threat to competition between Schneider, de Wendel, and Denain-Anzin surely did not lie in anything that might have transpired in the boardroom of SOMOSID, but in the connexions already existing between these three groups as owners of Knutange. On the other hand it must in fairness be admitted that the links between the three groups arising from their joint ownership of Knutange might have been of an extremely tenuous kind and that the High Authority's solution at least prevented a doubtfully competitive arrangement from degenerating into one that was wholly inimical to competition. Perhaps the main value of the SOMOSID case is that it will make clear to industry that the High Authority is now actively concerned with the problems of group control and is unlikely to take kindly to some possible extensions of it that might, if not checked, eventually involve increased connexions between major groups, perhaps even embracing competitors from several member states, and a corresponding erosion of the whole basis of business rivalry.

It is indeed probable that the High Authority is not only determined to prevent any weakening of the competitive structure in this way, but is actually intending to use the powers it possesses in these circumstances to bring about a structure that is in fact more conducive to competition. In other words, where dubious connexions, especially of a personal kind, exist between ostensible competitors, then a request by any such firm for approval of a concentration can always be made subject to conditions. The High Authority intends to impose conditions that will have the effect of breaking suspicious links, especially interlocking directorates, whenever the opportunity is presented. Unfortunately, of course, the High Authority cannot intervene actively but has to wait passively until a request for authorization is made, as this is the only circumstance in which it can influence

8*

this particular situation. To some extent this policy can be usefully applied in each of the member states—we have of course already seen how the authorization of the ATH-Phoenix merger was subject to conditions of this kind—but it is likely to be most relevant to the highly complex arrangement of interlocking shareholdings and directorates found in the French steel industry. As at the end of 1965 it was in fact very difficult to say with any confidence exactly where one French steel group ended and another began, such was the extent of the interrelationships between them. Just how complicated these interrelationships were may be judged by comparing the all too confusing Diagrams 2 and 3 (pp. 214–15). In the case of the German steel industry it is possible to distinguish eight main groups, but no such pattern can be established in the case of France. Of particular concern to the High Authority is the prevalence in the French steel industry of comparatively small shareholdings of one company in another when these are accompanied by a representative directorship—a listening post, in fact. The three parts of the French diagram that indicate some sort of break in the connecting links are where the High Authority, in being asked to approve a concentration, has been able to impose conditions that severed certain links. Obviously this policy, which has really only just begun to operate, has not had a chance to achieve any marked effects as yet, but its rationale is clear, commendable, and, it should be said, courageous.

3. STEEL CONCENTRATION: PERSPECTIVE AND PROSPECTS

If one regards the Community market as a unified whole, then the degree of proprietary concentration occurring there—at any rate in so far as this may be indicated by figures of crude steel production—is considerably less than in any other major steel market. This is shown clearly in Table 2 (p. 217).

The table shows that the largest group in the ECSC accounted for only 10 per cent of total crude steel production, whereas the corresponding figures for the other markets were US (28 per cent), UK (12 per cent), and Japan (25 per cent). Similarly, taking, say, the leading three or leading ten groups in each market, it emerges from the table that the degree of concentration

TABLE 2

Comparison of Degree of Concentration in the ECSC, US, UK, and Japanese Steel Industries
(per cent)

Size sequence of group or enterprise	ECSC (1961)	US (1960)	UK (1961-2)	Japan (1960-1)
The largest 1	10	28	12	25
The largest 3	25	52	34	52
The largest 10	59	80	82	80

Figures are rounded: ECSC data include ATH-Phoenix merger.
Source: Bull. ECSC, no. 47, 1964, p. 46.

is always lower in the Community than in any of the other three examples. Thus, in this basic structural sense, the steel industry in the Community is much closer to the requirements of competition than steel industries elsewhere. But the fact is that, whereas the US, for example, really is one large market, numerous factors such as long-standing links with customers, and, as we shall show subsequently in a detailed analysis of pricing in the steel market,[14] the policies of the individual governments, still result in at least some segmentation of the ECSC along national lines. Thus the degree of concentration in the ECSC steel industry is in fact a good deal greater than what would appear from Table 2. As time goes on, however, we may expect the full unification of the national markets to be made more and more of a reality. The technical economies of large-scale production that are one important cause of this trend will, however, simultaneously be responsible for ensuring that reconciliation of the needs of competition with the needs of production will remain a problem. That this is no remote possibility may be demonstrated by referring to a study of the economies of scale in the British steel industry carried out recently by C. Pratten and R. M. Dean. After a detailed study of cost and output relationships in each of the main stages of steel production, blast furnaces, steel furnaces, and finishing, the authors summarized their overall conclusions in the following significant paragraph:

[14] See below, ch. 9.

A feature of our study of economies of scale in the steel industry is that many of the estimates of these economies which we have obtained show no sign of costs ceasing to fall with scale even though the rate at which they fall declines. If works were constructed to produce, say 20 million tons of steel a year, there is no clear technical reason to doubt that yet larger scale plant would be designed and that there would be some economies of scale up to this level of output, provided the range of products was not affected by the level of output.[15]

4. THE EEC IN SEARCH OF A POLICY

The experience of the High Authority in dealing with concentrations has been characterized by a slow and none too willing awakening to the fact that the problem of size has a positive as well as a negative side. The Treaty of Rome in Article 86, and, indeed, the whole climate of discussion surrounding this constellation of problems in the general Common Market, breathes a very different spirit from that of Article 66 in the Paris Treaty, with its underlying presumption against the dangers of economic power and its insistence upon the preservation of competition. Perhaps the only connecting link between the two treaties in this sphere is that by far the loudest support for the widely divergent approaches embodied in each has come from the French in both cases. Thus the severity of the ECSC régime was largely the result of attempts to placate French fears, while the comparatively permissive attitude towards the establishment of dominant positions adopted in the Rome Treaty accords completely with the French view (although it is by no means exclusively a French view) that the size of enterprises in Europe is frequently far below what is necessary if the benefits of a large market are to be achieved.

In contrast to the detailed provisions regarding concentrations in the ECSC and the development of an important corpus of case law in that field, Article 86 of the Rome Treaty dealing with dominant enterprises is comparatively brief and has not so far (up to 1966) given rise to any decisions by the Commission.[16]

---

[15] C. Pratten and R. M. Dean, *The Economies of Large-scale Production in British Industry* (1965), p. 82.

[16] The Commission has, however, started one investigation. This concerns the Netherlands export monopoly for natural gas, NAM, which is jointly owned by Shell and Esso. According to a question raised in the European Parliament

This lack of case material is not, however, a sign of a total lack of activity on the part of the Commission. Thus, in an effort to gain as much insight as possible into the problems that would be encountered in implementing a policy towards dominant enterprises, the Commission appointed two groups of experts in 1963—

to examine the connection between concentration and the application and interpretation of Article 86 and also the possibilities of justifying compulsory notification for enterprises with a strong position on the market for mergers and for particular practices covered by Article 86; and

to investigate the connections between cartel policy (Article 85) and concentration.[17]

The Commission also requested an Institute of Comparative Law to make an inquiry into the forms of mergers allowed under the company law of the member states, the extent to which they hindered or promoted concentration, and the regulations governing publicity on mergers.

The Commission used the reports of these experts as a basis for a lengthy memorandum on the problem of business concentration in the Common Market and circulated this to the national governments at the end of 1965.[18] The most important problems discussed in this memorandum are the various ways in which fiscal and company law can influence the concentration processes, the special problems of small businesses, and what possibilities the Rome Treaty offers for the control of certain types of mergers. We revert to the specific matters raised in this memorandum later in this chapter after we have given a more general background account of the problems of business size in a Common Market context. Throughout this discussion we should bear in mind that the EEC is still very much in the early stages of working out the rationale of its policy in this field.

There is, of course, an almost infinite gap between the mere

---

by a Belgian Deputy, M. Tourbeau, it appears that NAM might have brought pressure to bear upon interests in Belgium, Germany and France, to increase its own share in distributing companies for Dutch gas. See Question no. 154 (1964–5), *JO*, 20 May 1965.

[17] EEC, *7th Gen. Rep.* (1964), pp. 58–59.

[18] EEC, *Das Problem der Unternehmenskonzentrazion im Gemeinsamen Markt* (1965). The substance of this is contained in EEC, Official Spokesman, *Concentration of Firms in the Common Market*, D Pl/66, Jan. 1966.

existence of business practices that may warrant investigation under Article 86 and a definite decision to the effect that the four criteria specified therein are in fact fulfilled in any particular case. For each of these four criteria presents the legal advisers of enterprises with considerable scope for manœuvre, and the Commission, as the main enforcement agency, with a correspondingly difficult brief. Let us consider some of the problems that would have to be settled if the four conditions necessary for the application of Article 86 were to be fulfilled.

To begin with, it is important to remember that Article 86 places the whole responsibility for all initiatives in this field entirely upon the enforcement agencies, which will probably mean in practice the Commission alone, although the anti-trust departments of the national administrations continue to enjoy a measure of competence also. Doubtless the Commission may occasionally be helped by complaints received from parties that consider themselves injured, although none in fact had been received up to 1966. But as Article 86 is not concerned with the establishment of a dominant position as such, but only with its abuse, it is not necessary for enterprises contemplating merging to notify the Commission of their intention, much less to obtain any authorization to proceed.[19] This places a definite burden upon the Commission, which will always be in the position of having to root out possible violations from scratch. This is in marked contrast to the procedure on cartels in which the work of the Commission in seeking out possible violations of Article 85 is greatly facilitated by the necessity of notification to obtain exemption, and, of course, the ECSC's authorization procedure for mergers.

As far as concerns the four conditions specified in Article 86, it is clear that each presents certain difficulties of interpretation and application. Consider first what might be regarded as an

---

[19] In Western Germany a proposed merger that would involve a 20 per cent share of the market or more must be notified to the BKA. This is supposed to enable the BKA to keep some sort of watch on possibly dangerous developments in the field of concentration, and to accumulate sufficient information to serve as the basis for any possible future changes in policy. But the BKA does not have the power to delay or prevent any merger, and, in practice, as firms tend to be uncertain as to whether the 20 per cent rule applies in any particular case, notifications tend to be infrequent, and the whole policy on mergers, such as it is, tends to be frustrated.

'abuse'. In an individual state an abuse would be some type of conduct that was not in the public interest, as defined ultimately by government. In the Community, however, there is as yet no corresponding Community interest, simply because there is no authority to define which interests are paramount. Abuse is, therefore, likely to be regarded as any conduct that frustrates the achievement of the goal that Article 86 is designed to realize. This is, according to Article 3(f) which specifies the main activities of the Community, 'the establishment of a system ensuring that competition shall not be distorted'. Thus, if normal conditions of competition may be equated with reasonable levels of prices and profits, attention to technical progress and so forth, then deviations from these criteria of normalcy could be considered as abuses.

The treaty in fact specifies some examples of business conduct that might constitute an abuse. As might be expected the first is the imposition of unfair buying or selling prices or other trading conditions, that is, the cruder forms of monopolistic exploitation. Next is mentioned the limitation of production, markets, and technical development to the detriment of consumers. A monopoly firm that failed to expand its output in line with increases in demand, preferring instead to enjoy higher prices as a result of scarcity, would probably be covered by this possibility, as might manipulations of patents or failure to exploit them. Price discrimination that results in a competitive disadvantage to the party affected is also cited as an abuse. This is an interesting possibility because it involves an attempt to give economic content along the lines of the US Robinson–Patman Act to a ban that could otherwise easily degenerate into a preoccupation with legalities. We show in the next chapter, in which we discuss the steel pricing régime, that one of the weaknesses of the ECSC's ban on price discrimination is that it fails to distinguish between economically deleterious discriminatory practices and those that do not have perceptibly objectionable effects.[20] By focusing attention directly on the anti-competitive effects that may arise from price discrimination, it may be possible to avoid some of the problems that have bedevilled the ECSC in trying to enforce its stricter rule. Finally, 'full line forcing' would constitute an abuse —that is, compelling customers by means of tie-in clauses to

[20] See ch. 9.

take additional goods not basically connected with the products actually required.

The second criterion that has to be fulfilled if Article 86 is to apply is that a position of 'dominance' in the market must be proved. Here the experience of the ECSC and US anti-trust is again of value. The revelant market will have to be defined in terms of product, geography, and time. Market shares will have to be assessed, and this will involve taking account of the role of imports. According to one distinguished commentator, continental legal doctrine and court practice will probably require a market share of 'at least 51 per cent . . . and probably considerably more' to establish dominance,[21] although the Director General for Competition in the EEC has stated that the Commission intends to assess monopoly in even more restrictive terms than the UK's one-third of the relevant market.[22] The availability of possible substitutes and countervailing power should also be considered in assessing this critical question.

Thirdly, the market that is dominated must be, if not the entire Common Market, then at least a 'substantial part' of it. What exactly might be meant by a substantial part in this context has been a matter of considerable dispute in legal circles. The rather legalistic debate has centred on the question of whether a substantial part of the Common Market could be equated with the territory of one particular state, or whether some part of the territory of at least two member states must be involved. The Commission has let it be known that in its opinion the 'substantial part' may lie within the confines of a single member state.[23] As we have seen in regard to the ECSC's treatment of the OKU case, a dominant position in one part of the Common Market, Southern Germany, was sufficient to bring that organization within the prohibited category[24] (although it should be borne in mind that the ECSC is not encumbered with an inter-state trade clause). From a non-technical standpoint, it would seem highly unsatisfactory if the Community were indifferent to the domination of, say, the German market of 55 million consumers

---

[21] Arved Deringer, 'The Common Market Competition Rules—Handicap or a Chance for British Industry?', *Europe House Paper*, no. 7, (1962), p. 6.

[22] P. Verloren van Themaat, in an address to a meeting of the Federal Trust Association on *Problems of Scale in Europe*, 22 Feb. 1966, p. 18.

[23] EEC, *Articles 85 and 86 of the EEC Treaty and the Relevant Regulations: Manual for Firms* (1962), p. 5.　　[24] See above, pp. 127–8

at the same time as it was actively concerned with the Belgium-Luxembourg market of 10 million simply because this involved two national states. But the common-sense view may not always prevail in a question like this where the issue could rapidly become one of states' rights v. supranationalism.

Fortunately, however, assessing the applicability of the fourth criterion laid down in Article 86—that trade between the member states must be affected—may in fact contribute to a clarification of some of the problems raised above. A dominant enterprise might affect the development of intra-Community trade, thereby frustrating the effects of tariffs and quota reductions, in a number of ways.

One such possibility might arise if transport costs and its own geographical position gave a firm a dominant position in a part of the Common Market only. Suppose that a firm in Rome was in a position to exploit the South of Italy as transport costs effectively sealed off that part of the Italian market from competition. It might then be in a position to discriminate with regard to price between the South and North of the country to such an extent that sales into the latter from, say, France or Germany, would be hindered by reason of the low prices there. This type of discriminatory pricing by an enterprise that was dominant in part of the Common Market only would impede the development of trade between the partners and, therefore, be of direct concern to the Community. An example of this kind of situation, although within a purely national framework, is provided by the policy of a West German sales syndicate, Zementkontor Unterelbe GmbH of Hamburg. The syndicate marketed cement in the lower Elbe region on both sides of the river. On the left of the river the sales area of the syndicate bordered on the sales areas of other German cement syndicates. On the right of the river the syndicate did not face any such competition, with the result that it was able to discriminate with regard to price between the two areas to the extent of DM4 per ton. The BKA found that the price difference was not justified by cost factors or other market conditions and ordered the Zementkontor Unterelbe to reduce its prices in the area to the right of the Elbe so that they should no longer exceed the prices it charged in the contested area to the left of the river.[25]

[25] OECD, *Guide to Legislation*, vol. ii, Germany 3, p. 38.

Suppose as a second possibility that the enterprise is dominant in one state only. It may distribute its output through a network of exclusive dealerships. In this case enterprises from other member states wishing to sell into the first state might find existing distribution channels virtually closed to them, and have to invest heavily in distribution facilities before any sales efforts could be mounted. An example that is to some extent analogous to this was the action of the dominant enterprise in the UK wallpaper trade, WPM. By its system of exclusive dealing arrangements with merchants and retailers WPM was able to deny outlets to its competitors. Besides restricting competition this may well have had the result of calling into being an excessive amount of capacity in distribution as other firms attempting to enter into the field had to establish their own distribution facilities.[26] It is clear that this kind of conduct, if repeated in a common market context, could prejudice the development of inter-state trade by adding to the costs of penetrating markets outside the national state. And as trade failed to develop, the benefits of competition would be excluded. Thus, these kinds of activities on the part of an enterprise that is dominant in one state only could run directly counter to agreed government policy of tariff and quota elimination and would, therefore, have to be controlled by the Community.

If an enterprise enjoying a dominant position in one member state did not take deliberate steps to preserve its monopoly position as tariffs were being dismantled, it would find its market area exposed to the possibility of invasion from firms in other member states. If prices in the first market were high enough, this might indeed encourage the entry of competitors. But if these potential competitors were themselves dominant firms in their own national markets, they might think twice about expanding into neighbouring states when the opportunity arises, as this might lead to retaliation and the kind of severe price competition that oligopolists have tended to eschew.

In such circumstances it might be in the interests of each of the dominant enterprises to refrain from trespassing in the other's home market. The point to stress here is that as long as each of the enterprises concerned pursued a fairly uniform price policy,

[26] The Monopolies Commission, *Report on the Supply of Wallpaper* (1964), para. 174.

there would be little scope for dealers shifting supplies from one part of the market to the other (that is to say the kind of action in which de Geus and UNEF were involved in the Bosch and Grundig–Consten cases), and, therefore, no need for the dominant enterprises to impose either exclusive-dealing or export-prohibition clauses upon domestic buyers. Thus the exploitation of its domestic market by each dominant enterprise could continue simply as a result of a consciously parallel course of action. It is this kind of apparently intractable situation that Article 86 can in fact deal with, as it is as much concerned with market domination by several enterprises as by one. For this reason alone, therefore, Article 86, in spite of its many appearances to the contrary, may yet turn out to be a potent weapon in the hands of the authorities.

It is also possible to see a threat to the integration of the Community in the case of an enterprise whose dominant position extends to two or more of the member states. By inserting export-prohibition clauses in its contracts with buyers the dominant enterprise could take advantage of different market conditions in the several states and discriminate among them with regard to price. The export prohibition would then serve to maintain the segmentation of the market—by maintaining different price-levels—much as tariffs have done in the past. In view of the Grundig–Consten Decision, this type of case would probably be more easily dealt with under Article 85.

However difficult it may prove to establish a case under each of the four criteria of Article 86, any unfavourable decision that does actually emerge can have the most far-reaching consequences for the enterprise or enterprises concerned. This is because the abuse has in fact been prohibited since it existed (strictly speaking, since March 1962 when Regulation 17 came into effect), and the decision of the Commission does not create the illegality but merely brings it out into the open. Thus, the possibility of substantial retroactive fines is quite real. Furthermore, the possibility of damage suits being raised by injured parties must at least be considered, although whether the law will in fact ultimately be construed as permitting this remains problematical. If it is finally construed in this way it will represent a new problem for European business, although one that US firms have lived with for a long time. Fines and damage suits are rare occurrences in the various national brands of anti-trust in both the UK and the Community, as the domestic anti-trust laws have tended to make illegality flow from the judgments of the Courts or the decisions of the enforcement agency, at which point the practice is usually stopped. Only in the rarest cases have specifically prohibited practices been continued. In the UK, for example, a remarkable case of contempt arose in 1965 from the failure of the members of the Galvanised Tank Manufacturers' Association to implement undertakings previously given to the Restrictive Practices Court. The firms' contempt in this case seemed to have been caused primarily by a mixture of incompetence and incomprehension rather than any deliberately conceived attempt to circumvent the law, although this may not have been entirely absent. At any rate the firms concerned were fined a total of £100,000, including £25,000 on Richard Thomas and Baldwins, the nationalized steel firm.[27] In France the authorities may make use of an unorthodox variation of the idea of fines: firms that have been implementing injurious practices may be invited to compound for their offences by making a significant contribution to the Treasury as a means of purging their guilt.[28] In the US, where the *per se* nature of the law has given rise to both fines and damage suits as well established remedies, the incidence of the latter may be considerably greater than the former. A striking example of this was provided by the recent electrical equipment case in which the actual fines imposed turned out to be a very small proportion indeed of the damages claimed.[29]

Thus the deterrent effect of the legal consequences that could follow from an offence under Article 86 may turn out to be quite considerable. It is, therefore, perhaps surprising to note that the other main anti-trust weapon that one would expect to be employed in this field, divestiture, has not in fact been specifically provided by the EEC. It may be that the absence of a specific provision for divestiture is inherent in the basic nature of Article 86 itself. By being solely concerned with the control of

[27] *The Economist*, 26 June 1965, p. 1555; *Reports of Restrictive Practices Cases*, v, pt. 5, Dec. 1965, p. 349. (See also the subsequent *Tyre Mileage Case*.)

[28] OECD, *Guide to Legislation on Restrictive Business Practice*, vol. iii France 2 (1964), p. 5.

[29] Gordon B. Spivack, 'Comparative Aspects of Enforcement—(1) The United States', *ICLQ*, Suppl. Publ. no. 6 (1963), p. 40.

abuse and not, in contrast to the approach adopted in the ECSC and US, with the preservation of competition as such, Article 86 fails to opt for the market as the main technique of control. This could well lead to considerable indirect supervision or control of dominant enterprises by the Commission.

5. CONCENTRATION, ECONOMIES OF SCALE, AND TECHNICAL PROGRESS

Among the most important changes that the operation of the EEC will require of industry in Europe is an adaptation to the size of the new market.

There are probably very few industries in which economies of scale are so important that an individual nation state of Western European dimensions (excluding, for example, the Benelux countries and Denmark) would not provide a market large enough to support one plant of technically optimum proportions. But the fact is that history has bequeathed to each national market large numbers of plants and firms that are embarrassingly small even by national standards. The advent of the large common market has underlined the inadequate size of many firms in European states and simultaneously made considerable concentration possible without jeopardizing competition. Competition and the existence of really large enterprises, perhaps uneasy bedfellows within the framework of the individual European nation state, become simultaneously feasible under conditions of integration.

The need to achieve a high enough level of output to make possible the full realization of potential scale economies is one important reason why a considerable amount of concentration and regroupment in European industry is not only to be expected but is to be positively welcomed. But the achievement of scale economies is in essence a static kind of adaptation in that it involves a redeployment of resources in accordance with known techniques. There is, however, a more fundamental reason to expect that concentrations will occur in European industry, either spontaneously through the initiative of business itself or as as a result of certain amount of government encouragement. This is because of the widely and deeply held view that competitive strength depends only partly upon the static advantages that large-scale operations can confer. A more important determinant of competitive strength lies in the application of scientific and technological research to industry. Since it is in the large firms that the bulk of such research is carried out, then the replacement of large numbers of small firms by a smaller number of larger firms will increase the research-mindedness of industry and improve its technological performance. Thus even if plant economies do not themselves require the creation of really large firms, the demands of research may still do so. This was in fact one of the reasons behind the large merger in the European photographic industry between Agfa and Gevaert—Kodak's expenditure on research being almost as high as Gevaert's total sales.

If this general line of argument is sound, then it implies (*a*) that the economic growth of the Community will be significantly influenced by the rate at which enterprises in fact adapt to the conditions of the large market; (*b*) that the competitiveness of Community firms in the internal market (that is, *vis-à-vis* imports from third countries) and, even more, actually in third countries, will be dependent upon their relative size as compared with those of the rest of the world—which primarily means those of the US at the present time; and (*c*) that business circles in the Community may see future schemes to liberalize world trade more as a threat than an opportunity as long as they consider themselves to be of inferior size to their American competitors. Already the principal industry association in the Community (UNICE) has referred specifically to the desirability of synchronizing concentration in Europe with the progress of the Kennedy Round.[30] In support of this kind of attitude UNICE and, even more, the main French business federation, the Patronat, tend to stress certain ways in which European efforts in research and development (R & D) contrast unfavourably with American, and to attribute much of the blame for Europe's shortcomings in this field to the smaller scale of enterprises there.

(*a*) *Economies of Large Scale*

Generally speaking there are available to firms in manufacturing industry economies of large-scale production and

---

[30] UNICE, *Aspekte ungleichgewichtiger Grossenstrukturen der EWG Spitzenunternehmen im Vergleich zu ihren Hauptkonkurrenten aus Drittländern*, 26 Feb. 1965, p. 1.

distribution which make it possible for them, by becoming larger, up to a certain point, to attain a lower cost per unit of output produced. As plants become larger, firms are able to exploit mass production techniques involving the specialization of labour on narrow specific tasks, the use of specialized machinery including capital equipment which is sometimes only available in very large minimum sizes (i.e. indivisibilities), specialization of managerial and supervisory personnel and so forth. To a large extent these are economies of large-scale plants.

Granted that there is an advantage in larger-scale plants, it is interesting to note that the size of plants in manufacturing in the US, measured in terms of employment, does appear to be bigger than that of the Six.

TABLE 3

Size of Plant in Manufacturing Industry in the US and the Six*
(Per cent of Total Employment by Establishment Size Class)

	1–49	*50–99*	*100–499*	*500–999*	*1,000+*
W. Germany (1958)	15·0	9·6	30·3	12·8	32·3
France (1954)	19·0	11·9	34·0	12·8	22·3
Italy (1955)	21·0	11·7	30·0	12·9	24·4
Belgium (1956)	28·0	10·4	27·2	11·4	23·0
US (1958)	14·6	8·7	28·0	12·4	36·3

*Data for Netherlands only available for enterprises.

Source: US Dept of Commerce, Bureau of the Census, *Statist. Abstract of the United States 1963* (1963), table no. 1094; P. L. Mandy and G. de Ghellinck, 'La structure de la dimension des enterprises dans des pays du Marché commun', *R. économique*, May 1960, p. 407.

The general picture is clear: the US has a smaller proportion of its employees engaged in plants of the smaller categories and a noticeably larger proportion in the 1,000+ category.[31] In the middle ranges there is no great contrast. The average size of plant, taking the Six as a whole, appears to be somewhat smaller

[31] Comparative data are not available about the bigger size classes, e.g. 2,000+ and 5,000+. Table 3 should also be treated with caution. The EEC industrial structure could be biased towards industries with a relatively small optimum plant-size, and vice-versa in the US.

than in the US—this appears to be most clearly so in the case of France, Italy, and Belgium. Average plant size in Western Germany on the other hand appears to be broadly comparable with the US. The other point of interest is that the percentage of total employment engaged in the 1,000+ class is smaller in France than in any of the other three EEC states. In part this fact no doubt explains the stress in French planning on the need for mergers and at the Community level explains the French insistence upon the need for policies designed to overcome the size disadvantage of EEC industry. The analysis in Table 3 based upon employment—an analysis based on value of turnover or physical output would provide a greater contrast because of greater US productivity.

Data concerning the ECSC steel industry indicate that despite the steady flow of mergers, joint ventures, and specialization agreements in recent years, the size of steel plants in the Six is well below that of Japan and the US. Thus in 1965 only 7·4 per cent of Community crude steel production came from plants of over 6 million metric tons annual capacity as against 81 per cent in the US and 49 per cent in Japan. On the other hand 39 per cent of production in the ECSC came from plants of less than 2 million tons capacity whereas in the US and Japan the figures were 15 per cent and 6 per cent.[32]

It may be, and indeed it seems likely, that a movement in the Six towards larger-scale plants is necessary—but this is not inevitable. Because plants are larger in the US does not imply that the latter enjoys an automatic advantage. The economies of large-scale production are not unlimited. The evidence collected by a distinguished research worker in this field indicates that over a range of increasing plant size cost per unit tends to fall but there is a critical size of plant beyond which no further economies are likely to be experienced.[33] Then again technical factors that initially dictate the construction of large plants sometimes develop subsequently in such a way as to make it possible in due course to build smaller plants that also incorporate the latest techniques. For example, the newest plants of General Electric are small even by European standards, with

---

[32] *Financial Times*, 24 May 1966.
[33] J. S. Bain, *Industrial Organization* (1959), ch. 5 and his *Barriers to New Competition* (1956), ch. 3.

50–1,000 employees. Also a study of the shoe industry in France showed that a technically optimum level of output could be reached at various levels, and that only between these levels was the competitive situation unfavourable.[34]

It should of course be remembered that the plant size position is not a static one. Over time existing plants may grow or decline and entirely new ones may be founded. Data is available for Germany showing at various dates the proportion of the total number of plants falling into certain employment size groups. This is reproduced below in Table 4.

TABLE 4

Industrial Plants by Size Categories as Proportion of Total Number of German Industrial Plants in Selected Industries

(*per cent*)

		Size of Plants (No. of Employees)			
		1–9	10–99	100–499	500+
Chemicals	1950	65	29	4	1
	1961	59	32	7	2
Electrical	1950	77	18	4	1
	1961	59	30	8	3
Plastic goods	1950	65	31	4	1
	1961	53	39	7	1
Textiles	1950	73	21	5	1
	1961	61	29	8	2

Source: Statistisches Bundesant, *Statistisches Jahrbuch für die Bundesrepublik Deutschland*, 1955, pp. 168–71; 1964, pp. 204–7.

Over the decade the relative importance of plants in the smallest size group has declined markedly. The question is not, of course, whether such a movement is occurring, but whether, granted that there are advantages in larger-scale plants, it is occurring fast enough.

(*b*) *Research and Development*
    (i) *Expenditure on R & D in Europe and USA.* Obviously the

---

[34] Verloren van Themaat, in Federal Trust Assoc., *Problems of Scale in Europe*, p. 17.

most daunting contrast between the US and any one European state is the considerable difference between the absolute volume of resources devoted to R & D in each. This is shown below in Table 5, which also sets out R & D expenditure as a percentage of GNP and on a per capita basis.

TABLE 5

Estimated Gross Expenditure on Research and Development in 1962

State	Expenditure ($ millions)	% of GNP @ MP	Expenditure in $ per head
USA	17,531	3·1	93·7
UK	1,775	2·2	33·5
France	1,108	1·5	23·6
Western Germany	1,105	1·3	20·1
Netherlands	239	1·8	20·3
Belgium	133	1·0	14·8

Source: OECD, *The Research and Development Effort* (1965), p. 71.

No matter which of the three headings in Table 5 is chosen, the lead of the US is quite remarkable. Within Europe itself, the position of the UK is very strong, with the nearest EEC member, France, making a considerably smaller effort in R & D, although one that has grown rapidly since 1959. Western Germany follows closely behind France, the two countries having changed their relative positions in the league since 1959. The general implications of these data for industry in each of the states concerned are clear enough, although some allowance—it is difficult to say how much—should be made for military spending within the above totals. If such allowance could be made the previous impressions would probably have to be modified to take account of the disproportionately large role of military spending on R & D in France as compared with the UK and, even more, with Western Germany.[35]

The figures given above are an unambiguous indication of the absolute and relative positions of science and technology in the economies concerned. But what is, perhaps, of equally great

[35] A detailed discussion of these types of comparisons may be found in ECE, *Some Factors in Economic Growth in Europe during the 1950s* (1964), ch. 5, p. 5.

importance to an understanding of European, particularly French, fears of American competition, is the fact that the vast sums devoted to R & D in the US are spent directly in the business sector to a relatively greater extent than is the case in European countries. This aspect of the situation is illustrated by the data in Table 6, which show, first, where the finance for R & D originated from and, secondly, where it was actually spent.

TABLE 6

Estimated Gross Expenditure on R & D by Sectors, 1962
(per cent)

	Funds provided by		Performed by	
	Business	*Government academic non-profit*	*Business*	*Government academic non-profit*
US	35	65	71	29
UK	36	64	63	37
France	30	70	48	52
W. Germany	60	40	61	39
Netherlands	65	35	60	40
Belgium	63	37	65	35

Source: OECD, *Research & Development Effort*, p. 72.

The broad distinction here is between the first three states in the table and the last three. In the former three, business spending on R & D is proportionately greater than the funds provided by business itself for these purposes, the contrast being greatest for the US, and, to a smaller extent the UK. In the latter three states business does not appear to be able to support any more R & D than it finances directly itself.

There can surely be little doubt that leading US firms are in the strongest position to benefit considerably in a purely technological sense *over the whole range of their activities*, from actually doing a considerable amount of R & D work on behalf of government in their own organizations. The fact that relatively more of such government-sponsored R & D work is done outside the business sector in Europe cannot but attenuate the impact of science and technology upon industry there.

There is also another economically telling contrast between the US (and, to a smaller extent, the UK) and France in this field of R & D financing, and this lies in the different proportions of R & D expenditure devoted to basic research on the one hand and applied research and development on the other. Approximate data on relative expenditure under each of these two headings are provided below in Table 7.

TABLE 7

Analysis of R & D Expenditure by Type

(per cent)

	US *(1959)*	UK *(1961)*	France* *(1959)*
Basic research	8	11	26
Applied research & development	92	89	74

* Data for France are not entirely comparable with US and UK.

Source: ECE, *Factors in Economic Growth*, ch. 5, p. 8.

It appears from the data in Table 7 (which should be considered in relation to those on the absolute level of R & D expenditure given in Table 5) that basic research acts rather in the manner of a fixed charge, with the result that it becomes easier to make substantial resources available for the economically crucial applied and development work when the total R & D budget is large.[36] The fact that the US is able to devote 92 per cent of its R & D expenditure to applied research and development, as compared with 74 per cent in France, underlines an important cause of the former's commanding position in the economic exploitation of technology. The position of the UK in this respect is much in advance of that of France. Unless con-

---

[36] The ECE, after warning that French data in these areas are not directly comparable with those in the US and UK, none the less concluded: 'it appears that France devoted at least twice as much of its research resources to basic research. There are some grounds for believing that the allocation of a high proportion of resources to basic research is a disadvantage, since the findings of basic research are currently published in scientific journals, and are readily available internationally. In other words, the *national* return on basic research is almost certainly less than in applied research' (*Factors in Economic Growth*, ch. 5, pp. 8–9).

siderable increases in the total French budget for R & D can be brought about, the only way that France, and probably, other individual European countries of similar size, could devote more resources to the applied and development sides would be to contract out of certain fields of basic research.

As a concluding indication of the commanding position of the US *vis-à-vis* European countries in the field of technology, we may cite briefly certain conclusions that have been drawn in an OECD study regarding the technological balance of payments between the former and the latter. Estimating the technological balance of payments is simply an attempt to show how a country's payments for technical know-how, licences, and patents compare with its receipts under these headings. Not surprisingly the position of European countries is bleak:

Despite limitations of the statistics, there can be no serious doubt that the United States has a very large and growing 'favourable balance', whilst the principal Western European countries have a large 'unfavourable balance' . . . Furthermore, the 'unfavourable balance' of the Western European countries arises principally from their heavy and growing deficit with the United States—two-thirds of the total French deficit and half the total German deficit were due to this. This points inescapably to a significant American development and technical lead in most industries, although not, of course, in all. The ratio of payments to receipts was 2·7 for both Germany (1963) and France (1962) for all transactions, but for their transactions with the United States the ratios were 4·8, and 5·0 respectively. The United Kingdom ratio for transactions with the United States in 1961 was very similar: 5·1.[37]

(b) *The Size of Firms in the Community and the US*

Industrialists in the Six, and especially the Patronat, emphasize the contrast between the size of firms in the emerging Common Market of 177 million and firms in the established single market of the US with its 187 million inhabitants. In terms of total population the EEC and US are indeed comparable but the size of the US market is, of course, considerably greater than that of the Community as per capita income is so much higher in the former. Notwithstanding this qualification, it is still instructive to compare the sizes of the leading Community

[37] OECD, *Research & Development Effort*, pp. 52–53.

firms in various industries with their counterparts in the US. This is done in Table 8 (below), which sets out for each of six major industries the sizes of the three largest Community firms, indicates their nationality, and compares their size with the corresponding three firms in the US.

Measuring the size of firms in terms of value of turnover in

TABLE 8

Comparisons of the Size of the Three Largest Enterprises in the Community and US by Industry, 1963*

	Community			United States		
		Nation-ality	*Size*		*Size*	*EEC/US %*
Automobiles	Volkswagen	G	1·7	General Motors	16·5	10
	Fiat	I	1·4	Ford	8·7	16
	Daimler Benz	G	1·2	Chrysler	3·5	35
Chemicals	Farbenfabriken Bayer	G	1·1	Du Pont	2·6	42
				Union Carbide	1·7	59
	Rhone-Poulenc	F	1·0	Proctor & Gamble	1·7	53
	Farbwerke Hoechst	G	0·9			
Rubber	Pirelli	I	0·6	Goodyear T & R	1·7	35
	Michelin	F	0·4	Firestone T & R	1·4	29
	Continental GW	G	0·2	General T & R	1·1	18
Electrical	Philips Gloeilampen	N	1·7	General Electric	4·9	35
				Western Electric	2·8	54
	Siemens	G	1·5	Westinghouse		
	AEG	G	0·8	Electric	2·1	38
Steel	ATH-Phoenix	G	1·3	US Steel	3·6	36
	Krupp	G	1·1	Bethlehem Steel	2·1	52
	Mannesmann	G	0·9	Republic Steel	1·1	82
Petroleum	Royal Dutch Petrol.	N	5·1	Standard Oil NJ	9·5	54
	Cie Fr. des Pétroles	F	0·8	Socony Mobil	3·9	21
	Gelsenkirchener BW	G	0·8	Texaco	3·3	24

* Size is measured by total turnover in $000 million; petroleum data are for 1962; figures for ATH-Phoenix obtained by summing the separate data for ATH and Phoenix.

Source: UNICE, *Aspekte ungleichgewichtiger Grossenstrukturen der EWG Spitzenunternehmen*, App. I & II and information provided by Michael S. Hood.

this way is a far from unexceptionable procedure, and we do not imply here that the data set out in Table 8 are exactly comparable with each other. But data on other aspects of size for specific industries (tons of steel or numbers of vehicles produced, for example) suggest that other criteria would not yield a vastly different impression from that conveyed by the admittedly imperfect turnover data actually used in the table.

If the data in Table 8 are at all representative of the sizes of the leading firms, then they point to two main conclusions.

Firstly, as far as the Community itself is concerned, it is clear that a big majority of the largest firms are West German, with France in second place but trailing well behind.

Secondly, the ratio of the size of a Community firm to its opposite number in the US, the percentage figure in the last column of the table, shows that, in two-thirds of the cases, the former is less than half of the size of the latter. Indeed, for the first four of the six industries mentioned in Table 8 even the third American enterprise is considerably larger than the largest corresponding Community firm.

There is a strong feeling in the Community that the kind of discrepancies in size that we have just shown are not confined to these particular industries but are on the contrary of more general validity. It is this kind of discrepancy between the size of firms in the Community as a whole and in America, and the poor French position in the Community itself, that is at the root of European fears, especially French fears, of American competition.

(c) *The Size of Firms and Research Activity*

In so far as Community firms are, in general, a good deal smaller than their American counterparts, it is important to try to gain some impression of the extent to which American (and other) experience in fact bears out the claims made by Europeans in support of the technological superiority of large firms. Are large firms more likely to carry out research than small, and do the large firms, especially the largest, in fact do the research that results in the significant technological advances?

The Report made by the OECD in 1963 on *Science, Economic Growth and Government Policy* provides information that is highly relevant to answering the first of these questions. The data concerned, which relate to the US and UK, are set out below in Table 9. Unfortunately, comparable detailed data for Community firms are not available, but there is no reason to believe that the situation there is materially different from that obtaining in the US and UK.

TABLE 9

Research & Development Related to Size of Enterprises in US and UK

	US (*1958*)			UK (*1959*)		
Size (employment)	*5,000 and above*	*1,000 to 4,999*	*less than 1,000*	*2,000 and above*	*300 to 1,999*	*less than 300*
Percentage of enterprises doing research	89	50	4	90	58	18
Percentage of total research expenditure	85	8	7	93	6	1

Source: OECD, *Science, Economic Growth and Government Policy*, p. 87.

Measuring firms' size in terms of numbers of employees and dividing firms into three main size-groups, Table 9 shows clearly for both US and UK that, while it is extremely unusual for firms in the smallest size-group to engage in research, it is virtually just as unusual for firms in the largest group not to. As the second row of the table shows, the vast bulk of research spending in industry was accounted for by the activities of the firms in the largest size-groups.

Why should the likelihood of firms embarking upon research increase with size? The answer to this is probably to be found in the fact that for each industry or section of an industry there is some initial threshold level of expenditure below which a serious research programme as dictated by the technology of the industry is simply not possible. The larger the firm, the easier it becomes to reach this threshold level.

A recent study of the electronic capital-goods industry contains an illuminating account of where this threshold might be for various sections of that industry, and the implications of this for competition within the industry.[38] In this industry competition is largely based upon technical innovation and service, for example the introduction by IBM of transistorized computers made the first-generation valve computers technically obsolete and compelled other producers to develop transistorized models if they wished to compete in the world EDP computer market. For various sections of the industry the minimum annual amount of spending on R & D that is necessary to keep a firm competitively viable varies quite considerably from perhaps £40,000–75,000 for radio communications receivers to £2–8 million for a communications satellite, these estimates being based upon European costs. It is important to stress that these figures, although necessarily approximations, refer to absolute levels of expenditure. A high ratio of R & D expenditure to sales might still mean that the absolute amount of expenditure is insufficient in the case of a small firm. Similarly, a low ratio of R & D expenditure to sales could be quite consistent with the necessary large absolute amount in the case of a large firm. The point that needs to be stressed is that, as with any other kind of overhead cost, the higher the R & D threshold, the greater is the necessity to spread these costs over a large output, and the greater the advantage, *cet. par.*, of the large firms. Thus, to the extent that the threshold nature of R & D costs makes them somewhat akin to an overhead cost, one might expect their relative impact often to be low in both small firms (as the threshold is simply beyond them and these costs are not incurred), and large firms (because they are spread).

It would certainly be wrong to argue that, because *large* firms are more likely to engage in R & D than small, then the *largest* firms in any industry should do relatively the most research. A number of recent American studies have tended to show that this is by no means the case. Jacob Schmookler cites evidence from six industries to show that in four cases (food and kindred products, fabricated metal products and ordnance, electrical equipment, and scientific and professional instruments) the percentage

[38] NIESR, *Econ. R.*, Nov. 1965, pp. 40–92.

9

of spending accounted for by research and development decreased in the largest firms.[39] Only in chemicals and machinery did the largest firms also make the greatest proportionate outlay on R & D. Another study of eight industries by James S. Worley also suggests that the very largest firm in an industry may not necessarily show the greatest relative interest in research. Measuring the research activity of a firm by the proportion of its total employees engaged in R & D work, Worley concluded:

Comparison of rank order of research and development personnel per thousand employees with rank order of employment size reveals no strong relationship. Instead, there appears a tendency for firms near the middle of the distribution to hire relatively more research-and-development personnel than do firms at either end, and in four of the eight industries the firm employing the relatively greatest number of research-and-development personnel is smaller in size than the firm employing relatively the smallest number.[40]

Again, in a separate study, Edwin Mansfield noted that

except for the chemical industry, there is no evidence that the largest firms in these industries spent more in 1945 on R & D, relative to sales, than did somewhat smaller firms. In the petroleum, drug, and glass industries, the largest firms spent significantly less. . . . During 1945–59, there was no indication in any of these industries of a systematic change in the effect of size of firm on the level R & D of expenditures.[41]

Whatever the relative or absolute amount of resources devoted to R & D activity, however, such activity is clearly not valuable for its own sake but for the economically exploitable innovations it actually yields. It is, therefore, vital to inquire whether fertility of innovation is significantly correlated with size. Mansfield has made a study in depth that is an important contribution to our understanding of this aspect of the problem. He studied three industries (iron and steel, petroleum refining, and bituminous coal production) and listed the main innovations that occurred in them over the period 1919–58. He assumed that if all firms were equally alert to innovations, then one would expect a firm's

---

[39] Jacob Schmookler, 'Bigness, Fewness and Research', *JPE*, Dec. 1959, pp. 631–2.

[40] James S. Worley, 'Industrial Research and the New Competition', ibid. Apr. 1961, p. 185.

[41] Edwin Mansfield, 'Industrial Research and Development Expenditures', ibid. Aug. 1964, pp. 337–8.

share in the total innovations in its industry to be approximately equal to its market share. Judged by this admittedly 'rather crude' standard the largest four coal and petroleum producers must be regarded favourably. On the other hand, the data for the steel industry tended to suggest that the four largest firms had not been responsible for as many significant innovations as one might have expected from their market shares. Within the steel industry, however, it was noted that the largest firm, the US Steel Corporation, had a better record than Bethlehem, the second largest producer. In all three industries, however, Mansfield noted that smaller firms have tended to become less important as innovators as time goes on. Clearly this could be accounted for by the rising development costs associated with the greater complexity of modern technology.[42] In the later and more extensive study previously cited Mansfield reached a number of conclusions that cannot be ignored by those who will have to shape European policy in these fields.

First, although the success of any one R & D project is always uncertain 'there seems to be a close relationship over the long run between the amount a firm spends on R & D and the total number of important innovations it produces'. Secondly, holding the level of R & D expenditure constant, the effect of firm size turns out to be negative. 'Thus, contrary to popular belief, the inventive output per dollar of R & D expenditure in most of these cases seems to be lower in the largest firms than in large and medium-sized firms.' And thirdly, when the size of firms is held constant and the innovative productivity of increasing amounts of R & D expenditure is estimated, then, except in the case of the chemical industry, 'the results do not indicate any marked advantages of the largest-scale research activities over large and medium-sized ones.'[43]

6. SIZE: THE LESSONS FOR TECHNOLOGY AND ANTI-TRUST

The current preoccupation in Europe with the virtues of

---

[42] Mansfield, 'Size of Firms, Market Structure and Innovation', *JPE*, Dec. 1963, pp. 560–1, 566 & 568.
[43] *JPE*, Aug. 1964, p. 336.

large-scale enterprises is based upon the belief that they are necessary to achieve the static economies of scale that the large market makes possible and that they are the spearhead of dynamic technological advance. The operation of both these factors is illustrated by the forces at present shaping the European aircraft industry.

In this industry, scale is as synonymous with immediate survival as with efficiency, both static and dynamic. This is so because the initial investment in R & D work that is involved in the construction of modern aircraft types, such as the supersonic Concorde, may amount to as much as £500 million, a sum not likely to be within the reach of private business in Europe and even beyond the reach of European governments unless shared. If the production of such aircraft can be geared to the requirements of several European airlines, then these enormous overheads can be spread and the cost per unit reduced. Thus the pooling of resources makes possible an initial investment on a scale that is probably beyond the reach of both individual companies and individual governments, and the widening of the market facilitates the volume of sales that will determine the ultimate viability of the entire project. And what is true of modern aircraft construction applies similarly over much of the field of advanced technology—computers, atomic power, space exploration, and telecommunications.[44] In each of these fields, and many others, there is much to be gained by eliminating the duplications that separate sub-optimal national efforts often entail, concentrating research, development, and production in a few large firms, and marketing throughout the entire integrated area. In this connexion the French government proposed at the beginning of 1965 that the Commission should compare industrial and scientific research policies in each of the Six and that the results of such a survey should then be used to promote rationalization and coordination in this field. Characteristically and, indeed, in our opinion, realistically, the French stressed the close relationship between technological performance in the

---

[44] A detailed discussion of the possibilities and problems in a number of important fields may be found in United Kingdom Council of the European Movement, *European Cooperation in Advanced Technology* (1965). As far as the UK aircraft industry is concerned these arguments were strikingly confirmed by the findings of the Plowden Report, Cmnd. 2853, 1965.

Community and the possibility of a liberal trade policy towards the rest of the world.[45]

The kind of industries mentioned in the previous paragraph tend to be those where the state plays a major role and their reorganization on a European scale requires primarily a co-ordination of state activities in the sectors concerned. In all of them technology has dictated a presumption in favour of size, and, as government is so deeply involved, there is an alternative mechanism to competition to ensure that the public interest is not lost sight of if concentration has to go very far. But what of the wide range of industries whose activities are more conventionally commercial in character? Here it is necessary to proceed more cautiously, for neither the static nor the dynamic superiority of the *largest* firms is so clearly marked as to justify any presumption in their favour. For example, an important study by J. S. Bain of twenty US industries suggested that, in at least half of all such industries, the leading firms were above optimum size for 'static' efficiency—that is, efficiency in production and distribution.[46] Furthermore, although the evidence cited in Table 9 (evidence that was necessarily limited to US and UK experience) suggests that industrial R & D work would indeed be stimulated if the small-sized firms that in practice do nothing in the way of R & D could be combined into a smaller number of larger enterprises each of the size at which R & D becomes more of a standard practice, there may be a limit to what should be expected from a continuation of this process in the long run, as Mansfield's studies suggest that fertility of research is not at a maximum in the largest firms. Thus if US experience is any guide, then neither the static nor the dynamic advantages of the largest-scale operations are so clear-cut as to rule out the need for a vigorous anti-trust policy towards big businesses.[47]

It can of course be argued that in some degree US experience is more a guide for the future than the present. Thus when it is pointed out that the largest firms do not appear to be superior and

---

[45] *Financial Times*, 17 Mar. 1965.
[46] Bain, *Industrial Organization*, p. 356.
[47] Further evidence stressing the extremely tenuous nature of the link between size of firm and the possibility of technological progressiveness may be found in the major studies by C. F. Carter and B. R. Williams, especially their *Industry and Technical Progress* (1957), p. 126, and J. Jewkes and others, *The Sources of Invention* (1958), pp. 168 & 249.

may indeed be inferior to large and medium ones, it should be recognized that many of the biggest European firms are almost certainly less than their large (and probably medium) US rivals. Therefore only after a considerable increase in size has occurred will European firms attain dimensions where further growth becomes a debatable advantage.

Nevertheless it would be wholly undesirable if the present justifiable interest in concentrations in European industry were allowed to degenerate into an anti-competitive megalomania. That there is a strong anti-competitive element in some of the reasoning used to stress the need for greater concentration can hardly be denied. For example, the past president of the Patronat has argued that

the way that leads to firms of European dimensions . . . often passes through the stage of agreements between firms. This is the moment to stress once again that a realistic and constructive application of the rules of competition of the Treaty of Rome is indispensable in deriving all the benefits attending unification.[48]

. M. Villiers's use of the word '*profits*' rather than '*bénéfices*' must remove any possibility of placing a wholly cynical interpretation upon his remarks. But here again it is important to learn from US experience, which in this respect surely teaches us that the most far-reaching ban on cartels is far from incompatible with—and could indeed be an important cause of—business concentration of the kind that European business is so concerned to achieve.

Just how well adapted are the policies of the Six to achieving the pragmatic but pro-competitive approach to larger-scale enterprises that seems on the balance of the evidence to be called for? There are in fact important reasons for believing that the policies of the member states and the Communities leave a certain amount to be desired—both from the standpoint of how far they contribute to establishing more desirable industrial structures, and what possibilities they offer in the anti-trust field for precluding or controlling the development of undesirable ones. This is because there are certain fields of policy, especially

---

[48] Président Villiers, 'Face a la concurrence américaine les enterprises européennes doivent concentrer leur moyens', *Patronat français*, Aug.–Sept. 1964.

those of fiscal and company law, that at the present time have the effect, for artificial exogenous reasons that have nothing to do with economic efficiency or competition, of promoting or hindering business concentrations. It is the policy of the Commission to attempt to adjust such factors wherever they arise and to make them *neutral* in their effects. Conversely, at the other end of the business spectrum, the Commission is seeking to improve the position of small businesses and to do this in ways that improve their efficiency without preserving archaic régimes. By these means it is hoped to permit a smooth adaptation of business structures to the conditions of the larger market.

(a) Fiscal Factors Affecting Business Concentration[49]

Apart from the effects of the multi-stage cascade turnover taxes which, as we have already shown in Chapter 2, can work to promote the vertical concentration of enterprises, there are certain other features of the national fiscal systems that can also bear upon concentration, either promoting it or discouraging it as the case may be. The various circumstances in which fiscal considerations might become relevant to concentrations may be divided into two main kinds. First, it is possible that fiscal difficulties may arise at the time of the actual act of concentration. Secondly, the fiscal position of the concentration for the years thereafter must be considered. Each of these two possibilities, the fiscal consequences of the intitial act of concentration itself, and the continuing fiscal consequences after the concentration has been completed, may also be subdivided into two other sets of circumstances. The first is when the concentration takes the form of a complete amalgamation involving the legal demise of one or both companies, and, in the latter case, the birth of an entirely new company. The second is when the concentration simply takes the form of the acquisition of a shareholding in one company by another.

Consider first the possible fiscal consequences of a once-for-all kind that might arise in the case of a complete amalgamation. The amalgamation will involve the end of at least one of the

---

[49] This discussion, and the following ones on corresponding problems raised by company law and policy on small businesses, is based upon the Commission's unpublished memorandum, *Das Problem der Unternehmenskonzentration im Gemeinsamen Markt* (1965). (See n. 18 on p. 219 above.)

companies as a separate legal entity, and, indeed, both companies would have to be dissolved if the amalgamation took the form of a mutual fusion into an entirely new company. Whatever taxes are involved at such a company dissolution would then become payable. Reserves and profits that had not been taxed up to that time would suddenly become liable to fiscal assessment. In particular the hidden reserves arising from the differences between the book value of the assets and their actual value would be revealed and would be liable to tax. In practice this latter kind of reserve might be very considerable, and taxation of them at the normal rate might make the cost of many amalgamations prohibitive. Within each of the member states, therefore, various concessions are granted by the national fiscal authorities that in practice do much to alleviate the difficulties that might otherwise arise in these circumstances. For example, taxes might be levied at a reduced rate, or payment might be permitted to extend over a number of years, or the amalgamation might be allowed to proceed without a definite settlement of the tax liability being made at the time, this being arranged in a mutually satisfactory way later on. Unfortunately, indeed inevitably, this understanding attitude on the part of the authorities usually vanishes when a cross-frontier amalgamation is under consideration. In particular the possibility of phasing tax payments over a number of years becomes unattractive to the administrative mind when the company on which the tax would be levied is due to disappear from the national scene. Finally, there also appears to be a possibility of double liability to corporation tax in certain types of amalgamations at the time when the assets of the company that is being dissolved are being transferred to the company that has assimilated it.

Secondly, a concentration may not involve an amalgamation but simply the acquisition of shares by one company in another. In this case it is broadly true to say that such acquisitions do not meet with either encouragement or encumbrance from the fiscal side.

This is also largely true of the third situation that has to be considered—namely what effects fiscal factors may have upon an amalgamation on a continuing basis in the years after it has been accomplished. The future change-over in five of the member states towards an added value tax on something like the

French model, which has now been agreed to in Council, will eliminate the fiscal incentive to amalgamation at present provided in varying degrees, but particularly in Western Germany, by the multi-stage cascade turnover tax. On the other hand a certain disincentive to amalgamation may exist in some of the member states by reason of the increased rates of profits tax that are levied upon larger enterprises. In this connexion it is useful to point out here that, assuming that the initial difficulties of bringing about cross-frontier amalgamations can be surmounted, then the differing national rates of profits tax will be one of the factors influencing the geographical direction that cross-frontier concentrations actually take. This, of course, is simply one aspect of the more general problem of the effects of differential rates of direct taxation on the choice of investment location which we have already discussed in Chapter 2.

We come now to the fourth and last possibility. Suppose that a concentration has occurred (or is being contemplated) that simply involves one company buying shares in another. What is the fiscal position of such a concentration once it has actually come into operation on a continuing basis? Here the potential threat is double taxation of the subsidiary company's dividends when they are paid into the parent company, thereby creating a disincentive to concentration. Providing that the degree of participation of the 'parent' in the 'subsidiary' is at least 25 per cent in Germany, the Netherlands, and Luxembourg, then the companies enjoy the *Schachtelprivileg*—that is they are considered by the fiscal authorities as a self-contained group and double taxation is completely avoided. Although the degree of participation of the parent in the subsidiary need only be 20 per cent in France, and in Belgium no minimum proportion of participation is laid down, these states do not appear to eliminate double taxation entirely on the dividends of the subsidiary company. When a company in one member state remits dividends to a company in another, the possibility of some double taxation is again quite real in the majority of cases, as Belgium, the Netherlands, and France automatically apply their own somewhat imperfect systems to profits from foreign subsidiaries, while Germany and Luxembourg only alleviate the problem if special arrangements are made between the fiscal authorities and the enterprises. Clearly a harmonization of policies relating to the

9*

taxation of the dividends of subsidiary companies is called for, as the present system militates to some extent against concentration by failing to eliminate double taxation completely, both in regard to national and, even more, to international remittances.

In general, it may be said that the existence of different fiscal provisions bearing on concentration in each of the member states is quite likely to lead to differential degrees of concentration, errors in siting, and distortions in competition that can only be avoided by co-ordination and harmonization of the relevant national laws.

(b) Company Law and Concentration

Although the Commission is interested in the artificial impediments to business concentration operative within individual states, its main problem lies in the field of combinations between enterprises in different member states, the term combination being understood in its widest sense. It has indeed been observed that in the field of international concentration there have been take-overs and joint ventures but hardly any real mergers uniting companies formerly operating separately in the Common Market.[50] Indeed the impression which emerges from the Dutch merger data in Table 10 is that links between American and European companies have been more easily established than purely intra-European links. It is not impossible to imagine that in time American business penetration in Europe may act as a catalyst to the concentration process within Europe itself.

As yet there is within the EEC no common regulation governing or facilitating the way in which companies in different member states may combine. At least three general solutions to this problem have been suggested. The first is that there should be a harmonization of national company laws so that the real and psychological obstacles caused by differences of rules can be eliminated. It has, however, been argued that the harmonization process is too slow, particularly in view of the need for European industry to adapt itself quickly to outside competition. Therefore an alternative approach has been suggested by the Directorate General for Competition of the EEC Commission. They have

[50] P. Dreyer, 'Interpenetration in the Common Market', in Federal Trust Assoc., *Problems of Scale in Europe*, p. 23.

TABLE 10

Mergers and other forms of Amalgamation in Dutch Industries
(1958 to mid-1965)

Sector	With Dutch enterprises	With foreign enterprises				Total	Total internal & foreign
		EEC	US & Canada	UK	Scandinavia & Switzerland		
Chemicals	49	7	25	8	2	42	91
Metals	54	1	8	7	3	19	73
Textiles	48	–	4	4	–	8	56
Paper	10	–	1	2	2	5	15
Rubber	6	–	–	–	–	–	6
Ceramics	5	–	3	1	–	4	9
Tobacco	3	–	1	4	–	5	8
Total	175	8	42	26	7	83	258

Source: Report of the (Netherlands) State Secretary for Economic Affairs to the President of the Second Chamber of the States General, 7 June 1966, p. 8.

suggested that a common form of European company—more precisely described as a commercial company of European statute—could be created.[51] The members states would through Community procedure draw up a convention containing common rules governing such a company. Companies wishing to combine with companies in other states could take the common European form, thus eliminating or at least reducing the problems posed by differences of national law. In 1965 the French government entered this field with a suggestion of its own.[52] It too was in favour of a form of European company. However, differences appear to exist between the Competition Directorate and the French government about the status of the law relating to this type of company. The Competition Directorate appears to envisage a Community law with final appeal to the European Court of Justice. The French appear to suggest a uniform law,

[51] EEC, *8th Gen. Rep.* (1965), p. 106. More recently the Commission has produced a memorandum on the subject—*Mémorandum de la Commission de la Communauté Économique Européenne sur la création d'une société commerciale européenne*, Document SEC (66) 1250, 22 Apr. 1966.

[52] Note du Gouvernement français sur la création d'une société commerciale de type européen (1965).

adopted by means of a convention between the Six, which would be introduced into the corpus of national law and would apparently be interpreted by national courts. The convention would be drawn up by an inter governmental working group with the participation of the Commission. Some commentators see in this proposal an attempt to whittle down the Community element as far as possible. We will merely restrict ourselves to observing that it would be a great pity if such a worth-while venture were to founder on some dispute about whether the arrangements should be inter governmental or Community in character.

It would however be a great mistake to assume that better legal arrangements for cross-frontier mergers within the Community are inevitably bound to have a dramatic effect. There is good reason to believe that international business affiliation is held back not just by legal and fiscal but also by more personal and psychological factors. Thus mergers across frontiers are likely to be inhibited by, for example, hostility on the part of French and Dutch enterprises to close business participation with German industry.

(e) *The Beginnings of a Policy on Small Businesses*

It has also been recognized by the Commission that neutrality in respect of size requires that some of the disadvantages experienced by small- and medium-sized firms be eliminated. In the fiscal field we have already alluded to the advantage which a cascade turnover tax confers upon vertically integrated firms. But there are other factors which tell against the smaller-sized firm. For example, the Commission refers to difficulties in gaining access to the capital markets, in obtaining guarantees for credit, in purchasing, in keeping abreast of technical progress, in distribution and market research, in gaining access to certain special markets in which demand is exercised by public authorities—for example defence contracting. The Commission has indicated, even before its investigations are complete, that certain positive steps are called for. These include measures to facilitate the access of small- and medium-sized firms to the capital market, approval of joint purchasing arrangements, and relaxation of the rules relating to common research, specialization, and rationalization agreements. The Commission is also of the opinion that assistance might be given to enable enterprises to adjust to new market conditions. The Commission intends to discuss with national governments what can be done in this field within the framework of the Rome Treaty. Obviously very little can be said about the implications of this kind of policy at the present time but it may be noted that the kind of proposals mentioned above seem to go a good deal beyond mere neutrality in the sense of offsetting the artificial disadvantages of small businesses.

7. POSSIBLE IMPROVEMENTS IN ANTI-TRUST IN RELATION TO LARGE ENTERPRISES

As far as the anti-trust policies towards large enterprises are concerned it is surely clear from our earlier discussion that the ECSC, with its rigorous insistence upon the preservation of competition, and the EEC, with its much milder prohibition of abuse of market power, cannot both be regarded as offering satisfactory solutions simultaneously. It would seem to us that each involves rather extreme positions and that a judicious mixture of the two approaches is now called for that would result in one uniform policy on concentration for both Communities.[53] The main ingredients of such a uniform composite policy would be as follows.

The ECSC would require to move away from the rather negative criteria that seemed so vital for political reasons to those who originally worked out the details of Article 66. Under the present system the High Authority can only authorize concentrations where competition is not jeopardized. Technically desirable concentrations may, therefore, have to be allowed in the future only by an increasingly generous interpretation of what constitutes a useful minimum of competition. It would surely be better to recognize that in certain circumstances (which will probably be very few and far between) there may be a genuine conflict between technical requirements and the needs of competition. In assessing the desirability of a proposed

[53] We have shown that there is no substantial difference between ECSC and EEC in the field of cartels—the establishment of a uniform policy on agreements for the entire Common Market would not, to that extent, present great problems. This view has recently been supported by a member of the High Authority, Dr Fritz Hellwig, who has also argued in favour of a single policy on concentrations—see *Europäische Gemeinschaft*, Apr. 1966, p. 3.

concentration as much weight should be given to its consequences for technological development as for competition,
rather than the latter alone, as is at present the case in ECSC.[54]
This would have the important psychological benefit of identi-
fying the anti-trust authorities in a positive sense with modern
industrial problems and eliminate the suspicion of business that
the former operate in a technological vacuum.

In introducing this kind of policy with a more positive emphasis
upon technology it would also be necessary to remove a further
weakness from the existing ECSC policy—namely the obligation
of the High Authority to take into account the size of existing
enterprises in the Community when assessing a proposed
concentration. This is a dangerous red herring. If certain enterprises as a result of self-financed growth or nationalization have
grown beyond the optimum size for economic efficiency, there
is no reason why this should be held in any way to justify, even
partially, the creation of further excessively large firms by the
process of concentration on the grounds of non-discrimination.
Similarly, if one large optimum firm exists, it by no means
follows that a merger of two smaller firms will automatically
result in a new enterprise of optimum proportions. Mergers that
substantially reduce competition but confer no real economies
should not be provided with any possibility of vicarious justification on the irrelevant grounds of equality of treatment.[55]

Certain features of the ECSC's concentration policy are,
however, extremely valuable and should be retained—these are
in particular the notification of significant merger proposals to
the authorities and their investigation and approval prior to
implementation. Similarly, the power to order divestiture,
however rarely it may be required in practice, should also be
preserved. Again, the ultimate power to fix prices and to allocate
production should remain with the authorities.

The differences between the above type of approach and that
at present embodied in the Rome Treaty are obvious enough. If

[54] It is perhaps worth noting that in the US some commentators have
suggested that in judging mergers the economies of scale should be considered
as an extenuating factor (see C. Kaysen and D. F. Turner, *Antitrust Policy;
an Economic and Legal Analysis* (1959), pp. 133–5).

[55] A more detailed discussion of some of the problems involved in the field
of merger policy may be found in McLachlan & Swann, 'Next Steps in Monopoly Policy', *Scottish JPE*, June 1964, pp. 141–4.

such a homogeneous policy for the whole Common Market were established it would imply the end of the present rather permissive approach to mergers in the EEC and acceptance of the principles of prior notification and scrutiny for those above a certain size.

It is true that the Commission in its memorandum on concentration has revealed itself aware of the need to maintain competition. But the position taken up on this question appears to stop a good deal short of the kind of policies that we are recommending here. This is probably because the Commission is at the present time trying to devise a policy that requires no more powers than those already provided by Article 86. The result is that only mergers that can be shown to be an abuse of a dominant position would be attacked. As one illustration of such a possibility the Commission cites the hypothetical example of a dominant enterprise selling below cost, driving another enterprise towards bankruptcy, and then forcing it to merge on unfair terms or against its will. This would, of course, be a clear offence against Article 86, and such a concentration could, therefore, be attacked under the existing powers.

A less clear-cut case would be:

Where a merger between one enterprise in a dominant position and another enterprise puts an end to competition which would otherwise have continued to exist on the market in question and so establishes a monopoly, it *can* have just the same detrimental effects for purchasers and consumers as the examples mentioned in Article 86. A monopoly position does in fact remove the incentive to further technical development and greater productivity, to mention only two of its harmful consequences. It has the result of limiting the level of production so much that maximization of profits is achieved by means of prices that are higher than they would be in a market where there is effective competition and therefore a higher level of production.

The Commission came to the conclusion that a concentration which establishes a *monopoly* on a market, and therefore prejudices the freedom of action of suppliers, purchasers and consumers, may *in a particular case* constitute abuse of a dominant position in the sense of Article 86 of the Treaty, and would therefore not be permissible.[56]

The weakness of the Commission's present approach is clear

[56] EEC Official Spokesman, *Concentration of Firms in the Common Market*, P-1/66, 1965, pp. 3–4, italics ours.

from these two cases: action can only be taken when one of the enterprises involved in the concentration is already in a dominant position. At the most, therefore, if this policy is actually put into practice, the Commission might sometimes be able to prevent a bad situation from becoming even worse, that is by preventing market domination from becoming actual monopoly. But on the vital question of what might be done to assess the desirability or otherwise of concentrations that might *result* in market domination the Commission has as yet been completely silent—officially at any rate. Under these circumstances it is not surprising to learn that the Commission has already begun to look covetously at those parts of the Paris Treaty that provide for prior approval of concentrations by the authorities, and, indeed, it has been encouraged to do so by one of the groups of professors appointed to advise on concentration policy. In a future merger of the Communities therefore, something like the ECSC policy on concentrations might come to prevail. If it does it would also make available two important weapons in the anti-trust armoury not at present provided for in the Rome Treaty— the possibility of divestiture and price and production control by the authorities.

There are, however, two highly valuable features of the Rome Treaty that should be incorporated in any new composite system. The first of these is the *per se* prohibition of abuse. By maintaining this principle large dominant firms will be forced to keep major aspects of policy continually under review if they are to avoid the possibility of substantial retroactive fines and, possibly, damage suits. In so far as this encourages them not to abuse their power, they would also avoid the possibility of intervention by the authorities in regard to prices and production. The second feature of the Rome Treaty's approach to market domination that should be maintained is its extension of that concept to include the possibility of domination by oligopolies as well as large single firms. This could well prove to be the most significant innovation in anti-trust for many years.

In short this kind of revised common policy would make a much more prominent feature of competition than does the EEC at present, and it would not detract in practice from the importance specifically attached to competition in the ECSC's concentration policy. But it would provide for the possibility that

there may on occasion be a genuine conflict between the maintenance of effective competition and technological requirements,
and it would also provide a wider selection of weapons for the
enforcement agencies than either the ECSC or EEC alone
provides.[57]

[57] The whole subject of the size of enterprise in the Six and the US, competition with US business and the relevance of all this to Community anti-trust,
is dealt with in greater detail in our PEP/RIIA paper, *Concentration or Competition: a European Dilemma?* (1966).

9

The ECSC Steel-Pricing Régime

ALTHOUGH the Paris Treaty sets up common rules regarding pricing and competition for both the coal and steel markets, a number of important factors have combined to make the coal market very much a special case. Among the most prominent of such factors are the following. First, in the coal market the elements of monopoly (public in France, private in Germany) are much more in evidence than they are in the case of steel. Secondly, the comparative inefficiency of the Belgian coal mines led to that country being sealed off deliberately from the rest of the coal market for a number of years while attempts were made by using subsidies to get Belgian costs down to something like a level that would be competitive with those in neighbouring states. Thirdly, and most important, the problems of the coal market cannot be understood except in the context of energy policy as a whole. We shall, therefore, consider coal separately in the general context of energy policy. By way of contrast, the steel market, subject to a number of important qualifications, has been allowed to function in a competitive manner, and an analysis of it as a competitive market is, therefore, meaningful.

Although the common market for steel has been functioning since 1953, and has been the subject of several studies, it still provides the challenge of an innovation and of a continuing experiment.[1] As an innovation, time was needed for firms and administrations to accustom themselves to it. As an experiment, it has lived at times with the prospect of failure. Our purpose in this chapter is to sketch the main features of the régime and to analyse its working critically. Our emphasis will be on quantification as far as this is possible.

[1] Among the most useful sources dealing fairly comprehensively with various aspects of the ECSC are: ECSC, *Le CECA 1952–1962* (1963) (Wagenführ Report); Diebold, *Schuman Plan;* Lister, *Europe's Coal and Steel Community;* D. L. Burn, *The Steel Industry 1939–1959* (1961); and H. H. Liesner's section on the ECSC in Meade, Liesner, & Wells.

I. THE GENERAL CHARACTER OF THE STEEL-PRICING RÉGIME

The most important single aspect of the ECSC's competitive régime is its hybrid, compromise quality. On the one hand it attempts, as we have shown, to prevent the reduction of competition by cartels or dominant enterprises and deliberately encourages price competition, while, on the other hand, the High Authority enjoys reserve powers to control prices (to prevent ruinous price competition in a recession or to prevent exploitation of the market in times of scarcity), to fix production quotas and consumption priorities, and—of the greatest importance in the long run for the workability of competition—to influence the course of investment in the industry. In discussing problems of competitive pricing in the steel market in the following pages we should, therefore, bear in mind the compromise nature of the régime that the High Authority is responsible for administering, and be on our guard against regarding the High Authority as simply a sort of European version of the US Federal Trade Commission with responsibility for anti-trust alone: clearly the work of the High Authority in promoting competition must be seen in the context of its entire responsibility.

In this field of pricing there are three requirements of the Paris Treaty that together fundamentally shape the character of the régime.

First, Article 2 lays down that the Community must 'progressively establish conditions which will in themselves assure the most rational distribution of production at the highest possible level of productivity'. Granted that this aim is not be pursued without regard to its effect on employment and general economic conditions in the member states, the words 'in themselves' make it clear that a competitive régime must be maintained, as only a competitive régime could be said to involve—however imperfectly—the required qualities of automatic adjustment. As we have mentioned, however, this reliance upon competition is by no means complete, because certain powers of intervention are also granted to the High Authority. But these powers of direct intervention with regard to production and the operation of the market are to be exercised 'only when circumstances make it absolutely necessary' (Article 5), for example in 'a period of manifest crisis' (Article 58); and then only when indirect means of action (such as co-operation with goverments to influence general consumption (Article 57)) appear inadequate. The qualification of the High Authority's reserve powers in this way was perhaps in some degree an early reflection of the reluctance of the national governments to grant too much power to a supranational agency even in fields where national interventions had been very prominent. However, a much more definite influence was the US which, as we indicated earlier, exercised a significant influence on the drafting of the treaty and was suspicious of *dirigiste* tendencies. These limitations on the conditions in which intervention by the High Authority may occur correspondingly reinforce the importance that is to be attached to the automatic controls of the market itself.

Secondly, the treaty makes a far-reaching prohibition of discriminatory pricing. It regards as incompatible with the common market, and therefore prohibited, 'measures or practices discriminating among producers, among buyers or among consumers, specifically as concerns prices, delivery terms and transportation rates' (Article 4). This is made more explicit in Article 60, which prohibits as unfair competition purely local price reductions the purpose of which is to acquire a monopoly within the common market, and defines as discriminatory the application by a seller of unequal conditions in comparable transactions—discrimination on grounds of nationality being singled out for particular condemnation. Both economic theory and the political needs of the member states provide reasons for this ban on discrimination. On the basis of static analysis price discrimination is usually held to impede the maximization of total welfare as it distorts the price ratios of goods as between different consumers.[2] But this technical argument, which is in any case far from flawless, is unlikely to have been uppermost in the minds of those who framed the ban on price discrimination. What is more likely is that, in the conditions of scarcity prevailing in the coal and steel markets during the years when the treaty was being negotiated, a ban on discriminatory treatment was necessary for the contribution it would make to political integration.

Thirdly, in an attempt to make the ban on discriminatory

[2] For a discussion of the basic welfare theory concerned see for example G. Stigler, *The Theory of Price* (1952), pp. 91–93.

practices effective and to discourage ill-considered price reductions, a system of price publicity is enforced. Steel producers
have to publish their price lists as applying at named locations
and sell at these prices without discrimination. The buyer pays
this basic price plus freight from this named location to his own
works. The producer remains free to change his price list after
giving the High Authority notice of his intention but not to
deviate from it except to 'align' his price on that of a competitor—
a possibility that we examine in greater detail below. Transport
rates for products coming under the ECSC rules must also be
either published or brought to the notice of the High Authority
(we shall ignore the problems raised by transport for the time
being and discuss them separately at the end of this chapter). In
principle, therefore, this ready availability of information (in
Community language, the transparency of the market) makes it
possible for consumers in any part of the common market to
ascertain the most advantageous terms on which they can buy
steel. And it is this availability of data on product prices and
transport rates that facilitates the supervision by the High
Authority of the ban on discrimination.

2. THE ECSC BASING POINT SYSTEM

Under the ECSC system a producer is free to name the location
at which his basic price list applies. This location is known as the
basing point and is the place at which a customer can in theory
take delivery of steel without incurring any transport charges. In
practice it is the point from which such charges are calculated.
To understand the economic significance of the basing point
system, and in particular to understand the criticisms that may
be made of it, it should be stated explicitly that the basing point
need not be, and in fact often is not, the producer's own works
from which the supplies originate. As basing point and mill are
usually at two different locations the probability is that the
customer will pay a transport charge quite different from the
actual transport cost involved, as the customer pays transport
costs from the basing point, whereas the goods actually travel
directly from the producer's mill to the customer's works.

This may be seen more clearly if we consider two hypothetical
examples in which the transport costs incurred by the customer

differ from those actually involved in the transaction. In Diagram I the relative positions of the Producer, the Basing Point, and the Customer are shown with the relevant costs of transport (in DM).

DIAGRAM I

Transport Costs in the ECSC Basing Point System

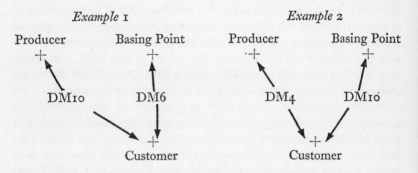

In Example 1 the customer is nearer to the basing point than to the producer. Supposing that the list price on the basing point were DM100, then the customer would have to pay a total delivered price of DM106. As it is the practice in the Community for the customer to pay the actual freight bill to the haulier (in this case DM10), then the producer has to adjust his invoice to the customer to take account of the fact that the latter has paid DM10 instead of DM6 for delivery. The customer finally pays the proper delivered price of DM106—that is, basing point price plus freight. But the actual price received by the producer is only DM96 as he has to 'absorb freight' to the extent of DM4—this being the excess of the actual freight over the notional figure.

In Example 2 the customer is nearer to the producer than to the basing point. If the list price at the basing point is DM100, then the customer must pay a total delivered price of DM110. If the customer pays the freight of DM4, then the producer will adjust the invoice so that the customer actually pays him DM106. Again, the customer will have paid the basing point price plus freight from the basing point to his own works. But the producer's receipts vary considerably in the two transactions with 'phantom freight' figuring prominently in the latter to his advantage.

If the producer chooses his own works or some fairly close

location as the basing point at which to apply his price list, then there is no substantial difference between the basing point and ex-works f.o.b. pricing. This is in fact what occurs predominantly in Italy and Benelux. But in Germany, and to some extent in France, there may be a considerable distance between the producer's mill and the basing point at which his price list applies. According to Liesner, over 85 per cent of steel output in Benelux, the Saar, and Italy was produced within 20 kilometres of the basing point in the period 1957–8, whereas in France only 50 per cent was produced within that limit, and in Western Germany only 40 per cent.[3]

The other related feature of the basing point system vital to an understanding of its effects on pricing and competition in the steel industry is the fact that a number of separate enterprises often select the same basing point for the application of their published price lists. This is most pronounced in Western Germany, but it also occurs, although to a rather smaller extent, in France. The result is that, broadly speaking, in Western Germany and France the number of enterprises producing a given product exceeds—sometimes greatly exceeds—the number of basing points at which their price lists apply, whereas in Italy and Benelux the number of basing points for any particular product corresponds rather more closely with the number of producers.

This may be seen from Table 1 (p. 262), in which we show for a range of products in each member state and the Community as a whole the number of basing points on which price lists are published (BP) and the number of enterprises producing the product in question (E).

In Western Germany the number of basing points for any product makes a striking contrast to the number of producers. Broadly speaking, the main producing centres are in the Ruhr and the Saar, but there are also certain important enterprises outside these two main areas, for example the Klöckner Werke at Bremen in the north, the Maximilianshütte in the south-east, and Ilseder-Peine and Salzgitter (which is state-owned) in the east. The Saar producers have all chosen common basing points in the Saar, either Saarbrücken or Dillingen according to the product. All other German producers, including those in the

---

[3] Meade, Liesner, & Wells, pp. 260–1.

TABLE I

Number of Basing Points compared with Number of Producers in ECSC (1962)

Product	Western Germany		France		Italy		Belgium		Nether-lands		Luxem-bourg		Communi*	
	BP	E	BP	E	BP	E	BP	E	BP	E	BP	E	BP	E
Rolled products (bars, angles, &c.)	2	33	21	32	58	104	10	12	1	1	3	3	95	179
Wire rods	2	15	6	11	15	19	4	4	1	1	2	2	30	53
Sections (joists, channels)	2	13	5	10	12	15	5	6	–	–	3	3	27	51
Hot-rolled strip	2	18	9	12	17	20	2	3	2	2	3	3	35	60
Heavy plates	2	14	11	19	10	12	5	6	1	1	1	1	30	55
Hot-rolled sheets (NPO)	2	16	12	18	11	12	5	7	1	1	1	1	32	55
Cold-reduced sheets (SPD)	3	15	10	16	6	6	4	5	1	1	1	1	25	44
Tinplate (electrolytic)	2	4	4	4	2	2	3	3	1	1	–	–	12	14

Source: Information made available by Iron and Steel Board.

outlying districts, have chosen common basing points in the Ruhr, for example Oberhausen for merchant bars, Siegen for sheets, and Essen for heavy plate. The economic significance of the choice of a common basing point by several enterprises is, of course, that it facilitates collusion: all enterprises basing their price lists on a given basing point publish identical prices—a practice no doubt gratefully inherited from the days of the pre-war steel cartels, as it can have the effect of making a customer indifferent as far as price is concerned between all the national producers.

Nor is this practice, or other forms of national collusion, confined to Germany. French firms in the major producing area around Thionville have selected common basing points within that area; and in general the prices set by the large firms are such that the customers in the major consuming area around Paris find themselves confronted by similar delivered prices from all the main producers. While it would seem at first sight from the much greater number of basing points in France as compared with Western Germany that the industry in the former state is the less rigid, it should be remembered that the French system of indicative planning does much to increase the spirit of co-operation in a nation of renowned individualists. With regard to Italy and Benelux, while it is true that producers tend to a greater extent to choose basing points at or near their own works, this is not itself sufficient to ensure that they follow completely independent pricing policies for, as we mentioned in our earlier discussion of the main type of restrictive practices in the Communities, it would appear that both trade associations and, even more, the national governments, exert some unifying influence.[4] On the whole it would probably be a fair summary to say that price competition on the basis of list prices between national producers is non-existent in Germany, is extremely unusual in France, and is only a little more common in Italy and Benelux. Because of this comparatively high degree of uniformity of list prices within each national price structure, the greatest importance must be attached to competition arising from differences in list prices as between enterprises in two or more member states, and to competition in the internal market against imports from third countries. To understand the strength and nature of such competition, it is necessary to describe the mechanism by which it occurs—the Community's rules on alignment.

3. ALIGNMENT

It is the alignment rule of the treaty, Article 60 (2,b), that is the means by which a measure of controlled competitive price flexibility is introduced into an otherwise comparatively rigid and compartmentalized oligopolistic market structure. Originally conceived as an attempt to obtain a modicum of controlled price flexibility in conditions of steel shortage, alignment has recently come to be the means to widespread and vigorous price competition. The alignment rule is presented by the treaty as an exception to the general rule that enterprises must at all times observe their published prices and conditions. It permits an enterprise to deviate from its published price lists in certain defined circumstances.

First, a deviation from published price lists is permitted to meet the competition of a producer selling on *another* basing

[4] See above, pp. 97–98.

point. Thus if producer A, selling on basing point A, finds that his list price plus delivery charges to customer B should be DM110 and that producer C, who perhaps has a lower list price or is using a more favourably located basing point at C, could offer B a delivered price of DM100, then it is open to A to reduce his delivered price to B down to DM100 also. Note that C need not actually have made any offer to customer B—the fact that he could have done so is alone sufficient to justify A's aligning down on to C's delivered price.

The example cited above would be known as a complete alignment. It is also, of course, possible for a firm to align by a smaller amount than that which would be necessary to equal the delivered price of its competitor. This would then be known as partial alignment. For either complete or partial alignment it is of the essence of the system that the maximum price reduction permitted is that which would result in the conditions of the competitor's price list being at most matched, but not undercut. The alignment rule clearly contains a recognition of the dangers of excessive price competition in the oligopolistic and cost conditions of the steel industry. For the system to work as it is meant to, the market must be transparent with regard to both steel prices and transport rates—conditions which have not in fact always been fulfilled satisfactorily, as we shall show.

A hypothetical example of alignment will demonstrate what the technique involves in practice. Let us take the simplest kind possible—where a producer in one country has to align down on the price list of another producer in that country. Suppose that Cockerill-Ougrée (Belgium) were selling SM heavy plate from its basing point at Seraing to a customer in Brussels and aligning on the price list of Forges de Clabecq at Clabecq. Cockerill-Ougrée would have to do the following calculation to ascertain how much alignment would be permitted:

Forges de Clabecq list price ex Clabecq basing point	BF 5,900
+ turnover tax of 6% basing point price	+354
+ transport Clabecq/Brussels	+55
Total price that would be paid by Brussels customer	6,309
— Transport Brussels/Seraing	—156
= Price (including 6% turnover tax) required ex Seraing to meet price ex Clabecq	6,153

Price required ex Seraing exclusive of 6% turnover tax   5,805
Cockerill-Ougrée list price ex Seraing   6,900
Maximum alignment permissible = (6,900–5,805)   1,095

Thus in this example Cockerill-Ougrée would be entitled to cut its list price for this transaction by up to BF 1,095 if a complete alignment was necessary.

Secondly, a similar form of controlled price competition is permitted between Community firms and imports from third countries. The rule here is that a Community producer may align his price down to the level of any offer *actually made* by an overseas supplier. As with domestic alignments, partial alignments are, of course, permissible.

The calculations required to make an alignment on an offer from a third country would be similar to those in the example of domestic alignment given above, except that the supplier starts with the knowledge of the delivered price required from him and therefore only has to calculate the equivalent of that delivered price related back to his own basing point.

Cases of alignment on offers from third countries must be reported to the High Authority giving the full details of the offer together with, if possible, a photostat copy of the order.[5] Alignments on third countries are only legal if the seller can prove that they are referring to an actual offer. Sellers must be faced with direct competition from third countries to justify departure from their own price lists.

The basic essentials of alignment are, therefore, fairly straightforward but it will be apparent that the successful operation of the process requires a considerable knowledge of general market conditions—in particular of the price lists and supply capabilities of competitors, of transport rates and turnover tax. In practice those firms that are attracted by the flexibility that alignment permits set up special departments to make sure that the necessary

---

[5] Until 1966 declaration of the details of such sales was only applicable in the case of alignments on third-country offers. However in November 1966 the High Authority announced that the system of declaring details of alignment sales would be extended to sales made by alignments on the prices of other Community producers. This was an attempt to deal with the extremely weak steel market conditions prevailing in 1966 and suggests that the High Authority believed that some of the weakness was due to abuse of the alignment rules. In November 1966 internal steel prices were reported to be as much as 20 per cent below list levels.

amount of accurate and up-to-date information is always available.

It is easy to demonstrate that in recent years alignment has offered definite scope for price competition. Table 2 below shows the basing points that were in a position to offer the lowest delivered prices for five steel products in each of eleven important consuming centres in 1963.

TABLE 2

Basing Points with Lowest Delivered Prices at Certain Consuming Centres (17 September 1963)

Product Consuming Centre	Billets	Merchant bars	Wire rod	Heavy plates	Sheet NPO
Hanover	Utrecht	Charleroi	Clabecq	Beverwijk Clabecq	Marchin
Duisburg	Utrecht	Oberhausen Charleroi	Clabecq	Clabecq	Marchin
Stuttgart	Milan	Thionville Charleroi	Clabecq	Clabecq	Marchin
Munich	Milan	Thionville	Clabecq	Clabecq	Marchin
Paris	Clabecq Milan	Charleroi	Clabecq	Clabecq	Marchin
Lille	Clabecq	Charleroi	Clabecq	Clabecq	Marchin
Bordeaux	Milan	Charleroi	Clabecq	Clabecq	Marchin
Brussels	Clabecq	Charleroi	Clabecq	Clabecq	Marchin
Eindhoven	Utrecht	Charleroi	Clabecq	Clabecq	Marchin
Rotterdam	Utrecht	Charleroi	Clabecq	Clabecq	Marchin
Milan	Milan	Novi Ligure	Clabecq	Clabecq	Marchin

Source: Information made available by the ECSC High Authority.

The above table shows clearly that even in Paris or the Ruhr, enterprises from outside the national state could offer better delivered prices than those of the national firms for these products. To retain their local customers firms in many cases would have to align on to lower delivered prices from competitors in other states of the Common Market. How great were the discrepancies between these various delivered prices? An estimate of this may be made by taking the example of one particular product, heavy plates, and indicating the delivered prices at which the main consuming centres could be supplied from certain basing points. Table 3 shows the delivered prices at each consuming centre expressed as a percentage of the cheapest of the eight possible sources of supply mentioned.

Table 3 also shows that buyers in all the consuming centres shown would, in the absence of any alignment possibilities, find it cheapest to buy at the Belgian basing point of Clabecq—that is,

TABLE 3

The Scope for Alignment

(*Indexes of Delivered Prices as Percentages of Lowest Prices—Heavy Plates, 16 September 1963*)

Basing Point / Consuming Centre	Essen	Saar-brücken	Seraing	Clabecq	Mont-médy	Dude-lange	Bever-wijk	Novi Ligure
anover	107	116	124	100	115	123	100	131
uisburg	108	120	125	100	118	126	102	133
uttgart	112	112	125	100	112	120	106	125
unich	108	110	122	100	110	118	103	118
aris	120	120	130	100	114	125	107	131
lle	120	122	130	100	116	127	107	135
ordeaux	119	119	127	100	114	123	107	125
russels	121	125	130	100	120	129	107	141
ndhoven	115	125	126	100	117	127	103	143
otterdam	116	126	128	100	119	129	101	143
ilan	112	113	124	100	111	118	110	107

Source: Information made available by ECSC High Authority.

in fact, from Forges de Clabecq. For this particular product (and indeed for others also) Belgian delivered prices from Clabecq were clearly strikingly competitive and must have been the cause of a considerable amount of alignment by other Community firms at the time. It should be mentioned at this point that the competitiveness of a Belgian or any other price has to be considered in relation to the supply position of the firm concerned. If the prices of Belgian producers are low but their order books are full, then Belgian firms do not present as great a competitive threat as would appear at first sight. There is no reason why producers selling ex Essen to customers in Duisburg need necessarily be perturbed if a Belgian firm appears to enjoy a price advantage on paper as long as the latter would in practice have difficulty in meeting orders from Duisburg quickly, perhaps due to capacity limitations. If the order books of the Belgian producers were full, it would not be necessary for the German producers to align down on the Clabecq price lists simply to prevent German orders going to Belgium. But if, at the same time, excess capacity was more in evidence in the German steel industry, it would be open to German producers to compete for orders among themselves on the basis of price by aligning down on to the lower delivered price of Clabecq. Thus in the recession of 1963, internal price competition among ECSC producers could manifest itself in three main ways. First, the small Belgian producers were in a position to quote highly favourable delivered prices in virtually all parts of the Common Market. Secondly, it was always open to any producer to bid for an order in any consuming centre by aligning his own price to the lowest delivered price at that centre. Thirdly, and of crucial importance, effective price competition would exist within each national steel industry by reason of national alignments on to the price lists of producers in other member states. Producers in the Ruhr, for example, when selling to local customers would compete for their business on a price basis by aligning down on to other more favourable delivered prices such as, of course, those of the smaller Belgian works.

It should be quite clear from the foregoing that the attitude of steel producers in the ECSC is anything but passive in the field of price policy, for the successful operation of the alignment possibilities requires the widest knowledge of price lists, transport rates, turnover taxes, and supply capabilities throughout the Community.

4. THE COURSE OF PRICES

Steel prices are an important part of the overall price level in any developed country and governments are very keenly interested in, if not actually involved in, the régimes within which they are determined. It is useful to consider some of the main phases in the development of steel prices in the internal market of the ECSC. To do this it is necessary to keep in mind that the published price lists of producers may not be exceeded (and that list prices may therefore be regarded as maximum prices) but that aligning on lower-price lists within the Community, and on to lower-priced offers from third countries, constitute legitimate methods of reducing prices in certain circumstances. As we explained in discussing alignment possibilities, data are available showing the amount of steel sold within the Community as a result of aligning on third-country offers, but no such data are available showing to what extent list prices are being cut by internal alignments. It is not, therefore, possible to make any accurate adjustment to indexes of list prices to show how actual transaction prices in the market are really moving at any particular period of time. This statistical gap is very serious indeed, although it should be possible in time to close it at least partially. An initial attempt might involve a study of quantities and values of steel products traded among the member states. At the present time, however, commentators have to make do with the fragmentary evidence that is available and piece together the true picture as best they can. This approach is no better for being that adopted by the national governments of the Six and the High Authority itself when framing policy decisions bearing on steel prices.

There are three particularly instructive phases in the development of steel prices in the Community.

The first, occurring almost as soon as the Community had come into existence, was connected with the reaction of producers to the recession of 1953/4.[6] According to the rules of the treaty, producers wishing to compete could have aligned down on to the lower list prices of other producers or reduced their own list prices (imports were not at that time a competitive proposition). In practice, the former possibility did not offer much prospect of price flexibility, as consultations between the national groups of steel producers before the opening of the common market had resulted in broadly similar prices in each of the member states.

[6] A more detailed account of the evolution of steel prices in the ECSC and comparisons between the Community's régime and those of the UK and US may be found in A. Forsyth, 'Steel Pricing Policies', *Planning* (PEP), xxx (Dec. 1964); and Swann & McLachlan, 'Steel Pricing in a Recession, an Analysis of UK and ECSC Experience', *Scottish JPE*, Feb. 1965.

If they had chosen the second course, producers would have been obliged by one of the first Decisions of the High Authority to observe a waiting period of five days before implementing their new price lists. In fact producers chose to ignore the treaty and granted concessions as they thought fit to individual customers. It is now clear that one of the reasons for this course of action was the belief of producers that a reduction in list prices duly publicized and notified to the High Authority, but implemented only after the statutory waiting period of five days, would simply result in a general reduction in prices all round with the result that those initiating the price cuts would not gain any competitive advantage. Competitive attempts by producers to increase their share of the market therefore required price reductions to be made secretly, and it would seem that the price cuts thus brought about may well have reached the order of 20 per cent.

The High Authority, aware that secret rebates, however indicative they might be of competition, would weaken its authority if allowed to continue unchecked, attempted to retrieve the situation by means of a compromise. It issued a Decision early in 1954 to the effect that producers could deviate from their published price lists provided that the average of such deviations over a period of 60 days did not exceed $2\frac{1}{2}$ per cent and that any future changes in list prices could be implemented after one day's notice rather than five. This attempt by the High Authority to encourage price flexibility within what came to be known as the 'Monnet margins' was, however, largely a failure. It is clear that once general deviations from published price lists are permitted, then discrimination among buyers is almost certain to occur—a result that is specifically forbidden by the treaty. Furthermore once list prices cease to be precisely applied, even the possibility of aligning in the manner laid down in the treaty is ruled out. It was for these reasons that the Court of Justice ruled against the Monnet margins at the end of 1954—by which time in fact demand had recovered sufficiently to make producers charge premia of up to $2\frac{1}{2}$ per cent rather than grant rebates that had been the original cause of the problem. On the other hand, the decision to reduce the waiting period required before the implementation of changes in list prices was both legitimate and conducive to competition in so far as it increased the prospects of quick gain for the price cutter—a lesson learned by the High Authority in embarrassing circumstances but which could in fact have been gleaned with much less trouble by consulting American experience of twenty years earlier with the Codes of Fair Competition set up under the National Recovery Administration.

The second phase in the development of steel prices that requires consideration is their behaviour in the conditions of expansion of 1957. On this occasion it was not the actions of producers but those of governments that required the attention of the High Authority. Both the French and German governments were at that time anxious to contain steel prices as part of their general campaigns against inflationary pressures. Direct government control of prices was ruled out by the treaty and an impression at least of producers' autonomy had to be preserved. In France government influence on steel prices therefore took the form of back pressure exerted via control of the price of steel-using industries and also, it would appear, 'expecting' a *quid pro quo* in the form of moderation in steel prices in return for certain fiscal concessions to the industry in the course of the Second Plan. The results of the policy appear to have been extremely successful in achieving their aim of moderating the rise of French steel prices, which were generally among the lowest in the Community up to 1962. But it should be noted that this kind of action on the part of one government tends to lead to a fragmentation of the price structure of the common market and to inhibit the accumulation of reserves by the enterprises concerned. This is a matter to which we return in the next section of this chapter.

In Germany, government attempts to temper the rise in prices of the boom of 1957 followed a very different pattern. When producers exercised their freedom under the treaty to increase prices, knowing that this would be regarded unfavourably by the government, the state-owned firm of Salzgitter was prevailed upon by the Ministry of Economics to maintain its existing prices. The result was the existence for a time of two divergent price levels in Germany—a situation quite out of keeping with the whole tradition of the industry, and which the private firms were only able to withstand by aligning down on to French prices to neutralize Salzgitter's advantage. (They could not formally align on to Salzgitter's price lists as the latter's, like their own, were based on Ruhr basing points, and the treaty

10

permits domestic alignment only on price lists quoted on other basing points.) This state of affairs lasted until the middle of 1958, when national price uniformity was restored by a compromise in which Salzgitter increased certain prices and the private firms reduced theirs to a common level. In so far as the private firms did reduce their prices to some extent, this could be held to be a victory—although not a complete one—for the government's price policy. But it was clear that the achievement of price uniformity in this particular manner was indicative of blatant collusion rather than mere parallelism. This element in the manœuvres was not lost upon the High Authority and fines were imposed upon the enterprises concerned for their breach of the cartel rules.[7] It was, perhaps, ironic that the competitive intervention of the Ministry of Economics should have ended in an anti-trust proceeding, while the comparatively blatant *dirigisme* of the French planning authorities should have resulted in a situation that did much to keep competition alive throughout the Community in subsequent years.

The third main phase in the development of prices in the Community—their reaction to the post-1960 recession—is perhaps the most instructive of all, as the course of events in the early 1960s was to a high degree implicit in the pricing régime rather than deviations from it by producers or governments.

The simultaneous impact of two sources of pressure on prices in the early years of the 1960s combined to make this recession particularly severe. Internally, demand for steel ceased to expand at its former rapid rate due to some slowing down in the rate of economic growth, especially in some steel-intensive sectors of the economy, and, to a smaller extent, to the increased competitiveness of substitute products for steel. Externally, demand from the traditional importing countries was affected by the development of domestic steel industries in those areas. On the supply side, capacity expanded continuously in the Community over the recession as investment projects already embarked upon came to fruition. But perhaps what does most to distinguish the recession of the early 1960s from that of 1958 or 1953 was the role of imports from third countries. The long post-war period of steel shortage and its associated mentality of scarcity seems to

[7] Hamburger, in Miller, *Competition, Cartels*, p. 373.

have come to an end as the boom of 1960 slid into the world-wide recession of 1963. Shortages gave way to surpluses that began to gravitate towards the most exposed markets. In this connexion the geographical proximity of the Community to the Eastern bloc made it an easy target for imports from that source, while its comparatively low level of external protection left it exposed to pressure from the low-priced Japanese supplies that were coming into the world market in increasing quantities. It was the presence of these low-priced offers from third countries that weakened the whole structure of steel prices in the Six during 1962 and 1963—and the mechanism by which this external pressure was transmitted was the alignment rule as applied to imports from third countries.

What happened during that recession was as follows. A Community producer would align his price on some Japanese or Eastern bloc offer and thereby prevent the foreign firm from obtaining that business. In many cases producers were happy to align in respect of very large quantities on very small tonnage offers from third countries. But this same quantity of foreign steel was then offered to another Community buyer, and would again provoke an alignment from an ECSC producer. In other words, a limited tonnage offered by overseas suppliers tended to be the cause of a disproportionate amount of alignment by ECSC firms. This leverage or multiplier effect continued until the foreign supplier had finally sold his steel or ceased trying to do so.

The weakness of the world market also affected the Community's internal market by way of the domestic alignment mechanism. This occurred towards the end of 1962 when Belgian exporters to third countries decided that such sales were so difficult that increased sales within the ECSC itself would be more profitable. To boost their internal sales quickly they made large reductions in their list prices, and ordinary domestic alignments, which became increasingly common as the recession deepened, were made upon these falling list prices. Thus, the end of 1962 and 1963 marked the conclusion of a long period during which French list prices had been the lowest in the Community, as some Belgian producers undercut their French competitors considerably in the worst stage of the recession.[8]

[8] ECSC, *12th Gen. Rep.* (1964), p. 162.

The increasing importance of sales by alignment on lower-priced third-country quotations is shown below in Table 4, which indicates that such sales increased almost tenfold during the course of the recession.

TABLE 4

Alignments on Third-country Quotations

(*metric tons*)

1960	1961	1962	1963
250,000	457,000	1,307,000	2,221,000

Source: ECSC, *12th Gen. Rep.* (1964), p. 165.

What sort of price reductions were involved in these alignments on third-country offers and lower list prices in the Community? It is clear that, as opposed to the gradual upward movement of mean list prices over the recession, actual market prices fell considerably.[9] In Table 5 we set out examples of the range of percentage reductions below list prices for five products at the lowest point of the recession.

TABLE 5

Range of Percentage Reductions below List Prices

	Coils	Merchant bars	Wire rod	Medium & heavy plate	Sheet
First quarter 1963	1–28	3–30	6–22	2–33	3–24
Second quarter 1963	1–29	5–30	3–29	2–41	3–28

Source: ECSC, Document no. 5858/63f, 23 Sept. 1963.

Estimates supplied to us from within the High Authority suggest that virtually all sales of steel products by ECSC producers within the Community market during 1963 were made by aligning below list prices, either on to lower Community list prices or on to low-priced foreign offers, and that the average

[9] The index of mean list prices in the Community rose steadily throughout the recession from 100 in 1960 to 105 in 1963.

degree of alignment for all sales by Community producers during 1963 was about 15–20 per cent.

Thus the weakness of the world market affected the internal price level of the Community primarily as a result of Community producers aligning their prices down to the level at which imports were offered. It would in fact appear that the situation was made worse than it need have been by the failure of some Community firms to observe the third-country alignment rule properly: cases were said to have occurred in which alignments were made on entirely fictitious offers. But the weakness of the world market also affected the internal price structure via the ordinary internal alignment mechanism. This happened, as we have seen, because Belgian producers retreated from the depressed export market during 1962 and intensified their sales efforts within the Community itself. To do this they in some cases actually reduced their list prices to the extremely low levels prevailing in the world market, which of course weakened the internal market still further as ordinary internal alignments then began to be made down to these abnormally low list prices.

As the foregoing attempts to measure the course of prices in the post-1960 recession are inevitably somewhat fragmentary and generalized, it is useful to cite here certain data that act as a rough cross-check on the reliability of these impressions of the extent of the price fall. C. H. Goudima, a financial analyst on the staff of the High Authority, has made a major recomputation in standardized form of the balance sheets of steel enterprises over this period.[10] His study sets out a so-called 'efficiency ratio' (or 'economic ratio') which may be broadly defined as the ratio of gross profits to capital employed. This ratio declined from 20 per cent in the boom year of 1960 to about 12 per cent in 1963 (the corresponding post-tax figures were 15 per cent and 9 per cent respectively). Unfortunately Goudima's figures necessarily include the non-steel earnings of companies whose interests extend beyond the steel industry and, of course, even the steel earnings of these and other companies include returns on exports to third countries. For these reasons alone, therefore, Goudima's figures should not be used as a direct measure of the course of

[10] C. H. Goudima, 'The Return on Capital employed in Iron and Steel Undertakings' (a paper read at the Knokke Conference of European Financial Analysts, Jan. 1965).

the recession in the internal steel market. Further indirect estimates of the extent of the price fall between 1960 and 1963 have been made internally by the High Authority. These suggest that the receipts of the steel companies in 1963 were about £700 million below their 1960 level. This estimate of a fall of £700 million in receipts may be compared with a figure of about £1,480 million for total investment in the ECSC steel industry in 1963.

Even allowing for the very real difficulties of quantification in this field, these data, and those set out earlier on the extent and degree of alignment, provide a striking contrast with the upward movement of list prices over the period and emphasize in an unmistakable way the fallibility of the latter as a guide to actual conditions in the market. For ECSC steel producers market conditions since 1962 have meant very definite price competition even when selling to traditional customers in their own national markets.

5. A CRITIQUE OF THE STEEL-PRICING RÉGIME

How far is the ECSC steel-pricing régime conducive to the realization of the fundamental aim of the Community laid down in Article 2, 'the establishment of conditions which will in themselves assure the most rational distribution of production at the highest possible level of productivity'?

Three main criticisms have been made of the system: that it has anti-competitive effects by promoting collusion in pricing, that it has adverse (static) effects upon the allocation of given resources, and that it weakens and distorts the (dynamic) long-run development of the Community's steel industry. Let us consider each of these criticisms in turn.

(a) Effects on Competition in Pricing

The most obvious criticism that is usually first made of the system, both as it is laid down in the treaty and as it is administered in practice, is that it fails to establish securely the kind of competitive régime that would most nearly guarantee the successful operation of automatic forces. This is not to say that the various interventionist measures provided for in the treaty (price-control possibilities, the establishment of general objectives, formal opinions on investment plans, and so forth) are in any way unduly prominent. The objection is not that the régime involves compromises of this kind, but, rather, that the competitive side of the compromise itself appears to involve a further compromise upon examination.

This is true as far as list prices are concerned, and it comes out most clearly in the operation of the basing point system with compulsory price publicity, which, as practised in Germany, and, to a smaller extent in the other member states, really builds collusion into the very foundation of the system. The superficial view that competition can work most effectively if prices are directly comparable by being based upon the same location ignores the fact that such competition, to be effective, pre-supposes the genuine possibility of different prices existing at the basing point—a state of affairs that conscious parallelism and industrial co-operation in government committees; in short the general desire as well as the general environment—do little to foster. Again, the obligation to publish prices means that the incentive to cut prices is reduced as any such initiative tends to be quickly matched by competitors. In any case compulsory price publicity identifies 'the fool who cuts' in an unmistakable way. In the socio-economic conditions prevailing in the national steel industries, a firm may well think twice before publicly stepping out of line with its industrial colleagues. The result is a cartel-like rigidity in list prices. Under these circumstances the otherwise laudable attempts by the High Authority to make sure that list prices are actually applied take on the character of unpaid police work to protect highly uncompetitive arrange-ments, if not actual cartels.

All this may be substantially true so far as list prices are con-cerned, but the fact is that the amount of price competition occurring in the ECSC simply cannot be inferred from the be-haviour of list prices alone. As we have shown, a considerable amount of price competition occurs as a result of the use of the alignment possibilities and, therefore, much of the criticism of the dubious arrangements regarding list prices falls wide of the mark. But two further criticisms may be made here. The first is that alignment is almost certain to involve discrimination, as the producer has the right, first, to align or not as he sees fit, and, secondly, when aligning, to fix whatever price he likes between the upper limit as determined by his own delivered price and the lower limit as determined by that of his competitor. It is surely reasonable to suppose that the decision whether or not to align, and the prices that are chosen within the permissible range of discretion, will often result in the application of different prices to comparable transactions, the whole outcome being determined by the producer's assessment of the commercial implications of each individual transaction. Thus if discrimination can in fact occur in this perfectly legal way (indeed desirable way, as alignment is in practice *the* means of price competition), it is difficult to see the justification for a rigid insistence on the strict observation and publication of price lists, especially when, as we have seen, this discourages price reductions and promotes collusion anyway. This is far from saying that information on prices and conditions is not important for the smooth working of market forces—of course it is—but it should not be impossible for the ordinary media of commercial intelligence to provide this. It is indeed very difficult to avoid the conclusion that the ECSC pricing system, with its basing points, its compulsory price publicity, and its waiting period was to some extent modelled upon American practices that were in fact abandoned there even before the Community came into existence.

The second criticism of the system is that, although alignment has been responsible for a substantial amount of real price competition, its effectiveness in this direction may not always be as great as it has been in the recent past. This is because it has been the presence of certain extremely low list prices that has made alignment so potent a vehicle of competitive pricing. But if the common market for steel is allowed to develop in a natural manner, the working of market forces might tend to bring list prices rather closer together than they have been in the recent phase of severe price competition. It should be borne in mind that the low level of French prices from 1957 to 1962 that undoubtedly caused a good deal of alignment elsewhere in the Community was the result of something extraneous to the system—in effect, of government price controls. Furthermore the low level of list prices of the smaller Belgian works that has prevailed since 1963 could turn out to be a transient phenomenon if these firms decided at any time to seek some kind of affiliation (specialization agreement or some kind of concentration) with enterprises less given to flexible price policies. In other words, it is not impossible to imagine that in the future the collusive potentialities of price lists published on a limited number of basing points may be much more inimical to competition than they are today. At that stage it would be difficult to postpone further a serious consideration of ex-works pricing coupled with something less rigid than compulsory price publicity. However, these are clearly criticisms of the way the system *might* develop, and economists should be the last to claim any special competence in clairvoyance.

Finally, as a historical tail-piece, it is worth pointing out that the system should also be judged not only by the way it induces price competition in periods of weaker market conditions, but also by the extent to which it inhibits price increases when demand is picking up. The important point to bear in mind here is that producers are not permitted to charge more than their list prices. There can be no question of a producer 'aligning up' for particular transactions in situations in which customers might well respond to pressure. On the contrary, the producer is only permitted to make a proper increase in his list prices and apply these in a non-discriminatory way. It would, therefore, seem that from the producer's standpoint, such increases are likely to be initiated only after very careful consideration of the permanency or otherwise of the situation.

(b) Static Effects on Resource Allocation

When basing points are a considerable distance from the producer's mill, some customers situated near the producer will be denied the benefits of their proximity by the imposition of fictitious transport charges. Liesner cites as an extreme possibility the example of customers in Nuremberg paying phantom freight as from the Ruhr basing point, although the producer's mill from which they are supplied is actually in the same city and transport costs are almost nil.[11] Although sales to such local customers would be extremely profitable to the producer (because of phantom freight), local customers would not in fact find it any more advantageous to obtain supplies in Nuremberg rather than the Ruhr, as the price is the same in either case. On the other

---

[11] Meade, Liesner, & Wells, p. 260.

hand, customers could well tend to site their own plants nearer to the Ruhr to minimize the impact of transport charges. Future investments in steel would then tend to gravitate towards the customers, and the result would be—as one feature of the mis-allocation of resources—an aggravation of the regional problem.

The practical significance of this criticism is, however, greatly reduced in reality for two reasons. The first is, as Liesner has pointed out, the German goverment's operation of a price equalization fund (*Preisausgleichskasse*) that imposes a levy on all German consumers and uses the proceeds to defray a proportion of the transport costs of buyers situated more than 220 kilometres from a basing point. The fund pays 80 per cent of the transport costs incurred in excess of the charge for 220 kilometres. Presumably the general intention of this fund is to reduce the transport disadvantage of consumers in areas remote from the Ruhr and the Saar, especially those in areas bordering on Eastern Germany. By helping consumers (such as those in Nuremberg) who are in fact close to a producer, the scheme partially offsets the artificial locational disadvantages that they suffer by reason of the basing point system. By helping consumers who are far from both a basing point and a steel mill the scheme simply reduces the importance of transport charges in location decisions and thereby encourages the uneconomic location of industrial plant. In both cases the burden of support is borne by customers who have chosen locations nearer the basing points—although even these locations are rational in only a formal sense due to the distance between many producers and their basing points.

But the main reason for doubting that the system has quite the adverse locational consequences that have been suggested is the existence of effective price competition. To take the example cited above, South Germany is one of the most contested steel markets in the entire Community; French, Belgian, and Italian delivered prices all being competitive there for various products, as was shown in Table 2 (p. 266). But a producer in Nuremberg would probably find that the phantom freight enjoyed on sales to local customers would give plenty of scope for alignment down on to the French, Belgian, or Italian delivered prices. It is, therefore, quite probable that the uneconomic effects of the system on locational decisions are nothing like as great as might at first be suspected.

But there is one way in which the system contributes to the misallocation of resources, and that is by its tendency to encourage a certain amount of cross-hauling. The system tends to lead to a situation where steel producers sell some part of their output in distant territory by absorbing freight, while mills in those areas ship identical products into the first producer's home territory. The products may even pass *en route*. Not even the wildest enthusiast for the cause of integration could wish it to be secured by methods such as these—particularly when such a result is quite unintentional.

(c) Dynamic Effects on Long-Run Development

Perhaps one of the most important criticisms that has been made of the ECSC system has been to the effect that in an industry such as steel (operating capital-intensively with durable equipment and in some fields with the most advanced technological innovations), price flexibility and the financial uncertainty that it creates militate against technological advance. This is in substance the kind of argument that certain UK steel makers advanced before the Restrictive Practices Court in 1964 when seeking to justify their price-fixing agreements for heavy steel products.[12] The argument is a perennial one in economics (it is one of the variations on the theme of the role of monopoly in economic growth) and its assertion by the British steel industry —a body that had not been immune to criticism on the grounds of inadequate attention to research[13] was a bold move, albeit an unsuccessful one. At one time the British steel industry, through its Federation, went so far as to make a direct comparison between its own record and that of the ECSC in the rate of application of a vital new technique in steel making—the introduction of oxygen converter processes in place of the traditional open-hearth processes.[14] The Federation was able to show that during

[12] 'Re British Heavy Steelmakers' Agreement', *Reports of Restrictive Practices Cases*, v. pt. 1, pp. 33–38.
[13] Iron and Steel Board, *Research in the Iron and Steel Industry* (*Special Report*) (1963). There was much to criticize and much to commend in the industry's record. But perhaps the most important conclusion of the Board's report was that 'a substantial increase is called for in the research effort of all branches of the industry' (p. 60).
[14] 'At the Technological Frontiers', *Steel R.*, July 1964, p. 25; 'Steel Pricing— A Lesson Retaught', ibid. Apr. 1964, p. 6.

the recession that developed after the 1960 boom, ECSC producers cut back their planned investments so much that this retarded the spread of the most modern steel-making processes in the Community, while, at the same time, British firms, operating a highly cartelized pricing system, were able to maintain the rate at which new techniques were introduced.

It must be admitted that the facts of the situation as stated by the Federation appeared consistent with the hypothesis that price competition inhibited innovation. But other facts besides those mentioned by the Federation are equally relevant to deciding whether the impact of financial security on technological progress is quite so direct as the Federation made out. In particular, the considerable amount of obsolete capacity in the British industry falling due for replacement in the early 1960s was an important cause of the industry's ability to press ahead rapidly with modernization at a time when the Community—with much of its plant probably of more recent construction—was forced to mark time. It would, therefore, appear as if the case against competitive pricing on these grounds is still unproven. Indeed, as part of its reaction to the adverse judgment of the Restrictive Practices Court in the Heavy Steel Case and the threat of nationalization, the British steel industry itself subsequently began to think in terms of a pricing system more like the ECSC's,[15] a deathbed repentance that would hardly commend itself if the penitent simultaneously believed that this course would put a brake on technological progress. However, the compatibility of the ECSC basing point system with national collusion on a grand scale could not have been overlooked by UK steel producers, and must make their interest in introducing that type of system into a purely national framework appear rather equivocal.

Two other points not directly connected with the technological implications of price flexibility may also be mentioned here. The first is that, as we have shown, price competition in the ECSC went to extremes in 1963. But the amount and severity of price

---

[15] British Iron & Steel Fed., *Ann. Rep. 1965* (1966), p. 37. In April 1966 one important section of the British steel industry began to implement this more independent pricing policy. John Summers, Richard Thomas and Baldwins, and the Steel Company of Wales all cut prices for sheet, and in so doing also considerably modified the previous system of zone delivered prices that had tended to make consumers indifferent as far as steel supplies were concerned between various locations.

competition internally is subject to influence by the High Authority and the member governments in a number of ways. Measures taken by both at the beginning of 1964 strengthened the Community market without involving any change in the basic nature of the régime. Secondly, the effects of price flexibility on buyers can hardly be overstressed. The decline in effective steel prices in the Six between 1960 and 1963 must have been of considerable assistance to steel-using industries there when selling in any market against British competition.

A further important criticism that has been made of the Community's system, or, rather, the way it has worked in practice, relates to the role of national governments in steel pricing. It is well known that French producers have been under considerable indirect pressure from their government to keep steel prices down as an important contribution to general price stability. Over a wide field French prices were well below those in the rest of the Community from 1957 almost to 1963, when they were undercut by the smaller Belgian works.

It is probable that this low level of prices was a reflection of the efficiency and natural advantages of the industry in France, as there is little evidence to suggest that input costs were subsidized there or otherwise made artificially favourable. Such distortions of competition would have fallen foul of both the High Authority and competitors in other member states. The absence of any real complaint along these lines from either of these quarters strongly suggests that the French industry was reasonably above suspicion on this score. The question therefore arises of whether an efficient industry was in any way held back by its government's measures.

In order to show what effects the indirect price control of the French government may have had upon the evolution of the Community steel industry, we may remind ourselves briefly of what would probably have happened to prices, trade, and production in an integrated competitive system that was free from these interventions.

Under such a system, in which producers attempt to maximize their profits, free trade would result in producers in the lower-cost state increasing their sales in the territory of their less-efficient partners, as greater profits could be made by the former if they switched sales from their own domestic market to the adjacent markets where prices were higher. Removing supplies from the home market would tend to push prices up there, while the invasion of the export market would bring about a lower level of prices there. A new common price level would be established between the former national price levels. Under static conditions production of the commodity concerned would rise in the state where it had been carried out more efficiently, and fall in the state where production costs were higher.

Under dynamic conditions of general expansion, no such absolute reduction in output is inevitable in the high-cost state, but the rate of expansion would probably be faster in the low-cost state as producers there increased their share of rising total sales. Similarly, with a commodity such as steel, for which transport rates are important, absolute price equality throughout the integrated area would not in fact be brought about by competition, but the differences in prices as between the various 'price islands' (the national basing points) would be determined by the condition that they should be no greater than the costs of transport between them. The economically-determined common price level (involving a rise in prices in the low-cost member state and a fall in prices in the higher-cost members) would also be reinforced in the ECSC by the legal prohibition of discriminatory pricing—sales by the French in the German market, for example, having to be conducted at prices equal to those charged to domestic buyers. The rising price level in the low-cost state would increase business profits there and thereby make possible future growth based on either self-financing or appeals to the capital market.

It is clear that for the above redistribution of resources to come about two main conditions must be fulfilled. First, producers who enjoy a cost advantage must be aware of their superior position and determined to exploit it. Secondly, they should not be prevented from behaving in this way.

It is quite possible that neither of these conditions has been satisfactorily fulfilled in practice in the circumstances of the ECSC. The over-cautious attitude of the French steel producers to expansion, the so-called Malthusian mentality, appears to have been a force to be reckoned with in the past. On the other hand, those in the *Commissariat du Plan* directly responsible for the steel industry appear to have been rather more expansionist minded than the industry itself, and their use of competition from other Community countries at a time when sections of the industry were dragging their feet on reorganization shows that they at any rate were fully alive to the opportunities presented by the common market.[16]

But the main reason for believing that the redistribution of the Community's resources towards lower-cost producers might have been hindered lies in the French government's indirect control of steel prices. As prices were in practice frozen for home sales, and the treaty made any possibility of dual pricing out of the question, French producers must have found that their profits were lower than they could have obtained in the absence of such restraints. Keeping profits down in this way would surely weaken the industry's ability to finance rapid expansion from internal sources and make it unattractive as a borrower in the capital market. The only other conceivable source of the large amount of finance necessary to promote the expansion of the industry in accordance with the requirements of the common market would be far-reaching fiscal concessions. French planning has certainly made considerable use of such devices, but whether the steel industry benefited from them to the extent necessary to offset its price constraints it is difficult to say. However difficult it might be to settle this type of question, it is regrettable that the High Authority has not seen fit to discuss it in greater detail in public as it relates to problems that are of considerable importance for the development of the Community industry.

6. TRANSPORT IN THE ECSC

In our description of the basing point system as implemented in the Community we deliberately avoided complicating the discussion by bringing in problems arising in the transport sector. It is now time to remedy this omission and to examine some of the work of the High Authority in this important field. It is important to bear in mind that the integration of the coal and steel industries in 1952 was a measure of partial integration only and that transport was brought within the ambit of the Community only to the limited extent that this was necessary to enable the coal and steel markets to function in the manner laid down in the treaty. The High Authority was not given powers

[16] Sheahan, p. 72.

over transport enterprises corresponding to its direct supranational authority over the producers of coal and steel. All such powers in the transport field remained expressly with the member governments, and action by the High Authority in transport matters has, therefore, largely amounted to pointing out to governments their obligations under the treaty and discussing with them how best they might fulfil these obligations.

But transport rates and conditions for coal and steel products, however important they may have appeared to the High Authority, have tended to be viewed by the governments not simply from the standpoint of their effects upon the working of the common markets for coal and steel, but equally from the angle of their compatibility with individual national transport policies. The result has been that, while the High Authority and the member governments have achieved notable successes in certain matters affecting the working of the coal and steel industries, some at least of the transport problems posed by the working of these two markets have proved virtually intractable within the framework of ECSC alone, and hope for a proper solution of them has been held out only within the wider framework of EEC transport policy as a whole.

The purpose of concluding this discussion of the working of the steel market with an account of the complications introduced by transport is twofold. First, it is to complete our account of the working of the steel market itself. We propose to do this in such a manner as to broach in a very preliminary way some of the aspects of transport that are of relevance to the general common-market transport policy of the EEC. This serves the second purpose of introducing questions that we discuss in greater detail in the next chapter dealing with the larger EEC transport policy itself.

(a) The Relevance of Transport to the Integrated Markets

The kind of pricing system set up by the treaty makes a prominent feature of market transparency: it endeavours to ensure that the coal and steel enterprises publish their price lists and that transport rates are likewise published, or at least made known by being brought to the attention of the High Authority. It is, therefore, possible in principle for customers to estimate the delivered price at which they can buy steel from any producer in the Community. Similarly, producers themselves, having equal access to the same information, can estimate the extent to which they would be entitled to align their prices should they wish to make a competitive bid for a particular order. Publication of price lists is also an important aspect of the enforcement of the ban on discriminatory pricing, and publicity of transport rates is a complementary aspect of the same policy, as it enables the check on non-discrimination to go right along the line to the final buyer. There is, therefore, a certain formal consistency between the sections of the treaty dealing with price publicity, alignment, non-discrimination, and transport.

But the relevance of transport to the coal and steel markets is, of course, far from being purely formal. The fact that coal and steel are products with a low ratio of value to bulk and that transport costs will, therefore, often add a considerable amount to the list prices of these products at their basing points means that the problems raised by transport for the Common Market— and especially this kind of common market—could be quite considerable.

Numerous examples could be quoted to show that transport costs account for a fairly large proportion of the final price paid by buyers for the integrated products. For coal, where the ratio of value to weight is lower than that for steel, transport costs might even account for more than 50 per cent of the delivered price paid by the buyer on a long run such as from the Ruhr or Lorraine to Italy. But even for steel the ratio is quite high. A rough estimate for the entire Community suggests that transport charges accounted for about 20 to 25 per cent of the delivered prices of rolled products in the early 1950s.[17] Thus, as transport costs are of very considerable importance in delivered prices, it is clear that any significant deviation by the transport industries from the requirements of the Common Market could have quite far-reaching consequences. That conditions in the transport sector were very much at variance with the needs of the Common Market was, of course, well known when the treaty was signed. Transport in fact raised three main kinds of issues for the integration of the coal and steel markets.

First, transport tariffs were often constructed in such a way that cross-frontier traffic paid higher charges than those for journeys of equivalent length within one member state. Such

[17] Diebold, p. 155.

transport charges would, therefore, tend to act in much the same way as tariffs on trade between the member states and would consequently impede the integration of the markets if allowed to continue—a discrepancy that became glaringly obvious when ordinary tariffs on trade were abolished almost entirely in one move as soon as the Community came into existence. Secondly, transport rates had often been manipulated by the member states in such a way as to give advantages to certain users. For example, in the interests of national regional policies, producers in outlying areas might have their costs subsidized by special support tariffs. Such producers might achieve advantages over their competitors by being able to transport their inputs of coal, coke, scrap, and ore at concessionary rates. As subsidies of any kind are a threat to the working of the Common Market, such special rates required careful scrutiny to ascertain whether they should be allowed to continue once it was opened. Thirdly, the proper operation of the pricing rules required a greater degree of transparency in the transport market than in fact existed. One of the High Authority's most difficult tasks has been to secure this necessary degree of publicity for transport rates.

Before going on to discuss each of these three problems in greater detail, it is useful to give some brief indication at this stage of the different relative importance of each of the main means of transport as far as the coal and steel markets are concerned. No figures appear to be available analysing the total movement of treaty products within the Community by each type of carrier, but a certain amount of information is available, mainly about inter-state trade, that probably gives a reasonable indication of the total picture. These are set out in Table 6 (p. 289).

The figures in the table below must be treated with the greatest caution. In the first place they do not really show the amount of transport actually performed as they refer to tons rather than ton/kilometres. Thus inter-state movements count both extremely short and extremely long hauls together, irrespective of the lengths of the routes involved. Lack of detailed statistics on road haulage in most of the member states makes it difficult to estimate the relative importance of each of the various transport media in the total transport of treaty products within the Community. But a survey has been made of long-distance road haulage in Western Germany that throws some light on the role

TABLE 6

Carriage of ECSC Products by Type of Carrier, 1961

(*per cent*)

	Tonnage transported between member states		Long-distance domestic transport (*W. Germany*)
	All ECSC products	*Rolled steel products*	*Rolled steel products*
Rail	54	53	60
Inland waterways	38	33	6
Sea transport	5	2	1
Road	3	12	35

Source: Statistical Office of the European Communities, *Transport von Gütern des EGKS Vertrages* (1962).

of road haulage internally. The relevant findings of this survey are shown in the last column of Table 6, and suggest that the importance of road haulage to the steel industry, especially if all internal hauls by road could be taken into account, may be very considerable. We shall show later why this is highly relevant to steel-pricing problems in the Community. Furthermore road haulage is probably increasing its relative share of the transport market, with the result that it has now become an active competitor for rail and inland waterways even in circumstances where its previous role was quite small.

(*b*) *Transport Rates as Tariffs*

Transport rate structures in the separate member states before the implementation of the treaty exhibited a number of features that placed international traffic in a relatively disadvantageous position as compared with purely internal traffic.

Perhaps the most obvious example of the way in which transport rates can act as a tariff on trade is when a discrimination in charges is made according to the country of origin or destination of the goods, with the result that goods of national origin are transported at more favourable rates than imports. By the end of 1953 the High Authority had secured the elimination of virtually all such discriminations by the railways and had achieved some success in the same field with regard to inland waterways and road haulage. While a variety of methods were used by the transport undertakings to eliminate the discriminations concerned, the new charges thus established represented on the whole a definite levelling down of rates and a saving in transport costs of about 24 million Belgian francs per annum.[18] These changes must have had some effect—how much it is difficult to say—in promoting more rational trade flows within the Community, especially as regards the bulky raw-material inputs of the steel industry.

Another feature of railway rate policy that tended to impede cross-frontier traffic, and therefore to act rather like a tariff on trade, was the existence of freight rates that were 'broken' at the frontier. Instead of regarding an international journey as an entity, the practice of the railway administrations had been to treat it as consisting of two separate national journeys. This involved two disadvantages for international traffic. First, there was the imposition of terminal charges for unloading and reloading at the frontier, even though such work did not in fact occur. The shorter the international journey, the more anomalous would such an inflation of charges appear, especially in the case of extremely short international hauls of which Strasbourg/Kehl is the classic example. Secondly, 'breaking' the journey at the frontier in this way meant that the advantages of tapering mileage charges were greatly reduced. In other words, for two routes of equal length, one national and one international, goods moving on the national route would obtain the full advantage of reductions in charges per ton/mile that are granted as the length of the journey increases, whereas goods moving on the international route would lose this advantage by being regarded as involved in two separate national journeys.

The solution to the problem of broken freight rates was the establishment of direct international tariffs. These through rates imposed one terminal charge only (the average of those of the two countries concerned) and a charge for distance that corresponded to the weighted average of the respective distance charges for internal journeys of equivalent length, the weights corresponding to the length of the international route lying in each state.

[18] *Wagenführ Report*, p. 391.

International through rates for intra-Community trade have been available for traffic moving via Switzerland since 1957 and via Austria since 1958.

The two examples that we have discussed—discrimination on grounds of nationality and broken freight rates—are both examples of ways in which transport rates were operated to the disadvantage of international transport as compared with internal journeys. There are, however, examples of fields in which international rates have been more favourable than internal ones, with the result that domestic journeys have, in some cases, suffered the kind of disadvantages that more usually occur on international routes. Both kinds of distortion are equally to be avoided if the transport sector is to play a proper part in resource allocation.

The possibility that transport could operate to the relative advantage of cross-frontier traffic arose because of the special position of inland waterways, especially Rhine shipping, in the Community. Broadly speaking, freight rates for purely domestic voyages on inland waterways are either fixed by the authorities of the state concerned or are controlled by various agreements or pools within the private sector. Such rates tend to be stable for quite long periods. On the other hand, international shipping on the Rhine is governed by the Mannheim Convention, under the terms of which governments refrain from influencing the determination of international freight rates, and the pull of market forces subjects such rates to much greater fluctuations than are experienced by the rates for internal voyages. The result is a structural or cyclical distortion between internal and international rates that can be quite extreme. In August 1957, for example, US coal carried on the international stretch of the Rhine from Rotterdam to Mannheim (580 kilometres) was paying a considerably lower rate than the internal rate from Ruhrort to Mannheim (350 kilometres)—3·35 DM/ton as against 8·5 DM/ton. As the member states were bound by their adherence to the Mannheim Convention to refrain from interfering with international rates on the Rhine, the High Authority has attempted to combat these distortions by promoting, in consultation with the governments concerned, schemes that would involve adjusting the internal rates to the international level. But little success has attended these endeavours, as a prolonged recession in shipping conditions on the Rhine commencing in 1959 resulted in the breakdown of the established rate schedules of the pools and thereby made the necessary comparisons impossible. Doubtless the recession also removed the main discrepancies as between internal and international rates faster than any feasible administrative action could have done.

(c) Special Tariffs

The measures described in the previous section relate to policies aimed at eliminating the economic significance of frontiers. They were very much the complement in the transport field of the elimination of tariffs on trade between the member states. In so far as increases in such trade may have contributed to a better international allocation of resources, the elimination of these distortions in the transport field has been a necessary step towards achieving the main goal of the treaty for the integrated products, 'the most rational distribution of production at the highest level of productivity' (Article 2). However, the realization of this goal equally requires the re-allocation of production within each member state away from high-cost enterprises towards more efficient ones. Subsidies of one kind or another that prevent or retard this process are incompatible with this fundamental objective. In order to promote this kind of internal re-allocation of resources, certain 'special' transport tariffs had to be scrutinized very critically by the High Authority to ascertain how far they were compatible with the treaty.

These special tariffs were forms of internal rather than international discrimination and were granted for two main reasons. First, to match a more favourable rate offered by another means of transport (a competitive tariff), or, secondly, for reasons of general economic policy such as aids to declining regions or eastern frontier areas of Western Germany (support tariffs). The importance of these special tariffs may easily be judged from the fact that at the opening of the common market 27 per cent of coal and up to 95 per cent of the ore carried by the German railways, and up to 30 per cent of the ore carried by the French railways were granted special rates.[19]

A special tariff of the former type—one offered for competitive reasons—does not necessarily fall foul of the treaty's ban on

[19] *Wagenführ Report*, p. 394.

discriminatory practices, as not all parts of the Community are equally well served by competitive forms of transport, and the existence of alternatives for some users only implies that not all users are in comparable conditions. But the second type of special tariff, a support tariff, has usually been disallowed by the High Authority, although it has permitted their withdrawal to be phased over periods of up to seven years. However, the High Authority has allowed certain support tariffs that favoured enterprises situated near the eastern frontier of Western Germany to be maintained on the grounds that the tariff in question did not give the enterprises any positive advantages over competitors, but simply offset the disadvantages suffered as a result of the division of Germany.[20] The removal of support tariffs has not been an easy task, as much opposition from vested interests has been encountered. Apart from the enterprises that would be affected, the High Authority has had to promote in this field a policy that runs counter to the entire tradition of the German railways, which have always been managed with a view to larger national rather than specific commercial interests.

None the less, some progress has been made in removing support tariffs. The German railways have now introduced a new tariff for coal, coke, and ore, moving in full train-loads, that applies equally to all users. This has had the effect of increasing the rates previously granted to favoured enterprises and conferring benefits upon others in the form of lower rates. Not only German firms have benefited by this change, as the large movements of coal from the Ruhr to Lorraine and Luxembourg have become perceptibly cheaper. The relative competitive position of the previously favoured firms has, therefore, been attacked from two directions simultaneously. Indeed the competitive position of some of them has been subject to further pressure as a result of the maintenance of competitive tariffs in areas in which transport by internal waterways forms a feasible alternative to the railways. For this reason, certain firms in the Ruhr, for example, continue to enjoy special competitive tariffs that cannot be granted to firms in more peripheral areas, such as Siegerland or Bavaria, that do not possess a competitive network of inland waterways. For similar reasons French firms in the

[20] Meade, Liesner, & Wells, p. 377.

Centre and Pyrenees are at a transport disadvantage as compared with those in other parts of France. In other words, the
maintenance of competitive tariffs is contributing to the centri-
petal tendencies of industrial location. As inland waterway rates
for international journeys have not been properly published,
however, and the true nature of some ostensibly competitive
railway tariffs cannot therefore be readily ascertained, it is quite
possible that a number of support tariffs have been maintained
by passing them off as being competitively justified. In summary,
both genuinely competitive tariffs and support tariffs successfully
passed off as competitive have tended to operate to the advantage
of enterprises in areas well served by inland waterways, that is,
the central areas of the Community, and to the relative disadvantage of enterprises in the more peripheral parts.

Clearly the existence of special tariffs may work to favour
higher-cost producers and thereby impede the transfer of resources to the more efficient enterprises. But other factors having
their origin in the transport sector have also contributed (to an
unknown extent) to frustrating the Community's aim of maximum productivity in the integrated industries. These factors
arise from the different principles of tariff construction applied
within the member states that have led, for example, to the
application of different degrees of tapering of the rates applying
to longer journeys, different concessions for complete truck or
train loads, and, perhaps of greater importance, differences
between the relative rates applicable to coal, coke, iron ore, and
scrap. Given the very high proportion of transport charges in the
delivered prices of these items to the steel producers, the latter
will find that transport costs are of great importance in deciding
the most profitable locations for their plant, and, of course, the
costs of these inputs will work themselves through to influence
the prices of other Community products. But as long as the ratios
of the rates on coal, coke, iron ore, and scrap vary for a diversity
of reasons as between the member states, the weight of the various
factors entering into a locational or pricing decision is distorted
as between enterprises in the different member states.[21] In this
connexion the relationship between the rates for coal and coke is
specially important. As coke has a lower specific weight than
coal, that is, a wagon filled with coke is 'full' before it is 'down'

[21] Meade, Liesner, & Wells, pp. 381–2.

(to borrow a term from the shipping industry), the utilization of wagons is lower for coke than for coal. If such inferior utilization were to be reflected in the charges for trasporting each, the rate per ton/kilometre for coke would have to be higher than that for coal, but in Germany the two rates are the same while diverse relativities exist in the other member states.

How much progress has been made in harmonizing policies of the member states in these various fields? It must be admitted that very little has in fact been achieved. The basic reason for this is inherent in the nature of the partial integration process itself. Given the diversity of purpose between the various national transport policies, the member governments were very unwilling to give concrete support to any particular tariff principles for ECSC products (such as that rates should reflect relative costs) when they were in fact pursuing very different policies in the rest of their respective national transport sectors. As a large proportion of the receipts of the transport undertakings was earned in the carriage of ECSC products, major revisions in rate making policies for these products could not but have had the most far-reaching consequences for the determination of rates for a large variety of other products also. Such a complete revision of tariff policy simply to satisfy the requirements of the ECSC could hardly commend itself either to the transport undertakings or the governments. In the event, such fundamental rethinking of tariff policy, necessarily going far beyond the scope of the ECSC, could only begin to be considered when the member states undertook in 1958 to extend their integration into all other sectors of economic life, and in so doing specifically recognized the need for a common transport policy.

(d) The Problem of Market Transparency

In the first few years of the Community's existence publication of transport rates does not appear to have been an important issue. This was because the role of the railways was even greater with regard to treaty products then than it is now and railway rates were generally published. It was, perhaps, also attributable to the fact that steel producers did not generally make much use of alignment possibilities until the recession of 1958. Up to that year, therefore, the High Authority was content to negotiate with the governments to try to secure a satisfactory amount of rate publicity for inland waterway transport and road haulage, the latter being particularly troublesome, as only Western Germany appears to have fulfilled its obligations under the treaty in this field.

But in the recession conditions of 1958 the lack of publicity for road haulage rates for treaty products began to have serious effects. The importance of road haulage had been growing steadily (for some steel products, such as sheets, many movements are now mainly by road),[22] and producers wishing to make use of the right of alignment began to experience difficulty in their attempts to compete in the manner laid down in the treaty. To prevent the loss of traffic to the road hauliers, railway administrations increasingly aligned their own rates on what they took to be the road haulage rates, and themselves resorted increasingly to secret rate contracts to improve their competitive position *vis-à-vis* the road hauliers. With the spread of secret rates to the railways, non-discrimination in transport is almost certain to have fallen by the wayside, price alignment itself became more arbitrary, and, probably, even more discriminatory, while the policing of the pricing régime by the High Authority was made very difficult because of the lack of reliable data on transport rates.

As the dangers of the situation became clear in 1958 the High Authority realized that something more robust than simply discussions with governments would be necessary to strike at the root of the problem and secure the publication of road haulage rates. It therefore issued Decision No. 18 of 1959 requiring the governments to bring about the necessary amount of publicity in this sector. The Italian and Dutch governments appealed to the Court against this Decision and it was reversed on largely formal legal grounds. The High Authority therefore issued a Recommendation to the same effect covering all means of transport, and the validity of this was confirmed by the Court in 1962 when the same two governments again appealed. Since then negotiations between the High Authority and the governments appear to have begun to have the desired results of increasing the transparency of the transport market.[23] However, as with the publication of product prices, one is left with the feeling that this strict insis-

---

[22] ECSC, *10th Gen. Rep.* (1962), p. 235.
[23] ECSC, *12th Gen. Rep.* (1964), pp. 206–11.

tence on the mechanics of the treaty has more to commend it on legal than on economic grounds. Competition in both the product and the transport markets may well require a more flexible attitude to the publication issue than has been characteristic of the ECSC.

PART III
Managing the Competitive Economy

IO

Managed Markets

MUCH of what the Rome Treaty seeks to do can be described as removing barriers to trade, increasing competition, and giving freer rein to the forces of the market. Nevertheless, neither the Rome Treaty (nor for that matter the Paris Treaty) provides for a system in which the course of events in every industry will be solely determined by the force of the market. In a few strategic industries the treaties either call for or permit an element of market control or supervision. The industries in question are transport, agriculture, and the coal industry, although policy here is framed as part of a broader overall energy policy. In this chapter we discuss each of these managed markets in turn.

At the outset we must emphasize that it is not our intention to provide a picture of all aspects of the common policies that are being evolved in these sectors. Rather our main focus of attention is upon those aspects of policy which involve exceptions to the competitive order discussed in Parts I and II. It would, of course, be foolish to deny that these common policies are also, in some degree, designed to remove certain distortions with a view to improving the working of the competitive system; and we shall draw attention to these aspects of the common policies in the course of our main discussion.

A. TRANSPORT

I. THE RELEVANCE OF THE COMMON TRANSPORT POLICY TO THE COMMON MARKET

Although the removal of state and private barriers—the kind of policies discussed in Parts I and II—should increase the flow of intra-Community trade, the lowering of transport costs can also contribute towards this end. Thus one of the overriding aims of the policy for transport must be to create an efficient transport system. The contribution which efficient transport can make to the development of the common market becomes increasingly obvious when consideration is given to the burden which transport costs sometimes assume. These are most burdensome when the goods carried are bulky or heavy and of relatively low value. For example, the German State Railways estimated that in 1957 railway freight charges added 50 per cent to the producer prices of stone and building materials and 9–26 per cent to that of bulk goods.[1] In discussing the relevance of transport to the integration of the coal and steel markets, we noted earlier that transport costs could add up to 50 per cent to the pithead price of coal on such long runs as, for example, Merlebach (Lorraine)/Tours, or Gelsenkirchen (Ruhr)/Munich.[2] In the UK it has been estimated that in 1955 rail freight charges for a 400-mile journey amounted to 28 per cent of the wholesale price of wheat, and 22 per cent of those of barley and oats.[3] (The impact of transport costs on agricultural products indicates the relevance of the common transport policy to the Community's agricultural policy.)

A common policy on transport is also essential because those who framed the treaty found themselves encumbered with a legacy of government interventions in the transport sphere. The fact that there is no common purpose in the various forms of intervention practised by member-state governments is itself a factor giving rise to distortions of the market. But, more important still, transport has been deliberately manipulated in such a way as to aid exports or protect home industries from imports. Discrimination on grounds of nationality had to be tackled at a very early stage in the integration of the national coal and steel markets, and this is a field in which corresponding problems arise in the implementation of the general common market also. For example, in Germany special rail tariff AT24A provided for the transport of wood, paper, cellulose, and artificial stones *for export* at between 14 and 22 per cent below the normal rate. In Italy all merchandise *for export*[4] carried more than 101 miles[5] on the Italian rail network was charged between 10 and 25 per cent

---

[1] S. Trench, 'Transport in the Common Market', *Planning* (PEP), xxix/ 473 (1963), pp. 228–9.
[2] See above, p. 287.   [3] Bayliss, table 1.
[4] Except ECSC products and several others.
[5] 201 miles in the case of horticultural products.

(according to distance) below the normal rate.[6] As an example of protection from imports, the tariffs of the Rhine/Herne and the Wesel/Datteln Canals can be cited. In both cases German-produced minerals were carried at tolls which were 90 per cent below the normal rate.[7] (In practice the Commission has already taken steps to deal with this kind of problem. It was reported at the end of 1964 that joint action had been taken to abolish or amend 251 transport tariffs applying differential rates and conditions as between the inland transport of a member state and its intra-Community transport.)[8]

Quite clearly, therefore, much of the impact of transport as it has been traditionally organized within separate national frameworks is at variance with the needs of a common market. Perhaps the most striking single aspect of national transport policies, when considered in the context of economic integration, is their lack of mutual coherence. In their attempts to create a harmonious common policy out of their disparate national systems, the member states have been compelled by the very incompatibility of their individual approaches to seek for a common policy that would make a prominent feature of a certain neutrality and objectivity. It is this which accounts for the emergence of the cost-oriented controlled competitive system whose general features we shall now examine.

2. MANAGEMENT OF THE TRANSPORT MARKET

The proposed basis of the common transport policy is revealed by the treaty Articles 74 to 84 and two subsequent documents produced by the Commission. The treaty itself is not very informative. The reason for this is that, at the time of drafting, the issues involved were so complex, and the differences between the states were so great, that no attempt was made to incorporate any detailed statement of policy in the treaty document. The detailed basis of the Commission's proposals are in fact contained in its *Memorandum on the General Lines of the Common Transport Policy*[9] (generally referred to simply as the Schaus Memorandum), which contains the general philosophy behind them, and its *Programme for Implementation of the Common Transport*

[6] Bayliss, p. 6.   [7] Ibid. p. 13.   [8] *Bull. EEC*, Dec. 1964, p. 33.
[9] EEC Commission, *Memorandum on the General Lines of the Common Transport policy*, VI COM (61) 50- E, Orig. F, 10 Apr. 1961.
11

Policy[10] (referred to from now on in this chapter as the Action Programme), which reveals the nature of the measures that the Commission proposed should be implemented. Following the requirements of the treaty, the common transport policy will apply directly to the transport of both goods and persons[11] by rail, road, and inland waterway. It will only apply to sea and air transport if, and to the extent that, the Council so decides by unanimous vote.[12]

The Schaus Memorandum and the Action Programme both make it clear that it is the intention of the Commission that the common transport policy should apply to national as well as international transport systems. This is a point upon which there has in the past been some difference of opinion between the member states, some maintaining that the policy should only apply to international transport. On a strict interpretation of the treaty, those who have taken the latter view might be said to be correct, since Article 75 speaks of a common transport policy which shall be implemented by 'laying down rules applicable to international transport'. On the other hand the same article provides for 'making any other appropriate provision' which is sufficiently wide to provide a legal basis for extending the policy to national systems. In practice it is clear that the logic of the treaty requires the application of the policy to national transport. There is indeed some analogy between the anti-trust rules and the requirements of the common transport policy. Thus an agreement which is on the face of it 'purely national' in character, for example an exclusive-dealing arrangement between manufacturers and dealers in one state, can clearly have restrictive effects on inter-state trade in the same way as an agreement between enterprises in the various states to respect each other's national market is restrictive of such trade. Similarly, it is clear that a common transport policy that applied only to inter-state transport would have serious inadequacies. For example, if the transport of a particular type of commodity between the manufacturer in Germany and consumers in Paris was subject to the common transport policy, but transport of similar goods from a

[10] EEC Commission, *Programme for Implementation of the Common Transport Policy*, VII COM (62) 88 final, 23 May 1962.

[11] In order to simplify matters, the ensuing account will refer only to goods transport.

[12] Rome Treaty, Art. 84.

French factory to Parisian consumers was outside the purview of that policy, it is possible that the freight rate per kilometre for the French goods could be set at an artificially low level, thus distorting the conditions of competition between French and German manufacturers. Similarly, distortions of competition could occur if transport of raw materials to the French factory were subsidized while the German manufacturer was not granted the same assistance. It is, therefore, difficult to see where a line can be drawn excluding certain forms of transport from the common policy, as in certain circumstances the development of industry and trade within the Community could logically be affected even by measures that appear to be very much limited to specifically national questions.

A prime feature of the common policy is the increased role which will be given to the forces of the market. In the words of one of the members of the Commission's staff responsible for transport:

Even a very superficial examination of the Treaty shows that the desired economic interpenetration is based on the general application of the concepts of a market economy and of competition. It would be no exaggeration to say that effective rules governing transport in the Community market can only be worked out if the principle of a market economy, which has been generally accepted for all other sectors, is applied here too. A dirigistic transport policy, subjecting all vital spheres of business, such as rates policy, to direct orders by national or supranational bureaucracies, thereby eliminating the guiding force of competition, would not be compatible with the fundamental character of our Community.[13]

In other words, the various forms of transport will be allowed to compete with each other and competition will exist within each form of transport. This means of course that enterprises will be free to set their rates (although within certain limits, as we shall show), and that the present system of government control which is in some cases very rigid, for example the German railways and, in some countries, inland waterway transport, will have to go.

This movement towards a more market-oriented transport policy in itself represents a fundamental new development since

[13] A. H. Reinarz, 'Transport Charges and Tariffs in the European Economic Community', Brit. Inst. Internat. & Compar. Law, Suppl. Publ., no. 2 (1963), p. 16.

in the past all the governments have in varying degrees impeded the working of market forces in the transport sector. This state intervention arose because of the monopolistic position acquired by the railways, which called for some form of regulation. In addition the principle of *Gemeinwirtschaftlichkeit* (the general economic good), or *service public,* had influenced the attitude of public authorities and has led to transport being used as an instrument of general economic policy. With the growth of competition from road transport, governments were led to impose restrictions on this competition in order to protect their investments.

From the play of market forces which the Commission would like to see established will come a better allocation of resources. Thus

funds available for investment—which are always scarce—can only be put to the best use in the Community where there is a rate which is in line with the real conditions of the market and clearly reflects the concentrated play of all the economic decisions, choices and preferences of the whole market.[14]

This better allocation of resources cannot, however, be achieved unless competition is undistorted. In Community language this means that competitors must start in comparable conditions. To achieve this end a number of conditions will have to be fulfilled. Within each state the following measures will be necessary.

All enterprises and forms of transport will in deciding rates, type and frequency of service, have to be free to base their decisions on commercial criteria. This will involve the freedom to close down services if necessary.

If some enterprise or form of transport is bound by some public service obligation, it should be compensated by the government.

All enterprises and forms of transport will have to be financially independent and seek to balance their accounts without the need for subsidization.

On the fiscal side there will have to be equality of treatment for each form of transport. In order to contribute towards this end, and as a contribution to making transport rates reflect costs, the states will have to recoup infrastructure costs according to the benefits received. It will also be necessary to harmonize the widely differing fiscal, technical, and social obligations imposed upon transport.

[14] Reinarz, in Brit. Inst. Internat. & Compar. Law, Suppl. Publ. no. 2, p. 16.

The Council's decision to investigate infrastructure costs with a view to apportioning them amongst users in a way that reflects benefits received is perhaps one of the most significant features of the proposed common transport policy. There would after all be little point in increasing the role of market forces if at the same time no attempt was made at a rational assessment of costs. The need for such an assessment, so that each branch of transport would receive equal treatment, has been strongly advocated by the Netherlands Government,[15] which undertook an investigation of the problem prior to the establishment of the European Economic Community. In 1960 a committee of government experts was set up to study the problem. However, it was found that the work of the committee could not bear fruit unless it was enabled to obtain actual data on infrastructure costs. As a result, the Commission decided to submit to the Council of Ministers a draft proposal to give a legal basis for an inquiry throughout the Community into the cost of the infrastructure of transport by rail, road, and inland waterway, and a Regulation to this effect was issued by the Council in 1964.[16] The inquiry was carried out with reference to the year 1966, and before the end of June 1968 the Commission is to submit to the Council of Ministers a report on the inquiry, together with a study of the way infrastructure costs are met and proposals for a uniform system of assessing and distributing them. The member states also conducted a road traffic census of the whole of their road traffic networks for the year 1965—a year in which a census of international road transport was in any case being made.[17]

But although the Commission's proposed policy was designed to give greater weight to market forces and the play of competition, some limitations were to continue to apply, and this differentiated the policy for transport from the general policy

[15] Ministry of Transport and Waterstaat, *Towards a European Transport Policy* (1964), p. 32. The importance of this problem was also highlighted in the first Kapteyn Report (ECSC, Common Assembly, *Rapport fait au nom de la Commission des transports sur la coordination des transports européens*, Doc. no. 6, session 1957–8, (1957), p. 22).

[16] *JO*, 29 June 1964.

[17] It is also worth noting in passing that the Commission has proposed that machinery be created to coordinate the transport infrastructure programmes of the member states. The basic idea here is to fit the various national projects into a programme for the development of a logical Community transport network.

approach of the treaty. Although one might have expected that the policy for transport would be based upon complete freedom of entry into the industry and the completely free play of prices, this would not be so if the Commission's view prevailed. Both at the national and international level, entry would in fact be con-controlled by licensing with the deliberate intention of adjusting the supply of transport to the demand for it.[18] But the fact that market forces were not to be entirely free is best illustrated by the rate bracket system under which transport enterprises would only be able to vary their rates between upper and lower rate brackets determined by the relevant authorities.[19] This feature of the proposed transport policy represented a compromise between two extremes: rates which were fixed by public authorities and publicized, and rates which were freely negotiated by the enterprises without the need for publicity.

An important feature of the proposed policy was that the consumer should be free to choose not only between alternative modes of transport[20] but also between transport services offered by enterprises of *all* member states. In order to give consumers more information about the range of possible offers—in Community language, to increase the transparency of the market—rate brackets were to be published and information would be provided *a posteriori* about actual rates charged. Two measures were proposed to enable consumers to choose between services offered by firms in any of the member states. One was that freedom of establishment was to be extended to transport, and this would throw national transport open to enterprises from all the member states. The second was that in international transport all arrangements, such as the bilateral agreements which restricted operations to nationals of the two signatories, were to be eliminated. Eventually international transport was to some extent to be open to all enterprises irrespective of nationality.

[18] This does not apply to own-account transport; the Commission favours complete liberalization in this sphere. It also requires that it be placed in a position comparable to that of hire-and-reward transport, particularly as regards fiscal charges and allocating infrastructure costs.

[19] Another qualification to the view that the common transport policy puts an increased stress on competition and market forces is the fact that Art. 75 (3) requires the unanimous consent of the Council of Ministers to transport measures that would adversely affect regional development.

[20] This also means that he should be free to choose own-account transport.

Although the treaty may be extremely uninformative on some aspects of the transport policy, it is quite clear about the approach to be adopted towards discriminatory and support tariffs. In line with the general philosophy of the treaty, discrimination on grounds of nationality is prohibited, and an instrument to implement this requirement has already been created. Support tariffs imposed by member-state governments to assist some particular enterprise or industry are likewise prohibited as from the beginning of the second stage.[21] This is very much in line with the kind of policy already being followed in the coal and steel markets. It is also worth noting that, again following ECSC experience, the Action Programme calls for the adoption, for example in the case of international rail transport, of international through rates.

With this outline of the basis of the proposed transport policy before us we can now proceed to discuss some aspects in greater detail, noting on the one hand the progress which has been made towards implementation of the policy and on the other the degree to which the actual policy decisions of the Council of Ministers are in line with the original proposals of the Commission.

3. ACCESS TO THE MARKET

One of the main features of the common transport policy is the creation of rules governing access to the transport market. This problem is most acute in the case of road transport, less so in inland waterway transport. Because of the particular position of railways the problem hardly arises in that case.

(a) Right of Establishment

The Rome Treaty envisages the progressive adoption of measures to bring about freedom of establishment, and this applies to transport also. In 1961 the Council of Ministers approved a general programme for the removal of restrictions on the freedom of establishment and on the freedom to supply services.[22] This programme requires that discrimination and other restrictions based on nationality, which limit freedom of establishment of road, rail, and inland waterway transport undertakings, be removed between 1 January 1966 (the beginning

---

[21] Both these prohibitions are subject to exemptions—see below, p. 325.
[22] *JO*, 15 Jan. 1962.

of the third stage) and 1 December 1967. The general programme also required that in respect of undertakings ancillary to transport such as transport agents and freight brokers, discrimination and other restrictions be removed by 31 January 1963. As a result of the implementation of these measures, enterprises of each member state are now able to establish themselves in any other member state and find themselves in conditions similar to those experienced by nationals.

It should, however, be stressed that although the above measures allow enterprises to establish themselves in any state of the Community, freedom of entry to the transport market is not automatically guaranteed, as some limitation on capacity will continue to be applied by means of licensing.

(b) Licences

Licensing is a well-established method by which governments limit freedom of activity in haulage whether by road or inland waterway. The régimes in respect of own-account transport have been relatively free from restriction, and the Commission has not experienced much difficulty in pursuing a policy of liberalization. For example, when the Commission came to review the situation it found that national road transport was fairly close to what it desired. Again in respect of international road transport the situation has been relatively liberal, and in 1964 the Commission was able to secure the Council's approval to complete liberalization in this sphere. By contrast, in the case of transport for hire and reward, the régimes have been relatively illiberal, and here the Commission has encountered more substantial problems. We shall not attempt an exhaustive account of these latter problems, but will confine ourselves to a discussion of the policies proposed in respect of hire-and-reward road transport.

(i) *International Road Transport for Hire and Reward.* This form of transport has in general been governed by means of agreements, written or oral, between the administrative authorities of the member states of the Community. The contents of the agreements vary, but typically they include the following features. Some have been bilateral, in which case each state has laid down the number and load capacity of vehicles from the other state to be allowed on its territory at any one time. In other cases there have been unilateral arrangements where only one state imposed a quota on the other.[23] In addition, apart from Benelux, these arrangements also require goods passing between two member states to be carried by transport undertakings of those states. In some cases carriers are forbidden to undertake return loads and are not allowed to perform a domestic haul in the country visited.[24]

It is clear that these systems have not contributed to a realization of the objectives of the Rome Treaty. In the first place, there appears to have been no effective machinery for expanding the size of the quotas as intra-Community trade expands.[25] The Commission's investigations revealed that bilateral quotas between certain member states had not been expanded to an extent corresponding to the growth of the trade between them.[26] These factors could restrict trade either through there being insufficient transport capacity or through a rise in freight rates. Secondly, restrictions such as those preventing return loads and domestic hauls in the state being visited (i.e. cabotage) tend to increase international freight rates. Thirdly, confining transport

[23] International transport between Benelux countries is entirely free of quotas There are no quantitative restrictions on international goods transported by inland waterway.

[24] G. Krauss, 'Licensing Policy in the European Economic Community', Brit. Inst. Internat. & Compar. Law, Suppl. Publ. no. 2, (1963), pp. 56–57.

[25] Trench, *Planning* (PEP), xxix/473 (1963), p. 270.

[26] Action Programme, para. 26. Not all commentators, however, consider that the relative rigidity of the quotas has been a restrictive influence. For example, Bayliss (pp. 140–1) argues that it is curious that the quantity of goods carried by international road hauliers has nevertheless increased. This he believes could be explained by greater vehicle carrying capacity or by greater use of own-account transport. Neither of these are acceptable explanations. It has always been the policy to use vehicles of the maximum size allowed by the law and no increase in the legal maxima has occurred. There is no evidence of a general increase in the use of own-account transport. Bayliss therefore concludes that bilateral quotas were underutilized and it is by this means that international road carriage (by hire and reward) has been able to increase. This does not mean that there have not been particular instances of quota rigidity having a restrictive effect. Thus in the case of transport between the Netherlands and Belgium, from the end of the last war until 1962 there was practically no increase in the number of hauliers for hire and reward who could enter Belgium. As a result Belgian licences commanded a high price in the Netherlands and increasing resort was had to own-account transport. Although Bayliss may be correct in his view that in 1958 there was considerable slack in the quotas, the Commission's approach is surely right in that the continued growth of trade is bound eventually to eliminate any such slack.

11*

between two states to transport enterprises of those states restricts the range of potential competition.

The Action Programme therefore proposed the following lines of policy. First, that bilateral quotas existing at the beginning of 1958 should be enlarged so as to bring them into line with the expansion of international trade. One of the problems involved here is the imposition of quotas on transport between Benelux states. Since this traffic is free of quantitative restrictions, any imposition would represent a retreat from an extremely liberal position. Secondly, that bilateral licensing systems should be progressively eliminated. Instead a Community Quota would be created. As the bilateral licences disappeared, Community licences would come into existence at a rate sufficient to compensate both for the disappearance of bilateral licences and for the growth of Community trade.[27]

In 1964 the Council of Ministers reached agreement upon the nature of the Community Quota, the main content of the accord being as follows. The Community Quota and the adaptation of bilateral quotas were to come into force on 1 January 1966. The Community Quota would be operated for four years, up to and including 1969. This was to be an experimental period—the Council being unwilling to commit itself to the Community Quota as a final system. The Council was to make a fresh decision, on the basis of a proposal by the Commission, in the light of experience. The initial Quota for 1966 was to consist of 880 authorizations to be divided among the member states as follows: Germany 210, France 210, Netherlands 176, Belgium 118, Italy 142, Luxembourg 42. In 1967, 1968, and 1969 the Quota would rise to 1,480, 1,930, and 2,380 authorizations respectively. The Commission would decide how the subsequent quotas were to be divided after consulting member states. Criteria for the allocation of authorizations would include the development of trade and the use made of authorizations with the proviso that no state

---

[27] It is questionable whether these proposals go far enough. Bayliss (p. 142) points out that the Commission has not made any proposals to deal with major problems such as: the division of countries into zones and the restriction of foreign hauliers in their access to some of these; the retention of foreign licences over a period of years by one haulier when these could be more intensively used if allowed to circulate; above all the elimination of the administrative difficulties and delays in obtaining foreign licences. The latter problem cannot be stressed too much. Indeed the obstacles to which administrative processes can give rise have a relevance over the whole field of Community policy.

should suffer a diminution of its absolute Quota. An authorization would entitle the holder to carry out transport over all
routes between member states and to unload his vehicles anywhere in the Common Market. Each authorization would be
made out in the name of a particular haulier and would cover one
vehicle. At the same time as the Community Quota was being
established the existing bilateral systems would be adapted to
transport needs by negotiations between member states.[28] The
Commission would take part on a consultative basis in all these
negotiations. If the member states could not secure agreement
within six months, the Commission would be required to formu-
late a proposal for submission to the Council. In some cases there
are no bilateral quotas on transport between states but transit
restrictions exist when such transport has to pass through
another state. Transit authorizations would therefore also have
to be increased by negotiation in line with the needs of trade.[29]

However as yet no Council Decision has been issued putting
the Community Quota into effect. The reason for this is that
French agreement to the quota arrangement was made con-
ditional upon agreement also being reached in respect of rate
brackets. As we shall see below, an outline agreement on the
subject of rate brackets was achieved at the very beginning of
July 1965. But the French boycott, which began on 5 July 1965,
prevented the Council from proceeding to issue a Decision on
the subject of brackets. At the time of writing this latter problem
is before the Council for final action and it is reasonable to
assume that a Decision in this field would be followed by one
dealing with the Community Quota.

In favour of the above arrangements it must be said that the
creation of an expanding Community Quota and the adjustment
of the bilateral quotas would make a considerable contribution
towards increasing the supply of international transport capacity
in line with the expansion which has clearly taken place in intra-
Community trade. Two criticisms can, however, be levelled at
them.

The first is that the idea of gradually eliminating the bilateral

[28] Transit countries, that is Common Market countries over which goods have
to pass when proceeding from one member state to another, will be involved
in these negotiations.
[29] The Commission will also make proposals to the Council if these negotiations fail.

quotas completely (as the Action Programme had originally proposed) and replacing them by the Community Quota has been dropped, at least for the present, possibly for good. To this extent the 'Community content' of this system has decreased.

Secondly, both the Community Quota and the bilateral quotas introduce an element of rigidity into the market. Thus, carriers in one state could qualify for licences while carriers in another state who might be more efficient could be debarred either by the size of their national allocation of the Community Quota or by the restrictions placed upon the size of bilateral quotas.

As has been pointed out earlier, the Commission has proposed that the Community Quota should be manipulated to keep the supply of road transport capacity in line with demand. Therefore although the Action Programme speaks of introducing a system of 'healthy competition', this should not be taken to mean leaving international road transport to the free play of the market. On the contrary: 'This is where the system of supervision of capacity, which the Commission considers essential, comes into play. The system would provide a flexible means of adjusting the supply of carrying capacity, to the demand for transport services.'[30]

Whether freights will be above or below the level dictated by healthy free competition will presumably depend upon the flexibility of the system, i.e. the extent to which the quota is increased (or decreased) as demand increases (or decreases). There is some room for doubting whether the arrangement is likely to be very flexible. Bilateral quotas would only be increased at intervals. The size of the Community Quota has been laid down well in advance of the growth of trade and could therefore prove to be inadequate.

(ii) *National Road Transport for Hire and Reward.* In all the member states some control is exercised over entry by requiring some form of licence or permit which is not freely granted.

The Action Programme proposed that such licensing should continue although the systems should be modified and harmonized.

In the first place the Commission believes that licence quotas have lacked flexibility and have in fact been restrictive, giving

---

[30] Krauss, in Brit. Inst. Internat. & Compar. Law, Suppl. Publ. no. 2, p. 60.

rise to a relatively high level of charges. An increase of quotas would therefore be required but the procedure for bringing this about would be left until later.

In the interim the Commission has proposed that certain steps should be taken to integrate national systems and allow a better use of international road-transport capacity, which would lead to some increase of national capacity. First, international carriers who do not have a Community licence (those for example who hold bilateral licences) should be allowed to carry out transport operations in the market of the member state[31] which is a party to the bilateral agreement. Secondly, those carriers who possess Community licences should be allowed to take part in national transport activity in all member states.

This penetration of national markets would, however, in some degree be frustrated unless there was a harmonization of national licensing systems. The granting of licences depends upon two sets of factors usually referred to as the subjective and objective conditions. Subjective conditions relate to the respectability, professional qualifications, and solvency of the applicants. Objective conditions refer to the system for determining the quantity of transport capacity deemed desirable. Some systems at present in use involve the fixing of a global capacity, others involve a flexible restriction of access so as to adjust supply to demand on the basis of a permanent study of the market, and yet others involve a compulsory waiting period operating transport not subject to licence. The first and third are regarded as too inflexible and so the Action Programme suggests the second.

Finally, by way of concluding this discussion of access to the transport market, it is worth considering how the Commission's proposals on road haulage licensing stand, first, in relation to the practice of member states and, secondly, in relation to the latest developments outside the Six. The general impression that emerges is that the licensing proposals of the Commission are not as liberal as those of some of the member states. But they do tend towards the relatively liberal position of the Italians and Dutch who, although they apply a licensing system, administer it in a

[31] This provision would be made more liberal by stages. Also common rules could be made which would, for example, stipulate that the national transport operation would have to take the vehicle close to the border between the two states.

way which does not significantly impede the growth of road transport. The Commission's proposals are, however, significantly more liberal than the licensing systems of Germany and France which are relatively restrictive, quotas having been increased very little since the last war.

However, it is significant that the proposed common transport policy in respect of licensing does not follow the trend, discernible in a number of countries outside the Community, towards the abandonment of licensing. Thus in Australia in 1954 all inter-state transport was freed from all forms of restriction. In Sweden legislation has been enacted to relax progressively the licensing systems for road transport with provision for total abolition in 1968 of the system whereby a carrier has to demonstrate the need for a proposed service and other carriers can object. Finally, in Great Britain the Geddes Report has recently recommended the complete scrapping of the licensing system.[32] There is a limited amount of evidence which suggests, hardly surprisingly, that licensing tends to raise freights and that the removal of restrictions has been followed by lower rates (and satisfactory service). This has for example been demonstrated in the case of agricultural and fishery products in the United States.[33] It is therefore a little surprising that, in the light of the EEC Commission's advocacy of competition and its desire for transport efficiency, it did not at least make an initial bid for a transport system free of all licensing restrictions.

4. RATE POLICY

(a) Rate Brackets

The Commission originally proposed that rates charged for transport within the Common Market should be controlled by a system of rate brackets. This system was to apply to rates charged

---

[32] Ministry of Transport, *Carriers' Licensing* (1965). It is interesting to note that the Geddes Report, while regarding the charges of inefficiency levelled against own-account operations ('C' licences) as being exaggerated, did consider that some improvement could be made by abandoning the licence system and thus allowing manufacturers &c. who own lorries to obtain better vehicle utilization by using them for hire and reward. The EEC Commission appears to be aware of the inefficiency problem connected with own-account but shows no sign of having considered breaking down the rigid distinction between own-account and hire-and-reward licences.

[33] Ibid. p. 37.

for road, rail, and inland waterway transport whether national or international. Own-account transport would be exempt from the system.

The rate bracket system was to specify a maximum and a minimum rate for different types of traffic and different routes. Carriers and consignors could negotiate the actual rates, which could lie anywhere within the two brackets but could not lie above the maximum or below the minimum bracket. The actual size of the spread between the brackets at the end of the transition phase of the transport policy was not revealed but the Commission envisaged in the initial period a spread of between 10 and 30 per cent. Thus if the maximum rate is represented by a figure of 100, then the minimum would be between 70 and 90. Within these forks it was to be permissible:

To adopt fixed rates and charges, or forked tariffs narrower than those approved officially or charges which have been freely negotiated and are valid for varying lengths of time or charges for each individual service performed. At the same time they could adopt several of these methods simultaneously.[34]

The Commission also suggested procedures for the proposal and approval of tariff brackets. Publicity was also provided for and controls and sanctions were envisaged.

So much for the basic proposal. What in fact was the reasoning which lay behind the proposal to adopt the bracket system?

Apparently an upper limit was to be set in order to prevent the abuse of monopoly positions and the possibility that in abnormal periods charges might rise excessively. The object of the lower limit was to prevent the appearance in transport of the detrimental effects of excessive competition.

In connexion with the latter the Commission maintained that freight transport, particularly by road and inland waterway, was subject to undesirable price fluctuations. This was said to be due to a marked inelasticity of supply and demand. Demand for freight transport as a whole is largely determined by the overall level of activity and at least *in the short term* a fall in freight rates will not stimulate an extension of demand.[35] On the supply side

---

[34] *Action Programme*, para. 94.
[35] In the short term there will, however, be a high cross elasticity of demand between the different forms of freight transport.

the Commission maintained that, partly as a result of the small-scale entrepreneurship in the industry, a fall in freight-rates would not lead to a contraction of the volume of supply. Vehicle owners would in fact seek to maintain or possibly augment their volume of supply in order to arrest a fall in the level of their earnings. Because of this twofold inelasticity, a fall in demand was likely to precipitate a steep fall in rates.

The Commission also appeared to have in mind the fact that this is an industry into which entry is easy, and ability to judge prospective profitability is likely to be poor because of the lack of professional training. In times of boom large numbers of small-scale entrepreneurs would be likely to be attracted into the industry. On the other hand in a period of recession or slump many of these entrepreneurs, particularly if they had only small financial reserves, would be likely to decide to leave the industry, but this process is not necessarily a rapid one. In the interim they would be prepared to accept rates that covered direct costs if they provided some additional contribution to overhead capital costs, however small. If there was a substantial number of such firms, extremely low rates might rule for a substantial period.[36] The Schaus Memorandum did not explain why low rates were un-desirable but it is reasonable to assume that the argument was based upon the likely effect on working conditions and profits for investment.

It is clear that the Commission regarded dangerous price fluctuations as a distinct possibility. To cope with such an eventuality two lines of defence were proposed. The first was licensing, which could be used to restrict the supply of transport capacity. The second was the system of rate brackets to restrict rate fluctuations. From the point of view of economic analysis it is legitimate to ask why two defences were needed. In principle increases or decreases in the supply of capacity via licensing could be employed to offset any increase or decrease in the demand for capacity, thus holding rates steady. The probable explanation is that licensing control has two drawbacks. The first is that it involves an administrative process which might be slow to operate. The second is that it is probably not sufficiently flexible. For example, once licences have been issued it might be difficult if not impossible to withdraw them to counteract falling

[36] Trench, *Planning* (PEP), xxix/473 (1963), p. 256.

rates. Also even if licences were freely available there might not be enough takers in a period of rising rates. In such circumstances the burden of holding rates up or down would have to fall on the rate brackets.

The Commission's original proposals are, however, open to a number of criticisms. First, we may ask whether the Commission's fear of dangerous rate fluctuations was justified. There is some evidence drawn from practical experience which suggests that it was not. Thus the Geddes Report refers to a number of countries which have freed part of their road traffic and have not experienced a severe fluctuation problem. In the United States certain classes of goods, particularly agricultural and fishery products, were exempted from licensing under the 1945 Motor Carrier Act. As a result any carrier, whether haulier or own-account operator, whether licensed or not, is entitled to carry such goods and charge what rate he pleases. Studies conducted by the US Department of Agriculture suggest that rates tend to be relatively stable, although there is some variation, because of seasonal fluctuations in demand. Thus 'exempt carrier rates, determined by unrestricted competition, have not been accompanied by instability within the industry or by uneconomic operations and high rates of bankruptcy'.[37]

In Australia, where inter-state road transport was freed from restriction in 1954, evidence indicates that, after an initial bout of severe competition with uneconomic low rates and numerous bankruptcies, rates have settled down and are low and stable.[38]

Secondly, it seems to us that the fear of monopoly and cut-throat competition was grossly exaggerated, a view which the authors of the Allais Report[39] (on transport pricing) also appear to have held. They appear to have felt that there was much to be said for setting rates free and seeing what would happen. If either monopoly or vicious rate cutting began to occur, a top or bottom bracket could be applied. In any case it was impossible to justify the application of both at one and the same time!

Thirdly, it cannot be doubted that the task of properly costing the brackets for all the routes in the Community would be a gigantic if not impossible task. Because of these difficulties, the

---

[37] Geddes Report, p. 37.   [38] Ibid. p. 39.
[39] EEC, *Options de la politique tarifaire dans les transports*, Études Série Transports, no. 1, 1965, especially ch. 32.

suspicion arises that, instead of costing the brackets, where, for example, fixed rates already existed, they would merely be determined by allowing a margin of fluctuation on either side of the fixed rate.

There is, of course, considerable reason to believe that the proposed use of the rate bracket system (and the same is true of other aspects of the common transport policy) was determined not so much by the kind of economic arguments presented by the Commission as by the need to achieve a compromise between the relatively free rate system practised by the Dutch and the rigid system of charges applied in Germany. The French operate a 30 per cent rate bracket system which lies somewhere in between the Dutch and German systems, and it therefore appears that the Commission's original proposals bear a fairly close resemblance to the French system. It is unfortunate that in the Commission's original basic documents on the common transport policy there was a tendency to argue the case for rate brackets as if they were entirely justified on economic grounds.

(b) The Dutch Opposition

The rate bracket and the allied rate publication proposals were the most contentious features of the proposed common transport policy and the inability to reach agreement upon them held back any substantial progress in transport policy for a number of years. The main resistance came from the Dutch, who were opposed to rate brackets—particularly in respect of international Rhine shipping. As a result of the Mannheim Convention of 1868 government control over charges for international traffic on the Rhine is prohibited, and the Dutch refused to alter the situation.[40] The Dutch publicly stated their objections, although it must be confessed that their argument was somewhat obscure.[41] Central to the Dutch interest in the international Rhine traffic system was the fact that they commanded, by virtue of their undoubted competitiveness, a large share of this traffic, and this made a substantial contribution to the Gross National Product and the balance of payments of the Netherlands. Thus in 1963

[40] This problem is not of course a new one. As we saw earlier it also arose in connexion with the ECSC (pp. 291).

[41] Ministry of Transport and Waterstaat, *Towards a European Transport Policy*, pp. 12–23.

66·6 million tons of freight was transported from or to the Netherlands on the Rhine, a large part of this traffic being transit trade. This constituted 61 per cent of all Rhine traffic and 53 per cent of it was carried under the Dutch flag.

The Dutch maintained that the common transport policy should be designed to allow the Community to reap the advantages of the division of labour in transportation, and they clearly and probably justifiably saw themselves as being among the most fitted to engage in international inland waterway traffic.[42] The bracket system was, however, seen as a threat to their position for reasons which were not clearly stated but which, by interpretation, seem to have been as follows. The first was that the rate bracket system would in effect tend to become either a legal minimum or a legal maximum price. In times of slump the former would obtain, but if prices were free the more efficient Dutch carriers would be able to underquote their rivals and pre-empt a large share of the trade. But since prices would not be allowed to fall below the lower bracket and, if this was set high enough, carriers other than the Dutch would be willing to continue to supply their services, the market share-out would be less advantageous to the Dutch. In times of boom under a free-rate system rates would tend to rise steeply but under the bracket system they would be constrained by the upper bracket. This would therefore limit the earning power of Dutch carriers and reduce the contribution of this trade to the Netherlands national income and balance of payments. The second Dutch objection related to rail competition. The Dutch feared the possibility that the railways, which under the Commission's original proposals would draw up their own tariff brackets, would artificially depress the rates on journeys competitive with inland waterways and would compensate by raising rates on routes where they had some degree of monopoly power. Inland waterway carriers who operated under competitive conditions would not have the same room for manoeuvre. Central to the Dutch interest was the future of the port of Rotterdam, an entrepôt through which the Rhine trade was channelled and from which the relatively large Dutch deep-sea fleet mainly operated. Any restriction which disadvantaged inland waterway traffic, to the benefit of the railways,

---

[42] The same could be said for international road haulage.

was bound to assist Rotterdam's competitors, Antwerp and Hamburg.

The other area of disagreement was rate publicity, to which the Dutch were opposed.[43] The Dutch approach to transport pricing has been essentially competitive with provision for individual negotiation of rates without the need for publicity. Presumably the assumption was that it would be easier to obtain business if competitors did not know how far they would have to reduce their bids to match the Dutch.

(c) The 1965 Agreement

In 1965, after a long stalemate and ironically just before the French boycott over agriculture began, a compromise agreement on tariffication and publicity was reached. Essentially this involved the formal abandonment by the French of the principle that tariff brackets be applied to all forms of transport, and agreement by the Dutch to a system of publicity. The basic features of the arrangement, which is experimental, are as follows:

In Stage One, which it is proposed will last for three years from 1 January 1967, the rate-bracket system will apply to international traffic only. There will be two forms of rate-bracket system—compulsory and reference. International road traffic (more than 50 kilometres) will come under the compulsory system, as will international rail traffic. In respect of rail traffic, however, it will be possible to conclude special contracts, where required to counter competition from other transport media, provided they are warranted. For international inland waterway traffic, however, a reference system will apply. The reference bracket is so called because it will be published and will serve as a guide to enterprises as to the rates to charge. It will not be compulsory to charge rates equal to or within the brackets, but when charging rates outside the bracket details will be published, whereas rates within the bracket do not require publication. Both compulsory and reference rate brackets will be published, as will any rates which deviate from them (i.e. rail and inland waterway).

In Stage Two—from 1 January 1969 to 1 January 1972—the bracket system will be applied to domestic transport as well. The

---

[43] Here again there is a parallel with earlier ECSC experience, where the spread of secret rate agreement in recent years greatly reduced the transparency of the coal and steel markets.

arrangements for international traffic will be the same as in Stage One, with the important difference that the reference rate system will be applicable to heavy merchandise. In the case of domestic transport the reference rate system will also apply to the transport of heavy merchandise. For the rest of domestic transport member states will be able to choose between the compulsory or reference systems. The publicity arrangements will continue to apply.

During the Final Stage beginning in 1972 the whole system of rate brackets will be reviewed.[44]

A number of basic problems still remain to be disposed of, including the width of the brackets (the Commission now proposes 20 per cent—that is 10 per cent above and below the basic rate), the criteria for special contracts outside the normal limits, the details of the publicity system, and the definition of heavy merchandise subject to the reference rate system.[45]

It is clear that there is no point in trying to explain or justify on economic grounds the decision to apply differing treatment to transport according to mode or destination of goods. These differences are purely the outcome of a political compromise. The difference of treatment does, however, carry with it certain economic consequences. One of the basic ideas behind the common transport policy is the avoidance of distortions which can arise from differences in transport policy in the various member states. The fact that, for example, at the national level for part at least of transport activity, states can choose between two different policies does make the Community's approach less of a common policy and to this extent seems to run counter to the logic of such a policy by leaving the door open to distortions. Time alone will show how serious a weakness this is in practice. On the other hand the 1965 agreement does have some merit. We have indicated that the rate bracket system must be regarded as extremely difficult if not impossible to administer— in so far as it is possible to operate it is likely to be highly inflexible. The Dutch stand has had the effect of allowing into Community rate policy a greater degree of freedom. To this extent the forces of the market and competition will be able to perform their guiding and

[44] *Bull. EEC*, no. 8, 1965, annexe 1.
[45] Details of the Commission's amended proposals in the light of the July 1965 agreement are to be found, ibid. no. 12, 1965, pp. 40–42.

selection functions. The fact that licensing will continue to be applied in some forms of transport even when pricing freedom has been accepted does of course mean that complete freedom for market forces will not automatically coincide with free pricing.

(d) *Discriminatory and Support Rates*

Article 7 of the Rome Treaty requires that there should be no discrimination on grounds of nationality, and in the transport title of the treaty this requirement is repeated by Article 79. In June 1960 the Council passed Regulation 11, which seeks to abolish discrimination in the field of transport.

The Regulation, which came into force in July 1961, applies to all transport within the Community by road, rail, and inland waterway (own-account transport being excluded). It forbids transport concerns to discriminate by making different charges or conditions for carrying the same goods along the same route because of the country of origin or destination of the goods. Transport enterprises are required to notify their respective governments of all existing rates, conditions, and agreements which involve such discrimination. They are also required to notify any future discrimination. Member states are required to pass on the information so acquired to the EEC Commission.

In order further to facilitate checks on discrimination, a transport document, giving full details of each transaction, is required for all movements of goods within the Community and accredited representatives of the Commission will have power to check the books and papers of transport undertakings. If a *prima facie* case of discrimination is uncovered, the transport undertaking must furnish proof that the action is not in violation of the provisions of the Regulation. This it can only do by proving that the difference in rates or conditions is justified on economic grounds and is not based on nationality. If it fails to do so, the Commission can levy a fine of up to twenty times the charge involved in the transaction. If the offence continues after it has been required to cease, a fine of up to 10,000 units of account can be imposed.

It is important to note that the prohibition of discrimination is not as sweeping as might at first sight appear, because Article 12 of the Regulation states that the making of different charges and conditions shall not be prohibited if such action 'results solely

from competition between transport concerns or is due to technical or economic operating factors peculiar to the transport in
question'. Such flexibility is likely to be necessary if competition
for freight is to be encouraged. It could, however, be a back door
for discrimination on grounds of nationality, but such practices
are less likely when enterprises base their policy on commercial
criteria and operate free of government interference in rate
policy.[46]

Apparently there have been a significant number of complaints
of discrimination. Up to 1963 about 300 cases, mostly in railway
transport, had been solved informally.

Article 80 of the treaty prohibits support rates. These are in
effect a form of state aid, since they take the form of favourable
transport rates imposed in order to support one or more particular commercial or industrial enterprises. The treaty declares
them to be prohibited as from the beginning of the second stage
(January 1962) but states that in specific circumstances they may
be authorized by the Commission. These special circumstances
are connected with regional policy, underdeveloped areas, and
areas seriously affected by political circumstances. The latter
refers to support tariffs applied by German railways to assist
areas on the East German border. Here again, in regard to both
discrimination on grounds of nationality and support rates, the
general common market is having to deal with much the same
kind of problems as arose earlier in connexion with the integration
of the coal and steel markets.

5. A BRIEF PROVISIONAL APPRAISAL

An assessment of a policy which is both experimental and
incomplete must necessarily take the form of an interim judgement. Some of its weaknesses have been discussed above. Its
three great strengths are these. First, it attempts to organize
transport on an economic basis rather than to employ it as a
servant of particular state interests. It seeks to do this by loosen-
ing the restrictive influences of the licensing and rate systems
applied in some member states. Transport is to be oriented more
towards competition between the different modes of conveyance

[46] Trench, *Planning* (PEP), xxix/473 (1963), p. 250.

based on a proper allocation of infrastructure costs and a harmonization of fiscal and other burdens. This seems to be a healthy path to follow. The only criticism is that it probably does not go far enough. The second main strength of the policy is that it is pragmatic. The Six have wisely, in their decisions about licensing and rate brackets, avoided attaching themselves irrevocably to any one blue-print for transport. Instead they have decided upon a period of experimentation. Thirdly, by specifically providing for a common transport policy and creating an independent Commission endowed with the necessary powers to carry it out, the Rome Treaty represents a distinct advance on the Paris Treaty. We showed earlier in our discussion of transport rates in the ECSC that the High Authority was severely handicapped by the fact that power in this field was very much left in the hands of the member states. As we indicated earlier, just as there is little point in reducing tariff barriers if cartels go unmolested, likewise trade liberalization and cartel policy can be rendered ineffective if distortions in the transport market are not dealt with.

B. AGRICULTURE

I. GENERAL

If one had to summarize in a single phrase what the EEC implies for its member states one might say that it involves the gradual substitution of unified internal market conditions throughout the area of the Six for their previously separate national policies. Unlike the industrial sector, where it is intended that competition shall determine relative prices, in agriculture competition has been to a very large extent rejected in favour of a central determination of prices. In agriculture, therefore, integration of the national markets and the establishment of common price levels is being brought about within a framework that involves market management on a vast scale. It should be added that the control to be exercised in agriculture is, generally speaking, bound to be more rigid than in the case of transport. In the latter, even when prices are to be controlled, there will nevertheless be some permitted margin of fluctuation. On the other hand in agriculture, in the case of certain important products, prices will be kept either very close to or at predetermined levels.

The purpose of managing the agricultural markets is, however, also much more than simply the establishment of one single unified market: the aim is equally the solution of certain specifically agricultural problems. Thus, the creation of unified internal market conditions is to take place in a way that will increase productivity by promoting structural reforms, mitigate the discrepancy between agricultural and industrial earnings, and guide production into the channels that seem to be indicated by the evolution of domestic and export markets.

In view of the fact that agriculture has provided perhaps the most intractable problems that the Community has had to tackle, we may wonder why it was included in the Rome Treaty in the first place. The member states might have adopted the approach of the EFTA countries and left each state to decide whether or not to protect its own agriculture and if so, how, and to what degree. Such a policy was, however, rejected. States such as France and the Netherlands felt that a Community based purely on free trade in industrial goods would be one-sided. Their industrial sectors would have had to face the competition of German industry whilst their farmers would have been denied the opportunity of making compensatory inroads into the German food market. As we can see from Table 1 below, all the evidence pointed to the fact that they would indeed have been able to make such inroads if given the chance.

Thus the table shows that of the nine products mentioned, France had the lowest prices in five of them and the Netherlands

TABLE I

Average Prices Received by Farmers, 1958/9 to 1959/60

(*Lowest price* = 100)

	Wheat	Barley	Potatoes	Sugar beet	Beef & veal	Pigmeat	Eggs	Milk
France	100	100	115	100	100	109	126	100
W. Germany	141	167	107	140	118	126	152	107
Italy	143	126	107	117	132	123	158	107
Netherlands	109	122	100	113	116	100	100	100
Belgium	131	128	103	125	106	102	141	101

Source: EEC, *Bilans et études*, Série B, no. 21.

in a further three, while German prices tended to be the highest or next to the highest. Provided that the price levels selected for the final stage of the common agricultural policy were significantly below those of Germany, then food exporters such as France and the Netherlands stood to gain considerably from free access to the German market.

There was in fact little or no chance of securing agreement to the creation of the EEC unless agriculture were to be included. In practice inclusion meant breaking down the protective barriers around each national agricultural industry by removing custom duties, quotas, and all other devices which would discriminate in favour of home produced agricultural products as opposed to those originating in other member states, and substituting common Community prices for national support programmes.

However, although national interests required the inclusion of agriculture within the jurisdiction of the Community arrangements, there is one reason connected with the logic of an economic union why agriculture had to be included. This reason is that if agricultural price levels had been left to be determined by each member state acting independently, the result would have been a considerable distortion of competition.

This would arise in some of the industries producing manufactured goods from raw materials produced by Community farmers. An industry drawing its supplies from an agricultural sector which was relatively highly protected could, despite its own efficiency in transforming these materials, be placed at a competitive disadvantage as compared with similar industries obtaining their supplies from less highly protected sources. The reality of this danger is illustrated by the fact that before the establishment of a common price level for agricultural products the EEC Commission has had to operate compensatory schemes to assist manufacturing industries that were placed in a disadvantageous position in this way.[47]

Of course, however important the economic reasons may have been for including agriculture in the Rome Treaty, there was clearly a compelling political fact requiring its inclusion. To have created an economic union that failed to embrace one of the

---

[47] This is discussed in greater detail by H. B. Krohn and G. Schmitt, 'The Common Agricultural Policy', in Junckerstorff, pp. 355–6.

largest and most politically sensitive industries would have belied the general declared intentions of the contracting parties in the field of political union.

2. NATIONAL SUPPORT POLICIES

Before discussing the main features of the common agricultural policy itself it is useful to provide a brief background account of the main aspects of national policy in this field as this helps to explain why the common policy has developed in the particular way it has.

(a) *Price Support Policy*

Before the signing of the Rome Treaty and the introduction of the common policy, the agricultural policy of the member states was one of protection, both from each other[48] and from the impact of low world-market prices. Generalizations about national policies are difficult because of differences in detail in the approach of the individual member states to the various agricultural products. However, as a broad generalization, it is basically true to say that the main approach of the Common Market countries has been to manipulate the demand for and supply of agricultural products within the domestic market so as to bring about a price level which would be high enough to remunerate the farmer directly. There are a number of ways in which this could be achieved. On the side of imports, supplies could be restricted by a number of devices such as variable levies, the size of the levy being adjusted so as to bridge the gap between the world price c.i.f. and the price to be maintained in the home market. Then again, imports could be directly restricted by the state or by some agency operating on its behalf. Alternatively the price of imports could be kept up by applying an import duty, or by the importing country negotiating a minimum export price with the exporting country. On the demand side, the domestic price level could be supported by such devices as compulsory incorporation of domestic grain in bread flour and animal feeding stuffs, or by officially sponsored purchases for stock, the stocks

---

[48] This is not entirely true. In the case of intra-Benelux trade in agricultural products, customs duties were eventually abolished, but on the other hand quotas and minimum export prices have in some cases been applied.

being either released later on the domestic market or being sold abroad, probably at a loss.

The approach adopted by the EEC states contrasts markedly with the policy of the UK where, at the risk of a broad generalization, official policy might be characterized as importing food at low world prices and then supporting domestic producers' prices at guaranteed levels specified in Annual Price Reviews by means of a system of deficiency payments.

The nature of the national system of protection adopted by EEC member states can be more fully understood by examining concrete cases in detail. But because of the complexity of some protection procedures, variations as between products, and changes from year to year, a discussion of the policy of each member state over the whole range of agricultural products would be an unduly lengthy process. The following discussion will therefore be confined to the price support policy of one member of the Community only (France), as the main techniques of market control in each of the member states have been strikingly similar in their economic essentials.

During the period between 1955 and 1960 there was no legal provision ensuring that the farming community as a whole would receive a guaranteed income, whether calculated on an absolute basis or in relation to other income groups within the economy. Nevertheless, when the Third Modernization and Equipment Plan (1958-61) was drawn up, the government indicated that it was intended that farming incomes should increase at the same rate as those in other economic sectors. This was to be in contrast with prior experience. For example, between 1950 and 1958, despite a 48 per cent increase in the productivity of the agricultural labour force, income per head in agriculture, although increasing absolutely, deteriorated markedly as compared with other sectors.[49]

In the first instance the function of the Third Plan was to calculate quantitative targets for agricultural production in 1961 (i.e. the last year of the Plan). These targets were to be based upon estimates of home consumption, of imports and, most important, of likely export outlets. The function of pricing was twofold. First, prices were to be such as to bring the composition

---

[49] OEEC, *Fifth Rep. on Agricultural Policies in Europe and North America* (1961), table 1, p. 137.

of agricultural output into line with the targets set out in the Plan. Secondly, on the basis of estimates of agricultural production and costs, prices would be fixed at a level which would secure the desired increase in incomes.[50]

The Plan recommended a coherent system of target prices and in the event a target price system was adopted for wheat, barley, maize, beef, and pork. The system was based on an indexing principle: prices were to be adjusted each autumn to take account of the rise in indices measuring the change in input costs and the retail cost of non-food goods. In 1959, however, following the introduction of a policy of financial reform it was decided that the indexing system would have to be abandoned because of its inflationary character. But in 1960 the French government once more reversed its policy by reinstating indexing on a partial basis, the authorities taking account in fixing target prices of the changes in indices of input costs, but not being obliged to concede the whole of the increase.

In fixing the price at which authorized stockpiling bodies had to buy the domestic production, the government had simultaneously to ensure that imported supplies would not prove more attractive to buyers. This it did by giving the National Cereals Office monopoly rights as a grain importer and so adjusting the flow of imports as the occasion required. Similarly, the National Cereals Office was the agency by which the authorities disposed of surplus domestic production abroad with the help of state aids.

Price support in the markets for dairy produce and wheat was essentially similar in that official agencies would buy or sell domestic production as required and control imports or subsidize exports as needed.

(b) Direct Grants

In addition to assisting their farmers by operating price support systems, each of the member states gives further assistance to farmers by making direct grants. These may be divided into two kinds, capital and current.

Capital grants are given for four main purposes. The first consists of grants for the improvement of farm structures, such

---

[50] OEEC, *Third Rep. on Agricultural Policies* . . . (1958), p. 361.

as the consolidation of fragments and the enlargement of farms. This kind of assistance is common to most of the member states. In Western Germany under the 1961 Federal Budget £42·2 million was allocated for land consolidation and enlargement of farms.[51] The French Fourth Plan authorized £17·6 million per annum to be expended on amalgamation and allocation. In the Netherlands direct grants in 1961-2 for land consolidation totalled £5·3 million and in Belgium the same item claimed £750,000 in 1961.[52] That there will continue to be a need in the EEC for a programme of structural reform in agriculture may be seen from Table 2 (p. 333), which shows that the structural problem (an important determinant of competitive strength in farming) is in fact of serious proportions throughout most of the Community. The second main type of capital grant consists of grants for the improvement of services. This covers expenditure on roads, water supplies, electricity, and drainage. The third consists of improvements to farm equipment. In France subsidies of between 10 and 15 per cent have been available on farm machinery and grants have been available for the improvement of farm buildings. In Germany grants have been made available for silos, manure pits, and hay driers and in Belgium for cowshed improvements. The fourth is expenditure on research, education, and advisory work.

The current items consist of subsidies on the cost of current inputs. In Germany, for example, in 1961 DM185 million was spent in reducing fertilizer prices. In Italy there was a remission of tax on fuel for agricultural purposes and a 50 per cent contribution to the purchase of selected seeds and a 35 per cent contribution to the cost of fertilizers used by mountain farmers.

3. PRICE DETERMINATION UNDER THE COMMON AGRICULTURAL POLICY

The main components of the EEC policy derive in large part from the existing national policies that are in process of being

---

[51] The data on grants are taken from G. McCrone, 'Agricultural Integration in Western Europe', *Planning* (PEP), xxix/470 (1963), App. table 7. The German allocation included £14 million credits.

[52] In Belgium further funds for this purpose were controlled by the local authorities and the Société Nationale de la Petite Propriété Terrienne.

superseded. The most important general principle of the common policy is that the return to the producer should be provided by the price paid by the buyer in the market. Because of this a large part of the economics of the common policy amounts to a study of the conditions under which prices will actually be determined—in other words, exactly how each market will be controlled. Broadly speaking, the commodity regulations that have now been agreed (and they cover over 90 per cent of the

TABLE 2

Size Distribution of Holdings (A), Distribution of Agricultural Land by Size of Holdings (B), and Fragmentation of Holdings (per cent)

Country	Census date	Size category of holdings (ha.)												No. of fragments per holding
		1–5		5–10		10–20		20–50		50–100		100+		
		A	*B*	*A*	*B*	*A*	*B*	*A*	*B*	*A*	*B*	*A*	*B*	
W. Germany	1960	44	12	25	18	21	30	9	28	1	7	–	4	11
France	1955	30	5	22	11	25	24	18	35	4	15	1	10	n.a.
Italy	1961	65	18	20	15	10	15	4	14	1	8	1	30	5
Netherlands	1959	38	10	27	20	23	33	11	31	1	5	–	2	4
Belgium	1959	48	16	27	23	18	30	6	21	1	8	–	2	6
Luxembourg	1960	32	6	18	10	26	29	22	47	2	8	–	1	16

Source: Statistical Office of the European Communities, *Statistique agricole*, no. 4, 1964, pp. 20–25.

EEC agricultural output) make provision for two contrasting approaches to price formation.

The first and most important is actual price fixing and support by the authorities. This will be the course adopted in the markets for grains, beef and veal, and milk and dairy products. If, because of an excess of supply over demand, prices fall below previously announced target or guide price levels, official agencies will be required to make support purchases once the market prices have fallen to the intervention level. Generally speaking the latter will be about 7½ per cent below the target or guide figure. In the case of milk and dairy products the price level will be supported by purchases of butter. Support purchases can be disposed of either in outside markets or on the home market when prices are above target or guide levels. In addition it is vital that the price level in the internal market should not be eroded by competition from third countries. Therefore two forms of external protection have been devised. In the case of grains a system of variable levies will be imposed upon imports into the Community, the actual level being adjusted so as to neutralize any price advantage that such imports might otherwise enjoy as compared with EEC target prices. In the case of beef and veal and milk and dairy products, the external protection consists of a customs duty which can, if necessary, be supplemented by a levy, the size of which can be varied to take account of the price level at which foreign produce is offered at the Community frontier.

A second approach is exhibited as regards fruit and vegetables, pigmeat, poultrymeat, and eggs. In the case of these products, and unlike, for example, grains, there is no predetermined target or guide price. Originally prices in the fruit and vegetable markets were to be left to be determined entirely by free market forces, but subsequently a form of support buying was agreed upon. Nevertheless market forces will still play a significant role because (during the initial trial period) support buying cannot begin until prices have fallen significantly further than is, for example, the case in grains, and official support only comes into operation when prices have fallen to a very considerable extent. Protection from outside competition is of course provided and this has become less liberal than the system originally envisaged. In the case of pigmeat, poultrymeat, and eggs, prices will be determined by the play of competitive market forces. The original regulation setting up the marketing organizations for these products made no provision for a common support buying policy. Even in these cases, however, the influence of the authorities will still be considerable, as the cost of feedgrain, the major input for the production of pigmeat, poultrymeat, and eggs, will be a fixed price, and the price of important competing products, beef and veal, will also be fixed. But although, given this cost constraint on the supply side, free competition will exist as between Community producers, a variety of devices can be applied at the

Community frontier in order to protect the internal price level from outside competition.

During the transitional phase of the common agricultural policy, which is characterized by the coexistence of different national price levels, in the case of most products variable levies are imposed on trade between member states although these are fixed at a slightly lower level than the corresponding levies on imports from third countries so as to establish a degree of Community preference. These internal levies will disappear in the final phase and common prices will come into existence. It is planned that the common target prices for grain will be achieved on 1 July 1967, the common guide prices for beef and veal should come into existence on 1 November 1967, and the common target prices for milk and dairy products are scheduled to be operative as from 1 April 1968. It has been agreed that internal trade in pigmeat, poultrymeat, and eggs should be freed of all levies simultaneously with the establishment of the common grain prices. The agricultural agreement of July 1966 provided for a common organization of the Community fruit and vegetable market by 1 January 1967.

In the following discussion we shall in the main confine our attention to the markets for grains as exemplifying the first approach (price fixing by the authorities) and the markets for fruit, vegetables, and pigmeat as examples of the second approach (comparatively free market prices).

We must emphasize that by concentrating our attention on these particular products, we are omitting any detailed discussion of certain other product markets that would have to be taken into account in any assessment of the common agricultural policy as a whole. The present study makes no claims to be a comprehensive account.

4. THE GRAIN MARKET

Much of the discussion of the common agricultural policy has centred upon the problem of achieving common prices for each of the various grains throughout the EEC. The reason for the prominence of grain questions in discussions of EEC farm policy is not far to seek. It is because of the interrelationship between grain prices and other agricultural prices, with the result that decisions about common grain prices are indirectly decisions about other components of the general agricultural price level.

This interrelationship comes about because the cost of animal feedgrain is the major element in the cost of production of pigmeat, eggs, and poultry. Pigmeat prices themselves, however, are related to beef prices by reason of competitive substitution, and beef prices in turn must stand in a certain relationship to milk prices if the raising of beef and dairy cattle is to be in line with the evolution of demand for these two products. Thus, once firm decisions about grain prices are taken, the area of possible uncertainty surrounding other aspects of agricultural policy is greatly reduced.

In considering the possible consequences of a harmonization of grain prices the member governments had to bear in mind how the Community's pattern of consumption and production had evolved over the last few years, and what these developments might imply as regards future changes in market outlets and supplies. These problems were the subject of a special study by the Commission.[53] On the basis of an analysis of the years 1951–9 the study suggests that the income elasticity of demand for direct wheat consumption is -0·24 and for rye -0·45. On the other hand a high positive elasticity (1·85) was observed for poultry, the production of which is to a very high degree simply indirect grain consumption. Given the population and income changes that occurred in the Six between 1951 and 1958, the net effect was an actual decline in the quantity of grain consumed directly as food (a fall from 24 to 23 million metric tons) but a considerable increase in the indirect consumption of grain as animal feed—a rise from 18 to 31 million metric tons. Given the likely rate of growth of population and income up to 1970, this basic pattern is expected to continue, with stagnant direct grain consumption but significant increases in the indirect demand for grain as a result of the increasing consumption of poultry, eggs, and pigmeat. Broadly speaking, the increasing consumption of grain in the Community up to 1970 is expected to be accounted for

---

[53] EEC Commission, Directorate General for Agriculture, *Le Marché commun des produits agricoles, Perspectives '1970'*. By H. B. Krohn and C. Mouton. *Étude 10* (1963). A summary of the section of this dealing with grains appears in translation as App. A in International Wheat Council, *Review of the World Wheat Situation 1962/63* (1963).

virtually entirely by an increase of one million tons annually in the use of grain as animal feed.

How did domestic EEC grain production evolve in response to this stimulus of increasing consumption, and how may it be expected to evolve over the next few years? Between 1951 and 1958 the area under grain was expanded slightly. But the big increase in EEC grain production over that period (about 26 per cent) was due predominantly to yields per hectare rising by about 3 per cent annually. While it is not expected that the years to 1970 will see a repetition of quite such a rapid increase in yields, total grain production is expected to increase by about 13 million tons from 1958 to 1970. In other words, successive increments in demand within the Community could be met entirely from domestic production, leaving the net annual demand for imported grains at about the same level of 9 million tons where it has been since 1951.

It should be emphasized here that the estimates of production in 1970 inevitably relied very heavily upon the extrapolation of past trends, and took into account only such deviations as seemed reasonably likely. But projections published in 1963 could not take into account one vitally important change—namely the equalization of grain prices that was decided in 1964 to take effect from 1967. Realizing that important changes in grain prices were likely to occur, the Commission's study did not overlook the possibility that domestic grain production might increase by much more than the figures that have been mentioned here. In fact the study suggests that reserves in France are such that that country alone could possibly expand grain production to such an extent as to meet virtually the entire increase in Community consumption up to 1970—provided price inducements were sufficiently favourable.

(a) The Transitional Period

At the present time (1966), as the transitional period rapidly draws to its close, grain prices in the Six are maintained at about their respective national target levels by national intervention agencies that buy from domestic producers whenever market prices fall 5–10 per cent below the national target figures. Only slight progress has been made towards harmonizing these prices and they still vary considerably as between the highest- and lowest-cost producing countries. To take a particularly important example, the target price per ton for soft wheat in the 1964/5 season was about $119 in the highest-cost producer (Germany) and only $100 in the lowest (France). Similar discrepancies occurred between the national target prices for the other grains.

In order to maintain their respective national grain prices, it has been necessary for the member states to protect their markets both from imports from other member states and from third countries. They have done so by introducing a standardized system of variable levies which since 1962 has taken the place of all other protective devices.

The levies are calculated in such a way as to eliminate entirely any price advantage that imports from third countries may have over domestic target prices and to have almost the same effect on imports from other member states. The levy is in essence the difference between the price of imports and the corresponding domestic target price at the main national marketing centre, allowance being made for transport costs. A hypothetical example will show how the levies are calculated and also define some of the terms used in this context.

Suppose that the target price for wheat in Brussels is $105 per ton and that the rate of freight per ton of wheat shipped from Antwerp (the point of entry for wheat imports from third countries) to Brussels is $5. Then the lowest price at Antwerp that is consistent with a price of $105 at Brussels is $100. This figure will then be the Belgian *threshold* price. If the lowest c.i.f. quotation for imported wheat at Antwerp is $60 per ton, then the Belgian authorities will apply a levy of $40 per ton to bring the price of imported supplies up to the national threshold level.

The variable levy system as such is not necessarily any more or less protective than the various systems that it has displaced. Some idea of the protection it has afforded may be gained from the fact that the highest levies in the first year of operation of the standardized system (those of Germany) had the effect of more than doubling the c.i.f. price of wheat at the port of importation. During that year, 1962/3, import levies as a percentage of c.i.f. wheat prices were 102–120 per cent in Germany, 84–98 per cent in Italy, 68–82 per cent in Belgium, 61–74 per cent in France, and 58–75 per cent in the Netherlands.[54]

[54] International Wheat Council, *World Wheat Situation*, 1962/3, p. 66.

Levies on imports from other member states are calculated in a substantially similar manner to the levies on imports from third countries. Calculating the intra-Community levy involves (*a*) determining the lowest price (the threshold price) at the national frontier that is consistent with the national target price in the importing state's major marketing centre; (*b*) determining the price of imports as delivered at the national frontier (the *free-at-frontier* price); (*c*) subtracting the latter from the former; and (*d*) subtracting a further fixed sum (the *standard amount* or *montant forfaitaire*) sufficient to make imports from a Community country marginally more attractive than imports from third countries. In practice the margin of Community preference has not been large enough to affect the flow of trade.

The levy system is, therefore, the technique by which the domestic price structure is protected against competition from imports. But it is also (when applied in reverse) the technique by which the refund payable on exports is calculated. In other words, disposing of surpluses either to other Community countries or into the world market, in the former case may, and in the latter will, require producers to be compensated to the extent of the difference between domestic and export prices.

(b) The Final Stage

The intra-Community levies become superflous and will disappear when common grain prices are introduced, but the levies on imports from third countries will continue to be applied, although they will become more uniform as they will then be protecting one common EEC price level rather than the six separate systems that exist at the time of writing.

Eliminating these present divergencies between the national price levels by establishing common target prices for each of the main grain products has required the member states to make a difficult compromise, the nature of which can best be understood by considering the two limiting extremes within which the specific figures had to be chosen. Consider, for example, the nature of the problem as it has been exemplified by the price of soft wheat.

At one extreme the member states could have adopted as the common price one approximating to the lowest of the six national target prices. The adoption of such a low price would, other things being equal, have made it virtually impossible for wheat production to have been continued by many farmers in the other member states, the incidence of the difficulty being roughly proportional to the degree to which their own national target prices differed from the low common price. Furthermore, the adoption of such a low common price—with its consequences for farm incomes—would not have accorded with the general policy objective of bringing agricultural earnings and conditions into line with those in the rest of the economy. Nor would such a low common price have done much to stimulate production in the least-cost member state; intra-Community trade would not have been significantly encouraged, and the Community would simply have increased its imports from third countries to make up for the loss of production in the high-cost member states. While such a course, which would have amounted to a major reduction in the average degree of agricultural support in the Community, might have had much to be said for it on general economic grounds, reasons of national political necessity precluded its serious consideration as a feasible choice.

The opposite alternative would have been to choose as a common EEC price something near the highest of the six national target prices. This would have enabled production in the highest-cost member states to be maintained, and would have acted as a considerable inducement to farmers in other member states to increase their production. Such an increase in production would have had to be sold (i.e. dumped) in world markets, as the maintenance of production in the high-cost member states would have made it impossible to dispose of the extra production within the EEC itself. This would simply have had the effect of re-phrasing the fundamental EEC agricultural problem from 'Who is to feel the pressure of competition?' to 'Who is to subsidize the exports?' Again, there would have been little prospect of increasing intra-EEC trade. On the other hand the considerable rise in grain prices in the low-cost member states would, simultaneously with its beneficial effect on farm incomes, have had an inflationary impact that might have been difficult to reconcile with other important national policy objectives: it should be recalled here that the final phase of the discussions on the common grain prices coincided with a period of financial stabilization in France.

Politically, the common target price eventually accepted had to be a compromise between these two extremes. Any such compromise would involve some curtailment of production (if only a relative one) in the highest-cost producers, and an increased penetration into that market by the lower-cost member states. It might or might not involve the emergence of a surplus, or, alternatively, greater dependence on imports from third countries, according to the level actually chosen.

In December 1964 the Six reached agreement upon the level of target prices to be applied throughout the Community from July 1967. As with the 1962 Decision on the commodity regulations, this agreement on the common grain prices was eventually reached only after a considerable battle, mainly between France and Germany, with Germany showing the greatest reluctance to reduce its grain prices and France threatening dire consequences if there was a failure to reach an agreement on this basis by the end of the year.

A basic feature of the new price system is the choice of one particular marketing centre as the base to which prices at all other marketing centres will have to be related. The centre chosen as the linchpin of the whole system is the greatest grain-deficit area of the Community, Duisburg, which will become for the Community as a whole what each major national centre is now in its own state. Once a price is fixed for Duisburg, 'regional' derivatives of this basic common price have to be established for each of the other main marketing centres of the Community. The main criteria involved in arriving at the regionalized common prices will be (*a*) the need to make it profitable for farmers in the large producing areas to incur the costs of transporting grain to the main deficit centres, and (*b*) the need to ensure that the resulting pattern of inter-regional trade is economically efficient in the sense of minimizing the movement of produce. This in turn requires the elimination of distortions in transport costs such as might be caused by subsidies.

The basic common target price for soft wheat will be DM425/ ton at Duisburg. In point of fact this price had originally been proposed by the Commission for implementation in 1964, and the other common grain prices that have been agreed are also either equal to or fairly close to the Commission's proposals. This is shown in Table 3 (p.342), which also indicates how the separate national prices compare with the new agreed common prices, and how big an adjustment of the former will be required by the implementation of the latter. It should be noted in passing that, as national prices relate to certain national marketing centres but the basic common price does not necessarily apply to all such centres, a true comparison between national and common price levels sometimes requires the basic price to be broken down into its regional derivatives for national marketing centres. This has been done in Table 3, and the relevant marketing centres, and other qualifications to the data are mentioned in the notes attached to the table.

TABLE 3

Comparison of National Grain Prices with Common Prices

Product	Common EEC target prices (DM/metric ton)		1964/5 national intervention prices as % of common intervention prices					
	Agreed for 1967	Proposed by Commission for 1964	W. Germany	Belg.	Neth.	Lux.	France	Italy
Soft wheat	425	425	111	100	101	118	91	107
Rye	375	375	114	90	83	123	84	–
Barley	365	370	112	99	94	98	88	79
Maize	362·5	370	–	–	–	–	108	75
Durum wheat	500	500	–	–	–	–	93 (75)	114 (92)

Notes: (a) The price relatives compare the actual intervention prices of 1964/5 at certain marketing centres with the derivatives of the common (Duisburg) prices for those centres. The centres concerned are: Germany (Mannheim); Belgium (Antwerp); Netherlands (Rotterdam); Luxembourg (Mersch); France (Marseilles; Orléans for rye); Italy (Genoa; Reggio Calabria for soft wheat).

(b) For durum wheat the figures in brackets are the ratios for 1964/5 intervention prices to the common guaranteed price of DM580/ton.

(c) The common intervention price has not yet been fixed for maize. The ratios are simply the comparison of national target prices with the common target price.

Sources: EEC Spokesman's Group, Information Memo P6/65 (Agric.), Jan. 1965; *Bull. EEC*, Feb. 1965, p. 12; FAO *Monthly Bull. Agric. Econ. Statist.*, Mar. 1965, p. 21.

5. THE MARKETS FOR PIGMEAT AND FRUIT
AND VEGETABLES

(a) Pigmeat

As about two-thirds of the cost of rearing pigs is accounted for by feed, much of which is grain, grain prices will be a major determinant of pigmeat prices. At the present time (the end of the transitional period) the prices of feedgrains still differ considerably between the member states, and there are corresponding differences between pigmeat prices. These ranged from about DM2·6 in the Netherlands to about DM3·5 per kilogramme in Germany in December 1964.[55]

The pigmeat regulation of January 1962 emphasized the close relationship between grain and pigmeat prices by establishing a technique of intra-Community protection involving two parts. The first, Part (a) of the intra-Community levy, is the sum necessary to protect pigmeat producers in a member state with high feedgrain prices from competition from a member state where feedgrain prices are low. Part (a) of the intra-Community levy is such as to offset these artificial differences in input costs. It will be eliminated from July 1967 onwards when grain prices are harmonized. The second part of the intra-Community levy, Part (b), was calculated in such a way as to offset the differing degrees of efficiency between the member states when the common form of market organization was introduced in 1962. It is being phased out automatically and will disappear completely from July 1967 onwards. The function of the intra-Community levy is, therefore, to protect the national markets from dislocations arising from distortions that are transient in character (that is, temporary discrepancies between feedgrain prices) and to expose them to competition from each other in a gradual manner.

The levies on imports from third countries involve similar techniques of calculation. They consist of two parts. The first part is such as to offset the lower price of feedgrains in the world market, and the second will eventually be the equivalent of a 7 per cent customs duty.

It should be noted that, as pigmeat prices are not (at present) fixed and supported by the authorities, as are grain prices, it becomes necessary to determine something resembling a

---

[55] EEC, *Newsletter on the Common Agricultural Policy*, Dec. 1964, p. 5.

threshold price for pigmeat to eliminate the possibility that imported supplies could disrupt the internal market even when levies are applied. A minimum import price is therefore fixed (known as the *sluicegate price*). If imports are offered below this price, the amount of the levy is increased accordingly.

(b) Fruit and Vegetables

As originally conceived in 1962 the prices of fruit and vege-tables within the Community were to be determined almost entirely by the free play of competition. Customs duties on trade between member states were gradually to be eliminated (with no internal levies to replace them). On the external side the only protection was to be that provided by the common external tariff. In practice the liberality of the régime has been pro-gressively whittled down. As part of its price for agreeing to the common grain price, Italy insisted on equally 'effective' arrange-ments for the fruit and vegetable markets. In 1965 the Council therefore agreed to this demand by instituting a reference price system. The latter is in effect a minimum import price in that if third-country supplies enter the Community market below this level, a countervailing charge will be imposed to bring the prices up to the reference level. The reference price is calculated on the basis of an average of Community *producer* prices during the preceding three years, plus a standard amount which is designed to bring the price of imported goods up to the *market* price level of home-produced goods.[56]

Even so, free competition within the Community, if it led to over-production, could cause prices to fall steeply. The Italian government was well aware of this and during the agricultural negotiations of July 1966 it secured a further concession de-signed to guard against this type of contingency. Basic prices will be fixed, and during the three-year experimental period 1967-9 producer organizations will be permitted to buy up produce when prices fall 15 per cent below the basic level, and governments will intervene and make support purchases when prices fall to crisis levels, that is below 70 per cent of the basic level. From 1970 onwards official support buying can begin when prices have fallen to 40-45 per cent of the basic price in the case of cauli-flowers and tomatoes, 50-55 per cent in the case of apples and

[56] *Bull. EEC*, no. 4, 1965, pp. 22-23.

pears, and 60–70 per cent for all other products, including citrus fruits, table grapes, and peaches.[57] It is clear that considerable scope for price fluctuation is still provided for, particularly in the post-1970 arrangements, but a limit has been set to it.

6. GRANTS AND THE PRICE MECHANISM

Just as the various national policies on price support have been complemented by various types of agricultural grants, so too it is necessary for the Community policies on prices to be filled out by a corresponding policy on grants.

The relevance of a policy on agricultural grants to the common price policies is clear enough. Once a given price is fixed for a certain product for the EEC as a whole, there will be an inherent tendency for farmers who find production difficult at that price to improve their methods, to switch to other products, or perhaps even to go out of business. Equally, farms that find the new common prices advantageous will seek to expand production. But this process could be distorted if national governments continued to intervene by providing, for example, subsidies to input costs such as fertilizer or mechanization subsidies. Production might then be maintained even in unfavourable locations and the result might be an aggravation of the surpluses problem.

It seems, therefore, as if the right policy to adopt towards subsidies to input costs is to abolish them entirely because of their distorting effects. This point of view gains added weight from the argument that, if it is the function of price support to maintain farm incomes, there seems little point in using grants to do this also, especially as grants that are controlled by national governments introduce an arbitrary element into the determination of farm incomes that will not help the cohesion of the Community. At the very least it would seem as if the equalization of such grants throughout the Six, under the general supervision of the Commission, was a basic condition for ensuring that price policy will bring about a realistic balance between production and outlets and at the same time reallocate production in more economic directions.

There are, however, other types of grant for which this kind of

[57] *European Community*, Sept. 1966, p. 3.

abolition or equalization treatment seems inappropriate. While subsidies to input costs do little or nothing to promote the ultimate viability of the recipients, grants to encourage consolidation of holdings, rural road building, and the like do improve the competitive capacity of the beneficiaries. To insist that even these grants be applied on a uniform basis throughout the Six would be to ignore the fact that farms in different areas may have quite different capacities for improvement, and the economic return from grants may, therefore, differ. In other words, only a highly discriminating policy in regard to grants of this type would be likely to satisfy objective criteria considered from the standpoint of the Community as a whole.

Conceptually at least the essentials of a common policy on grants are, therefore, reasonably clear. In practice, however, distinguishing between grants that are simply subsidies to costs and those that will improve efficiency is no easy task. Nor will it always be easy to assess the potentialities of an area for improvement, and to compare these objectively with the possibilities elsewhere. Considerable differences of opinion may well, therefore, arise among the member states on just how a policy on grants should be implemented; and such differences could result in conflicting policies, as control over grant payments, as opposed to actual price levels, still remains to a large extent with the national governments.

The Commission is, of course, aware that grant policy could turn out to be the vulnerable point in the logic of the common agricultural policy and has taken steps to reduce the likelihood of this happening. Although its proposals stop well short of taking responsibility for grants entirely out of the hands of the national governments and administering them on some strictly economic Community criteria, they do provide for measures that should eliminate the worst kind of national distortions.[58] What the Commission has done is to compile an inventory of state aids to agriculture in the member states (the list runs to about 500 examples) and to derive from this three broad classifications of aids, of descending degrees of compatibility with the common

[58] EEC, *Critères pour l'établissement d'une politique commune d'aides en agriculture* (proposition de la Commission au Conseil), Com (66) 60 final, 23 Mar. 1966; also *Newsletter on the Common Agricultural Policy*, no. 5, Apr. 1966.

agricultural policy. In Class 1 the Commission includes aids for consolidation of holdings, incentives to farmers to relinquish or take over farms in decline, and funds for scientific research and retraining. It is proposed that these aids be regarded as beneficial. They should be segregated forthwith from the main list of state aids, and not made subject to prior notification to the Commission for approval. Class 2 aids would include those that might conceivably distort competition in the long run, such as aids to encourage the purchase of selected seed and quality animals for breeding. These aids are considered to be potentially such as to affect competition in certain circumstances, but to present no very immediate threat. The Commission considers that it might be desirable for the member states to agree an upper limit on the extent of these aids and that these too might in time be freed from the obligation of prior notification. Class 3 aids are the crucial ones—aids given with regard to specific products. In this Class are included, for example, aids for the construction of hot-houses, buildings for rearing pigs and poultry, transport rate subsidies on inter-state shipments, aids for storage in excess of the actual costs involved, and so forth. The Commission will propose upper limits for the aids in Class 3 and will continue to require their prior notification.

In summary, therefore, the Commission is working to bring state aids to agriculture into the general framework already laid down in Articles 92–94 of the treaty. Its verdicts in particular cases will be based upon its assessment of the compatibility of the aids with the common agricultural policy and the extent to which the aids concerned encourage the adaptation of the existing structures to the needs of the new policy.

7. AGRICULTURAL PRICES AND INCOMES

So far we have been discussing agricultural prices from the standpoint of their role in integrating and unifying the national agricultural markets. But, as we pointed out at the beginning of this chapter, the common agricultural policy has to bring about the unification of the national markets in a way that contributes to the solution of certain specifically agricultural problems. Article 39 of the Rome Treaty setting out the objectives of the common agricultural policy lists a number of highly desirable ends such as the increase of agricultural efficiency, the stabilization of markets, guaranteeing of regular supplies and ensuring reasonable prices to consumers. The treaty also states as an important objective the need to ensure a fair standard of living for the agricultural population. In addition, as Mansholt has pointed out, as a highly industrialized area, the Community must maintain and increase opportunities for industrial exports. 'If it is to do so, it will be required to maintain liberal trade policies in industrial and agricultural products.'[59]

It is not difficult to see that if all these objectives are to be brought to bear simultaneously in deciding agricultural prices, then the common agricultural policy is bound to involve an element of compromise, since in some degree these objectives conflict. Thus although agricultural incomes could be improved by raising agricultural product prices, this would be in conflict with the interest of consumers. In some degree this conflict could be resolved by increasing agricultural efficiency. The net output of agricultural labour could be improved by creating a better structure of larger and less fragmented farms. As Mansholt has observed:

An examination of structural factors brings to light the true causes of the agricultural problems: the smallness of enterprises and their subdivision into too many units, farms inadequate to meet modern requirements (obsolete premises), unfavourable location of farmhouses in relation to the lands attached to them, inadequate infrastructure of rural areas, the disproportion between available labour and the work to be done (so-called concealed unemployment).[60]

It is equally true that a general increase in agricultural prices could lead to greater self-sufficiency and could therefore conflict with the needs of a liberal trade policy. The importance which, for example, the US attaches to agricultural outlets in Europe has been emphasized in the Kennedy Round negotiations.

Probably the most interesting of the objectives of the common agricultural policy is the one relating to the establishment of a fair standard of living for the agricultural population. Clearly

[59] Address by S. Mansholt to the American Farm Bureau Convention, Denver, 13 Dec. 1960, quoted in D. T. Healey, *British Agriculture and the Common Market* (1962), p. 11.

[60] S. Mansholt, 'An Agricultural Policy for the European Economic Community', *Progress*, xlvii/263 (1959).

there is considerable scope for improving the standard of living of the agricultural population as compared with that of the rest of the economy—a point which is illustrated in Table 4.

TABLE 4

Domestic Product per Employed Person in Agriculture Expressed as a % of Domestic Product per Employed Person in the Rest of the Economy in 1958

(*Gross Domestic Product at Factor Cost*)

Western Germany	45
France	45[*]
Italy	55
Belgium	65
Netherlands	96
Luxembourg	34
EEC	43

[*] 1955.

Source: Krohn & Schmitt, in Junckerstorff, table 4, p. 273.

Secondly, the establishment of a fair standard of living is sometimes stated rather crudely in terms of raising agricultural incomes to the industrial level. This is, however, an unduly simple view of the matter. The policy is best stated in the words of Mansholt. 'Provided labour in agriculture is properly employed, incomes in this sector must not compare unfavourably with those in others.'[61]

This implies bringing agricultural incomes upwards towards the level of the rest of the economy, although no specific sector or industry is referred to and absolute equivalence is not guaranteed. More important, however, the policy does not imply that all farms are to be guaranteed such an income level but only those where the labour is properly employed. Larger farms employing hired labour might normally be expected to be sufficiently efficient to be capable of surviving under the common agricultural policy, but quite early on when the policy was being formulated the problem of the family farm had to be faced. The Commission decided that the family farm would have a place in the

[61] Mansholt, in *Progress*, xlvii/263 (1959), p. 147.

European farming structure provided that it would efficiently occupy at least one or two workers full time and would also, by rational management, provide a reasonable income to each worker as compared with other groups.[62] In practice it seems reasonable to suppose that although the raising of the prices of agricultural products relative to those of industrial products and services may bring about part of this relative improvement, a good deal of reliance will be placed upon increased efficiency through structural reform, a policy that will be promoted by the Community via the Agricultural Guidance and Guarantee Fund whose first operations we examine in the next section of this chapter.

Thirdly, it seems worth noting that the establishment of fair incomes in farming must be regarded as being one of the most important proposals in the whole of Community economic and social policy. In view of the relatively low level of such incomes and the importance of farming within the Community economy, such a policy of improvement cannot fail to be of the highest significance. It is an example of the fact that the improvement of the standard of living of some of the less favoured regions and of one of the least favoured occupations is to be a 'managed' process rather than one which proceeds automatically from the working of a competitive market economy. Moreover, the fact that the Rome Treaty contains a commitment of such far-reaching economic and social significance goes a long way to explain why even those who are not necessarily enthusiastic about the idea of a competitive market-oriented economy in Europe can nevertheless subscribe to the Rome Treaty.

Any policy for improving in relative terms the income of the farming community requires some machinery for measuring the income levels of proprietors and workers on acceptably efficient farms, for determining the production costs of such farms and therefore the prices which are justifiable, and for judging how much progress has been made towards an approximation to incomes in other sectors. In the Netherlands and Belgium machinery has existed which, while not guaranteeing the farming community any particular share of the national income, has guaranteed a fair income for farmers. The phrase which is

[62] Whether such farms can ever be efficient in the light of modern production conditions requires some consideration.

generally used to describe the nature of the guarantee is that it is designed to achieve an adequate income for well-managed farms which are economically and socially justified. In the Dutch system, for example, guaranteed prices, based on cost-price calculations for a large number of agricultural regions, were arrived at by means of a farm accounts survey carried out by the Agricultural Economics Research Institute. The farms whose accounts were used were selected in consultation with the Agricultural Advisory Service and representatives of the Landbouwschap.[63] The farms involved had to be those whose size, land utilization, and livestock were representative of that particular region and they had to be well managed with a labour force adequately employed.[64]

Until quite recently little had been done at Community level to marshal evidence about farm incomes. In 1963, however, the Commission submitted to the Council of Ministers a proposal for the establishment of machinery to obtain information about the incomes of farms and the conduct of their business, and in 1965 the Council adopted a Regulation establishing such an information service.

The Community farm accounts survey will be organized as follows. The Community will be divided into thirty-six regions, each with a Regional Committee composed of representatives of the relevant government departments, the farming profession, and other experts. These committees will select the farms upon whose accounts the survey will be based. The selection of farms will be based on uniform Community standards. Accounting Offices will be created (in some cases they already exist) to gather in the data. A liaison office will be set up in each member state to maintain contact between the Brussels Commission and the Regional Committees. The Commission will also have supervisory powers over the bodies responsible for operating the survey. Finally, in processing and analysing the data it receives, the Commission will be assisted by a Community committee comprising officials of member states. The survey will begin by

---

[63] An organization representing farmers and land workers, whose board is appointed half by farmers' professional organizations and half by agricultural trade unions.

[64] In Germany too the Federal Government brings out annually the 'Green Report' based on the accounts of 8,000 farms.

covering 10,000 farms but this number will be increased to 30,000 in a few years. The survey will enable the Commission to produce comparative data on incomes in agriculture and industry, and this assessment and comparison of incomes will form the main part of a 'Report on the Situation in Agriculture and Agricultural Markets in the Community' to the Council and the European Parliament.

Thus with this version of an Annual Price Review, ironically the result of the negotiations with the UK, and deficiency payments on durum wheat, the Community has now shown itself quite capable of seeing virtues in policies that, up to January 1963, it had tended to regard rather unfavourably.

8. THE ROLE OF THE AGRICULTURAL GUIDANCE AND GUARANTEE FUND

In establishing the first common forms of market organization in 1962 the member states simultaneously created a new organ, the European Agricultural Guidance and Guarantee Fund. There are two reasons for discussing the role of the Fund here. The first and most obvious is that it is the instrument by which support buying and export refunds are financed. This is the work of the Guarantee Section of the Fund. But in addition the Fund has a Guidance Section that finances part of the expenditure by national governments on structural improvements in farming. Thus the Fund can be said to exercise some influence over the volume and direction of agricultural investment and therefore constitutes another example of management of the economic process.

As the exact financial implications of the agricultural programme could not be foreseen in 1962, it was agreed to define the Fund's role for only the first three years of its life, 1962/3, 1963/4, and 1964/5, it being understood that the Council of Ministers, on the basis of the experience gained in these first years, and in the light of further developments in the common agricultural policy, would reach agreement for the years subsequent to 1964/5 before 30 June 1965. In fact, of course, their failure to do so was the ostensible cause of the French boycott during the second half of 1965. However, the French return to the fold in January 1966 was followed by rapid progress towards a solution of the financing problem and at its May 1966 meeting the Council of Ministers agreed on the organization of the Fund for the remaining period up to 1970.

(a) *The 1962-5 Arrangements*

The Guarantee Section of the Fund was required to reimburse national governments one-sixth of the relevant expenditure incurred in 1962/3, two-sixths in 1963/4, and three-sixths in 1964/5. Under the heading of Guidance the Fund was required to make available a sum equal to 'about' one-third of whatever was paid out for guarantee purposes. Expenditure on guidance took the form of grants to national governments to cover up to 25 per cent of approved schemes of structural reform.

During this period the Fund's expenditure was financed entirely from national exchequers. In the first year of the Fund's operation member states contributed to its income in accordance with their proportionate scale of contributions to the general budget of the Community. Thereafter these contributions were increasingly weighted according to the volume of net agricultural imports into each state, although for the last year of the Fund's three-year trial period these were not to exceed 31 per cent for Germany, 28 per cent for Italy, 13 per cent for the Netherlands, and 10·5 per cent for Belgium/Luxembourg.

(i) *The First Payments from the Fund.* While the initial three-year trial period of the Fund was still in operation, agreement was reached in December 1964 on the common grain prices to be introduced from July 1967. As a result of this decision, which meant in effect achieving a substantial part of the common agricultural policy nearly three years before the deadline, it was agreed that the Fund would pay temporary and degressive subsidies to Germany, Italy, and Luxembourg as compensation for the effects of the lower grain prices. In calculating these sums the member states and the Commission had to make an assessment not only of the effects of lower grain prices themselves, but also of the indirect effects on farm incomes that would be caused by lower prices for conversion products. In the event it was agreed that the Fund should pay certain sums to the states that would be adversely affected: these are shown in Table 5.

TABLE 5

Compensation Payments from the Agricultural Fund

(*DM million*)

	1967/8	*1968/9*	*1969/70*
Western Germany	560	374	187
Italy	260	176	88
Luxembourg	5	3	2

Source: European Community, Jan. 1965, p. 3.

Of far greater potential interest than the payments listed in Table 5, which were of a wholly exceptional once-for-all kind, are those that were approved towards the end of 1965 in respect of the 1962/3 entitlements to assistance from the normal Guidance and Guarantee sections of the Fund. It is from the scale and nature of these that one can get a very preliminary impression of the work that will fall to the Fund as its sphere of responsibility is gradually widened. The relevant data are summarized in Table 6 (p. 355).

Under the Guarantee section the large share going to France underlines both that country's interest in obtaining a permanent solution to the problems of agricultural financing and the reluctance of her partners, especially Germany, to commit themselves too deeply in this field. In point of fact, about $22·3 million of the $28·7 million disbursed by the Guarantee section has been accounted for by export refunds, as distinct from contributions towards the expenses of intervening in the domestic markets. Under the Guidance section the projects that have been assisted by the Fund include extending or building co-operative dairies, irrigation schemes, canning plants, fruit marketing centres, and the like. Although the building of dairies in, say, Passau or Salerno does not at first sight strike one as the most important of economic events, a little reflection will show that the European commitment to the financing of such projects is one of the most tangible proofs yet of the degree to which, even at this very early stage, the common agricultural policy is making a direct impact upon European farming. It is also of course, as the last two

TABLE 6

The First Guidance and Guarantee Payments, 1962/3

(*$ million*)

	No. of projects	Guidance Amount	Guarantee Amount	Total national balance	
				% of contributions	% of disbursements
W. Germany	9	2·56	1·79	28	11·5
France	10	1·95	24·48	28	70·0
Italy	27	3·07	1·28	28	11·5
Belgium	7	0·7	0·31	7·9	2·7
Netherlands	4	0·77	0·86	7·9	4·3
Luxembourg	—	—	0·003	0·2	—
Total	57	9·06	28·7	100	100

Source: EEC Official Spokesman, *Information Memo*, P-64/65, Oct. 1965; *Press Release*, IP (65) 206, 16 Dec. 1965.

columns of Table 6 show, having a direct effect upon international income distribution and it is the great disproportion between contributions and disbursements nationally that accounted for the difficulty encountered in making a final settlement of the agricultural financing problems.

(b) The 1966 Agreement

It was agreed that for the year 1965/6 the Fund would meet four-sixths of the expenditure by national governments on price guarantees, five-sixths in 1966/7, and from 1 July 1967 the Community would be fully responsible for this expenditure. It was also agreed that for the years 1965/6 and 1966/7 the Fund would continue to be financed out of national exchequers, the percentage contributions being as shown in Table 7 (p. 356).

But from 1 July 1967 the finance of the Fund would be drawn from levies on food imports from third countries, 90 per cent of the proceeds of such levies being handed over to the Fund. This would in fact cover only about 45 per cent of the total Fund expenditure and the remaining 55 per cent or so would come from national exchequers in the proportions shown in Table 8. It was also agreed, at the suggestion of Western Germany, that the expenditure on guidance should no longer be based on the earlier one-third rule, but that it should be subject to a ceiling of $285

TABLE 7

The Percentage Contribution of Member States to the Financing of the Agricultural Guidance and Guarantee Fund decided for 1965/6 and 1966/7

	1965/6	*1966/7*
Western Germany	31·67	30·83
France	32·58	29·26
Italy	18·0	22·0
Belgium	7·95	7·95
Netherlands	9·58	9·74
Luxembourg	0·22	0·22

Source: EEC Council of Ministers, *Financement de la politique agricole commune*, Doc. 521/66 (AG 116), 11 May 1966.

TABLE 8

The Percentage Contribution of Member States to the Agricultural Guidance and Guarantee Fund to finance expenditure not covered by levies, 1 July 1967 to 1 January 1970

Western Germany	31·2
France	32·0
Italy	20·3
Belgium	8·1
Netherlands	8·2
Luxembourg	0·2

Source: EEC Council of Ministers, Doc. 521/66 (AG 116), 11 May 1966.

million per annum. Although the Fund cannot usually assist projects to the extent of more than 25 per cent of their cost, in special circumstances this can now be increased to 40 per cent.

The settlement also involved yet further once-for-all payments to particular countries—in this case the reason being that common marketing organizations for certain products had not come into effect according to earlier commitments. Italy was to receive $45 million in 1965/6 to be used to improve the production and marketing of olive oil and fruit and vegetables and $15 million in 1967/8 for improvements in the tobacco sector. In the case of Belgium, $4 million was payable in respect of the farm year 1965/6 to assist the marketing of sugar.[65]

(c) Some Implications

The combined result of these methods of determining the expenditure and income of the Fund could be a considerable international redistribution of income within the Community. While the member state with the greatest net imports (Germany) also has a poor farm structure, and may well, therefore, get a high priority for structural grants, it is very unlikely that the Fund will be called upon to make major disbursements in Germany for purposes of either market intervention or export restitution. But the new common price structure is, in general, very favourable to France, and it is, therefore, quite likely that French farmers will benefit considerably from the disbursements of the Fund under the two latter headings.

It is also quite clear that even the normal operations of the Fund will involve the disbursement of extremely large sums once the agricultural market is functioning as an integrated whole. The figure may be as much as $1,500 million from 1969 onwards. But it is also quite possible that claims upon the Fund could become unexpectedly great if the common target price levels act as greater stimuli to the low-cost producers than deterrents to the high-cost producers. In spite of assertions by the Commission that a soft-wheat price of DM425/ton should not over-stimulate production in France, a much more sceptical view has been expressed by the United Nations Food and Agriculture Organization. Considering the scope for improved yields and increased

[65] EEC Council of Ministers, Doc. 521/66 (AG 116), 11 May 1966.

acreage in France, and realizing that the reaction of German farming is likely to be a massive attempt to improve efficiency, with the result that output there may not fall very much, the FAO has suggested that the common grain prices 'will probably stimulate the Community's output of grains to an even greater extent than the marked technological advances in France and in other EEC countries since the war'.[66]

The FAO is further of the opinion that the Community financing of export refunds will lessen the interest of any one state in finding outlets within the Community, with the result that sales in the world market, perhaps even at concessionary rates, are likely to increase with a consequent pressure on world prices.

Finally, a point worth stressing is that the special Community treatment for Germany, Italy, and Luxembourg is both fixed in amount and limited in duration. In other words, agriculture in these countries is being given a breathing space in which to prepare itself for the full impact of the common agricultural policy. It must be expected, however, that even the most vigorous exertions by farmers in these three states will not prove quite sufficient to offset entirely the unfavourable price movements, and that some shift away from agriculture will characterize the development of their national economies as a consequence of the common agricultural policy over the next few years. In point of fact, of course, this process has been going on for a number of years already, and the implementation of the common agricultural policy will simply speed up the existing tendency for labour to leave agriculture for industry in these countries. In Germany, for example, the number of full-time workers in agriculture fell by over 2 million (about 40 per cent) over the period 1949-60.[67] There can be little doubt about the capacity of German industry to absorb labour (indeed, as we show later in Chapter 11 on Social and Regional Policy, Germany has been making considerable use of immigrant labour both from other Community countries and third countries), but whether any net surplus rural manpower in Italy will be as quickly absorbed is rather more doubtful. In other words, while the agricultural sectors of both

[66] FAO, *Monthly Bull. Agric. Econ. & Statist.*, Mar. 1965, p. 23.

[67] EEC, *The Effect on Farm Incomes in Federal Germany of Lower Prices within the EEC's Common Agricultural Policy*, Études—Agricultural Series no. 11, (1962), p. 58.

Germany and Italy will be affected rather adversely by certain aspects of the common agricultural policy, the capacity of industry in each to absorb manpower from agriculture is very different. It must, therefore, be apparent that only an active regional policy combined with occupational and geographical labour mobility will be able to solve this problem for Italy.

C. ENERGY

I. THE NECESSITY FOR A COMMON ENERGY POLICY

Broadly speaking there are two sets of reasons why the Communities need an energy policy.

(a) Security of Energy Supplies

The first arises from the importance of energy as a factor in general economic development. The location of the major centres of industrial development in Europe has been determined historically in no small measure by the availability of energy supplies, in this case indigenous coal. Conversely, the industrialization of certain areas, particularly Southern Italy, has been retarded by their absence. As development has proceeded, the demand for energy has increased slightly less than proportionately to the general rate of economic advance and, it is believed, European growth over the period 1965-75 will be somewhat more energy-intensive than it has been in the past.[68] As long as indigenous coal was well to the fore as the main source of primary energy in Europe, energy policy for the member states virtually meant assuring coal supplies on reasonable terms to all buyers. Hence the emphasis on non-discriminatory pricing in the Paris Treaty and its rigorous attitude to concentrations or cartels that could lead to market exploitation by the producers.

But over the years since the Paris Treaty was signed, the dominant position of the coal-owners in the European energy market has been greatly weakened. Coal's contribution to the total consumption of primary energy in the Six was about 74 per cent in 1950, but only 43 per cent in 1964. Oil's share of the market, on the other hand, increased from 10 to 40 per cent over

[68] ECSC, EEC, and EURATOM Executives, *Untersuchung über die langfristigen energiewirtschaftlichen Aussichten der Europäischen Gemeinschaft* (1964), p. 36.

the same period.[69] This relative switch from coal to oil has also occurred in the UK, USSR, and US,[70] but the process has gone furthest in the Community, which now, therefore, finds itself dependent upon imports to cover a substantial part of its energy requirements—a tendency that is intensified by the increased penetration of the Community market by imported coal, although this has tended to slow down more recently. If there was a world fuel shortage in the future the EEC would be the most vulnerable to its effects, as the other major blocs—the US and USSR—are by contrast almost self-sufficient. The first reason why the Community needs an energy policy is, therefore, this growing dependence upon imports. Whereas in the early 1950s the energy problem was basically one of coming to terms with indigenous coal's domination of the Community market, the energy problem of the 1960s and beyond is to devise a system that takes account of the consequences for the Community market of the predominance of imported petroleum. The problem posed by the growing importance of imported petroleum is not, of course, to be equated with any crudely mercantilist concern for the balance of payments. It is, rather, a realization that as the important sources of these supplies (the Eastern bloc and even more the Middle East) may both, for different reasons, be less than completely politically reliable, increasing dependence upon them exposes European industry to the risk of sudden disruption in the event of any interruption of supplies—as the Suez crisis showed. A very important element in the common energy policy is, therefore, the attempt to minimize the risks that are inherent in this kind of situation. In so far as the need to guarantee security of supply takes the form of aid to keep coal mines in production, the common energy policy also serves as a means of preventing the emergence of severe unemployment in coalmining regions.

(b) The Problem of Distortions

The second main reason why the Community needs an energy policy is because the cost of energy forms an important part of

---

[69] ECSC High Authority, *Europa + Energie* (1964), p. 11.

[70] L. Corradini, *The Place of Oil and Natural Gas in European Energy Policy* (1964), p. 3. (High Authority Document no. 6257/1/64 e; a paper presented at the Conference of Economic Co-operation, Oslo, 16 Oct. 1964.)

industrial costs in certain branches of the economy. The general cost of energy to Community enterprises will, therefore, be a factor determining the competitive strength of the Community in world markets. For the same reason, artificial differences in the cost of energy as between enterprises in the various member states will distort the conditions of competition between Community enterprises in the internal market. In this connexion, of course, the problem is more serious for some industries than others. The ratio of the cost of energy to the value of sales is in fact quite small for industry as a whole—perhaps 3 or 4 per cent;[71] and it is, therefore, tempting to minimize the seriousness of the effects of distortions in energy costs upon the competitive position of enterprises. But competition exists not in some vague general way throughout industry as a whole but specifically between enterprises in particular industries. And for certain industries the incidence of energy costs is sufficiently important to make firms far from indifferent to the terms on which it is acquired. Foremost among such industries would be iron and steel, where energy costs amount to 20-25 per cent of the total costs of production; transport (15-18 per cent inclusive of tax); chemicals, glass, pottery, and cement (about 15 per cent).[72] It is also interesting to note that 22 per cent of all the Community exports come from sectors in which energy costs represent 10 per cent or more of the value of production.[73]

As long as the member states continue to have different tariff and quota arrangements for coal imports from third countries, and as long as they continue to impose different taxes upon fuel oil, competition will continue to be distorted within the Community. Such distortions in the basic conditions of competition could, however, be temporarily ignored as long as each member state was at least partially sealed off from the others. But as trade between the member states has gradually become almost completely free, so has the necessity to eliminate such distortions increased, if competition across national frontiers is to have its full beneficial effects upon resource allocation.

[71] ECSC, EEC, and EURATOM Executives, *Memorandum on Energy Policy* (1962), p. 7.
[72] ECSC High Authority, *Europe + Energie*, p. 7.
[73] From a résumé of a forthcoming study on the economic impact of energy prices—*Bull. EEC*, no. 3, Mar. 1966, pp. 20-21.

2. THE ECONOMIC BACKGROUND TO THE SECURITY OF SUPPLY ARGUMENT[74]

The immediate post-war years and the early 1950s were years of coal shortage (that is, at prices that Governments were willing to contemplate). Intensive efforts were, therefore, made by the major coal-using industries to economize in the use of that fuel. This tendency expressed itself in two main ways. In the first place, in industries such as iron and steel, where the position of coal as the dominant fuel was largely dictated by technical factors, considerable progress was made in its more efficient utilization by curtailing heat losses. Secondly, where substitution between the various fuels was technically possible, decisions began to be taken against coal. Both these tendencies were at work throughout the 1950s, but their effect on the coal market was largely concealed by the rapid pace of economic development based on post-war reconstruction that reached its peak in 1956. In May of that year the OEEC published a report entitled *Europe's Growing Needs of Energy—How Can They be Met?* The whole burden of this report (the Hartley Report) was the danger of a possible shortage of energy in Europe with emphasis upon the balance of payments problems that are inherent in dependence upon imports.

The conclusions of the Hartley Report seemed to be strikingly vindicated within a few months of its publication. With the Suez crisis of late 1956, high ocean-freight rates for both petroleum imports and imports of coal from the US underlined the importance of Europe's indigenous coal supplies and made European governments begin to think seriously about the security of overseas supplies.

The longer-term consequences of the Suez crisis for the European energy market were as striking as its immediate impact had been. But these long-run effects were in the opposite direction to those foreseen by the Hartley Report. The major oil companies became anxious to develop alternative sources of supply outside the Middle East. New oil companies were established. Companies added to their tanker fleets. And Soviet oil again appeared in the

---

[74] This discussion also provides an economic background to the policy of state aid to Belgian coal mines discussed in ch. 3 (pp. 44–50), and ECSC social and regional policy discussed in ch. 11.

world market after a long absence. The collapse of the ocean freight market during 1957 brought the landed price of US coal at North European ports below the price for Ruhr coal (itself the cheapest in the Community). And this extension of supplies came at the very time when the pace of advance of the European economy temporarily slackened. A second report by the OEEC (the Robinson Report) was published in 1960 with the appropriate title *Towards a New Energy Pattern in Europe*. Its conclusions were virtually the reverse of those of the Hartley Report in that it looked forward to a long period of cheap energy supplies.

The results of this combination of factors on the energy market in Europe can best be summarized in the form of a table. Table 9 below shows, for what proved to be the worst years of the recession in the coal industry, the very considerable falls in the landed price of US coal and imported petroleum as compared with the upward movement of Ruhr coal prices.

TABLE 9

*Comparative Price Movements of Internal and Imported Energy Supplies**

($/ton approx.)

	Internal	Imported	
	Ruhr coal	US coal	Crude oil
1957	13	22	23
1962	15	13	18

* Prices are approximate only; grade of coal, coking fines; import prices are c.i.f. Rotterdam.

Source: ECSC, High Authority, *11th Gen. Rep.* (1963), pp. 598, 608, & 610.

This fundamental change in the situation in the energy market occurred at a time when the marketing arrangements of the mining enterprises were in any case under attack. The long-standing anti-competitive tendencies of the Ruhr coal-owners had resulted in the formation in 1952 of the monopoly selling agency for Ruhr coal, GEORG. In 1956, however, this was replaced by three other selling agencies (Geitling, Mausegatt, and Präsident) that were supposed to function independently. When it became clear that the Central Joint Office of the three agencies was allocating orders much as GEORG had done previously, they too came under a ban by the High Authority in 1959—at the very time when domestic coal production was feeling the greatest competition from imported coal and petroleum. Cartelization, therefore, could no longer be regarded by the producers as a major possibility for stabilizing the coal market. They accordingly turned increasingly for direct assistance to their national governments, who helped their own coal industries in various ways that contravened the spirit or the letter of the Paris Treaty, while the High Authority, by then deeply entangled in studies and abortive plans for a comprehensive energy policy, did little about it.[75]

But perhaps the most significant result of the post-Suez energy crisis in 1958 was the effect it had on coal output and employment in the mines. The figures provided below in Table 10, which refer again to the worst phase of the recession, show just how great this was.

TABLE 10

The Main Effects of the Recession in the Community Coal Industry

	Production (mill. metric tons)	Underground workers ('000)	No of pits	% of total output produced in fully-mechanized pits	Average output per man shift (kg.)
1957	249	659	413	20*	1,560
1962	227	470	280	55	2,174

* 1956.

Sources: ECSC, High Authority, *Europa + Energie*, p. 26; *13th Gen. Rep.* (1965), p. 407.

[75] It is probable that the lack of activity on the part of the High Authority also resulted from a fear that any initiative on its part would be disregarded by governments.

The effects of the recession are noticeable in the first place in the output figures, which show a definite decline. The fall in employment (about 29 per cent) was in fact far greater than that in output as the pressure of the recession brought about an intensive campaign of rationalization and mechanization which, while it led to a very considerable improvement in productivity, aggravated the fall in employment caused by reduced sales. Notwithstanding the improvement in productivity, however, rising input costs pushed coal prices upwards with the result that the competitive position of coal remained, and remains, weak.

The implications of the above data for policy in the Community are quite clear. The figures suggest that if the competitive strength of coal *vis-à-vis* oil does not improve, then the Community will have to reckon not only with a continued decline in employment in mining, but with a downward trend in production also.

As far as the employment problem is concerned, its importance lies not so much in the numbers of men who might be directly involved as in its specifically regional orientation. As Table 11 shows, the share of coalmining in total employment is in fact quite small, and reductions in such employment, if they were evenly spread throughout each economy, would not really constitute any major economic problem.

TABLE 11

The Proportion of Coalmining in Total Employment (1964)

	Working population ('000)	Total workers in coalmining ('000)	Mining as % of total employment
Western Germany	26,692	399	1·5
France	19,465	188	1·0
Italy	19,938	3	-
Belgium	3,622	91	2·5
Netherlands*	4,324	57	1·5
Luxembourg	138	—	—

* Netherlands refers to 1961.

Sources: EEC, Stat. Office, *Basic Statistics of the Community* (1963), p. 21; (1965), pp. 23 & 28; ECSC, *12th Gen. Rep.* (1964), p. 504.

But in fact reductions in mining employment, even in economies that are in general working at high levels of activity, tend to create disproportionately large problems, as the incidence of such unemployment is severely localized and can, therefore, contribute to the decay of entire regions. Nevertheless the regional unemployment problem, while admittedly difficult enough, is by no means insoluble, as the broad lines of remedial action are well known and suitable instruments of regional policy are at the disposal of both the Community and the member governments.

Whether the Community should be prepared to tolerate any further drop in actual production is, however, an entirely different question. It amounts in practice to asking whether the Community should continue to allow itself to become ever more dependent upon imports from third countries to meet its energy requirements and, if it should, whether anything should be done to slow down the rate at which the relative (or in this case the absolute) substitution proceeds. From the standpoint of energy policy it would only be sensible to contemplate substantial reductions of indigenous coal production if two conditions were fulfilled.

First, it would be necessary for something like the present ratio between the prices of indigenous coal and imported petroleum to be reasonably permanent. This is so because both geological and sociological factors combine to make pit closures and the dispersal of mining communities largely irreversible processes. European mines closed during the next few years could not be brought back into operation in the event of any future rise in energy prices except at extremely high cost. And given the long period of gestation of capital projects in mining (perhaps 10–15 years from starting to sink a pit to reaching a high rate of production), new investments could not be expected to make any contribution to supplies very quickly. If a marked increase in the relative price of imported energy is reasonably foreseeable, a case can certainly be made for temporarily supporting indigenous coal production until it materializes.

The second condition that would have to be fulfilled if the Community is to be able to contemplate a substantial reduction in indigenous coal production with equanimity is that the supplies of imported energy should be secure. If it is decided that the degree of risk attaching to oil imports is sufficiently large to require some kind of insurance, then support for indigenous coal is one possible method of achieving this.

We shall examine this second question of the security of oil supplies later in this chapter when we turn to consider the policy that the Community intends to adopt towards oil. Let us consider at this stage simply the first problem—the possible future trends in energy prices, especially the prices of imported supplies.

An attempt to throw light on this vital question of how permanent the present coal/oil price ratio is brings one immediately into the realm of economic forecasting. As we have seen from our references to the Hartley Report and the Robinson Report, this is treacherous ground indeed. Broadly speaking, some authorities prophesy a continuation of something like the present competitive pressure upon indigenous coal, while others stress that the present price relationships in the energy market are exceptional, and will ultimately change in a manner favourable to indigenous coal.

The former point of view was very much the standpoint adopted in the Robinson Report, and it is largely shared by the Executives of the three European Communities. While it is true that in their investigation into possible trends in energy prices the Executives discounted the possibility of import prices remaining as low as they had been in the early 1960s, none the less their considered opinion was that c.i.f. import prices for both coal and petroleum at European ports would still be sufficiently low to price nearly half of the Community's coal production out of the market by 1970 in the absence of some form of protection for coal.[76]

While the study in which this forecast is advanced examines internal demand and general supply conditions in considerable (some would say too much) detail, it does not appear—nor does the Robinson Report—to make any comparably detailed study of the likely rate of growth in demand for energy in the rest of the world. However difficult it might have been to refine the forecasts in this way, the fact that an important aspect of the problem has been dealt with only sketchily must tend to weaken to some extent the confidence with which one can accept the

[76] *Towards a New Energy Pattern in Europe*, p. 161.

13

conclusions of the study—especially those concerning the long-run price of imported fuels in Europe.

The opponents of those who anticipate a continuation of the present price level of imported energy supplies tend to place greater emphasis upon the likely growth of total world demand for primary energy (taking into account world demographic trends and probable rates of economic growth in both advanced and underdeveloped nations), and to minimize the contribution to supplies that might be expected from the most recently developed sources of energy such as atomic power and natural gas. Arguing along these lines it is suggested that a fuel shortage 10 or 15 years from now is more likely than a fuel surplus.[77]

Clearly this question of the future price level of imported supplies is the most crucial one of the whole debate on energy policy. Given the difficulty of answering the question in any completely satisfactory way, and bearing in mind the related secondary question of the place of indigenous coal in providing security of supplies, a rather modest degree of protection for European production might be a more prudent policy than to allow its fate to depend entirely on its competitive position. (Major developments in indigenous or North Sea oil and natural gas would, however, alter the case.) This policy would not obviate the necessity to close grossly uneconomic pits and intensify the mechanization of the remainder. But it would imply that successive increments in the Community's demand for energy would have to be met from other sources. And for the foreseeable future this will continue to involve a growing dependence upon imports.

3. OUTLINES OF A COHERENT ENERGY POLICY

Let us now turn to consider the steps that the member states are taking to devise a common policy.

The first positive step in this direction was taken in April 1964, when the Council of Ministers formally adopted a Protocol of Agreement on energy policy. This Protocol of Agreement is not, however, to be regarded as a formal statement of a detailed energy policy: to use a phrase that is familiar in another connexion, it is more in the nature of a declaration of intent. It

[77] E. F. Schumacher, 'The Struggle for a European Energy Policy', *J. Common Market Studies*, Mar. 1964, p. 205.

establishes certain broad objectives of policy, foremost among which are cheapness of supply, security of supply, fair conditions of competition between the various fuels, and an acceptance of the relationship of coal policy to regional employment questions. It was fully realized when this Protocol was negotiated that, while agreement on anything like a detailed energy policy was still a considerable time ahead, action was needed in certain directions more urgently than in others. The agreement discusses, therefore, how the general objectives of energy policy should be framed for each individual source of primary energy, but goes rather further in the particular case of coal for which the speedy implementation of a coordinated system of state aids is envisaged. Let us now consider the outlines of the policy that is to be adopted towards each of the main sources of primary energy, starting with coal where the common policy will first begin to show its effects.

(a) *Policy for Coal*

Any intervention in the energy market aimed at keeping the level of coal production above its natural competitive level (as determined by the present coal/oil price ratio) serves the purpose of both regional and energy policies. From the standpoint of energy policy, there are two main purposes underlying measures in support of coal. First, such measures are a hedge against the possibility of a future rise in the price of imported supplies. This would have the effect of making profitable once more some of the Community mines that are at present sub-marginal. Secondly, indigenous energy makes a contribution to the security of total energy supplies. By making cheapness of energy one of the cardinal objectives of policy, the Community has *ipso facto* chosen subsidies for coal, rather than duties, or taxes, or their equivalent, on oil, as its main method of support. In other words, the gap between coal and oil prices is to be narrowed, not by bringing the price of oil up to that of coal, but by measures that will enable the price of Community coal itself to become more competitive than its supply condition would warrant.

As a system of subsidies for coal is in marked contrast to the Community's system of agricultural support, it is worth mentioning here the reasons underlying the Community's decision to adopt this particular method. Access to low-cost energy supplies that will help to keep industrial costs down is one of the factors that will determine the Community's international competitive strength. Furthermore, agreement between the member states on low energy prices was probably easier to reach than a decision to protect coal by raising the price of competing fuels. This is so because Italian industry would have been placed in an extremely difficult situation by any deterioration in its energy supply conditions, and because opting for subsidies meant in practice very little more than the substitution of an overt and coordinated series of aids for the previous unsatisfactory half-concealed national subsidy arrangements that had been introduced in spite of the prohibitions of the Paris Treaty. As the member states adopting these questionable methods were only too anxious to regularize their unorthodox payments, this in turn meant that the awkward question of devising a Community-financed system of aids to replace the nationally-financed systems could be temporarily disregarded (although clearly not indefinitely).

Another reason that appears to be behind the decision to opt for subsidies is to be found in the changed structure of the energy market and in particular in the fact that indigenous coal now provides less than half of the Community's energy requirements and is declining in relative importance, while imported energy now (in 1966) covers one-half of internal consumption and will increase its relative share of the market. This latter fact appears to have been an important influence behind the choice of subsidies as the most appropriate measure to support coal. Thus although both a tax on imported fuel and a subsidy involve a fiscal burden, if the former were adopted the progressively increasing importance of imported fuel, mainly oil, would, other things being equal, involve a progressively increasing tax burden leading possibly to a situation in which the support of a relatively small amount of energy supplies (coal) would involve a very large tax burden. It is true that, in both cases, about the same quantity of resources that are uneconomic by present standards would be kept in production, but from the point of view of the fiscal burden a subsidy to domestic coal production is the more acceptable policy, particularly in the long run.[78]

[78] There is an element of guesswork in this fiscal burden argument. Certainly at the present it is by no means certain *a priori* that the fiscal burden of a tax on fuel imports would necessarily be greater than that of the tax that would have to

It may be noted that the argument in favour of a system of subsidies for coal rather than any alternative method of support is in practice at the present time an argument about the protection of an indigenous fuel against imports. But if we assume, as now seems inevitable, that the intensive search for oil and natural gas in the North Sea begun in 1965 will in a few years' time further weaken the competitive position of Community coal (particularly if the UK were to join the Common Market) then the current problems will still exist for coal, although in an exacerbated form. Europe might then find that the long-run price and security of energy supplies were no longer such pressing questions, and considerations of energy policy could not then be held to justify the continued support of coal. But if considerations of regional policy still required Community coal production to be maintained, subsidies would still be the most acceptable way of achieving this end.

The contrast between the agricultural and energy markets is, therefore, obvious. In agriculture the choice is a straight one between domestic production or imports and is not complicated by the possible emergence of a new indigenous or semi-indigenous source of supply. As the Community is about 84 per cent self-sufficient in food production, maintaining the present level of agricultural output by means of subsidies would involve a considerable fiscal burden as compared with simply increasing the price of the imported 16 per cent or so by levies. For the UK, however, which is only about 43 per cent self-sufficient in food production, the choice must be seen in very different terms— quite apart from whatever political advantages may lie in a cheap food policy.

The first positive steps towards a Community system of state aids to the coal mines came into effect in April 1965. As subsidies are expressly forbidden by the Paris Treaty, it was only possible to resort to their use by invoking Article 95 of the treaty, which allows for special decisions to be taken by the High Authority 'in all cases not expressly provided for in the Treaty', when this 'appears necessary to fulfil one of the objectives of the Community'. This was not the first time that the flexibility

---

be raised to pay coal subsidies. A definitive answer could only be arrived at in the light of the relevant elasticities of the supply and demand curves for energy in its various forms.

provided for in Article 95 had had to be invoked. At the very beginning of the recession in the coal market in 1958 the High Authority decided to allow special payments to the mines to finance the holding of pithead stocks (which in fact increased more than fourfold from 1957 to 1959). In 1959 the High Authority decided to grant a special allowance to Belgian miners to mitigate the consequences of short-time working there. And it was again invoked, as we have seen in our discussion of pricing in the steel market, in January 1964 to prohibit price alignments on offers from the Eastern Bloc and thereby help stabilize the internal price structure in the steel market. The decision by the High Authority in favour of a coordinated system of subsidies to the mines, which was (eventually) unanimously supported by the Council of Ministers, now provides the ECSC with an instrument for the application of a coordinated coal policy within the general framework for a common energy policy as a whole.

The basic principle underlying the new system is that measures of financial aid contemplated by the member states must in all cases be submitted to the High Authority's authorization and control. The decisions of the High Authority must be based upon Community criteria. They will involve assessing (*a*) how far the aids enable the collieries concerned to adjust to the realities of the situation in the coal market; (*b*) how far they will help maintain employment and avoid fundamental and persistent disturbances in the economies of the member states; and (*c*) how far they distort the conditions of competition as between the various mining enterprises.

Largely as a result of the type of measures already taken by the national governments, the High Authority is directing its scrutiny to two main types of aids.

The first of these are state contributions to the social security costs of the mining enterprises. As is well known, much of the expenditure on social security in Community countries is paid from funds largely financed by enterprises (in the form of supplementary labour costs) and by employees rather than by governments, as is the case in the UK. In 1960, for example, the state contributed about 52 per cent of social security revenue in the UK, while the contribution by the state in Belgium, the most similar Community country in this respect, was only 26 per cent (for the other members, the state's contribution ranged between

7 and 21 per cent).[79] The rapid reduction in the numbers of men employed in mining over the last few years has resulted in the impact of these social charges upon enterprises becoming proportionately greater as the income of the funds has been reduced by the decline in the number of employees, while expenditure has tended to increase with earlier retirements. The task of the High Authority is to make sure that any payment made by governments in schemes introduced since January 1965 to defray these excessive social security charges do no more than cover the abnormal costs of the schemes, and do not become positive subsidies that would place the recipients in a more advantageous position than their competitors. It is interesting to note that in its original draft proposals for these decisions, the High Authority had stated that all schemes introduced since January 1963 should be made subject to scrutiny.[80] The adoption of January 1965 as the operative date in the final text of the Decision[81] must give rise to doubts as to whether the change was prompted by the genuine belief that the policies adopted by member governments before that date were comparatively insignificant, or whether there was a certain reluctance on the part of the states to allow the High Authority to push its inquiries very far.

The second main heading under which governments have been subsidizing their collieries is by making aids available for rationalization. The High Authority now has the power to authorize such subsidies in so far as they serve to help the mines to adjust to the coal sales position and do not distort the conditions of competition within the industry. 'Rationalization' of the mines is considered for this purpose under two headings. First, negative rationalization (closure or partial closure of mines) may be encouraged by government grants to cover previously defined expenses, properly documented and accounted for. Secondly, the High Authority may also permit subsidies towards part of the expenses involved in schemes to increase general efficiency—positive rationalization. Such schemes could include greater concentration and link-up of pits and workings, capital

---

[79] G. L. Reid and D. J. Robertson, eds., *Fringe Benefits, Labour Costs and Social Security* (1965), p. 101.

[80] ECSC High Authority Spokesman, *Proposed Community Systems of State Aid to the European Coalmines, Information Background 12/64*, 8 Dec. 1964, p. 3.

[81] ECSC High Authority, *Decision on Community System of State Aids to the European Coalmines, Communiqué 11/65*, 18 Feb. 1965, p. 2.

projects to improve productivity per pit, introduction of improved methods of coal valorization, and investments to secure higher safety standards. Again, the High Authority may authorize the payment of subsidies towards the costs incurred in connexion with the recruitment, training, adaptation, and general employment stability of the personnel directly involved in the rationalization programme. This latter kind of help may be quite important in view of the difficulty of recruitment in some of the coal basins. Finally, the possibility is envisaged that certain mining areas may be so badly affected as to produce more general serious disturbances in parts of the Community. In such cases the possibility of extra assistance is provided for. In all the above cases the High Authority may make its authorization subject to certain conditions, and it is empowered to carry out checks on the collieries to ascertain whether such conditions are being fulfilled and generally to ensure that funds are being used for the purpose stipulated. In the event of misuse of the subsidies the High Authority may impose minimum prices upon the enterprise concerned and in addition withdraw or amend its authorization.

Such then are the first positive steps in the evolution of the common energy policy. Compared with the tasks that still remain to be done to bring about a full energy policy, they are modest enough indeed. But they do represent a definite attempt to attack those parts of the energy problem that have done most to endanger the cohesion of the Community—uncoordinated interventions by national governments. The fact that the High Authority now has specific powers and responsibilities in this field should enhance its ability to bring about the necessary additional policies that are required for coal, and possibly, in due course, the requisite complementary policies for the other sources of primary energy.

Perhaps the most important step that could be taken for coal would be a Community decision in favour of some level of total output or degree of support. At no stage in discussions on energy policy have definite figures been even tentatively considered by the Six. But if definite figures were decided upon, it would then be possible to start considering where future investments should be concentrated, and where regional development schemes should be most vigorously pursued. At the present time, however, decisions on the future level of Community output are in effect still being taken by the national governments acting independently. This has the effect of perpetuating the present division of the coal market into national compartments and makes the new supervisory role of the High Authority in relation to national subsidies appear somewhat equivocal to say the least.

But perhaps the main reasons for emphasizing just how much still remains to be done in the field of coal policy alone is that the existence of a nationally-financed system of subsidies amounts to an open recognition of the fact that the Six have as yet refused to recognize a specific Community responsibility for any very definite policy with regard to coal. The effect of the present system is largely to confirm the existing division of the coal market and this state of affairs is almost certain to persist until there is greater agreement among the Six about the long-run place of Community coal in energy policy. The most that can be said for the present system is that it at least represents some attempts to harmonize national interventions. As the evolution of the common agricultural policy has suggested, this could be the first step towards agreement on more substantial matters.

It is perhaps ironical to note that the present system of support for coal involves an extremely inequitable distribution of the burden of financing the maintenance of Community supplies. Thus Italy, a non-producer, is not involved (subject to the exception shown below) in any expenditure in support of production in the other member states. But if there emerged a shortage of fuel in the future, Italy would still be able to buy Community coal on the same non-discriminatory terms as nationals of the coal-producing countries themselves, who in the meantime will have contributed via their taxation to the payment of subsidies. A tax on imported fuel would at least have had the merit of distributing the burden involved in supporting coal more equitably between all the member states. In other words the present arrangements fall far short of being an attempt by the member states to adopt a truly Community approach.

(b) Subsidies for Coking Coal—the 1966 Initiative

In July 1966 the High Authority attempted to secure the agreement of the Council of Ministers to a system of subsidies

13*

for coking coal. This proposal was designed to deal with the difficulties arising out of the import into the Community of cheap American coking coal. Because there is no common external tariff and common commercial policy under the Paris Treaty, member states are free either to protect their own coal industries from such cheap imports or to take advantage of them. There are two aspects to this problem. First, the Netherlands and Italy particularly, whose steel plants have been sited on the coast, have taken advantage of cheap US supplies. On the other hand countries like West Germany are more dependent on domestically-produced supplies which are more costly. A distortion of competition in the steel industry inevitably arises under these circumstances, and in the intensively competitive conditions of 1966 the disadvantageous position, for example, of German steel producers was bound to be highlighted. Second, the cheap US coking coal tends to cause either a contraction of Community production or aggravates the surplus problem to such a degree that contraction becomes inevitable eventually.

The High Authority therefore proposed a subsidy system for Community coking coal (i.e. coal for industrial use, mainly in the steel industry, but not coal in general, including that for household use). Moreover the subsidy was not to be available in respect of all coking coal produced but only for that part of production which was exported from one member state to another—in practice this amounts to about a quarter of total Community production. The High Authority justified this proposal on the grounds that if no subsidy was given, the intra-Community trade in coking coal would decline as imports were switched from the Community to the US. A subsidy, by maintaining Community trade and production, would contribute to an avoidance of over-dependence on imported supplies. A tariff on imports of US coal was rejected on the grounds of the effect it would have on steel production costs. Internal and export prices of steel products were very low indeed at this point in time and a rise in costs would have been the last straw.

The intention was that the subsidy should be financed from a Community fund. The Community aspect had much to commend it since, as we indicated above, under a purely national subsidy system, countries such as the Netherlands and Italy would bear little or no part of the financial burden of keeping

Community mines in operation, but could always switch back to Community supplies, without discrimination, if cheap US supplies dried up.

However the Community system was rejected by the French. They took the view that national subsidies were the answer— although they were quick to add that such aids should be co-ordinated on a Community basis. If the latter condition was not fulfilled there was the prospect of a cost-cutting war. For example West Germany might subsidize the production of coking coal for internal use to such an extent that French steel producers would be disadvantaged. (The French government had just made a £220 million loan to its steel industry at a low-interest rate and had no desire to see the recipients succumbing to German competition.)

In November 1966 the High Authority returned to the attack. This time the French response was more encouraging. An agreement in principle was announced and the Council of Ministers called for the drawing up of detailed proposals. The basic idea was that there should be a Community fund for the payment of subsidies on coking coal entering into intra-Community trade. There were to be strict limits to the duration of the scheme and the quantity of sales eligible for subsidy. It was also envisaged that eventually the three-quarters of Community production consumed in the country of origin should be subject to national subsidies based on Community criteria. In February 1967 the Council achieved an agreement on these lines.

(c) *Policy for Oil and Natural Gas*

While the broad outlines of the policy to be followed with regard to oil and natural gas were sketched out in the Protocol of April 1964, no actual steps have yet been taken to bring into effect the policies there described. Very briefly, the aims of the policy on oil and natural gas would be as follows: (a) prices as low and stable as possible based upon diversified sources of supply; (b) promotion of the development of indigenous resources; (c) a common policy on stocks; (d) elimination of those features of national energy régimes that tend to discriminate against nationals of other member states; (e) a fiscal system for fuel oil (and, eventually, for other products) appropriate to the objectives of the energy policy.

Let us consider what some of the implications of this kind of policy may be in practice.

In the first place the policy for oil and natural gas takes for granted a continuation of the trend of recent years as a result of which oil's share of the Community's consumption of primary energy has grown rapidly owing to its price advantage over coal. It is realized, however, that this growing dependence upon imported energy supplies requires policy to take account of how secure these supplies really are—with regard to both price and physical availability. As we have seen, aid for the Community coal industry within the framework of energy policy as a whole could only be justified by reason of its contribution to the solution of these problems. But any practically conceivable level of support for indigenous coal would only reduce the problem of security, not eliminate it. As much of the Community's supplies of imported petroleum come from the Middle East, where various kinds of political disturbances could interrupt supplies, or Eastern bloc countries that again cannot be relied upon completely, the Community's policy on oil will eventually involve a definite element of insurance against the risks to which these supplies are exposed.

The first line of defence that is envisaged against a sudden interruption of supplies is the presence of adequate stocks in the Community itself. At one period in the development of Community thinking on these matters (1962) it was thought that such stocks ought to amount to about 4–6 months' current consumption.[82]

The second factor that will be relied upon to contribute to security is diversification of supply zones, so that if a crisis occurs in any particular one, it will be possible to call upon standby capacity and transport facilities in the others. To some extent such diversification is already inherent in the policy of the major oil companies. But the fact that the Middle East accounted for the same proportion of the world's oil reserves (about 61 per cent) in 1964 as it had in 1958 and 1954[83] suggests that the exploration pattern of the international oil companies is not that

---

[82] ECSC, EEC, and Euratom Executives, *Memorandum on Energy Policy*, p. 27.

[83] E. F. Schumacher, *Coal in the Fuel Economy* (1965), p. 10. A paper delivered to the Fourth International Mining Congress in London on 16 July 1965.

which would be ideally required in the interests of the Community's energy policy. On the other hand, over this same period the Community has diversified its main sources of supply, and of course natural gas developments in the North Sea are likely to change this pattern still further. The policy to be applied by the Community seems to go rather further than simply relying upon the international oil companies, in that emphasis is placed upon the role of European companies producing and marketing supplies derived from areas where European influence is strong (such as the development of Algerian and Libyan reserves by France). In line with this policy, the EEC Commission decided not to oppose the German government's request to be allowed to assist German companies in their search for hydrocarbons outside Germany. While disclaiming any hint of European 'nationalism' in this policy, one member of the staff of the High Authority has stated: 'But the fact remains that the majors, even though their outlook is gradually changing to a greater awareness of their public responsibility, are still not all sufficiently attuned to the needs and concerns of European consumers.'[84]

Whether 'nationalistically' inspired or not, however, the common policy for oil will work to maintain the present 'lively' situation in the oil market in which competition between numerous companies with diverse interests and resources serves to keep prices low. For its part the Community will not frustrate the basic purpose of its cheap energy policy by imposing heavy consumption taxes on fuel oil. This would not only weaken the competitive position of the fuel-consuming industries but would serve as a standing invitation to petroleum-exporting countries to attempt to press for larger royalties as the latter would be naturally aggrieved by the prospect of wealthy European governments benefiting to any greater extent from revenue derived from oil. Not only must taxes on oil be low, therefore, but they must also be of equal incidence in each member state if oil consumers in one state are not to be disadvantageously affected as compared with those in another. For example, harmonization of taxes on fuel oil is required by the common transport policy to eliminate distortions in competitive conditions in that sector. As any such harmonization of taxes will touch upon the fiscal

[84] Corradini, *Oil and Natural Gas in European Energy Policy*, p. 11.

autonomy of the member governments we may again expect rapid progress in the implementation of the common energy policy to be rather unlikely.

(d) *Nuclear Energy*

While the Community will continue and intensify its work on the industrial uses of nuclear energy via EURATOM, it is not really expected that nuclear energy will make any significant contribution to overall energy supplies in the foreseeable future. It is expected that energy from large-scale nuclear power plants will become competitive with energy produced from conventional sources by about 1970, and that even by 1975 only about 5 per cent of the Community's energy requirements will be supplied from this source. Whatever prospects it may hold out for the more distant future, nuclear power cannot be considered a rival to indigenous coal in terms of the contribution it can make to ensuring the security of supplies.

II

Social and Regional Policy

I. SOCIAL POLICY AND INTEGRATION

As has been mentioned in introducing the previous chapter dealing with managed markets, the economic policy of the Communities, although it attaches great importance to a proper functioning of competitive forces, can in no way be regarded as a blind surrender to outmoded notions of *laissez-faire*. Apart from the controlled régimes that are now beginning to be implemented in the transport, agriculture, and energy markets, the treaties have made substantial provision for various forms of action by the authorities in certain fields that modern states have judged to be of particular importance. These general areas of intervention may be broadly classed as social policy and employment policy, although inevitably there is no clear demarcation between the two. The member states have had to bring questions of social and employment policy within the ambit of the Communities for two distinct reasons. The first, a technical reason, is because of the possibility that various national policies pursued under these headings could impede the process of integration, especially by distorting the working of competition or hindering the flow of the factors of production. The second is because the kind of integration upon which the Six have embarked is more than just an economic union, however great a task that alone may represent. It is an economic approach to a fundamentally political objective, and it was necessary, therefore, that the Communities as such should make a clear demonstration of commitment in certain awkward social and economic fields that have often been sources of disunity even within individual states and which could *a fortiori* have weakened the cohesion of the Community as a whole if not brought into consideration from the outset.

Although the social security régimes in each of the six Common Market countries are extremely heterogeneous they none the less have one feature in common that sets them apart from the British and Scandinavian systems, and that is their much greater reliance upon the employer as a source of revenue. This emerges clearly from Table 1 below which shows the dominant role of the employer as a source of social security finance in the Six and the comparatively minor role of the state there, and indicates how the position in the UK is roughly the opposite of this.

TABLE 1

Sources of Social Security Revenue EEC and UK, 1962

(per cent)

	Insured	Employer	State	Other
Belgium	25	45	24	6
France	20	69	7	5
Western Germany	38	41	18	4
Italy*	15	69	11	5
Netherlands	46	38	7	10
UK†	27	21	52	1

* 1961.   † 1960.

Source: EEC, *Exposé sur l'évolution de la situation sociale dans la Communauté en 1963*, p. 320; *National Income and Expenditure* (HMSO, 1962).

These substantial employer contributions to social security in each of the Six are mostly the result of compulsory legislation that in effect finances social security by means of a payroll tax. To a smaller extent they have also originated in collective agreements in which employers have undertaken to finance social welfare programmes. In either case the result is that employers in the EEC find that their total labour costs are only partly accounted for by direct wage payments, and that a substantial proportion of supplementary labour costs have to be met on top of the actual wage bill. Some idea of how important these supplementary labour costs may be can be gained from Table 2 (p. 383), in which we show for two important industries, steel and chemicals, the extent by which hourly wage costs are increased by the addition of supplementary labour costs.

TABLE 2
Hourly Wage and Labour Costs in Steel and Chemicals
(Shillings/hour, 1961)

	Steel			Chemicals		
	Wage costs (A)	Labour costs (B)	$\frac{B}{A}$ (%)	Wage costs (A)	Labour costs (B)	$\frac{B}{A}$ (%)
Belgium	6·24	8·72	140	4·25	6·32	149
France	4·39	7·62	174	4·26	7·67	180
Western Germany	6·63	9·69	146	5·57	9·01	162
Italy	4·39	7·62	174	2·76	5·50	199
Netherlands	5·09	8·39	165	4·41	6·66	151
Luxembourg	7·31	10·23	140	—	—	—
UK	6·68	7·45	112	5·87	7·63	130

Source: Inst. National de la Statist. et des Études Écon., *Études et conjonctures*, Apr. 1962.

As the incidence of these supplementary labour costs paid by enterprises in any one particular industry clearly varies among the different member states, the question therefore arises as to whether they might not distort the conditions of competition.

The French in particular appear to have been worried that their own high level of compulsory social charges would adversely affect their competitive position, although in fact the proportionate impact of such charges is perhaps even greater in Italy, as is suggested in Table 2. Accordingly, when the ECSC Treaty was being negotiated the French tried to include provisions for the immediate equalization of the social costs of production. France's future partners were not prepared to go as far as this, however, and in the event the ECSC Treaty merely referred to a general intention to 'harmonize' social standards, but it did not give the High Authority any specific powers to bring this 'harmonization' about. In fact in this particular field of social harmonization the High Authority has been comparatively inactive. Quite apart from other possible reasons, there is a severely political reason for this comparative inactivity: changes in national social régimes in the ECSC industries would probably have required corresponding changes throughout each national security system and such a complete reorganization of social security could hardly have been expected merely to satisfy the requirements of ECSC. Much the same kind of problem arose in transport, of course, but in a much more acute form, as the ECSC Treaty requirements were more specific in that field and if implemented fully would almost certainly have brought about major alterations in transport tariffs going far beyond the ECSC products alone.

It would appear that when the Rome Treaty was being negotiated the French were still concerned about the impact of social charges on competitive conditions. Although the other five states do not appear to have been won over to this point of view, the Rome Treaty, as it eventually emerged, did contain definite concessions to the French position.[1] Very briefly, these concessions amounted to an agreement to introduce the principle of equal pay for men and women and to standardize the length of the working week above which overtime payments would have to be made.

Again, the general principle of harmonization was embodied in the treaty, but this time, although no specific policies were laid down in advance, the Commission was charged with promoting collaboration between the member states in the field of social policy and a special Directorate General for Social Affairs was established within the Commission. Thus social policy has in fact come to occupy a place of some importance in the integration process, but it should be noted that neither of the treaties links social policy directly to questions of competition.

Were the French right in their view that different policies on the level of compulsory social charges could affect the costs of production of enterprises and thereby distort the conditions of competition?

There are both theoretical and practical arguments for believing that any such distortion is extremely improbable in

[1] According to R. W. Cox in 'Social and Labour Policy in the EEC', *Brit. J. Industr. Relations*, i/1 (1963), p. 6, these concessions to the French were largely the result of the need to secure France's support for the EEC after the National Assembly had rejected an earlier proposal for a European Defence Community. It should be added that the French also demanded concessions in other fields, such as, for example, the association of member states' overseas territories and a veto on the passage from one stage of the transition period to another, see J. Pinder, *Britain and the Common Market* (1961), pp. 31–36.

reality. At the theoretical level a *comparative* advantage that a state enjoys in the production of certain commodities rather than others would not be altered by an equi-proportionate across-the-board increase in its entire cost structure such as might be held to result from, say, France's having a higher overall level of social charges than the rest of its trading partners. (The French export price level would of course become uncompetitive but this could be compensated for by an adjustment of the rate of exchange.) But if the incidence of such charges in the states concerned were not evenly distributed over the industries comprising their national economies, then a distortion of the conditions of comparative advantage might at first sight be thought likely. However, even this possibility must appear somewhat doubtful in practice as the reaction of employers to these schemes as they were gradually introduced many years ago would be such as to shift the burden of social-security charges.

This will have been achieved in the short run by employers raising prices whenever possible to cover themselves against increased social charges when they were originally imposed— the resultant price increases finally being reflected in exchange rate variations—and, of greater importance in the long run, by their resisting more strongly demands for actual wage increases. This amounts to saying that if employers are compelled to pay part of a factor's cost in one form (supplementary labour costs in the form of social security charges) they will take that into account when assessing other parts of that factor's remuneration over which, because of their equal voice in the collective bargaining process, they have a measure of control.

There is some tentative evidence that something like this kind of process has in fact probably taken place. In the first place, as we have shown in Table 2, states which have high social charges tend to have low wage rates and *vice versa*. When wages and social charges are aggregated in any particular industry then the spread of total labour costs is greatly narrowed. Furthermore a United Nations study also tends to point towards the same conclusion, in that it expresses the view that 'the percentage share of wages in the national income of France decreased between 1938 and 1950 by an amount corresponding to the increase in taxes on wages paid by employers'.[2]

[2] UN, *Econ. Bull. Europe*, Aug. 1952, p. 46.

There is, therefore, a high probability that different levels of social charges on employers in the several states do not normally have any crucial effect on the international conditions of competition. On the other hand, social security in each of the member states is also financed to some extent by the state, and the role of the state in this field does vary quite considerably, as Table 1 has shown. Might not the differing roles of the state with regard to social security financing be a cause of distortion in the conditions of competition within the Common Market—bearing in mind that the state's role is really made possible by taxation? The answer must surely be that any distortion which does arise is the result of the overall level of taxation and its detailed incidence within each state, rather than of the state's role in social security as such. State contributions to social security are only one of the reasons why governments use their powers to tax, and there is no reason why social security of itself should be singled out as a cause of fiscal distortions as long as other, even larger, recipients of public funds could be named. We have already shown in Part 1 of this book how divergent fiscal policies may affect the working of a common market, and we need not repeat our discussion of these problems here.

If, therefore, the preponderant weight of the foregoing argument is that not too much attention should be given to social-security questions as a potential source of distortion to competition, why then have the Communities come to devote a considerable amount of attention to social affairs? The answer is, of course, that economic integration is only a means to the wider goal of raising living standards and promoting political unity. The flexibility that economic integration requires itself makes social security schemes all the more important, while the closer relationship between the member states makes comparison between them that much easier. The result is that each state is becoming aware of certain ways in which it compares favourably and unfavourably with the others. To some extent such differences (for example the generous family allowances in France) may result from basic politics, but we are inclined to believe that such reasons for the well-known divergences between the different national régimes should not be overplayed, and that to some extent at any rate uneven development is purely fortuitous. The policy of the Community is in fact to harmonize these systems in such a way that the outstandingly good features in any particular national system are made the objectives of future changes in the other states.

2. REGIONAL POLICY IN THE COMMON MARKET

(a) *The Extent and Nature of Regional Disparities*

In spite of long-standing and widespread interest in regional economic problems, economists have only in comparatively recent years begun to develop anything like a systematic body of analysis on the subject. In the absence of any generally accepted analytical framework around which statistics could be assembled to form a meaningful map of regional economic activity, the rationale to justify statistical refinements has been lacking and data on regional economic problems have tended to remain inadequate. This is particularly true in the Communities, whose multi-national composition makes generalizations about the overall situation fraught with difficulties.

Nevertheless if the problem is not to be discussed entirely *in vacuo* it is necessary at least to mention some figures, although these should be understood to belong to the domain of ordinal rather than cardinal measurement.

One estimate for the year 1955 suggested that, dividing the Six into sixty-eight main regions and comparing per capita income in each region with the average Community figure of 100 then the proportionate range of the disparities might lie between 40 for certain southern European regions and 130 for highly developed regions such as North Rhine-Westphalia or the Paris region. In other words the standard of living in the wealthiest regions of the Community was about three times as high as that in the poorest.[3]

More recently perhaps the most authoritative brief statement of the size of the gap between rich and poor regions in the Community was provided by Lionello Levi Sandri, the member of the Commission with special responsibility for social affairs. According to Levi Sandri, at the time of the coming into force of the Rome Treaty in 1958, per capita income levels in the most favoured region (Hamburg) were about seven times the corresponding figure for the least favoured (Calabria).[4]

[3] EEC, *Berichte über die Regionalpolitik in der EWG* (1964), p. 21.
[4] Lionello Levi Sandri, 'The Contribution of Regional Action to the

These types of comparison between extremes, although useful as a first step, inevitably tend to create an exaggerated impression of the imbalances. However, further data cited by Levi Sandri on the same occasion also relative to 1958 only serve to strengthen the general impression that regional disparities are indeed very great. Out of 55 social and economic regions in the Community, only 20 exceeded the EEC average level of per capita income, while, of the remaining 35, at least 15 had income levels between 50 and 70 per cent below that average.

As the 1955 and 1958 data are clearly not directly comparable, it would be quite wrong to infer from them that regional disparities had increased over that period, least of all that the relative gap between rich and poor had doubled. However, if we take the important case of Italy, there appear to be some grounds for believing that the relative gap between North and South was widening, at least during the early part of the 1950s. During the first years of activity of the Cassa per il Mezzogiorno (1951–5), income per head in the South expanded at an annual rate of 1·8 per cent as against 5 per cent in the North. From 1955 to 1958 the gap between the growth rates was virtually closed, the respective figures for the South and North being 4·3 per cent and 4·7 per cent.[5] Over the whole period 1951–61, however, the figure for the South is the more favourable, 5·6 per cent as against 4·4 per cent in the North.[6] Evidence that the relative size of the gap between the wealthiest and the poorest Italian provinces has tended to close between 1951 and 1963 is set out in Table 3 (p. 389).

We may note, however, that even if the relative gap between the wealthiest and the poorest provinces has to some extent been reduced, the absolute gap has still widened considerably. Thus whereas the gap between the wealthiest and the poorest, measured in absolute terms was 284·2 thousand lire in 1951, this figure had almost doubled to 560·2 thousand lire in 1963, an increase far in excess of that which would be attributed to the 40 per cent increase in prices over the period.

Although the Italian situation is the most extreme in the Com-

---

Construction of Europe', a paper read at the Third International Congress of Regional Economics. Rome, May 1965, p. 7.

[5] EEC, *Dokumente der Konferenz über Fragen der regionalen Wirtschaft*, (1961), p. 118.

[6] EEC, *Berichte über die Regionalpolitik*, p. 125.

TABLE 3

Per Capita Income in Some Italian Provinces, 1951 and 1963

(*'ooo lire*)

	1951	*1963*
Wealthiest province	351·4	746·9
19th province	184·5	467·4
37th province	153·1	383·1
55th province	121.9	319.2
74th province	97·9	265·5
92nd (last) province	67·2	186·4
Wealthiest/poorest province (%)	523%	401%

Source: C. Duponte, 'Income Inequalities: Regions, Individuals, Nations, Some Analogical Aspects', Third (Rome) Congress, 1965, p. 7.

munity, and France too is characterized by fairly large and persistent regional imbalances, with large contrasts between the South and West on the one hand, and the Paris region on the other, the remaining member states do not appear to be affected by regional problems of anything like the same degree of severity. This is probably particularly true of Belgium and Western Germany. Data on income per head in nine Belgian provinces in 1959 are set out in Table 4 (p. 390).

From this table it would appear that the ratio between the wealthiest and poorest provinces is less than two to one in Belgium —a disparity which is considerably less than that found in Italy and which is probably being reduced further with time.

Again, for Western Germany and the Netherlands, in both of which regional imbalances have been comparatively minor (the Federal political structure of the former is to be stressed in this context) disparities are being further reduced.[7]

Before we go on to discuss how the implementation of the Common Market might affect these regional disparities and the relevant instruments that are at the disposal of the Commission and the national governments in this field, it is useful to sketch

[7] Levi Sandri, Third (Rome) Congress, 1965, p. 8.

TABLE 4

Internal Gross Product at Factor Cost per Inhabitant in 1959

('*000 Belgian francs*)

Brabant	69·1
Liège	57·6
Anvers	57·1
Namur	48·9
West Flanders	48·4
Hainault	47·8
East Flanders	42·4
Luxembourg	42·1
Limburg	36·6
Wealthiest/poorest province (%)	189%

Source: J. Geluck, 'Regional Action and National Economic Development in Belgium', Third (Rome) Congress, 1965, p. 1.

briefly the main outlines of the different kinds of regional problems that existed in the Six before integration was set in train. We can then discuss how integration might affect these regional problems and where it might create new ones.

At the risk of greatly over-simplifying the problem, we shall divide problem regions into two main categories.

The first are areas such as the Ruhr, the Sambre, and Lorraine that have been heavily industrialized for many years. Their take-off in the nineteenth century was based upon their proximity to coal and iron-ore reserves that made possible the development of steel and engineering industries. It is clear, however, that the weak competitive position of coal in the energy market, the growing importance of imported ores, and the emergence of domestic steel industries in the developing countries that have customarily been steel importers, all combine to weaken the traditional growth stimuli in these old industrial regions. Only engineering and, perhaps, steel can still be regarded as driving forces in these regions. Whether an old industrial region with this kind of industrial structure actually comes to constitute an employment problem depends upon the proportion of its labour force that is employed in the declining coalmining industry. For some regions, such as the Ruhr (where the mines are in general among the best in the Community) re-employment of displaced miners locally in expanding industries presents no real problem. For others, such as the Borinage, where mining employment has declined faster and where alternative forms of employment are not so easily found, there is a real threat of regional decay.

The other main type of regional problem is that found in certain predominantly agricultural areas. Throughout much of Southern Italy, Sicily, and Sardinia, and to a smaller extent in the West of France (all of these being regions of some considerable density of population by rural standards) agriculture is largely of the subsistence variety and standards of living low. What industry there may be is widely scattered and may be grossly inefficient, such as the Sicilian sulphur mines. On the other hand, a few large modern plants, probably introduced into these areas with state inducements, have tended to remain 'technically and psychologically isolated'.[8] They have not formed the springboard for any regional take-off and any fluctuation in employment in them has immediately created a severe problem due to the absence of favourable opportunities for local re-engagement. The surplus rural manpower, unable to find employment in industry locally, has migrated to regions that offer better prospects. Italians from the South move north to Milan and further on to other countries of the Community, and workers from Brittany and Normandy move to the Paris region. This regional emigration draws off surplus rural manpower and provides an opportunity to re-organize agriculture into bigger units. If this opportunity is not taken, as it does not appear to have been in certain areas of France south of the Loire, and west of the Rhône, then the last state is probably worse than the first, and what was rural migration takes on the character of depopulation.

(b) The Impact of Integration upon Regional Problems

There are three main ways in which the economic integration of the Six is likely to have an effect upon regional development.

(i) *The General Impact of Increased Competition.* For any particular industry in the Communities the integration process starts

---

[8] EEC, *Berichte über die Regionalpolitik*, p. 23.

from a situation in which enterprises in the various member states (and, but probably to a smaller extent, within the one state) exhibit different degrees of efficiency. In the absence of state aids and other distortions, and given the enforcement of anti-trust rules, the reduction and eventual elimination of tariff and quota barriers between the member states will create opportunities for the lower-cost firms to expand their output at the expense of their less efficient competitors. While some of the latter may well be stimulated by such competition to adopt improved production techniques, it is only to be expected that a number of others will find this beyond them and will be forced out of the industry. In one sense, of course, this is exactly what the forces of competition are supposed to accomplish within any one national economy. But there is a considerable amount of evidence to suggest that in a purely national market the working of this process is in practice rather sluggish, as a result of market imperfections and sociological considerations whose significance is implicitly minimized in economic theory. Thus, after studying twenty American industries, Bain concluded that in many there was an inefficient fringe of small plants that tended to persist over time.[9] Again, the experience of the French economy between the wars tends to suggest that if entrepreneurial Darwinism does have any affinity to the natural variety, it is largely in the length of time each takes to produce any noticeable changes.[10] The dismantling of trade barriers within the Six and the accompanying policies on anti-trust and state aids however, augment national with international competition and are transforming the separate and cohesive national groups into a wider and more impersonal environment in which entrepreneurs are forced to adapt themselves to market conditions and are not so easily able to adjust those changing conditions to their own ends. The economic structures of markets are changing and simultaneously the whole climate of competition is undergoing a qualitative metamorphosis.

With the creation of conditions approximating those of an internal market throughout the Communities we may, therefore, expect the normal pressures of competition to work more effectively. In the least disturbing combination of circumstances, when economic growth is sufficiently rapid, a change in the market shares of the firms constituting an industry may not involve any

---

[9] Bain, *Industrial Organization*, p. 353.   [10] Sheahan, ch. 14.

real absolute reduction in the output of the least efficient enterprises, even though successive increments of demand may be
captured entirely by aggressive competitors. But there will
probably be some cases when we should expect some absolute
adjustment to be called for, although even then we should not
expect this adjustment process to lead to the complete disappearance of a particular industry from a member state. But we may
quite reasonably expect the general impact of such competitive
adjustment to bear rather more upon some of the states than upon
others.

To the extent that certain industries tend to be concentrated in
rather limited geographical areas within the various states, we have
here one possible cause of a regional employment problem. One
of the first examples of this kind of problem in the context of the
Communities was, as we shall see, raised by the weak competitive position of some of the Belgian coalmines, especially those
in the Borinage. In this case, of course, the efficiency of the Belgian pits was so obviously below that of others in the ECSC that
the Community had to go out of its way for a number of years
to seal off the Belgian coal market from competition from the
rest of the ECSC, and the potential competitive threat was
deliberately held in check—a deviation that proves the reality of
this first possibility.

(ii) *Changes in the Pattern of Trade.* Conventional economic
theory also suggests another way in which the integration process
might raise problems in the field of regional development, and
that is through its effects on the direction and volume of international trade. The development of the common market for coal
and steel has been accompanied by a marked increase in intra-
Community trade in those products. Similarly, the experience
of the general common market has witnessed a swift growth of
trade between the member states to the relative (but not absolute)
detriment of their trade with the rest of the world. In this particular sense, it is of the essence of a common market that it is
'inward looking'. The significance of these changing trading
patterns (which may not of themselves be new but simply a
strengthening of existing tendencies) lies in the influence they
have on frontier regions of the member states. Where these
frontiers are contiguous with those of another member state, the

gradual integration of the separate economies is transposing the frontier regions concerned from being the peripheral areas of their own national states to a more central position in the larger market as it evolves. Thus, the development of certain frontier regions such as the Belgian Ardennes and the Eiffel–Hunsrück area in Western Germany will probably be facilitated by the disappearance of the economic frontiers on which they have been located. To an equal extent, however, the maintenance of the common external tariff means that other regions that are on the borders of their own states continue to be far removed from the economic centre of gravity of the enlarged market. Indeed, it might be said that they become even more remote. The relevance of this dichotomy of frontier areas to regional development in the Community is that some of the areas that already present the regional problem in the most uncompromising form—Southern Italy and parts of South and West France—are in the category that will not enjoy the sudden artificial push towards the centre, but will, on the contrary, continue to be remote from the centre of economic affairs. It is also relevant to point out here that certain regions such as the Hamburg–Bremen area of Germany that are, to say the least, far from being regarded as regional problems at the present time, may well find that these changing trade flows bring them rather less than their former share of economic activity. This is because their present prosperity is in large measure based upon their overseas trade, especially with states bordering on the North Sea and the Baltic, and the increasing westward bias of the German economy is unlikely to provide a proportionate stimulus to these traditional trades.

(iii) *The Cumulative Concentration of Economic Activity.* In these two ways, therefore, via the influence of competition and changing patterns of trade, the realization of the common market will tend to make for regionally different growth patterns within the Community. But it may be that the adjustments of this kind that would be suggested by conventional economic theory are little more than the mildest aspects of a problem that in fact goes much deeper—the kind of possibility that preoccupied Professor Byé in his minority contribution to the Ohlin Report, and which was certainly taken into account by the Six in the Spaak Report leading to the Rome Treaty. One need only visualize an economic map of the Six to realize that the most highly developed regions tend to form a definite block of concentrated activity centring roughly on the Rhine/Rhône axis. This block, stretching from the Netherlands to Northern Italy, takes in most of the main industrial centres, including the coalmining, iron and steel, engineering, and chemical industries. It has been estimated that this area covers about 35 per cent of the land area of the EEC, takes in about 45 per cent of its population, and produces about 60 per cent of its gross product.[11]

The problem therefore arises as to whether the existence of such a comparatively concentrated bloc of economic growth exerts a drawing power that results in its own further growth to the relative or even absolute detriment of regions remote from this zone. Further, does the process of integration make such an outcome more or less likely?

The existence of a large area of vigorous economic expansion affects the regional distribution of future growth as a result of the interaction of the two opposing sets of forces that respectively work to promote on the one hand the further concentration of economic activity within the original area of growth and, on the other, the wider distribution of this growth as a spill-over into economically related regions. The former factors have been analysed as (using what seems to us the most straightforward terminology) *polarization*[12] effects, and the latter as *spread*[13] effects.

The polarization effects are based partly upon objective factors, partly upon subjective factors in the realm of social psychology. In the former we should place specific physical advantages possessed by an area, and the whole range of advantages generally classed as external economies. In the latter we should put the growth-orientated mentality that the operation of the objective factors promotes, with the result that their mutual interaction becomes a cumulative process.

The spread effects, on the other hand, represent a leakage of growth stimuli from the point where the growth process originated to other economically related regions. The most obvious

[11] European Parliamentary Assembly, *Report on Regional Policy in the EEC* (Birkelbach Report) (1963), p. 29.
[12] Albert O. Hirschman, *The Strategy of Economic Development* (1963), pp. 183–201.
[13] G. Myrdal, *Economic Theory and Under-Developed Regions* (1957), pp. 23–38.

type of such an inter-regional relationship would be where an urban industrial complex promotes economic activity in the surrounding rural area by its purchases of food and raw materials.

The fact that there are two such opposing sets of forces operating, the one making for polarization and the other for a spread of growth, should not be taken necessarily to imply any balance between them, but only that the most extreme tendencies are damped down. Nor does this line of argument imply that there is absolutely no tendency to equalization of factor incomes in various regions as a result of the movement of factors and the consequent lowering of marginal products in the receiving area and the raising of them in the donor area. The point is rather that preoccupation with the latter kind of static adjustment at the expense of appreciating the deeper significance of cumulative causation in the growth process misconstrues the real nature of the regional problem and thereby leaves it as intractable as ever.

How, then, may we expect integration to affect the working of the polarization tendencies and the subsequent spread effects that they engender? To prove that integration will have a significant effect upon regional growth and stagnation we need to be able to show that it will affect one of the tendencies we have discussed rather more than the other. In actual fact, while it is clear that integration accelerates the working of both sets of forces—via its effects on intra-Community trade, labour, and capital movements—there is no strictly logical economic reason to believe that the polarization effects will prevail over the spread effects rather than vice-versa. However, as the whole economic rationale of the integration movement is based upon an intensified application of traditional economic principles (relating to size of markets, competition, economies of scale, specialization, and so forth), it seems safest to assume that the regional disparities produced by the operation of these forces in the past will increase rather than diminish as integration proceeds in the absence of deliberate interventions to stop this occurring.

From a more political standpoint it would also seem that integration presents regional policy with a real threat. In the past most of what is termed regional policy in national states has amounted to financial concessions from the central government that encourage infrastructure and other investments in the region concerned. It would be unduly idealistic to suppose that such concessions are other than the result primarily of the region's political significance in the national state. The considerable restrictions which are inevitably imposed on national governments when they embark on a course of far-reaching integration with neighbouring states suggest that regions could well find their strongest prop somewhat undermined. Only if the Communities as such emphasize the general desirability of national regional policies and simultaneously strengthen them by the development of specifically Community policies of their own will success in this field be made possible.

As the emergence of effective common political institutions in Europe is still prevented and there is, therefore, no supranational political authority that the regions may hope to cultivate, the greatest importance must be attached to the existing machinery in the national states and to the economic techniques built into the treaties to promote regional development.

3. BACKGROUND TO COMMUNITY REGIONAL POLICY

An important preliminary point that should be emphasized at the outset is that regional policy in the Communities remains in practice to a very large extent the responsibility of the national governments and their agencies.[14] It would be quite wrong to regard the centre of gravity in regional policy as being transferred to Brussels by the process of integration in anything like the same way that the common agricultural policy brings about such a reorientation in agricultural affairs. The role of the Communities in this field is rather to assist the national authorities —for example by encouraging exchange of views and analysis of experiences, by making sure that they are kept fully aware of the implications of the wider economic framework of which their work now forms a part, and in general to help ensure the consistency of national regional policies, both with each other and with the obligations that the states have incurred as a result of integration. Even the main instruments of regional policy that are at the disposal of the Communities as such—we shall describe their operation briefly presently—have been conceived largely as complementary to national policies.

[14] EEC, *Dokumente der Konferenz über Fragen der regionalen Wirtschaft 1961*, Introductory Report by R. Marjolin (1961), p. 29.

It would neither be possible nor appropriate in a book of this kind to describe and appraise the ways in which the member states have tackled regional questions, but plainly it is the efficiency of this national machinery that determines the chances of success in regional policy.[15] Broadly speaking, one gets the impression that up to very recent years policy in both the European countries and the UK has been held back by the lack of really rigorous economic analysis of regional activity, and that this accounts for an almost uniform staleness of approach based upon infrastructure investment by the authorities, their subsidization of heterogeneous forms of private capital that can be persuaded to move in, discriminatory transport rate structures, and bans on industrial development in the Paris type of region. After many years of policies of this kind only moderate positive progress can be seen, in that only states such as Belgium, the Netherlands, and Germany, where the regional problem has been less severe, present an encouraging picture, whereas the hard-core problem regions, such as Southern Italy and parts of Southern and Western France, continue to cause concern.

Be that as it may, our task here is not to evaluate the various national versions of regional policy, but the more limited one of giving some idea of the specifically Community policies that impinge directly on these questions.

Before beginning to discuss these policies, however, there are two general points that may be mentioned at this stage.

The first is that as a counterweight to the rather gloomy picture we have been tending to draw, there are certain features of the contemporary economic scene that can be used to advantage for regional development. The most important of these is economic growth itself. If this can be maintained at a fairly high rate the prospects for steering some of it into places where it is badly needed are great enhanced. This is all the more likely to be true when one considers that some of the industries that are likely to figure prominently in the growth of the European economy are comparatively footloose in a way that the old growth industries of the nineteenth century, tied to the sources of energy

---

[15] Apart from the 1961 and 1964 Conferences organized by the Commission and the 1965 Rome Congress cited here, further details of national regional policies are set out in ECSC, *Arrangements to Facilitate the Establishment of New Economic Activities* (1962).

and raw materials, never could be. And even proximity to the sources of energy and raw materials now no longer dictates location in the main industrial bloc of the Common Market. The complete change in the energy market brought about by imported petroleum, American coal, and natural gas, means that if energy supplies do have an important bearing on location decisions, then their effect is now increasingly centrifugal. This, together with the growing significance of imported iron-ore, has influenced a number of steel firms to choose coastal locations for their most modern plants. In this way some of the peripheral regions of the Community may find that certain fundamental developments are beginning to work in their favour.[16]

Secondly, it may be thought that the emphasis placed upon competition in integrating the national economies is inimical to the interventionism that regional policy, and indeed, active manpower policy in general, implies. However, such a view could only be based upon a superficial reading of the treaties. An impressive list of treaty quotations could be made to show how questions of social welfare and employment policy are given importance as objectives in their own right in the Communities.[17] A statement by Herr von der Groeben, member of the Commission with special responsibility for competition, who presumably has no vested interest in minimizing the importance of that side of the Commission's work, is worth reproducing in this context:

I am convinced that it will not suffice merely to establish a competitive order in our Common Market. Over and above that we are obliged to create a just social order, and because of that we also require . . . to carry out a regional policy. The European Economic Community must do everything to make sure that the differences in the levels of welfare between the regions of the member states do not grow. In particular the discrepancies between the levels of development in the peripheral agricultural regions and the central industrial regions should not be permitted to increase, but must be successively reduced simultaneously with the progressive development of the Common Market.[18]

[16] A. Prate, 'Marché commun et politique regionale', *R. d'Écon. Politique*, I (Jan./Feb. 1964).

[17] J. Dedieu, 'The European Economic Community', a paper given at the OECD International Trade Union Seminar on Active Manpower Policy, Vienna, Sept. 1963, pp. 94–97.

[18] H. von der Groeben in EEC, *Dokumente der Konferenz über Fragen der regionalen Wirtschaft 1961*, ii. 18.

Von der Groeben also mentioned in the same address various ways in which regional policy might be regarded as positively complementary to other of the common policies. He mentioned, for example, the general problem of overcrowding in the conurbations and the possible divergence between social and private costs particularly likely in such circumstances, the increased utilization of resources made possible by more balanced regional growth, and the possibility of more active competition in the conventional sense presented by new enterprises founded in the regions.

These observations notwithstanding, it is necessary to be aware that certain aspects of the common policies could have adverse effects on regional development if implemented without regard to these considerations. Obviously the clearest case of such a possibility is the common policy on competition which in Article 92 (1) of the treaty condemns state aids to enterprises. However, the third paragraph of that Article makes provision for exemption from the general ban for aids that are part of a coherent regional policy. For this reason, and, even more, because of the special Protocol for Italy annexed to the Rome Treaty, one has the impression that the Italian authorities have not had to worry too much about whether their own system of aids had the effect of distorting competition in a manner incompatible with the treaty.[19] Besides, a distortion in the conditions of competition would only arise if the concessions granted to firms locating in the development regions were more than sufficient to offset the disadvantages of being there. In the present imperfectly developed state of knowledge about regional economics and location problems it would be very difficult in the majority of cases to decide in practice whether any such distortion in fact occurred. For competition policy, therefore, 'an imperative arises, to improve the technical instruments which allow the evaluation with the utmost precision of the whole of the disadvantages involved'.[20]

The other common policies that could clearly have adverse effects on regional development are transport, agriculture, and

[19] The problem of the legality of Italy's policy with regard to the South in the light of Art. 92 and the Protocol for Italy has been examined at length by U. Leanza in *Legislazione per il Mezzogiorno e Mercato Commune Europeo*, Study no. 10 promoted by SVIMEZ.

[20] Levi Sandri, Third (Rome) Congress p. 6.

energy. In Chapter 10, in which we dealt with transport in the EEC, we described how favourable transport rates have sometimes been used as aids to regional development, especially in Western Germany. Aspects of the common transport policy that would have adverse effects on regional development will only be implemented if agreed unanimously by the Council of Ministers. The common agricultural policy, if it functions in the way that is intended as described in Chapter 10, will inevitably have pronounced consequences for regional development. Quite apart from agricultural-price-policy decisions having adverse effects in certain areas, the whole policy of structural reform and raising the standards of living of workers in agriculture nearer to those in industry will require large increases in labour productivity, and, therefore, if surpluses are to be avoided, an acceleration of the rate at which workers leave the land. The importance that must be attached to retraining and resettlement schemes under these circumstances needs no emphasis. Finally, the common energy policy, via its effects on the profitability of coalmining, has obvious regional implications. In employment terms, of course, the implementation of the common energy policy will simply present the High Authority with much the same kind of problem as it has already had to tackle in its previous work on behalf of the coal industry—and much the same instruments will probably remain at its disposal to deal with them. Let us consider what these instruments are and how they have been used in the past.

4. EMPLOYMENT POLICY IN ECSC

The authors of the Paris Treaty foresaw the possibility that the process of establishing a common market would in some cases affect particular enterprises adversely and lead to unemployment. Such a possibility was recognized in one of the early Reports of the High Authority, which pointed out that:

Competition in the common market is designed to make higher productivity possible. The investment policy should promote a constant improvement of equipment and a continued rise in productivity. But there is no progress without change, and change—no matter what precautions are taken or how long the period envisaged—means the adaptation or elimination of the inefficient producer.[21]

[21] ECSC, *2nd Gen. Rep.* (1954), p. 163.

Granted that unemployment was likely to arise, it was recognized that measures would have to be devised to protect the workers involved. The treaty therefore gave the High Authority certain powers in Article 56 (*a*) to facilitate the retraining and resettlement of workers—usually called in this context readaptation, and (*b*) to make loans to enterprises to stimulate employment locally by industrial redevelopment.

(*a*) Readaptation Policy

The High Authority was empowered to grant non-repayable assistance for the following purposes: 'to contribute to the payment of compensation to tide workers over until they were able to obtain new employment; to contribute to the granting of resettlement allowances; to contribute to the technical retraining of workers who were forced to find new jobs'.

In all the above cases of assistance to workers the High Authority undertook to pay one-half of the cost on the understanding that the member state government paid the other half. However, it is necessary to point out that, whereas in the period up to 1960 the High Authority was allowed to make these grants in a wide variety of circumstances, thereafter these provisions only applied to unemployment caused by technical change. In 1959, therefore, by which time the possibility of serious structural unemployment in coal was imminent, the High Authority proposed to the Council of Ministers that Article 56 be amended, and in 1960, having secured the necessary ministerial agreement, a second clause was added to Article 56 by an Act of the European Parliament. This clause provides that 'should profound changes in the marketing conditions of the coalmining or of the iron and steel industries, not directly connected with the introduction of the Common Market, make it necessary for certain enterprises permanently to discontinue, curtail or change their activities', then at the request of interested member state governments, the High Authority can extend the facilities provided in Article 56.

The policy of the High Authority in assisting workers discharged as a result of the closure of enterprises can best be illustrated by two examples.

The first case concerns a reorganization within the Belgian coal industry. During 1958 eight pits in the Centre, Charleroi, and Liège coalfields were closed. As a result up to September of that year 2,600 workers were discharged. The Belgian government therefore applied for help and the High Authority agreed to assist the workers involved. The assistance took the following form. For one year from discharge the High Authority undertook to pay the workers a tide-over allowance. This allowance was to be based on the wages previously earned and was to be paid at a descending rate as a means of encouraging workers either to find new jobs suited to their skills or to undertake retraining. During the first four months the allowance was equal to 100 per cent of the wages previously earned, in the second four months it fell to 80 per cent, and in the last four months to 60 per cent. If during this period the workers obtained re-employment or agreed to undertake retraining, their pay was made up to a level equal to that previously earned. If in order to obtain re-employment the discharged workers had to move, they were entitled to claim a settling-in allowance and transport and removal expenses. The High Authority also undertook to contribute to the costs of retraining centres in proportion to the number of discharged workers attending.[22] This example is typical of the kind of arrangements made in the earlier years.

Secondly, in some cases the competition arising from the establishment of the common market led firms to reorganize rather than to close down. Thus in 1954 four previously independent iron and steel firms in the Loire district undertook a scheme of rationalization and modernization which involved their amalgamation in the form of the Compagnie des Forges et Ateliers de la Loire. Arising out of this, the High Authority was requested to assist in a readaptation scheme covering 1,500 workers who were to become redundant, but who within two years, after technical retraining, could be re-employed either in producing iron and steel or in mechanical engineering. The scheme involved the expenditure of 300 million French francs which was borne equally by the High Authority and the French government. During the period of reconversion workers were to receive their basic wage for their particular trade for a 44-hour week together with social insurance benefits. They were either to be employed within the enterprise on work of a general nature or on work particularly connected with the production side, or they might attend vocational training courses at a training centre

[22] ECSC, *7th Gen. Rep.* (1959), p. 224.

or at the works.[23] In 1958 the High Authority was able to report that the company had carried out its modernization and concentration programme without discharging any workers.[24] In general it may be said that coal-miners have been most prominent among the beneficiaries of these readaptation schemes, although to some extent the steel industry, especially in Italy, has also made use of these arrangements, and in the last few years the closure of iron-ore mines in Lorraine and Siegerland has again emphasized the need for such facilities.

How successful has the High Authority's policy of readaptation been?

In terms of numbers of workers for whom readaptation aid was appropriated and the size of these appropriations, the policy has been quite impressive. In Table 5 (p. 405) we show the total appropriation from March 1954 through January 1966 broken down by country and industry.

This table clearly indicates that, in terms of numbers of workers to whom appropriations were made, Germany was the main beneficiary, followed by Belgium, with France and Italy tying third. The Netherlands and Luxembourg have not made any calls upon readaptation funds. Coalmining employees have been the main recipients of such assistance, Germany and Belgium heading the list. The average appropriation works out at about $300 per head. This, of course, is doubled by an equal contribution from the government concerned. In the final analysis, therefore, the High Authority has been associated with per capita payments averaging $600 for about 218,000 workers. This is a significant achievement.

On the other hand this assessment must be qualified by the fact that the High Authority has in the main been content to make financial assistance available to those who have been laid off, either temporarily or permanently, and has not had to tackle, to any significant extent, what could be the much more difficult task of creating jobs for the unemployed. The High Authority has in fact relied upon workers, with or without retraining, themselves finding jobs on the spot or reasonably close at hand. Fortunately this has in general proved relatively easy, particularly as a result of the growing scarcity of labour in the late 1950s.

---

[23] ECSC, *3rd Gen. Rep.* (1955), pp. 152–3.
[24] Ibid. *6th Gen. Rep.* (1958), p. 192.

TABLE 5

High Authority Readaptation Assistance

($'000)

Country	Coal		Iron ore		Steel		Total by country	
	Workers	*Amounts*	*Workers*	*Amounts*	*Workers*	*Amounts*	*Workers*	*Amounts*
W. Germany	108,990	26,286	8,054	1,283	4,686	723	121,730	28,292
Belgium	47,307	14,750	37	5	1,691	735	49,035	15,490
France	11,182	4,428	3,094	1,405	6,688	1,619	20,964	7,452
Italy	6,180	2,876	1,247	851	16,394	9,845	23,821	13,572
Netherlands	2,700	690	—	—	—	—	2,700	690
Community	176,359	49,030	12,432	3,544	29,459	12,922	218,250	65,496

Source: ECSC, *14th Gen. Rep.* (1966, French), p. 325.

The Belgian coal industry is a particularly good example of the relatively easy re-employment of workers. In 1961 the High Authority reported that between 1956 and September 1960 21,000 workers had been laid off as a result of reorganization, but that only 2,300 workers remained unemployed; the majority, particularly of those underground, found new jobs quite quickly.[25] In 1961 another 6,000 were laid off, but the High Authority reported that 'many collieries are now needing more workers, after some years of reduced recruitment'.[26] In other countries the situation was much the same. In Germany, for example, in 1961 six collieries were closed in the Ruhr, Lower Saxony, Saar, and Aachen coalfields but the High Authority was confident of quick re-employment: 'the nation-wide labour shortage and the rising manpower requirements of the coalmining industry itself making for quick reabsorption.'[27]

This general tendency has, however, been subject to exceptions. In the first place, up to 1960, of the four countries which benefited from readaptation assistance (Germany, Belgium, France, and Italy) workers in the first three were relatively easily absorbed, but this was not true of Italy. A particular instance of this occurred in the reorganization of collieries in the Sulcis coalfields in Sardinia, begun in 1957, which involved a concentration of production in the most economic pits. The High Authority agreed to assist workers made redundant by the reorganization, but in 1959 it had to report that the miners had experienced great difficulty in obtaining alternative employment and that it would be necessary for the Italian government to consider establishing new sources of employment in the Sulcis region.[28]

Secondly, although it is clear that in most countries workers were quickly reabsorbed, this did not apply to workers over fifty or to those suffering from physical disability.[29]

There can, however, be little doubt that if, particularly from the end of the 1950s onwards, when there was considerable structural unemployment in coal, there had not been a fairly general shortage of labour, the High Authority readaptation efforts would almost certainly have proved inadequate. Pockets

[25] ECSC, *9th Gen. Rep.* (1961), p. 276.
[26] Ibid. *10th Gen. Rep.* (1962), p. 427.
[27] Ibid. p. 426.   [28] ECSC, *7th Gen. Rep.* (1959), p. 225.
[29] Ibid. *9th Gen. Rep.* (1961), p. 275.

of unemployment could in this case only have been dealt with either by introducing new employment-creating opportunities in the areas affected, which is by no means an easy task, or by inducing workers to move to areas where jobs were available. In connexion with the latter it is clear from the experience gained by the High Authority in one of its earliest readaptation schemes that extreme difficulties would have been experienced if the latter course had been followed. Thus in 1954 the High Authority agreed to the request by the French government for financial assistance in connexion with a plan produced by the Charbonnages de France to close collieries in the Centre-Midi coalfield and to re-employ 5,000 miners so displaced in the Lorraine coalfield. Over a three-year period the scheme was to cost 1,000 million French francs to cover resettlement compensation, moving, and transportation expenses. The High Authority agreed to meet half the cost.[30] Great hopes were entertained that this first experiment in readaptation would prove a resounding success. In fact it proved to be something of a failure. In 1956 the High Authority reported that up to the end of 1955 560 miners had taken advantage of the Community's offer;[31] and it is significant that ultimately the High Authority proposed to the French government that they should join in examining opportunities for re-employment on the spot.

Basically the scheme failed because the Centre-Midi miners were highly immobile (a characteristic which the High Authority has more recently attributed to miners and iron and steelworkers in general). This immobility can be ascribed to many factors. First, and probably foremost, the miners were reluctant to leave their homes, to cut themselves off from their families, and to move to a new and strange part of the country where the climate and language were different, where assimilation would be difficult, and where discipline in the collieries was more rigorous. Their feelings were played on by a whole host of local forces in the Centre-Midi district which opposed the scheme, some calling for efforts to provide new employment on the spot.[32] Difficulties with housing for families and inadequate barracks for single miners also proved to be a deterrent to mobility.[33] There is also

---

[30] Ibid. *2nd Gen. Rep.* (1964), pp. 166–7.
[31] Ibid. *4th Gen. Rep.* (1956), p. 215.
[32] Diebold, p. 408.   [33] ECSC, *3rd Gen. Rep.* (1955), p. 152.

14*

some evidence that wages in the Lorraine collieries, at least at first, were below those enjoyed in the Centre-Midi coalfield.[34]

(b) Redevelopment Policy

This is the ECSC term for taking work to the workers—in this case by granting loans to enterprises to stimulate the demand for labour in certain areas. As with readaptation policy, the High Authority up to 1960 had a rather constrained legal basis from which to work, unsuitable for dealing with the structural unemployment that began to emerge in coal at the end of the 1950s. However, since the amendment of the treaty in 1960, the High Authority has been able to undertake certain initiatives in industrial redevelopment.

Up to the beginning of 1965 Italy was the main recipient of redevelopment finance, followed by Belgium, France, and Germany in that order, as emerges from Table 6 (p. 409).

Redevelopment in Belgium, which will serve as an illustration of High Authority policy, has been concentrated in the Liège coalfield and the Borinage. In 1961 a request was received from a Liège iron and steel enterprise, La Société Phoenix-Works that planned to instal additional galvanizing plant which would create 470 new jobs. The High Authority responded by granting a loan of about £700,000 for 20 years at 4⅞ per cent, the enterprise for its part undertaking to reserve a number of jobs for discharged mineworkers. In the same year the Société Provinciale d'Industrialisation de Liège was set up as a joint public-private company to speed up regional development. The company aimed to create 4,000 new jobs by building factories for rent or purchase, by creating a basic infrastructure of public utilities as an inducement to industrial development, and by preparing sites for factories. The High Authority loaned the company about £810,000 for 20 years at 4⅞ per cent with an initial redemption-free period of 4 years. The loan was guaranteed by the Belgian government, which agreed to reduce the interest rate to as little as 1 per cent in respect of some parts of the company's plan. In 1964 the High Authority was able to report that as a result of the company's activities a number of enterprises had been attracted, one making television sets and domestic radios.

In the Borinage the High Authority has sponsored two new

[34] Diebold, p. 409.

TABLE 6

ECSC Redevelopment Schemes

Company	Production	Location	Jobs created	High authority loan (£'000 approx.)
Aleurope	Aluminium	Ghlin-Baudour, Belgium	500	900
Phoenix-Works	Iron & steel	Liège, Belgium		700
Pirelli-Sacic	Rubber	Ghlin-Baudour	500–600	1,080
Soc. Prov. d'Industrialisation de Liège	Industrial estate	Liège	4,000	810
Alumétal	Metal framework	Champagnac, France	–	26
Soc. Bretonne de Fonderie et Mécanique	Castings	Lorient-Hennebont France	800	1,200
Soc. Chaudronnerie Tôlerie de l'Aveyron	Warm-air generators	Aubin, France	224	70
Esba	Seamless stockings	St. Éloy-les-Mines, France	250	115
Birbach	Needles & wires	Unna, Germany	70–90	18
Kautex-Werke	Thermoplastics	Wissen, Germany	300	227
Carbosarda	Coal & electricity	Porto Vesme, Sardinia	2,000–4,000	5,357
Total redevelopment loans by High Authority (approx.)				£10·5 *mill.*

Source: European Community, Apr. 1965, p. 11.

industrial ventures. In 1961 the Société Aleurope proposed to build an aluminium plant at Ghlin-Baudour capable of employing about 500 workers and producing initially about 12,000 metric tons of aluminium sheet per annum. The High Authority agreed to assist the project and granted a loan of about £900,000 on condition that the company recruited 30 per cent of its male workers and 25 per cent of its total workers from among miners discharged as a result of pit closures. In 1962 the High Authority granted the Société Pirelli-Sacic a loan of £1,080,000 to build, also at Ghlin-Baudour, a factory producing rubber products such as hosing, tubing, belting, foam, &c. The initial intake of workers was to be between 500 and 600, and 40 per cent of the new jobs for male workers were to be allocated to discharged miners.

The High Authority has estimated that the number of jobs provided by the eleven schemes that it has helped finance amounted to about 7,000, although it is not clear just how large a proportion of these were taken up by discharged ECSC workers, nor how much extra employment was created as an indirect result of these original investments. Table 6 above shows that the total value of the loans made in this connexion was about £10·5 million. According to M. Roger Reynaud, a member of the High Authority, this sum represents about 25 per cent of the total capital invested in the eleven projects.[35] The total investment actually required to create one new job was, therefore, running at about £6,000 on the average in the early 1960s, which compares (how directly it is difficult to say) with a figure of about £2,000–£3,000 for the UK.[36] There is every sign that the activity of the Communities in this field will be extended in the future, as agreement was reached in 1965 to provide redevelopment finance at more favourable interest rates in the future, and to increase the permissible degree of participation by the High Authority to a maximum of 30 per cent.

5. EMPLOYMENT POLICY IN EEC

(a) The Free Movement of Labour

Measures to promote the free movement of goods and factors of production within the Communities are part of a policy of creating unified internal market conditions. Labour mobility within the coal and steel industries was provided for in the Paris Treaty and has been extended to the general common market also. While the importance of labour mobility (especially of young workers) should be assessed in political as well as economic terms, it is only the latter that concern us here. This economic importance is clear enough. The ability of regions facing labour shortages to obtain additional supplies from areas with a surplus contributes to easing the immediate problems of both recipient and donor. On the other hand this is far from implying that in the

---

[35] R. Reynaud, 'New Trends in Industrial Redevelopment', *European Community*, Apr. 1965, p. 11.
[36] Information made available by government of Northern Ireland.

Communities migration is regarded as the best answer to regional problems. On the contrary, the Commission has gone on record as being of the opinion that 'whenever industry can move to the workers this is the best answer'.[37] Furthermore, migration must be seen in the perspective of the generally high employment rate prevailing throughout the greater part of the Common Market, five of the Six member states being as much in the full employment category as the UK, a full employment country by any reasonable standards. In practice, it is only Southern Italy that has been, and is likely to continue to be, a donor region on any significant scale. But the main impact of this Italian migration has been contained within Italy itself, and the net flow from Italy to other Community countries has tended to fall in recent years as national unemployment has been brought down.[38]

But however optimistic one may be about stimulating economic growth in regions of high unemployment or underemployment, or however small a proportion of the total labour force ultimately comes to be accounted for by migrant labour, it is only common sense to realize that some migration will continue to occur, and to devise policies that will allow this to be effected smoothly.

Article 48 of the Rome Treaty defines free movement of labour—which must be achieved by 1970—as the right to move freely throughout the Community to accept offers of employment actually made, to reside in any part of the Community for that purpose, and to live there after having been employed there. It prohibits any discrimination in employment between Community workers on grounds of nationality (although employment in public administration is not subject to these provisions). How has the Common Market in fact approached this goal of free labour mobility? Certainly not by any indiscriminate promotion of migration but by a carefully phased policy designed to achieve the desired goal without disruptions.

In the first phase, which ended in September 1962, vacancies were compulsorily notified in the labour exchanges of the home country for three weeks before they were passed on to other Community countries. Even in this first phase, however, the

[37] EEC, *5th Gen. Rep.* (1962), p. 147.
[38] Unemployment in Italy fell from 1,958,000 in 1954 to 1,162,000 in 1962 (Dedieu, OECD International Trade Union Seminar on Active Manpower Policy, p. 107).

temporary preference for the home market could be waived in special cases—where an employer asked for a worker by name, perhaps because of an existing family or trade relationship.

The fact that labour mobility made possible in this way could in fact be rendered nugatory by organizational impediments was, of course, recognized and taken into account. The most obvious of such impediments—non-transferable social security rights— was in fact made the subject of special attack by Article 51 of the Rome Treaty, and the results of this and the supplementary implementing regulations derived from it are (*a*) equality of entitlement to social security for all nationals of Community countries; (*b*) aggregation of periods of insurance and employment in more than one country, both for entitlement to benefit and for calculations of its amount; and (*c*) payment of most benefits in any Community country.[39] Again, the possibility that trade union recognition might cause similar practical difficulties seems to have been eliminated: workers of any Community country enjoy membership rights equivalent to those of nationals in the state where they wish to settle. This in turn has required co-operative efforts in drawing up agreed lists of acceptable qualifications and some harmonization of job classifications. Also, labour mobility is not frustrated in practice by placing difficulties in the way of a worker's family, as they too are endowed with all necessary residential and employment rights. A special bilateral labour agreement between Germany and Italy signed in February 1965 gives Italian labour in Germany equal status with German from practically every point of view. In the past, discrimination with regard to housing had weakened the effectiveness of previous schemes, but under the 1965 agreement such discrimination is directly attacked.

But perhaps the most important step taken during the first phase was the creation of an embryonic European Employment Exchange whose task is not only to match up workers and vacancies but to do so, as required by the treaty, in a way that avoids serious threats to labour's standards in the recipient regions and industries. Some idea of the early work of this European Coordination Office, as it is called, may be gained from the following brief account of its activities.

[39] J. J. Ribas, 'Social Security in the European Community', *Community Topics*, no. 18, 1965, p. 10.

The Office collates the statistical data supplied quarterly by the member states in accordance with identical schedules laid down by the Office. It draws up and distributes at the beginning of each quarter a list of regions and occupations scheduled by each country as having a shortage or surplus of manpower. It makes quarterly general reports and an annual report on clearing operations and placings within the Community. The Office is studying what 'uniform criteria' should be adopted to bring into line Member States' methods of assessing the labour market situation. Lastly it has begun to examine means of giving workers, employers, and labour exchanges more information on the manpower situation in each region of the Community.[40]

It might also be added that this early attempt at organizing the Community labour market is far from passive, as the Six are pursuing a common policy in vocational training based upon quantitative and qualitative forecasting of manpower requirements.

During the second phase of the policy on labour mobility, the creation of a Community labour market was pushed forward in several directions: the temporary preference for the domestic market allowed in the first phase was greatly reduced, and workers from other Community countries were allowed to acquire more rapidly the full rights of domestic workers in such matters as changing jobs and election to works' councils.

(b) The European Social Fund

The gradual introduction of free labour mobility that has been described relates, of course, to mobility in the geographical sense. But flexibility in the labour force also requires labour to be mobile between occupations as well as between geographical areas. It is the purpose of the Social Fund to facilitate in a practical way the realization of whatever degree of labour mobility of either kind is required in the Community.

The broad lines on which the Fund is to operate are laid down in Articles 123–8. The main feature of its policy is that, subject to certain conditions, it will reimburse the governments of the member states with 50 per cent of any expenditures they incur in retraining or resettling unemployed or underemployed labour, or in supporting the wage level of workers who are temporarily laid off or placed on short time as a result of the conversion of their

[40] EEC, *6th Gen. Rep.* (1963), p. 35.

enterprises to other lines of production. The retraining grants are only payable when retraining is the sole means of bringing the workers back into employment, and are then only paid when the worker has been employed for at least six months in his new occupation. Similarly, the resettlement allowance is only payable when the worker concerned has been obliged to change his place of residence, and then only when he has been employed for at least six months in his new post. Likewise, support given to workers' wages (up to a level of 90 per cent of their previous gross wages) is only paid with respect to reconversion schemes that have been submitted to the Commission via the government of the state concerned and have been approved by the former before implementation. It is not necessary for a worker to have to move out of his own country to benefit from the activity of the Fund, and the reconversion of an enterprise considered here need not be necessitated by the working of the new forces of Common Market. It is also important to mention that grants under all these three headings may only be paid direct to governments for schemes that they themselves organize or supervise, about sixty-eight agencies having been recognized for this purpose by 1965.[41] Funds are only payable *after* the relevant expenditure has been incurred. In other words, the initiative for the use of this Fund lies entirely with the member states. While this at least permits each government to adopt the kind of schemes best suited to its own requirements, it also, unfortunately, tends to permit the coexistence of schemes of differing intrinsic merit. For example, up to 1962 only France and Germany operated schemes to help migrating workers.[42] This is typically the kind of field where upward social harmonization seems desirable. It is likely to come about as a result of trade union pressure upon their respective governments to improve schemes where they compare poorly with those in other member states, and through increasing government awareness of alternative and superior approaches to these problems as national labour ministries liaise more closely. This is all the more likely to occur as the Fund does not have to operate within the limits of a fixed budget: it will be supplied by the member governments with any funds it needs to discharge its legitimate functions. The proportion of the

[41] EEC, *8th Gen. Rep.* (1965), p. 247.
[42] R. Colin Beever, *Trade Unions and the Common Market* (PEP, 1962), p. 67.

Fund's expenses that the various states have agreed to provide is different from the scale of their contributions to the general budget of the Community, as may be seen from Table 7.

TABLE 7

Scale of Contributions to the European Social Fund and the General Budget of the Community

(per cent)

	To the Social Fund	To general Community budget
Belgium	8·8	7·9
Western Germany	32	28
France	32	28
Italy	20	28
Luxembourg	0·2	0·2
Netherlands	7	7·9

Source: Rome Treaty, Art. 200.

It is not possible to decide exactly how these contributions were arrived at, but one would assume that the general intention was to help Italy; and some idea of the international redistribution of income in fact brought about by the Fund may be obtained by considering some aspects of its operations up to the present time.

(i) *Retraining and Resettlement.* Data on the operations of the Fund in these fields up to the end of 1964 are set out in Table 8 (p. 416).

The Fund made its first awards in 1962. These related to applications for grants in respect of retraining and resettlement schemes that had been effected in the very first years of the Common Market. In 1958 and 1959 a total of nearly 183,000 unemployed workers were found posts by means of schemes that later gained the support of the Fund. Of these, about 103,000 were retrained and 79,200 (all of them Italians) were resettled. France took most of these workers (48,000), followed by Germany (27,000) and the Benelux states (4,000). The sums paid over by

TABLE 8

Expenditure by the Social Fund on Retraining and Resettlement

Decision in		Retraining	Resettlement
1962	Total exp. $	11,500,000	800,000
	No. of workers	103,000	79,200
	$/worker	112	10
1963	Total exp. $	7,246,603	314,874
	No. of workers	38,430	41,898
	$/worker	189	8
1964	Total exp. $	4,259,875	379,644
	No. of workers	16,489	52,761
	$/worker	258	7
1965	Total exp. $	5,845,159	1,355,395
	No. of workers	16,309	105,566
	$/worker	358	13

Sources : Levi Sandri, *Premier bilan du fonds social européen*, Doc. no.
V/6043/63-F, 1963, p. 4; EEC, *6th Gen. Rep.* (1963), pp. 207–8;
7th Gen. Rep. (1964), pp. 243–4; *8th Gen. Rep.* (1965), p. 244;
9th Gen. Rep. (1966, German), pp. 264–5.

the Fund as its 50 per cent contribution to the expenses of retraining and resettling these 183,000 men amounted to about
$ 12·3 million.

In 1963 the Fund made disbursements of $7,561,477, by far
the largest proportion of which was for retraining as distinct
from resettlement, in respect of 80,328 workers.

In Belgium, France, Italy, and the Netherlands most of the
workers who were retrained were found employment in secondary industry, especially building and the metal trades. In
Germany, however, most of those retrained were placed in the
services sector. Of workers retrained in Italy, only a few, it
seems, were absorbed in the South. For most of them re-
employment involved a move either to the North or to another
country of the EEC, Germany being the Community country
that drew most upon the Italian labour market at that time.

As a result of its activities up to the end of 1965 the Fund had effected a net transfer of about $4·7 million to Italy and the Netherlands (nearly all of it in fact to the former) from other member states, especially Germany, whose excess of contributions over receipts was running at a level of about $3·3 million.

When discussing the general principles on which the Fund is operated we suggested that there would probably be some tendency for governments to improve those aspects of their schemes that compared unfavourably with those operated in other parts of the Common Market. There is some evidence that this has in fact tended to occur. Thus, while per capita disbursements from the Fund on retraining schemes were about $112 in 1962, this figure had risen to $189 in 1963, to $258 in 1964, and again to $358 in 1965. As disbursements from the Fund cover only 50 per cent of the costs of approved schemes, the actual cost of the schemes was running at over $700 in the last period, which probably represents something more than purely nominal retraining. On the other hand the low figure for disbursements for resettlement probably represents little more than the 50 per cent contribution to the cost of a railway ticket.

(ii) *Support of Wages during Conversion of Enterprises.* The work of the Social Fund up to 1963 was concerned entirely with retraining and resettlement schemes. But there is, as we have mentioned, a further type of activity that comes within the ambit of the Fund. It is empowered to make governments grants of 50 per cent of any expenses they incur in supporting at 90 per cent of their normal level the wages of workers who are temporarily laid off or put on short time as a result of the conversion of their enterprises to different types of production. The necessity for such conversion need not be attributable to the operation of the Common Market itself, nor need the firm concerned be a purely Common Market enterprise in character. Indeed, the only request to the Fund under this heading would have been inadmissible had the latter criterion been relevant. The particular case involved is especially interesting as it is complicated by the fact that a state aid to the enterprise concerned was an integral part of the scheme.

Very briefly, the details of this case were as follows.[43] The

---

[43] Comité du Fonds Social Européen, *Avis du Comité du Fonds social européen*

management of the Belgian Ford Motor Company's factory at
Antwerp wished to discontinue the assembly of cars and trucks
there and to concentrate the work of the factory on the manufacture of certain parts for tractors, and the assembly of tractors
using additional parts supplied from other Ford plants. The
tractors would be marketed both within the Community and in
third countries. Ford's assembly of cars and trucks would be
switched from the Antwerp works to other Ford plants, especially
to a new one at Genk in Limbourg, a region that was in need of
the extra employment. This reorganization would require the
temporary suspension of 1,164 of the 2,223 workers at the
Antwerp plant. To support the wages of these workers at about
90 per cent of their normal level during their period of redundancy would cost the Belgian government about $1,085,453. To
qualify for a grant of 50 per cent from the Fund for such expenses, the Belgian government had to submit the whole scheme
to the Committee on the Social Fund and to obtain the latter's
prior approval. Besides being willing to support the wages of the
workers during the reorganization of the plant, the Belgian
government was intending to grant the Ford Company a loan of
about $20 million, with a 3·5 per cent reduction in the interest
rate to facilitate the implementation of the scheme. The Committee on the Social Fund ruled that it was prepared to make the
50 per cent grant in support of the employees' wages on condition that the subsidy element in the rest of the scheme met the
approval of the Commission and that the effects of the project on
the general employment situation in the Community would not
be unfavourable.

It is here that the difficulty seems to have arisen. For the
competitive process to function satisfactorily it was necessary
that the treaty should prohibit distortions in the conditions of
competition such as would arise from subsidies. It was recognized,
of course, that such subsidies might be justified in certain
circumstances—as instruments of regional policy, for example—
but that would be a question for the Commission to decide on the
facts of specific cases. In the case of the Ford factory at Antwerp
it would seem that the subsidy could not be justified in any of

---

*à la Commission concernant une demande d'approbation préalable présentée à la
Commission pour un projet de reconversion; Belgique—S. A. Ford Motor Company
Belgium à Anvers, V/4007/64–F.*

the ways permitted by the treaty. Antwerp was not a region with an abnormally low standard of living, nor was unemployment or underemployment serious there, nor was the proposed manufacture of tractors an important project of common European interest. Quite the reverse, existing capacity in the Community was already in excess of output and this expansion in Belgium would create further difficulties for French and German producers. As a result of these considerations, therefore, the Commission requested the Belgian government to withdraw its subsidy before the end of October 1965,[44] the Social Fund withheld any support from the maintenance of wages during the conversion, and the embarrassment of having a European welfare fund make the first grant on behalf of one of the wealthiest American companies was avoided.

Although the Social Fund has been operating for only a comparatively limited period, it seems that this experience has been enough to suggest various ways in which its scope and administration might be improved. Broadly speaking, criticisms of the Fund have been made to the effect that its administrative provisions are unnecessarily rigid and that its limitation to dealing with the cruder existing kinds of unemployment and underemployment is increasingly irrelevant to present economic conditions.

On the first point it does seem as if the procedure for obtaining aid from the Fund is unduly complicated. Firms contemplating conversion to other activities have to get prior approval from both their national governments and the Commission. For workers to qualify for benefit they must register at the employment exchange and no other suitable work must be available for them. They may well, therefore, be lost to other firms in this process, which in any event might imply a higher degree of publicity for a firm's investment plans than is desirable in a competitive situation.

But the second criticism—that the scope of the Fund was not conceived widely enough—is the more fundamental. For example, the Fund can help support wages but cannot make any contribution to the costs of technical conversion of plants, which are

---

[44] EEC, *8th Gen. Rep.* (1965), p. 81; in answer to Written Question no. 79 in the European Parliament addressed to the Commission by M. Laan, the former confirmed in February 1966 that the Belgian government had met its obligations in this matter.

likely to be much higher. Also, the conversions that the Fund can support seem to be limited to complete changes in the range of production and to exclude conversion to the manufacture of related products even when new plant needs to be installed. Finally, and of crucial importance, the Fund cannot take any initiative to anticipate difficulties in the labour market by supporting retraining for workers whose jobs are threatened but who are not yet actually unemployed.

These general criticisms are indirectly borne out by the data in Table 8. Each successive year has seen a reduction in the total number of men being retrained. This is because such support is limited to those who are actually unemployed and the incidence of unemployment has been greatly reduced. It is in the more difficult tasks of anticipation, prevention, and guidance that the Social Fund could play an important role in improving the adaptability of manpower in the Community. Aware of these problems and prospects, the Commission submitted certain proposals to the Council of Ministers in January 1965 for extending the scope of the Fund. These proposals included (*a*) support of retraining for those not actually unemployed but threatened with unemployment; (*b*) support of wages for unemployed workers pending location of a new enterprise in their locality; (*c*) contribution to the expenses of constructing vocational training centres in areas where they are especially needed; and (*d*) contributions to special housing schemes for migrant workers.

(c) *The European Investment Bank*

The concern of the founders of the EEC with regional questions is most clearly expressed by their action in creating a special institution—the European Investment Bank—which would have foremost among its objectives the support of projects for developing the less developed regions of the Community.

The existence of the bank, whose operations should be seen against the background of the rest of the economic policy of the Community, especially those parts that are discussed in this chapter, represents a specific Community commitment in what has previously been one of the most intractable fields of national policy. The treaty designates in Article 30 three spheres of operations for the bank. It is to use its resources in financing underdeveloped regions of the Community. In fact, as early as 1958 the board of governors laid down that a substantial proportion of its loans would be available for this purpose. Secondly, the bank may make loans available to enterprises that are forced to convert or modernize by the development of the Common Market if the projects concerned cannot be entirely financed by the usual sources of capital in the member states. In this case there must be a definite causal connexion between these investments and the reductions of tariffs, quantitative restrictions, state aids, &c. brought about by the implementation of the Common Market. Thirdly, the bank may participate in projects that are of common interest to several member states and which cannot be entirely financed by their ordinary resources. In 1963 the bank's sphere of lending was extended to the Associated States (Greece and Turkey) and in 1964 to the eighteen Associated African States and Madagascar and the overseas territories of the Six.

The advantage of the existence of the bank to the regional economies lies in the fact that, operating on a non-profit basis, it disposes of funds that are specially earmarked for these purposes (the $1,000 million of its capital) subscribed by the member states, and that it may also divert further resources into these channels by its ability to raise loans cheaply as a first-class borrower on the international capital market. Although the bank has a separate legal identity (unlike the Social Fund) it is required to work in the closest co-operation with the governments of the member states and the Commission in order that its actions may be consistent with those instigated by these authorities. The bank also co-operates with the World Bank (in 1959 its first three loans in Southern Italy were made in co-operation with the latter) and with the High Authority, with which it jointly financed a project in Southern Italy in 1960. Indeed this aspect of the bank's lending policy—that is, its participation in projects alongside other sources of finance—is one of its most important features. It limits its lending to the last increment of finance (*Spitzenfinanz-ierung*) that is still needed to start a scheme when all other sources of funds have been exhausted. In this way its role is comparable with that of the High Authority in financing developments in the coal and steel industries (we discuss this aspect of the work of the High Authority in our 'Note on Investment Planning in the ECSC' (pp. 428–9). The significance of the bank's participation is, therefore, much greater than the sums involved would of themselves suggest. Like the High Authority again, its borrowing is not limited to the capital markets of the Community (nor, for that matter, is its lending limited to Community firms) but it floats loans in whatever it judges to be the most favourable centre. Thus in 1961 it raised funds in Switzerland as well as the Netherlands. In the event of the bank's not being able

TABLE 9

European Investment Bank—Sources of Capital and Distribution of Loans 1958 through 1964

Countries	% contribution to bank's capital*	No. of projects	EIB loans ($ mill.)	Each country's share in the total (%)
I. Ordinary Loans				
Member countries				
Belgium	8·65	1	4·8	1
Germany	30	3	32·4	7
France	30	11	71·0	15
Italy	24	59	310·7	67
Luxembourg	0·2	1	4·0	1
Netherlands	7·15	—	—	—
	100	75	422·9	91
Associated countries				
Greece	—	8	36·8	8
	100	83	459·7	99
II. Special Loans				
Turkey	—	2	5·4	1
Grand total	100	85	465·1	100

* As at the end of 1964 only 25 per cent of the bank's capital was paid up.

Source: European Investment Bank, *Ann. Rep. for 1964* (1965), p. 53.

to raise funds on suitable terms from the capital markets, the governments of the member states have undertaken to provide it with special loans in such circumstances to the tune of $100 million annually up to a maximum of $400 million.

As with the Social Fund, the best way of summarizing the scope and nature of the bank's activities is to tabulate its sources of finance and the distribution of its loans. This is done in Table 9 (p. 422).

This table clearly shows that the bulk of the bank's lending has been directed towards Italy and France: in fact, the loans have, of course, gone to the needy southern parts of these countries. It is also instructive to inquire what kind of activities have gained the support of the bank, and an analysis of its lending by industries is therefore set out in Table 10.

TABLE 10

Breakdown of EIB Loans by Economic Sector, at 31 December 1964

(Ordinary and special loans)

Sector	No. of projects	EIB loans $m.	Each sector's share in total (%)
Agricultural improvements	4	33·8	7
Transport	11	132·2	29
Power	11	79·6	17
Telecommunications	1	16·0	3
Industry:	58	203·5	44
Mining	2	2·0	
Iron & steel	3	48·9	
Building materials	7	13·5	
Glass & pottery	4	6·4	
Paper pulp & paper	4	17·5	
Mechanical engineering	13	26·1	
Chemicals	11	74·0	
Textiles & clothing	3	3·1	
Leather	1	0·3	
Foodstuffs	10	11·7	
Total	85	465·1	100

Source: European Investment Bank, *Ann. Rep. for 1964*, p. 54.

The large proportion (44 per cent) going to industry is note-worthy. While many of the bank's first loans were to large enter-prises it is now tending to increase its lending to medium-sized concerns. In all cases, of course, the bank has only provided a small proportion of the total finance needed by a project—on the average in the region of $5·5 million or about 23 per cent. The sizes of the loans have, however, varied from $24 million, to aid the construction of a motorway from the Brenner Pass to Bolzano or steelworks in Naples-Bagnoli, to much smaller sums, such as $400,000 to a shirt factory in Chieti-Scalo (Abruzzi).

(d) *Italconsult's 1965 Plan for Southern Italy*

The Rome Treaty contains a basic commitment to balanced expansion. Southern Italy represents the most unmistakable challenge to this idea in its regional application. How is the EEC proposing to contribute to a solution of the problem?

Obviously the Italian government has been actively concerned with this extreme example of economic dualism for many years and has evolved certain policies in this field ranging from the grants and loans of the Cassa per il Mezzogiorno to a legal requirement that all state enterprises should locate at least 40 per cent of their new investments in the South. But although the relative gap between the North and the South may not have been increasing in recent years, the absolute gap is almost certain to be widening still. That great efforts have been made to stimulate industrial development in the South is evident from the scale and type of plants that have located there in recent years. These include Italsider's £240 million steelworks at Taranto, ENI's £90 million petrochemical plant at Gela, Sicily, the Montecatini-Shell £600 million petrochemical plant, and big investments by the Breda Group in heavy- and precision-engineering plants at Brindisi, and ENI's £25 million petrochemical plant at Ferradina. But despite all these basic investments there has been no cumulative concentration of further industrial economic activity around these major plants. There exist only industries processing local farm produce and a few others such as building materials enjoying natural protection. The big new steel, engineering, and chemical plants remain isolated instances of economic advancement in a region that is still dominated by a backward agriculture. Industry, both implanted and local, is

what has been called (not too helpfully) the 'short-cycle' type—
that is, its development is comparatively self-contained and has
not called into being the host of ancillary trades that give to the
big industrial zones both their dynamism and their cohesion. In
the Commission's view the failure of additional enterprises to
locate in the South was basically because the external economies
of locating there compared badly with the multiplicity of opportunities in the North.

For the Commission, therefore, the basic questions that had to
be answered for Southern Italy were these. Starting with the
existing dispersed short-cycle industries, how could they be
linked up together? How many and what types of other enterprises should be encouraged to move into parts of the South to
result in—necessarily in a modest way—the kind of extensive and
self-sustaining industrial growth zone already found in more
fortunate parts of the Community? In other words, how could
the conditions in which external economies arise actually be
created? This was the problem as seen by the Commission and
which it handed over in 1962 to an important firm of economic
consultants, Italconsult, for detailed consideration.

Italconsult made a 300-column input-output table of the Bari–
Ferradina–Taranto–Brindisi area, showing the goods and services
used and produced in each of the main productive activities of the
region. With a detailed map of the economic life of the region
before them, the consultants then had to consider what activities
might be able to make use of these particular resources as they
existed in the given location. In other words, what industries would
be attracted by the existence of steel, engineering, and plastics
industries, abundant cheap labour and sites, and proximity
to the Mediterranean markets. It was in looking for specific
industries that might fit these requirements that Italconsult
came to place great emphasis upon a particular aspect of external
economies. To be precise, it was found that the existence of
many firms presupposed the existence of certain other specialized
firms supplying them with components or providing maintenance
for plant. In many ways it is the firms doing this subcontracting or
subsidiary work that are of critical importance in the development process, for such firms cannot be competitive themselves
unless they too are able to operate on a large scale. Thus as the
Commission has put it:

it is quite clear that, for 'complex cycle' industries, an entrepreneur can only reasonably envisage manufacturing a finished product in centres where he can find all the industries ancillary to his own branch. Conversely, a subcontractor will only set up in an area with both an adequate market in the shape of firms requiring his specialised services and also the ancillary industries without which he himself cannot operate.[45]

In its essentials, therefore, Italconsult's plan is to establish simultaneously all the ancillary trades needed by the main branch which it is desired to promote, and to establish a sufficient number of users in that branch to provide a large enough market to support at least one firm of optimum size in each of the ancillary trades.

The main industrial branch chosen for development in this way was engineering, based on the existing facilities at Taranto and Brindisi. Eight sub-branches of the engineering industry (termed the 'motor' industries) are to be established. These are: (1) the manufacture of heavy structures such as bridges; (2) cooking stoves, baths, radiators, hollow metalware; (3) fuel-oil burners and centrifugal pumps; (4) agricultural machinery other than tractors (reapers, binders, &c.); (5) machine tools, such as milling machines, lathes, &c; (6) earth-moving equipment and a mobile crane plant; (7) cranes and continuous mechanical conveyors; (8) lifting and carrier trucks.

In addition to these main motor industries it is proposed that about twenty-two subsidiary concerns should be set up around these eight main units, covering tool shops, subcontracting works, maintenance and repair shops, nut and bolt works, foundries, &c.

It is estimated that the plan should provide about 8,000 jobs in the new plants that are to be established and that this will require a total investment in the order of about £46 million giving an average figure of investment per job created of about £5,700.[46] The intention is to start construction of the first plants in 1967 and that the entire complex, or the development pole, as it is called, should be functioning as a whole towards the end of 1970.

[45] EEC, 'The Commission proposes to the Italian Government a new method for promoting industrial development in Southern Italy', *Information Memo*, P/68, 19 Nov. 1965, p. 3.

[46] EEC, Generaldirektion Wirtschaft und Finanzen, *Vorlage der Studie über die Förderung eines industriellen Entwicklungschwerpunkts in Süditalien*, 312/II/66, 18 Jan. 1966, pp. 39–42.

Both the usual Italian incentives for the South and the special resources of the European Investment Bank are likely to play prominent parts in financing the investment, although the whole emphasis is upon creating a pole that will eventually attract further industries by its own inherent advantages rather than on the basis of continuous outside support.

Obviously no appraisal of this ambitious plan is possible at this stage, but the general line of thought that it embodies has been very well received. As a pilot scheme for the industrialization of backward areas in the EEC and with wider implications for some developing countries, the progress of the scheme will be watched with more than the usual amount of interest.

A NOTE ON INVESTMENT PLANNING IN THE ECSC

In the foregoing two chapters we have stressed that *laissez-faire* is not the universal rule of the Paris and Rome Treaties. As far as the former treaty is concerned this fact is further illustrated by the quite unambiguous obligation to practise, on behalf of the industries for which the High Authority is responsible, a type of planning that goes well beyond being merely indicative and exhortative.

For basic industries such as coal and steel, whose performance has widespread repercussions throughout the entire economic system, it is especially important that capacity and demand should evolve together in a reasonably smooth parallel manner through time. If capacity were to lag behind demand the general expansion of the economy would be retarded. If their capacity were to run ahead of demand, then scarce resources would be wasted in under-utilized plants. The exact process by which competitive industry is supposed to adjust its output to changed demand conditions is a subject that economic theory has tended to neglect in the past, although the traditional cobweb analysis of certain agricultural markets suggests *a priori* that the beneficent effects of the market mechanism in this field are hardly self-evident. The problem really arises because it cannot be taken for granted that the aggregate investment decisions of independent entrepreneurs will be such as to make total capacity adjust by the right amount. If entrepreneurial investment decisions in response to an increase in demand are staggered, then a step by step movement to an equilibrium can be achieved, but if the decisions are taken more or less simultaneously, then the inevitable ignorance about the volume of competitive investments simultaneously being undertaken could lead to overinvestment and consequent cut-throat competition. This problem is likely to be most acute in industries where technical considerations dictate large-scale plants of a durable nature and where demand is increasing only slowly, so that over-optimistic investments by enterpreneurs are not quickly compensated by favourable demand movements.[1]

[1] G. B. Richardson, *Information and Investment* (1960), particularly chs. 1 & 2.

However much these practical difficulties of adjustment may have been pushed into the background by economic theory, the facts of life have required that they be given a prominent place in practical business policy. Rather than undertake costly capital schemes without knowing whether, and to what extent, other enterprises have embarked upon such ventures, business has often preferred to reduce the area of uncertainty surrounding these decisions by having them discussed in the convenient forum of a cartel. However much one may sympathize with business in this predicament, the fact is that once these investment decisions are made as a result of co-operation between firms in the industry, then the possibility of exploitation of the market becomes quite real. It is the great virtue of the ECSC's approach to industrial planning that it meets the legitimate need of business for sufficient information about the development of demand and the construction of capacity but does so in a way that avoids the possibility of this information being used to secure monopoly profits.

There are two related elements to this branch of ECSC policy. The first is the task of forecasting demand. On the basis of such forecasts General Objectives are drawn up which are in effect statements of the size, shape, and technical composition of the industry that the High Authority will endeavour to bring about by a certain date. The second is bringing influence to bear upon the construction of capacity so that industry actually achieves the General Objectives. Let us deal with each of these elements briefly in turn.

(a) Forecasting Demand and Establishing General Objectives

We propose to illustrate this with reference to the steel market only. The High Authority has made four major studies of the evolution of demand for steel: in 1953, 1957, 1962, and 1965. The results of the last, which will relate to the year 1970, have not yet been published, so we shall confine our discussion to the forecast made in 1962 of the level of demand that could be expected in 1965.[2] This has the advantage of making possible both a *post mortem* and an account of methodology. The methods followed by the High Authority involved estimating the total

[2] Full details of the General Objectives for 1965 are contained in ECSC, *10th Gen. Rep.* (1962), p. 312.

internal demand for steel, then taking into account the impact of exports and imports. It is of the greatest importance to stress a procedural matter at this point. These studies are not made by the High Authority from any position of Olympian isolation but only as a result of careful discussions with governments, producers, and consumers. Although the High Authority takes final responsibility for them, they are to an important extent a joint effort.

Estimates of internal demand depend upon estimates of the economic growth of the Six. Two methods were adopted in the forecasts made in 1962, one global and the other sectoral. The global method consisted, first, of taking a standard measure of growth such as the index of GNP or the index of industrial production. Secondly, estimates were then made of the growth of these indices to 1965. Thirdly, on the basis of past relations between internal demand for steel and these indices, an extrapolation of the demand for steel was made. Two alternative relations between the variables were used, one being linear and the other being of constant elasticity (linear between the logarithms of the variables).

The attraction of the above approach is its simplicity. Its weaknesses are: (*a*) mistakes may be made in estimating the growth of GNP or industrial production. This in fact occurred with the first forecast made in 1953 of internal steel demand in 1956 and 1961. GNP actually grew at about twice the forecast rate. (*b*) It assumes that the observed relation between the growth of GNP or industrial production and steel requirements in the past is going to reproduce itself in the future. But this may not be so, either because the composition of output in the future may be different from what it has been in the past, with a relative change towards or away from steel-intensive industries, or because, even if the composition of output remains unchanged, substitutes for steel might be employed. Again, the 1953 forecast for 1956 and 1961 erred by underestimating the coefficient of elasticity of demand for steel with respect to GNP. The combined effect of underestimating both the elasticity coefficient and the growth of GNP meant that the level of internal demand forecast for 1961 was in fact virtually reached in 1956.

Because of the weaknesses of the global approach (which, however, as refined and used in the 1957 forecast made a fairly accurate prediction for 1960) sectoral techniques were also employed for the 1962 forecast. Twenty steel-consuming sectors were distinguished and estimates made of the likely level of production in each of these in 1965. In working out what this would imply for the specific demand for steel in each of them, special attention was paid to the role of technical progress and the substitution of other materials for steel. By converting these data on likely demand for particular products in each sector into crude steel equivalent, the results of the sectoral method could then be compared with those of the global forecasts. It was in fact found that the sectoral method yielded perceptibly lower predictions than either of the global methods as the latter could not take into account the slowing down of the rate of growth of certain steel-intensive sectors. In particular, the results of the global method using a constant coefficient of elasticity were ruled out as they involved the assumption of a continuation of the remarkably rapid increase in demand for steel in Italy, which was regarded as exceptional. For this reason the global method using a constant elasticity was disregarded and the upper and lower limits of Community demand as forecasts for 1965 were 78·4 million metric tons (using the global method with the index of industrial production) and 74·7 (using the sectoral approach).

Once the likely level of internal demand has been estimated, it is then necessary to calculate how much additional demand will be generated by exports to third countries and how much of the internal market's demand will in fact be supplied by imports from third countries. The difficulties in both these directions are substantial and estimates of both exports and imports may contain a wide margin of error.

Exports were forecast by considering the likely evolution of demand in the main consuming areas, taking into account how much of this might be met from the establishment or expansion of national steel industries, and how much of the consequent demand for imports might accrue to the Community, an attempt being made to take into account the changed competitive relationship between the Community and its main rivals in these markets, the UK and Japan.

The method of estimating imports into the Community is not revealed in any great detail and one suspects that there is again room for quite important errors here.

Exports and imports are then set against each other to give a figure of net exports which is added to internal demand in the Community to give a figure of total demand likely to confront ECSC producers in 1965.

How accurate have these various forecasts been? Table 1 sets out the three main forecasts that have been published and compares them as far as possible with what actually happened.

We have already discussed in passing the reasons for the inaccuracy of the 1953 forecast for 1956 and noted how the 1957 forecast for 1960 must be regarded as highly creditable. What

TABLE I

ECSC Steel Production: Comparison of Forecasts and Actual Results

(million metric tons of crude steel)

Forecast made in	Relating to 1956	1960	1961	1962	1965	1970	1975
			Forecast limits				
1953	46·5–50	–	52·6–56	–	–	–	–
1957	–	60·5–73·5	–	–	71–86	–	105
1962	–	–	–	–	89–94	–	–
			Actual results				
	56·8	72·8	73·2	72·7	85·9		

Source: Wagenführ Report, p. 528, and information made available by Statistical Office of the European Communities.

must now appear rather discouraging is that the comparatively unsophisticated 1957 forecast for 1965 in fact yielded a much more accurate prediction than did the more elaborate 1962 forecast for the year that we have described. What were the main reasons for this discrepancy between the 1962 forecast and the actual results achieved in 1965? The High Authority started its *post mortem* even before the period covered by the forecast had expired. Obviously the reasons must lie in the actual development of internal steel consumption and the behaviour of net exports. Under the former heading it appears that not even the sectoral forecasts made sufficient allowance for the changed composition of national output, the use of lighter but equally strong steel products, and competition from substitutes. And net exports were below expectations due to the world-wide excess capacity in steel which had emerged even before the ink was dry on the 1962 forecasts.

(b) Short-term Forecasting

Apart from the long-term forecasts described above, which are intended to be the main guides for investment decisions affecting the quantity and type of capacity to be constructed, the High Authority also makes short-term forecasts quarterly and annually that are intended to indicate to business whether it should be thinking in terms of increasing or decreasing the output from existing capacity and hence the kind of pressure that is likely to occur on prices. Table 2 (p. 434) compares the accuracy of these quarterly forecasts with the results achieved.

As would be expected, the short-term forecasts yielded a fairly high level of accuracy for the main item of crude steel production. But the difficulty of forecasting the export side is again obvious, as even these short-term forecasts were not infrequently wrong by a margin of 10 per cent or even more.

As was indicated in Chapter 9, 1966 was an extremely difficult year for the ECSC. Export prices of steel products fell markedly and internally price falls of up to 20 per cent below list levels were reported. The fall in the internal level of prices was the result of over-production—home demand failed to keep up with the expansion of capacity—together with pressure on prices from the continued operation of obsolescent but fully amortized plant. Various devices were considered by the High Authority for bringing about a better balance between production and demand, and in November 1966 the High Authority decided to make even greater use of the quarterly forecasts. Up to that date the forecasts had only been broken down into output, consumption, exports, and imports of crude steel by country. The High Authority decided that the forecasts should also be broken down into categories of steel products and that such data should be sent to individual firms. The intention was that this would induce firms to adjust production to the forecasts, thus causing the pressure on prices to abate.

TABLE 2

The Accuracy of Short-term Forecasts: Results as a Percentage of Forecasts

		Steel production	Steel exports
1956	II	100	125
	III	101	117
	IV	100	106
1957	I	101	107
	II	97	103
	III	98	88
	IV	100	95
1958	I	100	98
	II	98	124
	III	101	147
	IV	97	110
1959	I	103	94
	II	109	109
	III	101	94
	IV	104	118
1960	I	103	110
	II	99	104
	III	101	88
	IV	100	107
1961	I	102	91
	II	100	103
	III	98	92
	IV	99	106
1962	I	105	87
	II	99	95
	III	99	89
	IV	99	90

TABLE 2 *(cont.)*

The Accuracy of Short-term Forecasts: Results as a Percentage of Forecasts

		Steel production	Steel exports
1963	I	102	90
	II	102	98
	III	98	87
	IV	100	97
1964	I	106	101
	II	100	100
	III	103	102
	IV	105	119
1965	I	106	112
	II	101	119
	III	103	116
	IV	100	122

Source: Wagenführ Report, pp. 549–50, and information made available by Statistical Office of the European Communities.

(c) Influencing Investment Decisions

Exactly what kind of powers were to be given to the High Authority in this field was a matter of some considerable dispute in 1950 and 1951 in the negotiations leading up to the establishment of the ECSC. In fact the powers finally given to the High Authority in Article 54 make it clear that there is no question of any form of compulsion being brought to bear upon enterprises. Instead, the High Authority is empowered to bring certain forms of influence to bear, although this is done in a continuous manner and not just as sporadic interventions when some sort of emergency threatens. The fact that industry has been actively associated with the High Authority in the preparation of the General Objectives makes co-operation in their implementation that much more likely. The main ways in which the High Authority brings its influence to bear are as follows.

(i) *Information and Opinions.* Information on the expected

development of demand is, of course, supplied by the short-term quarterly and annual forecasts, and in a major way by the General Objectives. Similarly, information on the supply side of the picture takes several different forms. Perhaps the most important are the annual investment surveys which estimate total capital expenditure on plant and total capacity available in the current and immediately subsequent years. This is done under the main headings of iron-making, steel-producing and rolling, and within each category, further detail is provided for each type of process. The dissemination of this detailed information enables it to be used by enterprises as a guide to the advisability of installing certain types of plant. It may be noted that, while demand forecasting is a commonplace in formulating economic policy in many industries, there are probably no other industries in the Six so well served with data on capital development as are those subject to the régime of the High Authority.

The work of collecting data on current and anticipated investment projects is facilitated by the Decision of the High Authority in 1955 requiring enterprises to submit proposed capital schemes for scrutiny and comment: new investments in excess of half a million dollars, and replacement investments in excess of one million dollars, have to be reported to the High Authority at least three months before work on them is due to start. The High Authority then considers them to see how far they accord with the General Objectives and, possibly after discussion with the enterprise during which the original plans may be modified, issues a reasoned opinion on them. (In 1966, because of the tendency for Community steel production to exceed internal demand, the High Authority was considering a change in its system of scrutinizing investment projects. It was considered that if a longer period of notice was given, the High Authority would be in a stronger position since it could exercise influence well before final investment decisions were taken.)

Well over one thousand projects have been scrutinized by the High Authority in this way. The essence of an opinion, which may be favourable or unfavourable, is that it is advice to the enterprise concerned and is not in any way mandatory—the freedom of decision of the enterprise remains unimpaired. However, the contents of the opinion are made known to the government concerned and the fact that an opinion has been given on a particular scheme is mentioned in the Official Gazette, although the nature of the opinion is not published. How much influence these reasoned opinions may have had upon the recipients is difficult to judge, but they are thought to have had some influence on coal-mining enterprises by encouraging the construction of pithead power stations, and on steel enterprises by slowing down too rapid a development of electric furnaces and the production of warm- and cold-reduced wide strip.[3]

But the real efficacy of the opinions of the High Authority is most apparent when a company is looking for some sort of outside finance to enable it to undertake a particular scheme. If a company can finance a project entirely from its own resources, then an unfavourable opinion from the High Authority might in the final analysis do nothing to stop it. But when a company has to look beyond its own resources for finance, then lenders, being aware that an opinion has been given, ask the enterprise to inform them of it in detail, and assess the advisability of the loan in the light of that.

(ii) *Financial Support of Investment Projects by the High Authority*. The High Authority raises loans as a first-class borrower in the international capital markets and re-lends the proceeds to ECSC enterprises to help them undertake certain investments. Even allowing for the fact that the High Authority re-lends to business at a slightly higher interest rate than that at which it borrows from the international market, the rate to the enterprise is still very favourable when compared with the rates ruling in six countries for similar loans of equivalent duration. The first seven loans raised by the High Authority in the US and Switzerland incurred rates of interest between $3\frac{7}{8}$ per cent and $5\frac{1}{4}$ per cent: these formed the basis of loans to industry at rates between $4\frac{1}{10}$ per cent and $5\frac{3}{4}$ per cent when market rates were more like 7 per cent.

The loans granted to the enterprises by the High Authority

---

[3] In 1966, in order to restrain the expansion of productive capacity in steel, the High Authority was considering ways of achieving an even more effective means of co-ordinating investment plans. Recognizing the existence of national governmental steel plans, the High Authority suggested that under Article 26 of the Paris Treaty (which calls for harmonization of High Authority and member government policies) there should be a regular confrontation of member country plans and the Community General Objectives.

only cover a small proportion of the total finance needed to complete a project. In this way the High Authority is able to spread its influence in the widest possible manner. Obviously the High Authority will not give financial support to any project on which it has issued an unfavourable opinion—it may be doubted whether any other lender would either—and, conversely, it directs its lending towards those kinds of investments that it most wishes to encourage. For example, because of the tight supply situation as regards scrap and coke in the early years of the ECSC, ore preparation and sintering plants were given priority. Later on priority was given to increasing iron-making capacity at coastal plants and the construction of large integrated iron and steel works. Most recently preference has been given to promoting the commercial application of oxygen steel-making processes and to plans for rationalization and specialization of production.

Besides granting loans itself, the High Authority is also prepared to guarantee loans from third parties for projects which it specially approves. In this way it has helped in the construction of large integrated steel works on the French coast and in Lower Saxony.

(iii) *Promotion of Technical Research.* The significance of technical research and the rapid application of its results to industrial processes needs no stressing. It is perhaps of particularly great importance for the coal and steel industries as they face a competitive squeeze from two directions simultaneously. Competition from newer industries within the Common Market is one source of such competition, and their conditions of production in terms of geological endowments and proximity of raw materials probably place Community producers in a more unfavourable situation than their counterparts in the USA and USSR.

The High Authority encourages research by a variety of grants in a number of ways. For example, it may play a subsidiary role in supporting the existing research of an organization that is working in a promising field. Or it may take the initiative itself and stimulate research in a particular direction. Or it may help with development costs and the cost of pilot plants. In all cases the main concern of the High Authority is to promote the kind of work that will strengthen the competitive position of ECSC enterprises. It has supported research into new processes at each of the three main stages of steel-making—iron-making, steel production, and rolling—in particular into new techniques in the blast furnaces, reduction of heat wastage, and the development of automated plants. The High Authority supports industry financially in the costs of maintaining the extensive technical literature that research requires, and also facilitates the translation and evaluation of technical documentation from the Eastern bloc. All research supported by the High Authority has to be made available to the widest circle of firms in the ECSC and, if it results in a patented process, this has to be licensed to other Community firms.

PART IV
Conclusion

I2

A Concluding Assessment

COMPETITION policy is an important part of general economic policy in any system that is based wholly or to a large extent upon the principles of a market economy. In the Communities it is expected to contribute to exactly the same type of goals as it does in the ordinary national economic framework—lower prices, faster technical progress, and a fairer distribution of income, for example. But in the context of integration competition is also a medium to expedite the unification of the national economies into one larger common market. In the Communities competition policy has a wider task than it has within the framework of an ordinary national market economy. It is in fulfilling this wider aspect of its role that its special character in the Communities is most clearly revealed. Its distinctive features arise from the opportunities and problems presented by the integration process itself.

As far as the opportunities are concerned the great significance of integration for competition is that, by freeing trade over a wider area, it supplements or even supplants national with international competition. Not only will market structures be changed by the increase in the number of competitors, but there will be a qualitative metamorphosis in the whole character of competition as established coteries of national producers are undermined by competition from imported supplies. In assessing the strength of competition in the Communities, the greatest importance must, therefore, be attached to the extent to which the national markets have been invaded by imports from the other member states. For both the ECSC and the EEC it is possible to provide quantitative evidence of the extent to which this has happened.

In the case of the ECSC the position is clearest in the steel industry. Indeed, the coal industry, with one part of the market at one time deliberately sealed off from the rest, and subsidies widely used, can hardly be regarded as an example of the effects of freer trading conditions unless it is as the exception that proves the rule. In the steel industry, however, the market has been comparatively free from interventions and it is interesting to see how trade between the member states has expanded in these freer circumstances. In Table 1 below we show this increased penetration—as it has occurred in the case of finished laminated steel products—by expressing intra-Community imports of such products as a percentage of the Community's production of them. The data for 1954, the first full year of the common market for iron and steel products (but not special steels), is compared with 1964 (the last full year for which data was available at the time of writing), by which time the interpenetration process had had time to show definite results.

TABLE I

Production and Intra-Community Imports of Finished Laminated Steel Products 1954 and 1964

('ooo metric tons)

	Production A	Intra-Community imports B	$\frac{B}{A}\%$
1954	29,669	3,044	10
1964	58,553	10,652	18

Sources: ECSC, *Bull. statistique*, 1958, no. 3, tables 16A and 45A; Statistical Office of the European Communities, *Sidérurgie*, no. 1, 1966, tables 29 & 77.

Over the period 1954–64, production increased by 97 per cent —on the other hand intra-Community imports increased by 249 per cent. This differential growth is shown in Table 1 by the rise of the trade/production ratio from 10 to 18 per cent.

The increased penetration of markets has proceeded at different rates according to product. In order to measure this a penetration coefficient can be employed. This is simply the ratio of deliveries of a particular product passing over national boundaries to total deliveries (both those passing over national boundaries and those supplied directly to the national market). For treaty products as a whole the average coefficient of penetration rose from 6·5 per cent in 1952 to 17 per cent in 1962. The increase for particular products is shown in Table 2 below.

TABLE 2

Interpenetration of Markets by Product 1952-62

(*per cent*)

Product	1952	1962
Tinplate	6·7	25
Joints, sections	6·8	23·4
Galvanized sheet	2·6	20·1
Sheet	7·0	20
Wire rod	5·9	18·6
Heavy & medium plate	6·5	17·6
Ingots & semi-finished products for re-rolling	4·9	17·1
Magnetic sheet	5·4	17·1
Merchant bars	9·4	17
Hoop & strip for tubes	4·6	16
Coils for re-rolling	1·1	15·8

Source: Reproduced from J. J. Comhaire and C. A. Oury, 'L'expérience de l'intégration dans la sidérurgie', in Collège d'Europe, Bruges, *Intégration européenne et réalité économique*, 1964, table H, 2, p. 245.

The growth of specialization is evident in the case of some of these products. Tinplate had the greatest rate of interpenetration in 1962. This is a product of relatively high value to weight and bulk and can therefore be transported over relatively long distances with minimum competitive disadvantage. There has been a rapid expansion in the Community demand for this product and a considerable degree of specialization has been achieved. In the case of sections there has been a noticeable development of specialization—this has been aided by technical developments which have helped to counteract the fact that transport costs are high because of the relatively low value/bulk-weight ratio. Sheet steel is another product which had a relatively high penetration coefficient in 1962, and is one in which a relatively high value/bulk-weight ratio has aided the development of specialization.

This increased penetration is only another way of saying that the national steel industries of the Six have since 1953 experienced increasing competition within their own national markets. Increasingly it is clear that national markets have ceased to be mainly the sole preserve of national industries—increasingly national demand has actually been, or has had the opportunity of being, satisfied by imports from other member states. The other side of the coin has been that the national markets of other member states have been opened up to those firms which had the drive and efficiency to take advantage of them.

Within the wider common market of the EEC reductions of trade barriers have again contributed to a sharp increase in the rate of expansion of intra-Community imports. There has also been an increase in the rate of expansion of the Community's imports from third countries, though of modest proportions by comparison. The data are shown in Table 3.

TABLE 3

The Value of Intra-Community Imports and Imports from Rest of World

(*$ million*)

	Intra-Community imports	% increase	Average annual % increase	Imports from rest of world	% increase	Average annual % increase
1953	3,954 ⎫			10,964 ⎫		
		71	14·2		47	9·4
1958	6,790 ⎬			16,156 ⎬		
		200	28·5		76	10·8
1965	20,417 ⎭			28,562 ⎭		

Source: Statistical Office of the European Communities, *Commerce extérieur statistique mensuelle*, 1966, table 1.

The contrast between the growth in intra-EEC trade and that with third countries is most clearly brought out by the figure of average annual increase in imports in pre- and post-Rome Treaty periods. Whereas the average annual rate of increase of imports from third countries has risen from 9·4 to 10·8 per cent, intra-Community imports have doubled their rate of increase since the treaty came into effect. This latter fact is a vivid illustration of the effect of removing barriers to trade between the member states.

It is possible to build up a picture of what intra-Community imports might have looked like if the Rome Treaty had not been signed and other liberalizations had not occurred in its place. This can be done by calculating the trend relationship between Community GNP (Y) and intra-Community imports (I) prior to the cuts in trade barriers between the Six. This has been done by means of the ordinary least squares technique. This relationship can then be projected forward and deviations of actual intra-Community imports (I) from their trend value ($\hat{I}$) can be observed. In Table 4 we show the relationship between GNP (Y) and actual and extrapolated intra-Community imports (I and $\hat{I}$ respectively). Diagram 1 presents the same data in its more striking graphical form.

TABLE 4

Comparison of Actual Intra-Community Imports with their 1953-8 Trend

	Y Index of Community GNP	$\hat{I}$ Intra-Community imports on basis of 1953–8 trend relationship	I Index of actual intra-Community imports	I–$\hat{I}$
1953	100	104	100	−4
1954	106	119	121	2
1955	114	138	141	3
1956	120	153	156	3
1957	126	167	169	2
1958	129	174	169	−5
1959	136	191	210	19
1960	145	213	256	43
1961	155	237	295	58
1962	162	254	336	82
1963	168	269	390	121
1964	179	296	441	145

Source: Statistical Office of the European Communities, *Basic Statistics of Fifteen European Countries* (1962), table 13; *Basic Statistics of the Community* (1965), table 13, *Commerce extérieur statistique mensuelle,* no. 2, 1966, table 1.

DIAGRAM I

Intra-Community Imports in (I) *Relation to 1953-8 Trend* $(\hat{I})$

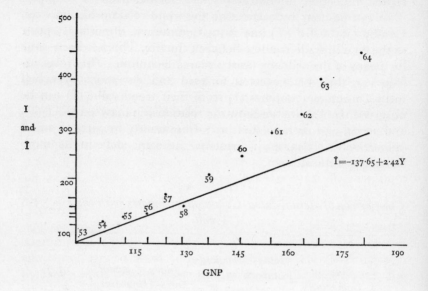

GNP

The relationship between 1953 and 1958 is one of almost total linearity (R^2 being 0·9743 and the regression equation being $\hat{I} = -137·65 + 2·42\,Y$). The fact that after 1958 the actual trade figures lie increasingly away from the trend line indicates the increase in the ratio of intra-Community imports to Community GNP. All the signs are that this increased interpenetration of markets is giving rise to greater competition. Directly, this is occurring as goods from the other member states increasingly enter into competition in their domestic markets with those produced by national firms. Indirectly, the same result is being brought about by the effects of integration upon established methods of national planning. As the discipline of the treaties limits the range of instruments at the disposal of national governments for planning purposes (that is, the use of tariffs, subsidies, fiscal concessions, discriminatory transport rates, and so forth is largely ruled out), national firms are gradually led to realize that their survival and success in the future will be determined by their own efforts alone. Traditional accommodating relationships among national firms are gradually being replaced by an individualism more appropriate to the new order.

That trade between the member states has increased considerably with the progress of the common market is certainly a cause for satisfaction but not for complacency. The fact is that the policy of dismantling tariff and quota barriers to trade, which has proceeded so smoothly and is now virtually complete, should really be seen as only the first part of a more general reorientation of government activities towards what is required by the integration process. It is in these other fields—policy on direct and indirect taxation, state aids, state monopolies, and the harmonization of technical and professional standards—that the Communities still have a long way to go. Thus, even when the customs union is complete from 1968, the full potentialities of such freedom will not be realized as long as, for example, differences in national fiscal policies continue to result in distortions to competition and fiscal frontiers. If the basic conditions of competition are distorted it cannot be assumed that freer trade will have the beneficial effects on resource allocation expected of it under normal circumstances. If fiscal frontiers exist it can be assumed that the growth of trade is being to some extent held back even though tariff and quota barriers are eliminated. But fiscal frontiers are not the only obstacles to trade. Divergent technical standards, especially in such fields as electrical equipment, continue to effect to some degree a national segmentation of the common market. It may be too much to expect any really rapid progress, on, for example, fiscal harmonization, as this touches governments in what is probably the most sensitive area of national economic sovereignty. But the same cannot be said of technical standards. A powerful stimulus to integration and greater economic efficiency (by increasing the possibility of achieving scale economies) would seem to be well within the reach of the member states now if determined efforts are made on harmonization of standards. The results here could be fairly important and fairly rapid: equally, further failure to advance significantly in this field would be more than regrettable.

When considering the way in which national governments can

impede the attainment of the goals set by the two treaties, we should not neglect the kind of relationships built up between government and industry. We have drawn attention to the way in which government policy in the steel market has served to make the existing *national* oligopoly situation more overtly collusive. Then again there are extremely important problems arising out of the purchasing policies of central and local government and bodies such as the nationalized industries. Clearly the achievement of greater inter-state competition is likely to be hamstrung if such authorities pursue a policy of supporting their own firms when awarding contracts. In this context it is interesting to note the observation by Sheahan, in his study of French industrial policy, 'The government firms "buy French" with decidedly few exceptions.'[1] It was alleged before the Select Committee on Nationalized Industries in 1962 that Électricité de France was firmly wedded to French suppliers. At that date its imports from other Common Market countries were negligible. It was also alleged, though not proven, that Électricité de France allowed French suppliers to recoup their research and development overheads in the prices charged for home orders—thus allowing exports to be sold below full cost. It was also pointed out that in several member states financial and other links existed between firms generating electricity and those supplying the generating equipment.[2]

Just as certain government policies are incompatible with securing the full benefits of the integrated market, so too are certain private practices that have the effect of maintaining the economic identity of the national markets. The private practices concerned are most obviously those of international cartels within the integrated area. Such agreements very often provide that each partner will 'respect' in some specified manner the domestic markets of the others. Less obvious, but equally antithetical to the integration process, would be a purely national cartel involving producers and dealers in one state only if this had the result of preventing or impeding the access of suppliers from other member states to the national market in question. An international cartel that took the form of a simple price agreement

---

[1] Sheahan, p. 201.
[2] *Report from the Select Committee on Nationalized Industries* (1963), iii. 349, iii, 284–5.

would tend to make buyers indifferent as between low- and high-cost sources of supplies and would thereby affect the flow of trade between the states concerned. It would tend to impede the reallocation of production to the more efficient firms, i.e. it would help to perpetuate a less efficient distribution of resources than competition would bring about, thereby holding back the general rate of economic advance. In reality most international cartels probably practise more than one kind of restriction and thereby compound the threat they present. That they are in principle a threat to both integration and economic growth is beyond serious dispute. That they are so in practice also should be clear from their ubiquity, well known to all businessmen, and clearly demonstrated in many places including an earlier chapter of this book. Any idea that international cartels were only prevalent in the pre-war depression years is simply wrong. Their existence and activities today are on such a scale as to be relevant not only to far-reaching integration of the EEC type, but also all other schemes aimed at bringing about freer trading conditions. That their activities appear to be largely ignored in practice in EFTA, GATT, the Dillon Round, and the Kennedy Round is evidence more of the shortcomings of international economic policy than of any lack of potency on the part of cartels.

The shortcomings of international economic policy in this field have obvious causes. The most obvious is the lack of any kind of agreed attitude to anti-trust in the wider international community. But even if a meaningful amount of common ground could be found, the international juridical problems of embodying this into actual laws and creating enforcement agencies are probably insurmountable except within an EEC-type of supranational framework. The possibility of having some kind of international convention administered by separate national authorities is a pathetically poor alternative. To say the least it would be unwise to expect too much action from national authorities when their own firms are in danger of being submerged by a blast of real international competition. It is here, in the tightness of the link between economic logic and realism on the one hand, and legal and institutional reality on the other, that the Communities come uniquely into their own. Acting under treaties that have the full force of law in each of the member states, and subject ultimately only to the equally supranational authority of the Court of Justice, the executives of the Communities have been endowed with sufficient power to act effectively. Moreover, the mere existence of such effective power must have gone some way to discourage some at least of the grosser practices of international cartels in the Communities. It would be a great mistake to equate the effectiveness of anti-trust in the Communities solely with the number of Decisions and Judgments that have been handed down. It is quite clear from the considerable attention given by business and its legal advisers to the anti-trust rules that the latter must have had a definite impact on the formulation of business policy. By having responsibilities in a host of other branches of economic policy, the common market executives are in a position to work for sufficient harmony between them to ensure that action in one field is not rendered nugatory by contradiction or failures elsewhere. The logical interconnexion between various facets of economic life means that tariff reductions and anti-trust policies lose much of their meaning if discriminatory national policies in transport rates, government procurement policies, and state aids are allowed to go unchecked. We cannot stress too strongly what we would call the unity of competition policy—that is the fact that it cannot be pursued successfully other than simultaneously on a number of fronts.

Although it is in the complexities of its international character that much of the interest in Community anti-trust lies, it is important to remember that these policies are adopted not solely to promote integration but also to help achieve the same kind of general aims as anti-trust in any national market economy. Inevitably one is led to assess the Community version along very much the same lines as one would any of the leading national brands.

In the field of cartels both ECSC and EEC adopt such similar approaches that they can realistically be considered as one. Their approach is to prohibit cartels unless these can be shown to fulfil certain requirements. In principle this appears to be a middle of the road policy that steers clear of both the more severe approach of *per se* prohibition, as exemplified in American anti-trust, and the feeble policy of only penalizing proved abuse that characterized a number of European countries for many years. As there were great differences of opinion between the

member states on anti-trust questions, it is not surprising that
their common policy should appear something of a compromise
between the more extreme possibilities open to them. The important question here of course is whether the exemption
possibilities will prove too widely drawn. If it is difficult to get
agreements through the gateway, then the approach of the
Communities will in practice have much in common with the
US approach. That a fairly vigorous policy will be applied is
evidenced by the Commission's treatment of the Pottery and
Cement cartels and, in particular, by its Decision in the Grundig–
Consten case, which was substantially confirmed by the Court of
Justice in July 1966. If, in the nature of things, the strictest
approach to cartels was ruled out from the start, the Community
version is probably about the strictest alternative. Its great virtue
lies in the way in which the exemption gateway has been framed:
a cartel can only be approved if it does not eliminate competition in respect of a substantial part of the relevant goods, and
does result in definite benefits to the public. The importance
of maintaining competition is recognized in practice but
there is an element of flexibility that can be turned to good
account.

But whatever the legal approach adopted there will always be a
tendency in some business circles to look for ways of circum-
venting the existing rules, for example by the utilization of
information agreements to achieve much the same results as
ordinary cartels. In the long run there is a definite danger of this
in the Communities as the very existence of the executives has
compelled business to form Community-wide industrial federations. At present the Commission still finds the existence of such
offices in Brussels highly convenient for sounding out business
opinion on numerous matters, but it may yet see the day when
such organizations have to be regarded in a more critical manner.
The work of business federations at the Community level could
gradually erode the basis of entrepreneurial diversity that is an
important cause of the competitive nature of the Community at
present. Once such a change in the competitive climate had
occurred, it would be but a short step towards information
agreements and the like. How well adapted Community policy
might be for dealing with this kind of situation it is impossible to
say. But one can say that the time to start thinking about this is

now—not when the problem has taken some distinctly practical turn.

If a provisional judgement on Community (but, in particular, EEC) cartel policy may be ventured at all at such an early stage in its evolution, it should, in our view, be a reasonably favourable one. Unfortunately the same cannot be said for the policy that seems to be evolving as regards market domination, although it must be stressed that 'policy' in this field has not yet gone beyond the discussion of principles.

The absence of any Decisions so far on market domination is both surprising and disappointing. Market domination at the national level (if nothing more) is certain to exist in some industries in the EEC, and, judging by UK experience, there is a definite possibility that market power will be abused in a number of the cases where it exists. For dominant individual firms, the reports of the Monopolies Commission on matches, oxygen, fertilizers, wallpaper, and colour films are ample evidence of this. For domination by oligopolistic groups the reports of the Commission on the supply of petrol to retailers and household detergents are again evidence of the reality of this problem. Even allowing for the fact that all the special circumstances of Article 86 have to be met before any unfavourable decision can emerge, one cannot help feeling that the failure to come to grips with the problem in a practical way is perhaps the result of an excessive preoccupation with the *minutiæ* of the cartel side of the anti-trust policy.

Admittedly, the problem of market domination is not an easy one. The gist of it is that although certain aspects of the behaviour of large enterprises, whether oligopolists or particularly large individual firms, may adversely affect the working of an integrated market economy, large enterprises may be the very ones whose activities in both production and R & D are on such a scale as to be a precondition for obtaining the benefits of integration. Whereas there must be a presumption against cartels because they freeze important aspects of economic life, there must be an equal but opposite presumption in favour of large enterprises in the conditions of a larger market. Admittedly it is not possible to make any completely watertight general case in favour of them but the whole balance of the arguments discussed earlier seem to us to add up to a very definite practical presumption to this effect in the context of the present stage of European integration.

The policy proposals of the EEC Commission in such fields as taxation and company law are therefore particularly apposite. It is true that they are not designed purely to bring about greater size—indeed the accepted form of common turnover tax will remove a stimulus to vertical concentration. Rather they seek to introduce a greater degree of neutrality into the impact of taxation and company law upon business size. This does, however, mean that in so far as they sweep away artificial obstacles to greater size, they will facilitate the growth of firms to the point where they will be most effective as regards the economies of scale and technical progressiveness.

Inevitably the question arises, if the obstacles to growth by merger are removed, may Europe not run headlong into the problems of bigness, whether in the form of oligopoly or monopoly? Is there not in fact a dilemma here in that the search for greater efficiency and progressiveness through concentration may also carry with it a threat to competition? As a result of their size and market power companies may be able to make unduly high profits at the expense of the consumer. Recently, to take the UK as an example again, we have witnessed the case of Kodak Ltd, a firm which in 1964 was responsible for 77 per cent (by value) of all colour film supplied. Kodak had been in a position to charge prices that enabled it to earn in that year 55 per cent on the relevant part of its capital. Alternatively the consumer could suffer in the sense that competition, in so far as it exists under conditions of oligopoly or duopoly, could take the form of excessive promotional efforts, such as advertising, free offers, and so forth, at the expense of a lower price level which the consumer would in all probability prefer. The 1966 Monopolies Commission report on household detergents illustrated just such a situation in the UK.

In the immediate future such an anti-competitive threat, at least in general form, is doubtful in the Communities. The process of merging national markets to form a common market makes a powerful contribution to the maintenance of competition. It is true that if the search for the optimum size of firm (whether defined statically or dynamically) is pursued within a purely national context, then the result could and probably would be a monopolistic or highly oligopolistic industrial structure. But when the process of concentration takes place within the context of a common market the threat to competition is automatically reduced; the monopolist in one state competes with the monopolist in another and oligopolies compete with oligopolies. In short, the degree of concentration at the Community level is less than the degree of concentration at the national level. With this in mind, it seems reasonable to say that, even if the merger movement proceeded apace for a number of years, conditions in most (but not of course all) Community industries would still be a good deal short of anything like monopoly of the larger market.

Nevertheless, in the longer run (and in the shorter run and even now in particular industries) a continuing merger movement could begin to throw up anti-trust problems. It is for this reason that we emphasize the need for a positive policy on mergers within the European Community. This should follow the example of the US, UK, and ECSC in so far as they provide means for nipping incipient market power in the bud. Thus some mergers may be dictated purely by the desire to exploit the consumer. Unfortunately, Article 86 is not well designed to deal with such a situation, since it only operates when a dominant position is being abused, whereas it would be desirable to prevent the power to abuse from emerging in the first place, provided that there were no compensating advantages from greater size. When it comes to mergers, Article 86 seems to lock the stable door after the horse has bolted.

But of course the heart of the dilemma between concentration and competition arises from the fact that *in some cases* greater size, with a consequent emergence of monopoly or oligopoly, may be indispensable if the economies of scale are to be fully reaped, or R & D thresholds surmounted. Indeed the likelihood that such a situation will emerge is considerably greater in the EEC than in the US. This arises from the fact that if, in order to compete with US industry, European enterprises have to emulate their US counterparts in the matter of size, then by virtue of the fact that the US market is more than twice the size of that of the Community, it follows that the Community market will support fewer optimum sized enterprises than that of the US. The degree of concentration in the Community would therefore be greater than that in the US. As a result, to a greater extent in Europe than in the US, market power and oligopolistic market behaviour may be an inevitable concomitant of optimum size.

With this fact in mind, it would in our view be desirable that a Community policy for controlling mergers should be introduced that follows the pragmatic British practice of recognizing that although monopoly and oligopoly pose problems, there may be compensating advantages to be derived from size, and these should be taken into account in deciding whether or not a merger should be permitted. The approach adopted in the US and ECSC of not, at least explicitly, taking account of the economies of scale in assessing mergers is not one which the Six should adopt. It would be a great mistake to transplant the US approach into Europe in an uncritical fashion. In so far as US firms often tend to be larger than their European counterparts and as a consequence are either closer to or at the optimum size, and are thus well able to compete with foreign enterprises, the American policy of only taking account of reductions of competition makes at least some sense. But for Europe, where firms more often appear to fall below the optimum, the American approach to mergers must be described as a luxury which it can ill afford.

For this reason Europe should develop a distinctive form of anti-trust policy which aims less at forbidding firms from merging when problems of size are in prospect and more at regulating their behaviour (if competition is substantially affected) when they attain their optimum size. Here a genuine conflict arises but it would in our opinion be a mistake if, recognizing that difficult problems of monopoly and oligopoly were likely to arise, those responsible for European anti-trust policy shied away from them by taking refuge in punitive anti-merger policy. Rather the path of European anti-trust should be to recognize that sometimes, in order to achieve an efficient industrial structure, the classical model of competition has to be sacrificed. This would involve recognizing the necessity of employing techniques of control which would be a substitute for, or a supplement to, the force of competition. In this way it might prove possible to escape from the dilemma. It goes without saying, of course, that mergers that substantially reduce competition but do not offer correspondingly substantial technical economies should not be permitted.

✸ The EEC already has one extremely powerful weapon at its disposal and that is the threat of the consequences that could flow from a violation of Article 86. It will be recalled that this Article prohibits the abuse of a dominant position by one or several firms. Monopolists and oligopolists in the EEC already have every incentive therefore to avoid the attentions of the Commission, as substantial fines could result from any unfavourable decision by the latter. But the Community could also learn with advantage from the experience of the UK and, interestingly enough, from that of the US. For example, in the latter the technique of the consent decree has been employed with some success. In civil cases, when the Department of Justice has brought a firm to court, it has been possible for the respondent firm to negotiate with the Department, giving the latter the satisfaction it needs by accepting injunctions and prohibitions relating to its future conduct. Upon receiving the consent of the court, such injunctions and prohibitions are legally binding. This has a number of advantages of which the avoidance of the costs of legal proceedings and speed in reaching a mutually satisfactory result are the most important. Even in litigated cases the judiciary has sometimes preferred similar techniques of regulation. For example in the case of *United States* v. *the United Shoe Machinery Corporation* in 1953[3]—a case of monopolization —the Department of Justice proposed that the corporation be split up into three companies, but Judge Wyzanski instead preferred to place a series of injunctions upon the corporation which sought to regulate the technique of leasing shoe machines about which the charge of monopolization had originally been made. In the UK the recent Kodak case has indicated how the authorities can induce a dominant firm to moderate its profits and pass on some of the benefit to consumers in the form of lower prices. In another case (household detergents) the aim has been to regulate the nature of competition between duopolists by securing a reduction of promotional expenditures. There are also other techniques which could be incorporated in a European anti-trust armoury. For example, Galbraith, discussing the prob-

---

[3] D. Mass. 1953.

lem of oligopoly in the US, has drawn attention to the beneficial effect of countervailing power, the essence of his argument being that powerful buyers, whether in other manufacturing industries or retailing, tend to spring up to counterbalance the market power exercised by oligopolists. It is questionable whether the emergence of such power is quite as spontaneous as Galbraith suggests, and as far as the consumer is concerned it could merely mean the substitution of one powerful seller by another, but the concept does suggest that the governments of the Six, as major purchasers, could exercise this type of influence and their impact would be all the more powerful if coordinated. There are, of course, considerable political problems involved in getting governments to co-operate in putting pressure on their own national enterprises.

What prospect is there that Community anti-trust policy will develop on the lines we have been discussing? As far as mergers are concerned the EEC Commission as a whole appears to recognize that there is a gap in its armoury. But a number of problems arise in connexion with filling it. There is, for example, no guarantee that the Commission will be successful in stretching the interpretation of Article 86 in such a way as to make it a comprehensive weapon of merger control, although it may be applied successfully in certain particular situations. Some indication that there is a lack of confidence about the outcome can be gleaned from the fact that envious glances have been simultaneously cast in the direction of Article 66 of the Paris Treaty. The opportunity for making a bid to adopt that Article, in modified form we would suggest, would arise if and when the treaties are fused, although there does not seem to be any inevitability about success on either of these points. The French probably still regard a policy for controlling mergers as an unnecessary luxury at the present time, being mesmerized by their own particularly acute problem of small firms. And they can probably count on powerful support from within the Commission in the form of M. Marjolin who is sometimes regarded as being rather sceptical about these matters and more inclined to emphasize the overriding importance of structural change at the present time.

As for the idea that anti-trust policy will in some cases have to consist of regulating the exercise of market power rather than preventing its emergence, this does not seem to have received

much consideration as yet. It is true that in some degree the
pressure of present problems is bound to push thinking about
the longer run into the background. But it is our impression that
within the Brussels Competition Directorate there are some who
doubt whether the economies of scale and the needs of R & D are
of such a nature as to require enterprises of a size which imply
significant market power. Because there is some reluctance to
accept this as a real problem, thinking and, still more, active
policy-making may be retarded. Perhaps in some degree this
reluctance springs from a desire not to get too deeply embroiled
in active industrial policy-making, but nevertheless this is a field
into which, in our opinion, the EEC Commission will eventually
have to enter.

Policies to promote greater competition, by increasing trade
within the Community and by simultaneously implementing an
anti-trust policy in order to maintain that competition in existence are not ends in themselves. They are economically desirable
in so far as they contribute to improved industrial performance
for the benefit of the consumer. While having every respect for
the logic of those who would caution against inferring that
economic events in the Six are necessarily caused by the operation of the Common Market itself, we feel that some changes at
least are so closely related to the policies followed by the Communities that to deny a substantial element of causality is
bordering on perversity.

The Community automobile industry provides a good example
of the effects of increased competition. Table 5 (p. 461) shows
that, although between 1953 and 1958 intra-Community imports
of motor vehicles (measured in units) increased, the ratio of such
imports to Community production actually fell slightly. However between 1958 and 1963 the ratio increased sharply to 11·2
per cent.

The EEC Commission has arranged a study of the effect of the
Common Market upon competition in automobiles. In drawing
upon the study the Commission refers to the appreciably keener
competition between manufacturers which has stemmed from
the tariff reductions and removal of quantitative restrictions. The
Commission observes:

To maintain their position on the home markets or to penetrate those of the other EEC countries, firms have vied with each other in all fields: price, quality of vehicles, delivery dates, frequent changes of model etc. They have stepped up investment, increased rationalization, and sometimes made greater efforts to regroup their production. Similarly, marketing and other sales service networks have been extended and modernized.[4]

TABLE 5

Intra-Community Imports and Production of Motor Vehicles 1953, 1958, and 1963

(*'000 units*)

	EEC production A	Intra-Community imports B	$\frac{B}{A}$ %
1953	1,164	50·5	4·3
1958	3,027	128·0	4·2
1963	5,575	627·5	11·2

Source: UN, *Monthly Bull. of Statist.*, 1966, tables 45 & 46, pp. 74–77; and EEC, *8th Gen. Rep.* (1965), p. 131.

List prices for vehicles (which do not take account of reductions granted by dealers to purchasers) have increased much less rapidly since 1958 than retail prices in general. This is even more significant when it is recognized that substantial technical improvements have been made to some products. It is also significant that competition has compelled manufacturers and distributors to pass on tariff cuts in the form of lower prices (although this is not true in the case of other products, electric razors for example, where tariff reductions have not been clearly reflected in the shops). Another sign of increased competition is the more frequent change of models. Certain French models remained unchanged for some ten years. But in the last few years French manufacturers have launched a whole new range of models over a relatively short period of time. A sign of increased interest in the markets of other member states by national producers is the development of models for the whole Common

[4] EEC, *8th Gen. Rep.* (1965), p. 130.

Market, for example Renault R4, R8, Caravelle; Simca 1000; Citroen AMI-6; Opel Kadett; Ford Taunus 12M &c.[5] Another sign of increased competition is that other aspects of marketing have been improved, such as delivery dates. In France at the end of the 1950s delivery dates were 1–2 years but they have now been reduced to 1–2 months.

· The French refrigerator industry is a particularly dramatic example of what the forces of competition have achieved, particularly in respect of its effect in contributing to the rationalization of the structure of the industry. In 1958 there were forty-five refrigerator manufacturers in France, which when the advantages of long runs and standardized components are considered, can hardly be described as an ideal industrial structure. However, the opening up of the French market to Italian competition led, as we saw in Chapter 1, to a flood of Italian refrigerators. In 1965 French refrigerator imports amounted to 527,000 units of which 80 per cent were Italian. The increased competition had a galvanizing effect upon the French industry. Some firms abandoned production, others merged, and by 1966 the number of firms in France producing refrigerators had fallen to six. French refrigerator production has fallen—it was 1,075,000 units in 1964 (an all-time high) and 875,000 in 1965. The main effect from the consumer point of view however is that increased competition and a more efficient industrial structure has led to a marked fall in prices. In 1949 the index number of refrigerator prices stood at 100, but in 1965 the figure was only 80—a not inconsiderable achievement in a period of inflation. But if we bear in mind that in the US with its much larger market there are only eight producers of refrigerators, it is clear that this industry in the EEC could benefit from still further rationalization.

But perhaps the most impressive example of the effects of greater competition is provided by comparing the steel industry in the ECSC with that in the UK. Both industries are old and serve economies at very much the same stage of development: in 1964, for example, 87 per cent of ECSC steel was produced in Western Germany, France, and Belgium-Luxembourg. But the great contrast between them is that whereas competition has been

---

[5] M. Ouin, 'L'industrie automobile et l'intégration européenne, in College, d'Europe, Bruges, *Intégration européenne*, pp. 283-4.

a reality in the ECSC, particularly in times of slacker demand, competition in the UK industry, both between domestic enterprises and between domestic enterprises and imported supplies has been, at least until 1966, virtually non-existent. We do not need to labour the point that, certainly until the Restrictive Practices Court judgment on the Heavy Steel Case in 1964, the UK industry regarded the Iron and Steel Board's maximum prices as minimum prices to be observed by all. Thus although between 1960 and 1963 the rate of utilization of capacity in the UK steel industry fell from 94 to 74 per cent, and between 1961 and 1963 imports of iron and steel products increased by 130 per cent, the price level was held—this being in material contrast to developments in the ECSC during the same period.

In so far as the ECSC enterprises have actively competed both amongst themselves and with third-country suppliers, it would be reasonable to expect, if conventional economic thinking is any guide, that this will have provided a stimulus to greater efficiency which has been lacking in the UK. If the prices of UK steel products have risen faster than those of the ECSC industry over the years since the opening of the common market this would suggest a differential change in efficiency favourable to the ECSC.

Data are available concerning the course of prices in the ECSC and UK between 1958 and 1966—(see Table 6, p. 464).

The contrast between the UK and ECSC is stark indeed. In the former the prices of all these products increased, the increases ranging between 26 and 44 per cent. In the latter only two of the nine products showed price increases and the overall trend of prices was downwards, with some products showing quite significant falls. Moreover we see that for most products ECSC prices lay well below UK prices—this is highly significant when it is recognized that in all cases in 1953 ECSC prices lay above those of the UK. However, two important qualifications have to be kept in mind in assessing the validity of the above type of comparison.

As indicated in Table 6 the prices taken as representing the ECSC are in fact the low Belgian prices. On the face of it the assumption that these prices represent prices for the ECSC industry as a whole may seem unwarranted—it could be objected that Belgian prices merely relate to the Belgian industry. But the

16

TABLE 6

The Percentage Change in Steel Prices in the ECSC and UK
1953 to 1966 and their Relative Levels in 1966

	Concrete reinforcing rounds	Bars	Angles	Joists	Wire rod	Strip	Heavy plate	Tin-plate	Sheet (cold)
UK	+31	+26	+44	+43	+34	+34	+38	+38	+36
ECSC (Belgian low prices)	−11·6	−1·6	−1·6	−1·2	−2·9	+12·9	−21·4	−6·5	+9·0
ECSC prices below (−) or above (+) UK prices in 1966 (%)	−27.3	−14·9	−12·6	−16·6	−23·2	−2·9	−11·3	+2·9	+9·7

Notes: Prices are exclusive of taxes and refer to May 1953 and Feb.
1966; SM steel in all cases except ECSC heavy plate and sheet (cold)
which are Thomas steel.

Source: Data made available by ECSC High Authority.

Belgian steel industry is part of the common market for steel and,
as we showed in Chapter 9, steel enterprises in other member
states can and do compete with Belgian enterprises by aligning
down on the low Belgian list prices. Also, for example, competition between two German steel enterprises can and does take
place by both of them aligning down on Belgian prices even if a
competing Belgian offer is not actually being made. In February 1966 Belgian low prices were in fact setting the pace in
steel pricing in the Community, as indeed they had been during
much of the early 1960s. These particular Belgian prices are
therefore not only indicative of the position of the important
Belgian section of the ECSC industry, but in our opinion they are
not unreasonable indications of the position in the rest of the
Community also. Clearly an ideal comparison would require a
study of actual prices received by producers but, as we indicated
earlier in Chapter 9, such information is not available. Despite
all the reservations that surround the data in Table 6, it seems
that the basic contrast between the price performance of the two
industries cannot be dismissed on the grounds of the inadequacy
of the price data.

The second qualification to the comparison is this. It could be
objected that the actual fall (in most cases) in steel prices in the
ECSC as compared with the UK was simply a reflection of a

more favourable trend of input costs there, rather than any indication of superior performance by the steel industry itself.

How did input costs change? As we are assuming (we believe with reasonable justification) that Belgian steel prices are genuinely indicative of the trend of transactions prices throughout much of the ECSC, let us also assume that changes in input costs of Belgian producers are indicative of changes in such costs throughout the ECSC. In fact this is rather unlikely, as OECD data on input costs suggest that the experience of Germany and France in this field has been less fortunate than that of Belgium. But using our assumption increases the possibility of the ECSC's price performance being attributable to favourable input cost movements and therefore biases any comparison between prices there and in the UK in a manner favourable to the latter.

Comparative data on changes in input costs in the UK and Belgium are set out below in Table 7.

TABLE 7

The Movement of Input Costs in the UK and Belgian Steel Industries 1956–65

(1956 = 100)

	Imported ore		Home ore		Coke		Scrap		Labour costs	
	1956	1965	1956	1965	1956	1965	1956	1965	1956	1965
UK	100	73	100	126	100	133	100	100	100	174
Belgium	100	77	100	118	100	79	100	74	100	175

Source: OEEC, *The Iron and Steel Industry in Europe*, 1959, pp. 59–62; OECD, *The Iron and Steel Industry in 1964 and Trends in 1965*, 1965, pp. 40–44; Statistical Office of the European Communities, *Basic Statistics of the Communities*, 1965, table 87; Iron and Steel Board— British Iron and Steel Federation, *Annual Statistics*, 1956, table 74, 1964, table 84. (Data for home ore and labour costs only available up to 1963.)

If we take an unweighted average of the increases in these five main cost items over the period, then the general increase was about 21 per cent in the UK and 5 per cent in Belgium. A roughly weighted average suggested increases of 22 per cent and nil respectively. As the unweighted average increase in price of the nine products specified in Table 6 was 36 per cent in the UK

16*

but – 3 per cent in Belgium, it is clear that the Belgian performance must still be regarded as something of an achievement and the UK's as a definite disappointment.

There are other contrasts between the performance of the UK steel industry and that in the ECSC. According to a paper given by Sir Robert Shone in 1961, the main source of the superiority of a new steel plant over an old high-cost one lies in the reduced outlay on manpower required for each ton of steel produced.[6] This in fact accounts for over 50 per cent of the new plant's advantage. In other words, increasing efficiency in the steel industry is to a high degree synonymous with increasing the productivity of labour. In this field too the UK comes out unfavourably in comparison with the ECSC (see Table 8).

TABLE 8

Labour Productivity in the UK and ECSC Steel Industries

	1954	*1964*
UK	100	128
ECSC	100	176

Source: ECSC, *Bull. statistique*, no. 3, 1958, tables A2 & A31; Statistical Office of the European Communities, *Sidérurgie*, no. 1, 1966, tables 3 & 46; Iron and Steel Board—British Iron & Steel Federation, *Annual Statistics* (1956), table 73; (1964), tables 1 & 83.

The figures given above have been derived by dividing total crude-steel output in each market by the total number of process, maintenance, and administrative workers. They reflect very creditably upon the ECSC by showing its ability to change inputs into outputs by techniques that are above all labour-saving.

On the vital matters of pursuit of technological innovation and industrial rationalization the balance of advantage again appears to lie with the ECSC. It is difficult to say much about relative expenditure by the UK and ECSC steel industries on research; but according to the special report on this subject prepared by the Iron and Steel Board in 1963, expenditure on research in the French steel industry amounted to over 1 per cent of the value of

[6] Robert Shone, *The Economic Development of the United Kingdom Steel Industry* (1961), p. 11.

gross output in 1959 whereas the corresponding figure for the UK was less than half this.

But it is in the matter of structural reorganization and rationalization that the greatest contrast is to be found between the experiences of the UK and ECSC steel industries. A considerable amount of regroupment and rationalization has occurred in the ECSC, while in the UK such changes have been conspicuously absent. Activity in the ECSC has taken two forms. One has been the creation of larger groups involving various kinds of proprietary connexions. The other has been the formation of specialization agreements between otherwise independent firms.

In Table 9 below we compare the size of the largest groups in the ECSC with the largest in the UK.

TABLE 9

A Comparison of the Size of Steel-making Groups in the ECSC and UK in 1966

(*Ingot capacity*)

ECSC	m. tons	UK	m. tons
Hoogovens/Hoesch-DHH	10·04	Richard Thomas &	
Italsider/Finsider	9·93	Baldwins	3·6
Thyssen Group	8·87	United Steel	3·5
de Wendel/Pont-à-		Colvilles	3·4
Mousson	7·97	Steel Company of Wales	3·0
Cockerill/Providence, &c.	7·27	Dorman Long	2·6
ARBED	5·32	Stewarts & Lloyds	2·4
Krupp Group	4·87	John Summers	2·3
Usinor	4·7	GKN	2·3
Klöckner	3·67	South Durham	2·0
Mannesmann	2·68	Tube Investments	1·3
Lorraine-Escaut	2·67	Consett	1·1
Hüttenwerk Oberhausen	2·66	English Steel	0·869

Source: Financial Times, 17 Feb. 1966, p. 12.

The contrast in size between the largest ECSC producers and their UK counterparts is very clear. The largest UK group[7]

[7] However, in November 1966 it was announced that a merger between Dorman Long, South Durham Steel & Iron, and Stewarts & Lloyds was planned, which will put the new company about half-way down the ECSC list.

would come tenth in the ECSC list. It is of course easy to be carried away with mere size. But it is true that the optimum size of steel-making plants is tending to rise—that is to say the economies of scale are principally to be found at the plant level and not at the level of the firm to which the data in Table 9 refer. However, to dismiss the data thus would be to fail to acknowledge the benefits which such large groupings can confer. One is that the large size of efficient modern plants can mean that only large groups have the resources to finance their construction. Secondly, such arrangements are often a vehicle for specialization which confers the benefits of economies of long runs. Thus in the case of the new Hoogovens/Hoesch-Dortmund Hörder grouping the Dutch plant, being located on the coast, is well placed to receive cheap imported ore and produce pig iron and crude steel up to a semi-finished state. On the other hand the two German companies on the Ruhr close to consumers are better placed to expand on the finished steel side. The grouping also confers many other advantages. To avoid the cost of duplicating capacity by building a second hot-strip mill Hoesch will buy semi-finished steel from Hoogovens. The merger also allows the melting of high phosphorus ore in one plant and low phosphorus ore in another thus avoiding the cost of melting both in the same one. Rolling can also be concentrated so that plant does not have to be adjusted frequently to deal with products of different sizes and shapes.

Similar economies can also be gained from the other main type of rationalization that the ECSC has followed—the conclusion of specialization agreements between otherwise independent enterprises. Two important examples of such agreements in recent years have been the Stab-und-Formstahl-Kontor, Essen, and the agreements between Ilseder and Salzgitter.

In the former case Dortmund-Hörder Hüttenunion, Hoesch AG, Hüttenwerk Oberhausen AG, and Mannesmann AG have entered into an agreement providing for pooling and reallocation of orders for merchant-mill products and sections. The member firms have to submit all orders for products covered by the agreement to a joint Board of Officers who will then allocate orders to the various mills in accordance with the rolling programmes agreed for them. The main feature of the agreement is that for a certain time in each quarterly period each mill will concentrate on a reduced number of dimensions and qualities. A subsidiary feature of the agreement is that a mill will not be permanently specializing in given dimensions and qualities; as each mill will take it in turn over successive periods so to change its programme that over a longer period it will have produced more than just the limited range laid down in the first rolling programme. Obviously this kind of close working arrangement will in practice eliminate competition between the enterprises, at least as far as the products covered by the agreement are concerned, and for this reason the High Authority had to be satisfied that competition would still be provided in these markets by other producers. The High Authority authorized the arrangement in July 1965 on condition that a report on the effects of the rationalization be submitted to it annually. These reports should be invaluable in the future for making really detailed assessments of the benefits of this kind of arrangement.

Ilseder and Salzgitter on the other hand have concluded a number of agreements that involve specialization on a more permanent basis. In 1961 the High Authority authorized an agreement between the two producers as a result of which Ilseder ceased to make certain flat products and tubes, and Salzgitter undertook not to produce certain sections and pilings. This agreement also involved the joint selling of merchant bars mainly through Ilseder's sales organization. In 1962 a further agreement was authorized between the same producers relating to the production of wire rod. Salzgitter constructed a rod mill with half the capital being supplied by Ilseder, the latter undertaking not to construct a rod mill of its own.

In summary, the result of the concentration and specialization movements has been a marked reduction in the number of enterprises producing many ECSC products, this being particularly noticeable in the case of sheet. This must surely have improved efficiency by permitting scale economies and longer production runs. On the other hand the creation of the common market, the anti-trust rules, and the competitive pricing régime mean that this process has been able to occur without jeopardizing competition. On the contrary, this is keener in the ECSC now than when the Community was first established.

In the final analysis, however, it is not by the performance of particular industries that an economic system will be judged, but rather by its overall performance, especially its ability to sustain and even increase the rate of economic growth. It is true of course that much of the impressive economic growth recorded in the Six in the post-war period has been connected with reconstruction investment. For example, the high annual growth rates in the Community of GNP at constant prices (5·3 per cent) and GNP per capita (4·4 per cent) over the period 1953-8 must be seen in this context. But in the post-Rome Treaty years 1958-64, by which time the reconstruction argument is beginning to show signs of wear, these growth rates had in fact increased to 5·6 and 4·5 per cent respectively. One effect of these high growth rates has been to bring about a painful change in relative positions in the league table of international affluence. In 1959 real product per head in the UK was higher than in France, Germany, and the Netherlands. By 1965 the Netherlands had drawn level with the UK, while France and Germany had both achieved higher figures of real product per head.[8]

Exactly how much competition has contributed to this impressive performance in the Six is of course a matter that is open to dispute. What is not open to dispute is that competition has necessitated considerable modifications to existing policies and practices throughout the entire fabric of government and business life in the Communities. If the cumulative impact of these changes has not been at least an important cause of the high rate of economic growth, then other explanations should be found for such a significant phenomenon. So far they seem to be conspicuously absent.

[8] NIESR, *Econ. R.* Feb. 1966, chart 22, p. 54. (In 1966 the Netherlands moved ahead of the UK.)

SELECT BIBLIOGRAPHY

Balassa, B. *The Theory of Economic Integration*. London, Allen & Unwin, 1962.

Bayliss, B. T. *European Transport*. London, Mason, 1965.

Collège d'Europe. *Intégration européenne et réalité économique*. Bruges, De Tempel, 1964.

Diebold, W. *The Schuman Plan*. New York, Praeger, 1959.

Forsyth, M. 'Cartel Policy and the Common Market'. *Planning* (PEP) xxviii/464 (1962).

Honig, F., and others. *Cartel Law of the European Economic Community*. London, Butterworth, 1963.

Junckerstorff, H. A. K., ed. *International Manual on the European Economic Community*. St. Louis University Press, 1963.

Lister, L. *Europe's Coal and Steel Community*. New York, Twentieth Century Fund, 1960.

McCrone, G. 'Agricultural Integration in Western Europe'. *Planning* (PEP), xxix/470 (1963).

Meade, J. E. *The Theory of Customs Unions*. Amsterdam, North Holland Publishing Co., 1955.

Meade, J. E., H. H. Liesner, and S. J. Wells. *Case Studies in European Economic Union*. London, Oxford University Press for RIIA, 1962.

Neale, A. D. *The Antitrust Laws of the USA*. Cambridge University Press, 1960.

OECD. *Guide to Legislation on Restrictive Business Practices*. Paris, 1964. 5 vols.

Scitovsky, T. *Economic Theory and Western European Integration*. London, Allen & Unwin, 1958.

Sheahan, J. *Promotion and Control of Industry in Postwar France*. Cambridge, Mass., Harvard University Press, 1963.

Trench, Sylvia. 'Transport in the Common Market'. *Planning* (PEP), xxix/473 (1963).

Wagenführ, R., and partners. *CECA 1952-1962*. Luxembourg, ECSC High Authority, 1963.

INDEX